Augustine the Educator

Nihil obstat:
    RT. REV. JOHN K. RYAN
    Censor Deputatus

Imprimatur:
    PATRICK A. O'BOYLE, D.D.
    Archbishop of Washington

May 20, 1963

Augustine
the Educator

*A Study in the Fundamentals
of Christian Formation*

by Eugene Kevane
The Catholic University of America

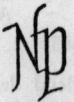

THE NEWMAN PRESS • WESTMINSTER, MARYLAND
1964

TO THE QUEEN OF THE UNIVERSE
IN FILIAL DEVOTION

Tu solus ante saecula
Spes atque centrum temporum . . .
Jesu, tibi sit gloria
Qui sceptra mundi temperas.

ROMAN BREVIARY

"*But Augustine would seem to have wrested the palm from all (the Fathers of the Church). Of a most powerful genius and thoroughly saturated with sacred and profane learning, with the loftiest faith and equal knowledge, he combated most vigorously all the errors of his age . . . (and) laid the safe foundations and sure structure of human science. . . .*" Pope Leo XIII, *Aeterni Patris* (1879)

"*St. Augustine was the great Doctor of the Church who before all others conceived and executed the plan of the philosophy of history. Those who deserve mention after his time in this branch of philosophy always took Augustine for their master and guide, and derived their inspiration from his writings. On the other hand, those who have departed from the path laid down by this great man, have suffered a variety of errors and have ended far from the truth. The reason for this is the fact that they who contemplate and narrate the pathway and development of human societies apart from St. Augustine's position, will lack a true knowledge of the causes which govern the temporal process of humanity.*" Pope Leo XIII, *Saepenumero considerantes* (1883)

"*We have retraced, Venerable Brethren, the life and merits of a man, with whom one will not find another to compare, or certainly very few, from the beginning of the world to the present day, on account of the power of his penetrating genius, the sublimity of his holiness, and the victorious combat which he undertook to defend Catholic truth. . . . Surely no one is unaware of the admirable manner in which St. Augustine wrote of the divine government of all things and all events of history in his noble work on* The City of God. *For he made use of everything he drew from an assiduous study of the Bible on the one hand, and from the fullness of the human culture of his day on the other hand, in order to produce one integrated concept of the history of the world.*" Pope Pius XI, *Ad salutem humani generis* (1930)

"*The Roman Pontiffs have extolled St. Augustine with the highest praise; the solemn Councils of the Church, whether in earlier or more recent times, have used his words more than once in their work of declaring and safeguarding the dogmas of the Catholic religion; and the holy Fathers and Doctors were wont frequently to borrow strong and wise teaching from his works in their defense of Christian truth from error. . . . The doctrine of St. Augustine, since it offers excellent instruments for refuting and defeating the fallacies of our own times as well, ought to be expounded in the fullness of its light.*" Pope Pius XII, *Quamquam Ecclesia* (1954)

Foreword

THE question concerning St. Augustine's doctrine on catechetics and education arises naturally from that return to the sources which characterizes the life of the Church in our time. This return, which has taken place under the inspiration and leadership of the Holy See, concerns the biblical and liturgical foundations of Christian life.[1] In the Christian education of youth, this leads directly to a renewed interest in the educational theory and practice of the Fathers of the Church. For they were the pioneers in establishing the deeply biblical and liturgical mode of teaching which was to produce the fruits of Christian culture which have distinguished the Christian era. A return to the sources in the Christian education of youth means a study of the pedagogical positions of the Fathers of the Church.

St. Augustine is generally acknowledged to occupy a preeminent place among the Fathers, completing their doctrinal work and handing it forward to the schools of Christendom. Indeed, as Cardinal Newman writes, he is the teacher who "has formed the intellect of Christian Europe." [2] It is commonly recognized that more is involved here than the in-

[1] With regard to the Bible, the encyclical *Providentissimus Deus* of Leo XIII on the study of Holy Scripture (Nov. 18, 1893) comes readily to mind, and in matters of the liturgy, the acts of the pontificate of Pope St. Pius X.

[2] John Henry Newman, *Apologia pro Vita Sua* (New York: Longmans, 1908), p. 264.

fluence of the theological writings of St. Augustine: he was a member of the teaching profession, and remained in some way related to the field of education throughout his life, as his *De catechizandis rudibus* and *De doctrina christiana* bear witness. The present work addresses itself to the study of this relationship of St. Augustine's life and work to the field of education.

Two separate questions are involved. The first in order of time for the author was the practical one of St. Augustine's pedagogical principles in their bearing upon the modern Catholic school. For the practical approach of St. Augustine concerns the teaching of religion. The study of St. Augustine's catechetical method reveals the academic teacher at work, and offers good hope to the religion teacher for a better unity of a solid academic teaching and at the same time of a genuine catechetical apostolate in the classroom.

This leads to the second question. The relevance of St. Augustine's educational principles for contemporary problems presupposes a clear perception of the nature of those principles and of his position in relation to the abiding features of Catholic educational philosophy. For the study of his catechetical treatise leads directly to the *De civitate Dei* on the one hand, and to the *De doctrina christiana* on the other, and raises the further and more fundamental question whether his contact with the field of education is perhaps deeper and more significant than commonly supposed.

A study of St. Augustine's earlier works, those written in the years immediately following his conversion, offers evidence pointing toward this conclusion. His resignation from the chair of rhetoric at Milan did not necessarily mean that he left the field of education and his teaching profession. The contrary is the case. He entered more fully and directly into it than ever, and indeed began his extensive literary career as a result of his profound plan for educational regeneration and renewal. This immediately opens wider possibilities for the study of St. Augustine's educational philosophy, and its relevance to contemporary problems.

The present study of the apostolate of the Bishop of Hippo arrives at a precise conclusion concerning his life and work, that he remained consciously and intentionally in the teaching profession after his conversion, and that his works prior to his ordination are largely characterized by a specifically Catholic pedagogical undertaking which he had in mind.

An authentic humanism and a soundly philosophical approach to the humanities, full in the footsteps of Plato and of Cicero, formed the essential features of this pedagogical undertaking, an achievement that opens perspectives toward the richly varied development of humanism in the Western civilization still to come. For St. Augustine's emphasis upon the quadrivium laid the basis in Western education for the massive breakthrough of the natural sciences in recent times; and his insistence upon the central role of philosophy in the humanities led directly to the brilliant Quattrocento with its transcendence of mere philology and its discussion of the great questions and issues of mankind in its study of the humanities. All of this, furthermore, is conceived within the over-arching frame of an approach sufficiently comprehensive, sufficiently human, and sufficiently open to the higher intelligible order of reality and value, to offer contemporary educators the sound and practical solution to the impasse of "The Two Cultures."

The way opens in this fashion to a study of St. Augustine's contact with the field of education as a consistent feature of his entire life, and leads to a recognition of the educational relevance and intent of several of his works which usually have been considered exclusively philosophical. St. Augustine's Christian philosophy is seen to arise, as a consequence, in closest union with his educational interests and his practical pedagogical undertaking, both after his conversion and after his ordination. This procedure tends to clarify and to solidify the exact nature of his philosophy of education, and indeed to reveal it as a strikingly rich and comprehensive body of educational doctrine. After the evidence is gathered for these fundamental positions on St. Augustine's pedagogical teaching, their contemporary relevance and significance are discussed. May the resulting picture of the great Patristic educator be of benefit to the Sister, Brother, Priest and Catholic Lay Teacher engaged today upon the same apostolate of the classroom, and indeed to all who are concerned with guarding the natural and supernatural heritage of mankind.

EUGENE KEVANE

Feast of the Immaculate Conception
December 8, 1963

Contents

xiii

Augustine the Educator

1

History,
Philosophy and
Classical Education

IN THE attempt to place St. Augustine's philosophy of history and hence his educational doctrine in proper perspective, it is incorrect to look upon him as a mere speculative thinker standing isolated and unrelated in late Roman times, constructing for himself a "system" like that of Voltaire or Hegel or Marx or Toynbee. Actually antiquity is not an unrelieved plain broken here and there by a few philosophers and classical authors. Thanks to the archaeological and documentary discoveries of the past century the Graeco-Roman civilization stands out now with its proper characteristics in sharper relief than ever, but at the same time with its beginning rooted in the older culture of the Orient and its ending fifteen centuries later involved in what Toynbee calls its affiliation with our own Western civilization.[1]

In this perspective St. Augustine's philosophy of history assumes a new stature and special importance, standing as it does precisely at this affiliation, at this unique juncture which even a contemporary philosopher like Karl Jaspers sees as the "Axial Period" of universal history.[2] St. Augustine's understanding of history cannot be dismissed lightly as simply another system constructed in abstract philosophical speculation, for out of it came that typical approach to education which formed the mind of the West and made it the home of a new and distinctive civilization—distinctive, although affiliated with the Classical civilization which was ending as he wrote his *De civitate Dei*.[3]

Even with this, however, the work of St. Augustine is not yet adequately located. There remains its connection with the beginning of Classical civilization and with the process of ever-increasing secularization which characterized the centuries of Greece and Rome. In this perspective St. Augustine's philosophy of history and its application in education take their place as an integral part of the vast restoration and renewal of the religious life of mankind which the Catholic Church has been accomplishing throughout the Christian era.

If we can state this properly, according to the evidence now available from scholarship in comparative religion, it will bring the fundamental importance as well as the abiding humanistic value of the Augustinian philosophy of education into striking relief.

The Initiation Schools

Moved by an inner *elán* which is one of its most distinctive and even unique properties, Western Christendom in recent centuries has gone forth to the rest of mankind, establishing contact with practically all human tribes and tongues and peoples and nations on earth. "Columbus and Magellan opened up a new world to the scholar," writes the Director of the Philippine Studies Program at the University of Chicago, "and the ordering, analysis and interpretation of the cultures of the non-Western world gradually became the province of the cultural anthropologist. At first the emphasis was evolutionary or historical, in keeping with the intellectual climate of the nineteenth century. More recently there has been a shift in the direction of comparative and general-

4

izing interests, and the gradual differentiation of social anthropology as a separate subdiscipline." [4]

This shift is nowhere more apparent than in the area of comparative religion. Here missionaries have always noted the initiation rites and ceremonies met repeatedly in the widest variety of places, always in connection with puberty and the advent of adult responsibilities in the life of the young person. Specialized students of these phenomena, following in the wake of the missionaries, began to observe a certain constancy of pattern in these matters from tribe to tribe and people to people around the entire circuit of the earth. At first they seemed to be nothing but religious ceremonies, obscured and distorted by human weakness and error and cruelty.

Gradually, however, their true nature emerged into full view before Western scholars in comparative religion. They are more than religious rites conducted as it were at random. They are schools, processes of religious education, whereby the tribe forms its young generation in the religious knowledge, values and motivation which characterize and preserve the social life of the group. Indeed, the term "initiation school" is coming into use as a technical term for these educational processes. "In his chapter on education in *Man and His Works*," writes Prof. Hart, "Herskovitz finds it necessary to stress that the training of the young in the simpler societies of the world is carried on . . . in the rather formidable apparatus of what is usually called in the anthropological literature the initiation ceremonies or the initiation schools. [This] initiation education takes place outside the home and is worthy to be called schooling, for it contrasts with the education the child receives around the household and the village long before the initiation period begins." [5]

It is the curriculum in these schools which interests us here, the means used, as the natives say, "to teach a boy to become a man." Surprisingly enough, continues Prof. Hart,

"It is hard to find in the literature any case where the initiation curriculum contains what might be called 'practical subjects,' or how to make a basic living. . . . The basic food-getting skills of the simpler peoples are never imparted in the initiation schools. . . . The curricula cover instead quite a different series of subjects, which I am tempted to call 'cultural subjects.' . . . There is much variation from tribe to tribe and region to region, but the imparting of religious knowledge always occupies a prominent place. This . . . includes such things as the learning of the myths, the tribal accounts of the tribe's own origin and history, and the performance, the meaning, and the sacred connections and connotations of the ceremonials. In brief, the novices are taught theology, which in primitive society is inextricably mixed up with astronomy, geology, geography, biology, (the mysteries of birth and sex), philosophy, art, and music—in short, the whole cultural heritage of the tribe." [6]

Describing the Igorots of the Philippines, Prof. Eggan writes, "The older boys supervise the younger group and teach them their tasks. The old men, in turn, teach the boys the history and the rituals of the ward and village and allow them to learn the prayers by assisting and observing." [7]

The point we wish to underline here is this universally-recurring pattern of religious education involving instruction in a sacred understanding of the human past and participation in the social life of prayer and liturgical worship. Prof. Eliade, Director of the Department of History of Religions at the University of Chicago, synthesizes the monographs of many scholars in his luminous description of the teaching of sacred history in the initiation schools. "Initiation introduces the candidate into the human community," he writes, "and into the world of spiritual and cultural values. He learns not only the behavior patterns, the techniques and the institutions of adults but also the sacred myths and traditions of the tribe, the names of the gods and the history of their works; above all, he learns the mystical relations between the tribe and the Supernatural Beings as those relations were established at the beginning of Time. Every primitive society possesses a consistent body of mythical traditions, a 'conception of the world'; and it is this conception that is gradually revealed to the novice in the course of his initiation. . . . The world is the work of Supernatural Beings—a divine work and hence sacred in its very structure. . . . The world has a 'history': first, its creation by Supernatural Beings; then, everything that took place after that—the coming of the civilizing Hero or the mythical Ancestor, their cultural activities, their demiurgic adventures, and at last their disappearance. This 'sacred history' . . . not only relates how things came to be; it also lays the foundations for all human behavior and all social and cultural institutions." [8]

This lucid summary shows that the science of comparative religion at last is coming to a more true and more human understanding of its object, an understanding which is of vital importance in relation to St. Augustine's philosophy of history and his manner of organizing the teaching of sacred doctrine. "To know the myths," continues Prof. Eliade, "is not (as was thought in the past century) to become aware of certain cosmic phenomena. . . . It is, first of all, to know what has happened in the world, has *really* happened, what the Gods and the civilizing Heroes *did*—their works, adventures, dramas. Thus it is to know a divine history—which nonetheless remains a 'history,' that is, a series of events that are unforeseeable, though consistent and significant. . . . It is, in short, the history of everything significant that has happened since the Creation of the world, of all the events that contributed to making man as he is today. The novice whom initiation introduces to the mythological traditions of the tribe is introduced to the sacred history of the world and humanity." [9]

We meet here, then, a concretely organized institution and process of religious education for what we now call the high school age-group. This education teaches a complete understanding of human development as a sacred history, and it forms the mind and will of the young person to con-

7

ceive and project his own personal living in terms of its values. It was this kind of religious schooling which brought men of the ancient East to the dawn of civilization, which colored the entire development of the Archaic civilization, and which formed the mind and spirit of the early Greeks. It set the stage for the familiar features of classical antiquity: its religion, its *paideia* in education, and the rise of its philosophy.

Paideia

Every human culture possesses a distinctive system and process of education, else it could not live in history for inability to transmit its essential values to its young generation. The Classical civilization of Greece and Rome therefore possessed its own proper way of educating its young. This was the *paideia* or *humanitas,* the distinctive classical education which corresponded to the initiation schools and was the accepted instrumentality in classical antiquity for teaching a boy to become a man.[10] Concentrating as we are upon the background for relating St. Augustine's philosophy of history and philosophy of education, we shall do no more here than summarize briefly the relationship of classical philosophy to this *paideia,* before going on to the "Myth of the Eternal Return" which is so important alike in Greek philosophy and classical education, and which St. Augustine was at such pains to refute.[11]

Classical civilization and its education begin with Homer, recognized throughout antiquity as the educator of Greece. Hesiod himself first appears as a rhapsodist, a poetic teacher reciting Homer. "Throughout its history," writes Marrou, "Greek literary education kept Homer as its basic text, the focus of all its studies." [12] "The poet's function is to educate," he continues; "The aim of poetry is not essentially aesthetic but the immortalization of the hero. The poet, as Plato was to say, 'clothes all the great deeds accomplished by the men of old with glory, *and thus educates those who come after.*' I have emphasized the last few words because they seem absolutely fundamental. To understand Homer's educational influence one has only to read him and see what his method is, . . . to set before them the great examples to be found in the old legends and so to arouse the agonistic instinct, the competitive spirit." [13]

Thus in method and in content the Homeric *paideia* of classical Greece continues the world-wide and history-deep tradition of the initiation school. While in one sense it appears secularized in comparison with the profoundly religious character of the initiation school as we still find it today among simpler peoples, nevertheless the same basic religious reference, the same respect for moral value, and the same imitation of divine or quasi-divine models and instructions set up for human living *in illo tempore,* reappear throughout the Homeric education.[14] This fundamental religious orientation of the classical *paideia* makes intelligible the generally religious character of personal outlook and social living in classical times described with profuse detail in *The Ancient City.*[15]

This is the reason why the Sophist approach to education was such an anomaly, developing as it did "in the direction of a relativistic humanism" and "brazen in its cynical pragmatism." [16] Socrates, Plato and Aristotle dedicated themselves to a restoration and safeguarding of the heritage of traditional values by moving the entire system of *paideia* over to a philosophical foundation supporting—and to a degree replacing—the simple and unreflected older approach to value-education through the study and appreciation of the poets.[17]

This meant, however, a further de-emphasis of the concept of sacred history which lay behind the Homeric *paideia.* "The work of Homer," writes Collingwood, "is not research, it is legend; and to a great extent it is theocratic legend. The gods appear in Homer as intervening in human affairs in a way not very different from the way in which they appear in the theocratic histories of the Near East." [18] Furthermore, in Homer there is still a genuinely humanistic education toward

9

intellectual understanding of these models and values for human living, which is based on a true concept of human freedom and moral responsibility. Men are still considered to have the innately human power to fashion their living according to these elevated and even glorious and heroic examples. In Homer, fate is still the will of Zeus. After him, a new view creeps into Greek religion, into the poetry which teaches about it, and gradually pervades the Greek mind. It is the concept of Fate, *fatum,* that dark *moira* which weighs ever more heavily on the thought of classical antiquity. *Moira* stands above even the gods and envelops both them and *physis*—this natural cosmos including men and human history—in her saddening and often tragic shroud.[19] This is the concept of time taught by the myth of the eternal return, a concept which not even Plato and Aristotle could escape, and which came to characterize the world-view of classical antiquity. Since a philosophical concept of time underlies any philosophy of history, this new anti-historical current in classical antiquity forms another important component for the background of St. Augustine's work in philosophy, history and education.

Eternal Recurrence

The religious life of man's simpler and even primitive cultures, based upon an intelligent and free imitation of divine models and examples held up *in illo tempore,* and preserved by careful fidelity to the pattern of education which taught them to the young, was unable to endure in unadulterated form. This was especially true in connection with the rise of civilization in the Near East, when the view of time characteristic of archaic man began to suffer change to the cyclic concept ruled by fate and necessity.

"In the third century B.C.," writes Prof. Eliade, "Berossus popularized the Chaldean doctrine of the 'Great Year' in a form that spread through the entire Hellenic world (whence it later passed to the Romans and the Byzantines). According to this doctrine, the universe is eternal but it is periodically destroyed and reconstituted every Great Year." [20] But a brief review of pre-Socratic philosophy will show that the doctrine of cyclic time had much earlier roots in Greek thought.

The earliest Greek philosophers are called "physicists" from the fact that the object of their thought was the *physis,* the *nature* which constitutes the cosmos. This idea of *physis* fills the world of Homer and the poets, who equate *natura* with the divine: *physis* is the entire universe conceived always as animated, living, and therefore in some sense divine. Aristotle considered this one of mankind's most ancient and sacred traditions.[21] Some historians of philosophy seem to hold that these early Greek thinkers denoted by *physis* a static and motionless substance. But this is not so. Originally, Greek philosophy was entirely compatible with the concept of historical growth, process and change. Aristotle made this clear when he pointed out that growth is the etymological sense of *physis.* "Nature means the genesis of growing things," he writes, "the meaning which would be suggested if one were to pronounce the Y in *physis* long. . . . From what has been said, it is plain that 'nature' in the primary and strict sense is the essence of things which have in themselves, as such, a source of movement; and . . . processes of becoming and growing are called nature because they are movements proceeding from this." [22]

Rightly understood, then, it appears that Greek philosophy deals with process, here on earth and in historical mankind. For process leads directly to history. It concerns the genesis, growth, development and maturation of things. History concerns such developmental processes when they take place in human groups. The Greek thinkers, however, were never able to rise to a linear and purposive concept of time and therefore of history, but rather succumbed more and more to cyclism, to the myth of the eternal return. "The vision of reality given us by the first philosophical speculation of the Greeks," writes Professor Diano, "is a historical view. That 'nature' (*physis*) which Anaximander and Anaximenes sought to explain . . . is actually the birth of things considered in the principle which generates them. . . . But time closes itself into a circle . . . and thus this historicity becomes cyclical. Because worlds are generated, grow and die away while the principle abides, it is 'the divine.' " [23]

Leaving the Ionians we find even more pronounced among the Pythagoreans the cycle of eternal recurrence interwoven with the complementary concept of transmigration. "The Pythagoreans," wrote Eudemus of Rhodes at that time, "teach that things return in a cycle individually identical. I therefore shall find myself staff in hand narrating the same myths to you in the future and you will be seated then just as you are now. Everything will be the same. It follows that time itself will be the same . . . for change itself recurs one and the same." [24]

Heraclitus, born about 500 B.C., herald of the great age of Greek philosophy, philosopher of the *logos* or reasoned purpose in the world-process, seems likewise to teach the cyclic concept. An important fragment emphasizes his denial of the creation of matter. "This ordered universe (cosmos) . . . was not created by anyone of the gods or mankind, but it was ever, and is, and shall be ever-living fire, kindled in measure and quenched in measure." [25] Greek philosophy, even in Plato and Aristotle, never breaks free of this cyclic concept nor rises to the concept of the creation of heaven and earth and all things by almighty God.

In Plato's *Phaedrus* we find that the cyclic doctrine lies at the very root of his theory of knowledge based on pre-existence and thus becomes the foundation of his *paideia* of reminiscence. "For the revolution of the spheres," he writes, "carries the immortal souls around, and they behold the world beyond. . . . And the intelligent soul . . . feeding upon the sight of truth is replenished, until the revolution of the world brings her round again to the same place." [26] Plato at times speaks of fate in terms of an iron necessity,[27] then again recovers his native humanism sufficiently to deplore astral fatalism and to deny eternal recurrence in the strict sense of Stoicism.[28]

Aristotle assembled the instruments of thought for break-

ing the spell of the cyclic view with his penetrating metaphysical analysis of the causes and his powerful passages on
the mode of existence and the operation of the eternal Prime
Mover. Even he, however, was unable to use his tools to full
effect. He too remained bound to the turning wheel, power-
less to rise to the concept of a material world created and
controlled by a Supernatural Being, which is so common in
the religious thought of the simpler peoples around the
world.

If, then, on the one hand Aristotle sees the distinction
between necessity and contingency,[29] on the other he seems
to embrace the world-system which makes the latter, and with
it genuine history, untenable. "For we maintain," he says in
the Meterology, "that the same opinions recur in rotation
among men, not once or twice or occasionally, but infinitely
often." [30]

Zeno the Stoic (336-264 B.C.) constructed the philosophical system and school which dominated the entire last half
of the Classical civilization through his far-reaching influence on the educated class of imperial Rome. Chrysippus, his
disciple, summarizes his teaching: "The substance (that is,
the world) is transformed by fire to its original state and from
it returns again in the identical order as before. . . . At peri-
odical intervals of time there is a conflagration in which all
things perish, then return again to form this same world.
For just as the stars turn around in the same orbits, so the
events of the cycle just past recur identically the same. Socrates and Plato will exist anew, and so too all men, identically, with the same friends and neighbors. And the same
things will be believed and discussed, and every city, every
village and every landscape will rise again identical. This
return of all things happens not just once but many times—in
fact, things will recur in this way forever without any end
unto infinity." [31]

Clearly the cyclic concept of the world-process and of
human history is ripening into full expression. History is not
composed of unique, contingent events. Neither time nor hu-

man freedom have any real significance. "Fate is the *logos* of the world," continues Chrysippus; "Fate is the *logos* of the things which providence administers in the world. . . . Fate is the eternal motion, continuous and ordered, . . . the series of the causes. Chance is but a cause unknown to human reasoning. . . . God is defined as providence: the purpose of divinity is to give order to the course of things and to provide for human affairs." [32]

In this fashion the philosophical thought of classical antiquity was corrupting the very words used to express the ancient religious belief in a personal, flexible Divine Providence, compatible with the contingency of human life and history, utterly different from this mechanical fatalism which has hardened reality and even human history into these inexorable cycles. Man is called "free" by the Stoics, but in the manner of the modern Marxists: free to obey necessity willingly, recognizing this "nature of history," lest he have to submit unwillingly.

Thus the poetry which the classical *paideia* uses to form minds and spirits, as well as the philosophy which was to safeguard and rejuvenate the ancient ethical and religious values of classical humanism, have both succumbed to the irrationalism which weighs ever more heavily upon the Graeco-Roman conception of the world and human history in the centuries of Karl Jasper's "Axial Period."

"The concept of the eternal return," writes Prof. Padovani, "aside from a few insignificant exceptions, dominates all Greek thought. The endless turning of all becoming before the immutable One, the everlasting repetition of all things and all events—this is the mind of antiquity. From this there follows the failure to achieve a rational concept of human history, because the human actors therein depend on the irrationality of matter, not created by God: they are born, they live, they die, without reason and without purpose. This is the fundamental basis of that concept of Fate, the irrational necessity which presses darkly on all events and binds them like iron. This is that fearful and obscure Destiny upon which in the end even the gods, suffering like men, depend. For even the Greek gods have ended bound up within the cosmic cycles of the eternal return." [33]

Since history is the web of human doings, a philosophy of history must entail a basic outlook upon human life and destiny. It is this fatalistic and hopeless outlook of the cyclic view of time which explains the pessimism and the note of emptiness and of the monotony of human life, even of tragedy, which sounds through Greek literature—together with the reverse counsel to enjoy the present moment.

The spread and the victory of this myth of the eternal return represents the corruption of traditional religious thought. Instead of offering human freedom paradigms and examples of divine origin, instead of teaching divine interventions freely entering and ordering human affairs, thinking has declined into myths which destroy the meaningfulness of time and history and hence of personal living. In the cyclic and fatalistic view of time there can be no genuine hope and no real happiness for man. He has left only to turn to the transitory things of earthly life and to live in them as though there were no God.

With this, and its attendant secularizing influence on life and education, we turn to a final consideration in the background for St. Augustine's philosophy of history and of education. It is the place of the classical historians in Graeco-Roman education, and the question whether the cyclic philosophy of historical time affected this type of historical teaching, even as the "sacred history" which lay behind the Homeric *paideia* has been disrupted by the myth of the eternal return.

The Classical Historians and Education

It is characteristic of man to preserve and to cherish the memory of his past. This memory is not a vague abstraction concerning mankind as a whole, but a concrete and vivid heritage of information about the significant events in the past life of each man's own group, his own tribe or people or nation—significant because of their relation to the essential character and values of the particular human society concerned. This concept embraces to the fullest extent the sacred history which is the most important feature, as we have seen, of the curriculum of the initiation schools described by the social anthropologists.

It is for this reason, furthermore, that more advanced societies have kept their annals.[34] "Historiography," says C. F. Jean of the Louvre, writing of pre-Hellenic Mesopotamia, "is represented by official inscriptions commemorating the building of palaces and of temples. The theocratic style of the scribes attributes everything to the action of the divinity." [35] This "theocratic style" probably is nothing else than the reflection of the close union between religion and social living which always has characterized mankind, at least in principle, apart from the last two centuries in the West. It manifests the bond between annalistic writing on the one hand, and religious worship, education and literature on the other. Aristotle, who considered poetry more truly "history" than the annals, draws a distinction which illuminates anew the Homeric *paideia* and shows its continuity with the earlier religious education of mankind. "The poet's function," he writes, "is to describe not the thing that has happened, but a kind of thing that might happen. . . . The distinction between historian and poet is not in the one writing prose and the other verse—you might put the work of Herodotus into verse, and it would still be a species of history; it consists really in this, that the one describes the thing that has been, and the other a kind of thing that might be. Hence poetry is something more philosophic and of graver import than history, since its statements are of the nature rather of universals, whereas those of history are singulars." [36]

Hence a *paideia* resting fundamentally on the poets will contain and teach essential values, universally valid patterns which are paradigms for right conduct. Thus the *paideia* forms the on-coming generation toward true and integral humanism. This is the idea of a school. It is in this sense that Plato in the passage already cited deems poetry, as poetry was understood in Greece, educational. Due to the religious nature of these patterns and paradigms resulting from divine intervention *in illo tempore* and reported by the "sacred histories" taught in the initiation schools, mankind as a whole always has had a deeply religious education. As we have noted, more or less broken remnants of this concept of sacred history remained in the poets and gave the Homeric *paideia* the aura at least of a religious education and formation of youth.[37]

Naturally the Greeks also had their annalistic history, their records to assist their human memory of their group-life. Speaking of Hippias, one of the early professional educators of Greece, Marrou writes: "Hippias' own works included geographical tables (names of peoples), 'archaeological' tables (mythology, biography, genealogy), and above all historical tables such as his catalogue of Olympic winners— the first of a whole series of similar investigations and the beginning of scientific chronology in Greek history, of scientific history in the modern sense of the word." [38] No doubt only a small fraction has survived of the writings produced by "the constant succession of new historians" of whom Livy speaks in his preface—the familiar classics which found a lasting home in the schools and with which St. Augustine was so familiar. It is these histories of Herodotus, Thucydides, Polybius, Sallust, Livy and Tacitus which we wish to consider briefly here as the final component of the background of St. Augustine's work.

"History is a Greek word meaning simply an investigation or inquiry," writes Collingwood. "Herodotus, who uses it in the title of his work, thereby marks a literary revolution. . . . Previous writers had been 'logographers,' writers-down of current stories [while] the historian . . . sets out to 'find' the truth. It is this use of the word, and its implications, that make Herodotus the father of history." [39]

Collingwood's philosophy does not permit him to see the

possibility of a "theocratic history," a divine intervention in human affairs, which can be known precisely by the "scientific history" introduced by Herodotus. St. Augustine will have no such philosophical limitations upon his intellectual freedom—nor indeed did the classical historians themselves, as their respectful attitude toward the "myths" and "theocratic legends" indicates, when they descend from too remote a time to reach by their method of using eyewitnesses or the surviving reports of eyewitnesses. "Such traditions," writes Livy, "as belong to the time before the city was founded, or rather was presently to be founded, and are rather adorned with poetic legends than based upon trustworthy historical proofs, I purpose neither to affirm or to refute. It is the privilege of antiquity to mingle divine things with human, and so to add dignity to the beginnings of cities. . . ." [40]

So much for recent philosophical presuppositions and prejudices. The fact remains that the classical historians were scientific in their concept of eyewitness reports about happenings, and that they did not arbitrarily exclude the possibility of finding divine facts, what the Hebrews call the *mirabilia Dei,* among them.

Herodotus and Thucydides wrote of particular incidents in the life of Athens. With Polybius the scene shifts to Rome, the Rome with which St. Augustine will be concerned, and it is Livy who composed the first "world history" which, instead of descending from above as the sacred histories, rises up from the human scene and the annalist's viewpoint. He was able to do so, welding together earlier particular histories into one universal history, because Rome had become his whole world, the one great social reality embracing all the tribes and peoples and cities. This set the frame of mind for the Christian thinker upon historical becoming, for Eusebius and St. Jerome in the *Chronicles* and for St. Augustine in the *De civitate Dei.*

The classical historians were not untouched by the cyclic philosophy of time. Herodotus and Thucydides prosecuted historical knowledge for its value in affairs and Livy wishes to teach the virtues of early Rome when society was uncorrupted. But in Polybius one learns only the inner success of Stoicism, not how to master circumstance but only to bear bravely whatever fortune brings: Polybius has imported into history "a new element of determinism." [41]

Nevertheless the classical historians as a whole manifest an alternate view of history to that of the philosophers and their eternal recurrence.[42] It is optimistic, not pessimistic, an investigation into the observable behavior of men for Thucydides, a history of the rise and development of the Roman civil and social order for the Greek Polybius and his Latin successors, as the magnificent goal toward which all mankind has been on a long upward climb.[43] This too is deeply significant for the proper understanding of St. Augustine's philosophy of history, and indeed for comprehending the shudder which passed over antiquity at the sack of Rome in A.D. 410. It was this shocking event which caused St. Augustine to write the *De civitate Dei,* convinced that Catholic thought alone could answer the question raised on every side: were the philosophers of the cyclical recurrence right after all? Was the world conflagration at hand? Was the concept of historical progress a chimera and the secular faith in "Eternal Rome" an illusion? Did not this secular faith need the worship of the gods to secure its hope? Or could Christian historical understanding discern a sense in which both "progress" and the "Eternity of Rome" are true? Finally, could Christian historical thought disprove once and for all the myth of the eternal return?

Such in broad sketch was the general significance of the great historians of classical antiquity and their relationship to the work of St. Augustine. It remains to review their role in classical education.

It is difficult to obtain a clear concept of the place of historical studies in the classical *paideia.* Some authorities deny that history was taught at all; others assert that it had a place on the circle of the arts as a separate discipline. Perhaps this obscurity of the case is precisely the knowledge one needs in order to appreciate the nature of the curriculum in St. Augustine's philosophy of education and the fact that the restoration and renewal of historical scholarship and thought came to the Bishop of Hippo from Jerusalem rather than from Athens and Rome.[44]

The fact is, however, that Isocrates included Herodotus on his curriculum of studies, and that henceforward the historians were read together with the poets and the philosophers as an integral part of the classical *paideia*.[45] When so eminent a classicist as Wilamowitz, therefore, states that "The Greeks and the Romans had no education in history," and that "No man in antiquity ever gave lectures on history," it is clear that some distinction must be made.[46]

The truth is that history was studied, indeed, in classical antiquity, but in a manner quite different from that which is characteristic of Western civilization.[47] The classical *paideia*, it seems, did not possess a systematic teaching of history in the schools with a meaningful chronology, not even in the schools of Rome after Livy wrote. History lay almost completely under the sway of rhetoric and was cultivated partly for the examples it offered for teaching moral virtue but even more for the models it contained for composing fine speeches as in Thucydides or for learning an elegant style like that of Livy. Thus the history of the historians had become separated almost entirely, from the viewpoint of education, from that meaningful history of the initiation schools, the sacred history which had deposited remnants still visible in the poets and to some degree, as Collingwood complains, even in the classical historians.[48] The annalistic history of the historians has become by a slow and gradual drift almost completely divorced from sacred history. It lives, so to speak, a separate, secularized existence. In practice it has even lost chronological meaningfulness of any kind, having become but a quarry for random examples. Worse still there was the attitude which so disgusted St. Augustine after his conversion, but which Cicero had explicitly approved, that orators and rhetoricians might lie in recounting events in order to make a point more effective.[49]

All this, as we noted, is an educational approach to history quite different from that which has always characterized Western civilization—even in the distortions and aberrations of the last two centuries. It is not too much to say that this is the feature, speaking from the viewpoint of educational structure, which chiefly distinguishes this new civilization, arising in the West after the Patristic Age, from its classical predecessor. Nor is it too much to say that we have here the proper background for studying the essential feature of St. Augustine's philosophy of education and for appreciating its indispensable contribution to Western culture.

Moira and Secularization

It is fair to say, therefore, that history in classical antiquity existed in a quite secularized form, reflecting a concept of earthly social and cultural progress finalized in the Roman Empire. It is safe to say, furthermore, that the classical *paideia*, while it was familiar with the works of the historians, did not really teach history at all.

What is the case regarding religion? Discussing "Education in Antiquity in Relation to Religion," Grasberger writes: "In this chapter it must be remembered throughout that there was no apparatus for instruction in religion, either among the Greeks or the Romans. Such an arrangement is to be found only in the centuries after Christ, from the time when a fourth subject was added to the three original simple components of the elementary level of education, reading, writing and arithmetic—namely a course of instruction in the Christian Religion arranged for the school." [50] We have seen, as Fustel de Coulanges points out, that there is a sense in which the entire classical *paideia* was, or at least wanted to be, a religious education and formation of youth. The fact remains, however, that it was so deeply secularized that in comparison with the Christian centuries to come, or with the other civilizations and simpler cultures of mankind, it could appear to provide no place for religion at all. Fustel de Coulanges himself admits this indirectly, for he sees clearly the progressive secularization which overtook the Classical civilization and left it at the end hollow and empty. "We have sought," he writes, "to place in a clear light this social system of the ancients, where religion was absolute master, both in public and private life. . . . But little by little, as we have seen, society became modified. . . . Already, in the fifth century which preceded Christianity, the alliance was no longer so close between religion on the one hand and law and politics on the other." [51]

A progressive growth of the dark doctrines of *Moira,* therefore, the cyclical fatalism which removed real meaning and genuine happiness from human life, coupled with progressive secularization: such proved to be the development of those fifteen centuries of the Classical civilization at the end of which St. Augustine stood. In all of this the Homeric *paideia* has been deeply involved, and its fundamental inability to cope with the human situation became ever more manifest.

In the vast restoration and renewal of mankind's religious life which the Catholic Church had begun, there would follow quite naturally a renovation of the education of youth in both content and structure. This is the significance and proper location of St. Augustine's philosophy of education, which applies in school work, in the initiation of Christian youth to Christian adulthood, that altogether different linear view of history which had been confined to the Chosen People in Palestine during most of the classical centuries.

With this as a background, then, locating St. Augustine at the end of the "axial period" in universal history, at the point of affiliation between Classical civilization and our own Christian culture, we can proceed to determine St. Augustine's philosophy of history, his philosophy of education, his practical career as a schoolman, and the contemporary relevance of his work in the face of the Voltairean understanding of mankind's past.

Notes from Chapter One

1 That the history of the Greeks and the Romans must be viewed "as an integral part of an historical development going back to the fourth millenium in Egypt, Mesopotamia and the Aegean lands" is now too commonly admitted to need documentation. "Man erkennt heute immer klarer dass die griechisch-römische Antike in ihren Anfängen unter dem übermächtigen Eindruck der altorientalischen Kultur stand." Siegfried Lauffer, "Der Antike Fortschrittsgedanke," *Actes du XIe Congrès International de Philosophie* (Louvain: Nauwelaerts, 1953), p. 37. The "affiliation" of the modern West to the classical civilization through the creative activity of the Catholic Church likewise has come to be recognized as a fact. For this cf. for example, Gustav Schnürer, *Kirche und Kultur im Mittelalter* (Paderborn: Schöningh, 1936), Erster Band; Christopher Dawson, *The Making of Europe* (New York: Sheed and Ward, 1938); and Arnold Toynbee, *A Study of History* (London: Oxford University Press, 1934 ff.), *passim*, but especially Vol. I, pp. 52-63. It should be noted that H.-I. Marrou, in his *Saint Augustin et la fin de la culture antique*, studies the Bishop of Hippo in his role as the predominant figure in this affiliation which made the Western world what it is as a civilization.

2 Cf. Karl Jaspers, *The Origin and Goal of History* (London: Routledge, 1953), chart facing p. 26.

3 The assertion that St. Augustine's philosophy of education was actually related in this fashion to the mind of the West will be studied further below. For the present we cite Marrou's summary: "Meanwhile, a new curve was already rising from below; and at the end of this book we shall see how, beginning from one small section of the Christian society—the monasteries—a new course of development was rising which would in the end lead to a new type of education, that which was to dominate Western Christendom during the Middle Ages." *A History of Education in Antiquity* (New York: Sheed and Ward, 1956), pp. xiii-xiv. It is the "newness" of this new type of education which is the object of the present study, a quality which is possessed by virtue of its relationship to St. Augustine's philosophy of history.

4 Fred Eggan, "Social Anthropology and the Educational System," *The School Review*, LXV (1957), 249.

5 C. W. M. Hart, "Contrasts between Prepubertal and Postpubertal Education," in George D. Spindler (ed.), *Education and Anthropology* (Stanford: Stanford University Press, 1955), pp. 127-128.

6 *Ibid.*, pp. 137-38. Cf. George A. Pettitt, *Primitive Education in North America* (Los Angeles: University of California Press, 1946), p. 3: "Primitive education . . . was a constant challenge to the elders to review, analyze, dramatize, and defend their cultural heritage"; and *passim*.

7 Fred Eggan, *loc. cit.*, 252.

8 Mircea Eliade, *Birth and Rebirth* (New York: Harper, 1958), pp. x-xi.

9 *Ibid.*, p. xv.

10 Cf. Marrou, *A History of Education in Antiquity* (New York: Sheed and Ward, 1956), pp. xii-xiii: "[Classical antiquity] stretches over a period of

fifteen hundred years—in round numbers, from 1000 B.C. to A.D. 500. This allows room for several stages of development. The subject is, however, more unified and more closely defined than we should expect, for the ancient Mediterranean world knew only one classical education, only one coherent and clearly defined educational system."

11 For this relationship between philosophy and education in antiquity, cf. Marrou, *op. cit.*; the older work of Lorenz Grasberger, *Erziehung und Unterricht im Klassischen Alterthum: Mit besonderer Rücksicht auf die Bedürfnisse der Gegenwart*, Vol. I-III (Würzburg: Stabel'schen Buchhandlung, 1864, 1875, 1881), of which Marrou remarks, "For education in Antiquity as a whole still the basic work . . ." (*op. cit.*, p. 353); Werner Jaeger, *Paideia: The Ideals of Greek Culture, Vol. I-III*, Transl. Gilbert Highet (New York: Oxford University Press, 1936, 1944); Ignatius Brady, *A History of Ancient Philosophy* (Milwaukee: Bruce, 1959), especially the manner of expounding Plato's philosophy in terms of *paideia*, pp. 80-107.

12 Marrou, *op. cit.*, p. 9.

13 *Ibid.*, p. 12.

14 Cf. Marrou, *op. cit.*, Chapter I, "Education in Homeric Times," pp. 3-13, and his own reference (p. 359) to Werner Jaeger, *Paideia*, Vol. I, pp. 46-105, "the most illuminating pages I know . . . on this subject."

15 Cf. Fustel de Coulanges, *The Ancient City* (New York: Doubleday Anchor Books, 1956), *passim*; cf., for example, p. 216: "The Athenian whom we picture to ourselves as so inconstant, such a free-thinker, has, on the contrary, a singular respect for ancient traditions and ancient rites. His principal religion—that which secures his most fervent devotion—is the worship of ancestors and heroes. . . . Whatever relates to antiquity is sacred to the Athenian. . . . If a priest introduces the slightest innovation into the worship, he is punished with death."

16 Marrou, *op. cit.*, p. 51.

17 Cf. Marrou, *ibid.*, pp. 58 ff. (for Socrates) and pp. 66 ff. (for Plato). Aristotle was explicit in his respect for the religious traditions handed down from mankind's distant path: "Our forefathers in the most remote ages have handed down to their posterity a tradition, in the form of a myth, that these [heavenly] bodies are gods and that the divine encloses the whole of nature . . . [and] one must regard this as an inspired utterance."—*Metaphysics*, XII, 8, in Richard McKeon, *The Basic Works of Aristotle* (New York, Random House, 1941), p. 884.

18 R. G. Collingwood, *The Idea of History* (New York: Oxford University Press, 1956), p. 18. Collingwood of course misses the point of archaic myth and legend, but his witness to the bond between Homer and the archaic religions with their "sacred histories" is important.

19 Cf. W. C. Greene, *Moira: Fate, Good, and Evil in Greek Thought* (Cambridge: Harvard University Press, 1944), pp. 14-16.

20 Mircea Eliade, *Cosmos and History: The Myth of the Eternal Return* (New York: Harper Torchbooks, 1959), p. 87.

21 *Meta.*, XII, 8.

22 Aristotle, *Metaphysics*, V, 4, in McKeon, *op. cit.*, pp. 755-756.

23 Carlo Diano, "Il concetto della storia nella filosofia dei Greci," *Grande Antologia Filosofica*, II, 248.

24 *Grande Antologia Filosofica*, II, 355.

25 K. Freeman, *Ancilla to the Pre-Socratic Philosophers: A Complete Translation of the Fragments in Diels' Fragmente der Vorsokratiker* (Oxford: Basil Blackwell, 1948), p. 26 (Heraclitus, Frag. 30). Cf. Mircea Eliade, *Cosmos*

and History, p. 87: "It is probable that this doctrine of periodic universal conflagration was also held by Heraclitus." Cf. *ibid.*, p. 120, "The universal conflagration is . . . also accepted by Heraclitus." Ignatius Brady is categorical: "Heraclitus emphasizes a circular process . . ." (*op. cit.*, p. 45).

26 B. Jowett, *The Dialogues of Plato* (New York: Bigelow and Brown, n.d.), Vol. III, pp. 405-6.

27 E.g., in the Myth of ER, *Republic*, Book X (in W. H. D. Rouse, *Great Dialogues of Plato* (New York: Mentor Books, 1956), pp. 415-422.

28 Cf. *Republic*, Book VIII; Mircea Eliade, *Cosmos and History*, p. 132.

29 Cf. Aristotle, *On Interpretation*, IX; *Metaphysics*, VI, 2 (McKeon, *op. cit.*, pp. 45-48; 779-781).

30 Lee, H. D. P. (transl.), *Aristotle Meterologica* (Cambridge: Harvard University Press, 1952), p. 13.

31 In the *Grande Antologica Filosofica*, II, 403, citing Von Arnim, *Stoicorum veterum fragmenta* (Leipzig: Teubner, 1923), Vol. II, *Chrysippi fragmenta*, 625.

32 *Ibid.*, II, 403-404. Cf. C. R. Haines (transl.), *Marcus Aurelius Antoninus: The Communings with Himself* (New York: Putnam's, 1916), Book XI, 1 (p. 293) for the echo of this doctrine in the Roman world, taught with the authority of the Philosopher-Emperor in the second century A.D.

33 Umberto A. Padovani, "I caratteri filosofici del pensiero classico," *Grande Antologia Filosofica*, Vol. I, XVI-XVII (premessa).

34 The most comprehensive collection of the annals of the various peoples of the ancient world, a primary historical source to this day, is the chronology of Eusebius, translated and brought to date by St. Jerome. It is the *Chronicorum libri duo*, Migne, P.G. (Paris: 1857), Tom. XIX, col. 101-598. St. Augustine had this fundamental treatise before him as he composed his *De civitate Dei*. We shall return to it below. For a full study of Eusebius' work, cf. A. Schoene, *Die Weltchronik des Eusebius* (Berlin: Weidmann, 1900).

35 Charles F. Jean, "The East," in Edward Eyre (ed.), *European Civilization, Its Origin and Development* (London: Oxford University Press, 1935), Vol. I, p. 260. Cf. *ibid.* for a typical example translated from the records of Lagash in Sumer. Numerous complete annalistic documents in English translation are to be found in James B. Pritchard (ed.), *Ancient Near Eastern Texts* (Princeton: Princeton University Press, 1950), Part III, "Historical Texts," pp. 225-322.

36 Aristotle, *Poetics*, IX, 1451b (McKeon, *op. cit.*, pp. 1463-1464).

37 "Children were taught gymnastics, because the body of a man was an arm for the city, and it was best that this arm should be as strong and as skilful as possible. They were also taught religious songs and hymns and the sacred dances, because this knowledge was necessary to the correct performance of the sacrifices of the city."—Fustel de Coulanges, *The Ancient City* (New York: Doubleday Anchor Books, 1956), p. 222, citing Aristophanes, *Clouds*, 966-968. The position of Grasberger on the total lack of religious education in antiquity, as we shall see below, can be accepted only with certain distinctions and reservations.

38 Marrou, *A History of Education in Antiquity* (New York: Sheed and Ward, 1956), p. 55.

39 R. G. Collingwood, *op. cit.*, p. 19.

40 Livy, I, 1, preface: B. O. Foster (Transl.), *Livy* (Cambridge: Harvard University Press, 1952), p. 5. Collingwood's manner of reading back into the minds of the classical historians the attitude of the modern atheist who has prejudged the very possibility of authentic and historically verifiable divine

interventions into human history can only be viewed as arbitrary, anachronistic and unhistorical. The classical historians were not "scientific students," as he calls them (ibid.), in contrast with the earlier "theocratic historians" and with Homer and Hesiod, as if they were modern philosophical positivists. Rather, their minds were open to possible divine interventions not so remote in the past as to lie beyond the reach of the actual eyewitnesses sought by Herodotus, or the documentary records of eyewitness reports sought by his successors. This primacy of philosophy as such over philosophy of history is of fundamental importance in understanding St. Augustine.

41 R. G. Collingwood, op. cit., p. 36.

42 For cyclism and fatalism as they affected Herodotus, cf. Charles Norris Cochrane, Christianity and Classical Culture: A Study of Thought and Action from Augustus to Augustine (London: Oxford University Press, 1944), pp. 461-469.

43 Cf. Siegfried Lauffer, "Der Antike Fortschrittsgedanke," Actes du XIe Congrès Internationale de Philosophie (Louvain: Nauwelaerts, 1953), 37-44.

44 Cf. William M. Green, "Augustine on the Teaching of History," University of California Publications in Classical Philology, 12 (1944), 315-332. "The statement has been made that the subject was not admitted into the schools until the modern era," p. 315, with the references cited. Professor Green, however, states categorically that "some knowledge of past events has been taught . . . in schools of every period" (ibid.), and documents his position with the epitomes and textbooks of history which were used in the ancient schools. "In the rhetorical schools, however," he admits, "attention was devoted not so much to the comprehensive view of history as to the stories which afforded illustrations for commonplace topics" (ibid., 317).

45 H.-I. Marrou, A History of Education in Antiquity, p. 83: "Isocrates recommended an interesting addition, 'the knowledge of the past, of events and their consequences.' This was doubtless a reflection of the progress of contemporary culture, which had taken into its field the work of the historians and elevated Herodotus and Thucydides to the rank of classics." "Poetry was supreme because it was to be found at the very origin of Greek culture," Marrou notes elsewhere, "but Hellenistic schools also had a place for prose. . . . The prose writers were mainly historians . . ." (ibid., p. 164). The most complete and explicit treatment of the role of history in the circle of studies found by the writer is in Werner Jaeger, Paideia: The Ideals of Greek Culture, Vol. III (New York: Oxford University Press, 1944), pp. 100-103, where he contrasts the two currents of educational philosophy issuing from the contemporaries Plato and Isocrates. Cf. also Theodore Haarhoff, Schools of Gaul (London: Oxford University Press, 1920), pp. 209-219.

46 Quoted by Haarhoff, op. cit., p. 210.

47 "It is quite clear that history was studied in a very haphazard way." Haarhoff, op. cit., p. 213.

48 R. G. Collingwood, op. cit., p. 18: "Nor is it to say that these legendary elements, theocratic or mythical as the case may be, are entirely absent even from the works of the fifth-century historians."

49 Cf. William M. Green, op. cit., 318; Cicero, Brutus, c. 42; and St. Augustine, Confessions, IX, c. 2, where he deems his "burden of teaching," his previous literary work and worldly career, nothing else than "that chair of lies."

50 L. Grasberger, op. cit., Vol. III, p. 532.

51 Fustel de Coulanges, op. cit., pp. 389-390.

2

Augustine's
Career in the
Pagan Schools

I T IS difficult to encompass St. Augustine. So great is the
intellectual stature of this "genius of western civilization," [1] so varied are his contacts with the life and teaching
of the Catholic Church and with the fundamentals of Christian culture that one or the other easily can lose proper
perspective or even fall out of view.

Something like this seems to have happened to his contact with the field of education. Although he was a professional teacher in the school system of classical antiquity until he joined the Catholic Church, and a bishop, a member
of its official teaching body, for over thirty years more, the
exact nature of his work in education has been studied less
frequently than his accomplishment with grace, for example,
or ecclesiology, or Christian philosophy, or the philosophy of
history, or the analysis of the nature and experience of time. [2]

Our purpose here is to gather some of the evidence for
this contact with the field of education in an effort to determine better which of his writings are educational in nature. Perhaps the listing needs to be lengthened. Frequently
the works of St. Augustine float free, as it were, from the concrete institutional framework of education in which he lived
most of his life. It is this relationship to education which

we seek to clarify, establishing whatever contact of his life and work with the field of education which the evidence will support, as a preparation and guide for the study of the Augustinian philosophy of education.[3]

The Study of St. Augustine's Life

It has been observed many times with justice that we know St. Augustine better than any other personality of ancient times. There is first of all his own famous autobiography, *The Confessions,* sufficient by itself to make men always aware of its author.[4] Then there are the numerous biographical references scattered through his works, particularly his sermons with their unique confidences to his hearers; the Benedictines have gathered these into a "Life of St. Augustine" written in a sense by himself.[5] St. Augustine, furthermore, had a friend and disciple in Possidius, who wrote an indispensable eye-witness biography based upon forty years of first-hand observation.[6]

Standing directly or indirectly behind modern biography of St. Augustine is the fundamental work of Tillemont, whose thirteenth volume is devoted entirely to the life of St. Augustine in a scholarly study which reflects the close association of the author with the Benedictines of St. Maur.[7] We shall return to the general character of Tillemont's approach after a brief survey of the more recent biographies.

Over a century ago Bindemann's major three-volume life of St. Augustine appeared in Germany under Lutheran auspices.[8] The first volume follows the *Confessions* and the *Dialogues* as purely personal and philosophical reflections; the second and third analyze and describe the sermons and the works against the various heresies engaged by St. Augustine. The discussion prescinds from education and its institutional forms, whether in the rhetorical schools of classical antiquity or in the teaching Church, and thus seems to reflect the basic approach of Tillemont.

At the same time Jean Poujoulat was publishing his comprehensive biography, likewise in three volumes. It had immediate success: the third edition appeared within seven years.[9] Again the description prescinds from the field of education. St. Augustine's activity in the schools of rhetoric is incidental, hardly mentioned. Cassiciacum is a *retraite* and nothing more. His life as a priest and bishop is portrayed in terms of his sermons and his contact with the heresies of his day in North Africa.

At the end of the century Wolfsgruber and Portalié published major studies of St. Augustine. The former, basing his work on the scholarly material left behind by Cardinal Rauscher, produced an excellent systematic survey of St. Augustine's life and work, clarifying especially his role as a Father of the Church through the writings which he bequeathed to Catholic posterity.[10] There is a chapter on the student and the professor, but again this educational framework of St. Augustine's life is touched only lightly, as incidental to the inner wrestling described in the *Confessions*. Over two-thirds of the book is devoted to his life as a bishop, analyzing his written works without reference to any pedagogical activity. Portalié's work is the well-known general introduction published in the *Dictionnaire de théologie catholique,* and recently in English translation.[11] It is, of course, not the intention of the author to do a biography of St. Augustine, but rather to present "an account of the history of his thought" and "his life as a scholar." [12] This is accomplished so well that his work remains the standard point of departure for the study of St. Augustine's writings. It is still true, however, that these writings are not presented in relation to Augustine's activity in the educational institutions within which his life unfolded. The very words "doctrine," "education," "liberal arts," "rhetoric" and "school" are missing in the index.

While it is not a life of St. Augustine, Eggersdorfer's study at the beginning of the century was a pioneering analysis of his work in the field of education which merits special mention here.[13]

In the series "Les grandes philosophes" Jules Martin's biography has won wide recognition.[14] His study remains fundamental for research on St. Augustine's contact with the field of education, for it expounds carefully and with excellent bibliographies those aspects of Augustinian philosophical thought which touch teaching and learning most closely.[15]

The fifteenth centenary of Augustine's death, 1930, brought forth several biographies and many special studies, opening a period of renewed interest in "the Christian Plato" which continues to the present. Hugh Pope contributed a valuable study in English, based on a series of conferences in 1930, containing a wealth of technical information about Augustine's life and works. The relationship of them to the educational reality in which Augustine lived, however, is almost wholly lacking.[16]

Lesaar's biography studies "The Professor at Carthage and Rome," and devotes most of his book to "The Doctor of Grace," an analysis of St. Augustine's works as priest and bishop.[17] While Augustine's role as a teacher both before and after his conversion appears more clearly in Lesaar's book, education as such is incidental to the real course of Augustine's life. It is as if "His Conflicts Concerning God" (Part II) were separate from his profession as *rhetor;* and as if that profession ended when he found "the peace of God" and retired to do his writings in a totally new situation.

The French patristic scholar, Gustave Bardy, contributed an excellent life which has gone through several editions. Again, however, a contact with the field of education is not developed.[18]

Vernon J. Bourke's well-known and substantial work singles out Augustine's philosophy, as the subtitle indicates, as the aspect of his life which is given special study. While considerable attention is devoted to his thought and work in education, the contact continues to appear incidental.[19]

M. F. Sciacca, the noted Italian Augustinian philosopher,

in his three-volume study likewise has little which bears directly on an intrinsic contact with the field of education as such, although his analyses of St. Augustine's teaching on philosophical questions adjacent to education are excellent.[20] Lucien Fabre's biography is distinguished by an excellent chapter on the impact of Cicero's *Hortensius* upon St. Augustine, but even this does not relate the episode to classical education, nor does Augustine's later life appear in contact with the field of education.[21] Simon's biography concentrates on St. Augustine's ecclesiology and theology of history: education is almost entirely omitted from the treatment.[22] In the same year, 1954, O'Meara published his detailed study of the growth of St. Augustine's mind up to his conversion.[23] Here indeed we find a scholarly discussion of Augustine's life as a student, a *rhetor* and a "philosopher" at Cassiciacum, to which we shall return; it is not within the author's intention to study the later years with a possible educational relevance, in a special sense, of his life as a priest and bishop. To conclude this survey, there is the recent major biography by Sizoo, containing chapters on Augustine's student days and his life as a *rhetor* at Carthage, Rome and Milan.[24] But again his inner quest of wisdom is not seen in direct relationship to the field of education; and, after his conversion, it drops out of view entirely: Augustine is a clergyman, a preacher, a letter-writer, a publisher of books, and the formidable opponent of Manicheism, Donatism, and Pelagianism.

These works, of course, do not exhaust the more recent lives of St. Augustine, not even all of those listed in the bibliography. They will perhaps suffice, however, to provide an overview of the general trend in portraying his biography. Nor is this survey intended in a spirit of criticism of these lives of St. Augustine. Beginning with Tillemont, each is an excellent work of scholarship, making clear and substantiating some approach to or aspect of the many-sided activity of the Bishop of Hippo. For various reasons, they simply prescind, for the most part, from a contact of Augustine's life and work with the field of education. It is perfectly natural, in fact, that they should do so. Since Tillemont, St. Augustine has been perceived and studied as the greatest Father of the Church, whose works have long since become detached from the concrete social situation which gave them birth.

The particular practical interest of the present study demands a review of this original framework in which St. Augustine lived and wrote—and thought—because it was entirely educational in nature, whether in the Schools of Rhetoric, or in the Bishop's Cathedral School which he established at Hippo.[25] Indeed, as they tell us who know St. Augustine's character best, it was not in him to compose his books apart from the concrete situation of his life and the immediate challenge and need of his work. Several advantages might result from a close scrutiny of this institutional framework of education. Increased unity might be brought into our knowledge of St. Augustine's thought and life—a unity which we expect in the case of so great a man and so strong a mind. The deliberate choice of the terrain of education as the point of view might throw unexpected light on the relationship between the *Dialogues of Cassiciacum* and the *Confessions*, and thus upon the now-protracted dispute which one might well call the Alfaric–Boyer controversy.[26] Above all, it may assist in determining better which of his writings are relevant to the field of education, and in what way.[27] This is an important preliminary to the study of St. Augustine's philosophy of education and a necessary prerequisite for a proper "return to the sources" in Catholic education today.[28]

Augustine's Student Days

We turn, then, to a review of the original social and institutional framework of Augustine's life and writings.

He was born in 354 of a mixed marriage, of good parents, Possidius tells us, who "carefully attended to his upbringing themselves." [29] "Augustine received a Christian education," Portalié asserts flatly,[30] and describes the basic religious ideas which the boy learned at home: the providence of God, the practice of prayer, the Holy Name of Christ which abided with him [31] and the thought of judgment which never left him.[32] As a full-grown young man of nineteen, at his conversion to philosophy, he had no thought of actually finding wisdom apart from Christ.

"I was stirred up," he tells us, ". . . to love and pursue . . . wisdom itself, whatsoever it might be. In so great a blaze only this checked me, that the name of Christ was not in it. For this name, O Lord, according to your mercy, this name of my Savior, your Son, my tender heart had holily drunken in with my mother's milk and kept deep down within itself. Whatever lacked this name, no matter how learned and polished and veracious it was, could not wholly capture me." [33]

There was, then, a definite and positive Catholic formation from his home and perhaps to some degree from the catechumenate in which his mother enrolled him.[34] It was not, however, an "education," nor was it sufficiently strong to withstand the influences of the institution to which he had to go for his education. Recalling these things later on as a bishop, he could not but think of "the safe way in which children should walk." [35] As we shall see, this safe way was nothing else than the theory and the practice of Catholic education which played so large a role in his pastoral care of souls. For the Church had not yet had the time or the opportunity to acquire the social strength needed to provide an education for the children of her catechumens and her members. Indeed, the unfinished patristic blueprint for such an education was awaiting the one who would complete it in theory and exemplify it in action, here at the historic juncture between the period concerned with the reception of adult converts and that coming time which had to care for the children of a now largely Catholic population.

Thus it was that this Catholic boy entered the educational system of classical antiquity quite unprepared spiritually to cope with it. He lacked even the first prerequisite, the solid backing of a serious-minded Catholic father.[36] When he left that system many years later after achieving the very pinnacle of success in it, he understood its emptiness thoroughly and saw through its inadequacy for Catholic children with a piercing insight unsurpassed by any ancient thinker. It is the very drama of classical antiquity itself, its decline and fall through inner decay as well as its renewal and transfiguration in the times of Christendom, which unfolds before our eyes in the brilliant career which this Catholic boy will have in the schools of rhetoric, and in the educational work and mission which he will continue after turning in his resignation from the chair at Milan.

His parents, therefore, "carefully attended to his upbringing themselves and he was educated at their expense, chiefly in secular literature; in other words, he took all the subjects that are included in what we call a liberal education." [37]

These words of Possidius define with standard terminology the educational institution and system of classical antiquity. It had a venerable past by Augustine's time, indeed it stood there as a majestic cultural phenomenon with untold achievements, including the very administration of the mighty Empire itself, to support the general recognition of its essential soundness and true humanism. "The ancient Mediterranean world," writes Marrou, "knew only one classical education, only one coherent and clearly defined educational system. It is true that this did not appear at the beginning in its final, fully-developed form. It reached this only at a comparatively late date, which I place after the decisive contributions of the two great educators—Plato (d. 348) and Isocrates (d. 338)." [38] "The period of time . . . ," Marrou continues, "stretches over a period of fifteen hundred years—in round figures, from 1000 B.C. to A.D. 500." [39] The Sorbonne professor documents this important fact throughout his work. "This whole long period," he says in connection with Hellenistic teaching methods, ". . . is not one which shows any signs of evolution in the proper sense of the word—i.e., a gradual transformation ending in a complete renewal. There are many changes, but no alternation in the basic structure." [40] Marrou deems his three chapters on "The Roman Schools" in a sense unnecessary, for "the change-over to a Latin-speaking society . . . from their Hellenistic prototypes caused no important modification in teaching. . . . It was not even a case of imitating; it was on the whole a pure and simple transfer." [41]

The Nature of the Classical System

It was indeed a mighty institution which Augustine entered as a boy, and a venerable one.[42] His career as a student and a professor reflects its stages and wrestles with its inner qualitative tensions so truly and so fully that we could reconstruct that educational system from his life and writings alone. Apuleius of Madaura, writing in the second century, describes its basic structure in words which convey a sense of that swollen intellectual pride which Augustine came so to detest.

"At a banquet," Apuleius tells us, "the first cup is for thirst, the second for joy, the third for sensual delight, and the fourth for folly. At the feasts of the Muses, on the other hand, the more we are given to drink, the more our soul gains in wisdom and reason. The first cup is poured for us by the *litterator* who begins to polish the roughness of our mind. Then comes the *grammaticus* who adorns us with varied knowledge. Finally it is the *rhetor's* turn who puts in our hands the weapon of eloquence." [43]

It is as if classical education had no philosophical problems in the realm of qualitative excellence. It is as if the schools of rhetoric culminated a bright and lucid process leading directly to all knowledge, all wisdom, to the sovereign good and happiness of man.

Such was emphatically not the case, as we know both from the philosophical developments within classical education and from St. Augustine's description of his own inner experience of the system. For the two are actually one: it is here that we can perceive the first intrinsic connection of the life of St. Augustine with the field of education. His *Confessions* reflect the philosophical tension in classical education which goes back to the opposition between Plato and Isocrates and which reappears in the effort made by Cicero and Quintilian to save Roman education from mere externalized verbalism reflecting the gradual loss of inner substance and content, both in the order of truth and in that of moral training.

"The most obvious danger," writes Gwynn, "was that it tended to become a purely literary education, with facility in rhetorical composition as its ideal accomplishment. In Greece, where the national tradition of education was strong, this tendency was perhaps less marked, though it always existed. . . . In Rome the tendency to subordinate the artes liberales to Rhetoric was strong from the first. Cicero fought against it in his *De oratore* and *Hortensius;* but the society for which he wrote ceased to exist within a generation of his death and rhetoric carried all before it in the early Empire." [44]

We stand in the presence here not of an isolated and secondary fact, but before the very life-drama of the classical civilization. St. Augustine lived and worked at the end of an educational process which had harbored within itself since the days of Plato and Isocrates this philosophical tension, this fundamental controversy on qualitative excellence.

"There is no doubt," writes Marrou, "that Isocrates . . . is the supreme master of oratorical culture, the literary kind of education that was to become the dominant feature of the classical tradition—despite the dialectical tension created at the very heart of that tradition by the permanent opportunity of choice that had been opened up by the critical philosophy. On the whole it was Isocrates, not Plato, who educated fourth-century Greece and subsequently the Hellenistic worlds." [45]

It is here that the greatness and historical importance of Cicero, educated in Athens as he was, comes fully into view.

He opposed the emptying of education of intellectual content and moral purpose, seeing the cult of rhetoric for its own sake as a dire threat to the Roman society which he loved. "It makes young men ignorant even in their knowledge." [46] Therefore he insists "on the ideal of a cultured orator, *doctus orator* . . . , who shall combine the excellences of both orator and philosopher. . . ." [47] It follows that educators must hold all the arts and disciplines called the liberal studies in due respect. Who can fail to recognize here the future Augustine, indeed the Bishop writing *De doctrina christiana?* "Later in life," Gwynn points out, "under the stress of public calamities, Cicero tended to lay greater emphasis on philosophy as the sole moral and intellectual guide for men; and the *Hortensius* . . . was written to convey this lesson." [48]

Augustine's Indictment of Classical Education

With this sketch of the philosophical situation of classical education, and with this insight into the triumph of a type of education which had progressively lost intellectual content and moral substance and even concern or awareness in the matter, we are in a position to return to the youthful St. Augustine. For, seen in this light, even his *Confessions* appear to express an intrinsic contact with the field of education.

Relevant here are the unforgettable passages which describe the moral emptiness and even turpitude which had fastened upon the classical *paideia*.[49] It had become almost completely secularized and even worse. Augustine holds the educational system partially responsible for the moral helplessness into which he fell and for his concomitant and resulting gradual alienation from God. Worst of all was the fateful fall into the common attitude of spiritual and intellectual pride with which the system was imbued. "One must concede to Augustine," writes Eggersdorfer, "that this education was not without blame for the moral condition of its young people, which it looked upon coolly and with an indifferent eye." [50]

Let us hear the central core of Augustine's indictment. "What wonder was it," he cried in anguished memory, "that I was thus carried away into vain practices and went far from you, my God? For the men set up for my models were utterly dejected when caught in a barbarism or solecism while telling about some of their own acts, even though the acts themselves were not bad. But if they would describe some of their lustful deeds in detail and good order and with correct and well-placed words, did they not glory in the praise they got? . . . Regard, O Lord my God, . . . how carefully the sons of men observe the proprieties as to letters and syllables . . . , and how they neglect everlasting covenants of eternal salvation which they have received from you." [51]

An excessively and even exclusively rhetorical education, with the solid intellectual content of the sciences and disciplines neglected and—which is still worse—any kind of moral formation abandoned on principle. Does not the Bishop who is the founder of Christian philosophy seem to be speaking out of the pedagogical tradition of Plato and Aristotle, Cicero and Quintilian? A young man of Augustine's powerful talent, coupled with the fact of his Catholic conscience, could not but experience acutely the intellectual one-sidedness and moral emptiness of the educational content which his progress through the system encountered. [52]

More than that: Augustine, even though a contemporary, is able to sweep with his mind's eye that entire corrupted and secularized classical civilization which he too represents, perhaps because he is at the same time the educational pioneer of the coming Christian culture. [53] "Woe to you, O torrent of men's ways!" He writes with the insight of a modern sociologist or philosopher of the *Zeitgeist*. "Who will stand against you? How long will it be until you are dried up? How long will you sweep the sons of Eve down into that mighty and hideous ocean . . . ? Have I not read in you of Jove,

both thunderer and adulterer? . . . The story is told so
that authority would be provided to imitate the true adultery while the false thunder cloaks it over . . . so that debauchery might not be accounted debauchery. . . . O hellish
flood, the sons of men are thrown into you with fees paid,
so that they may learn these fables. . . . You dash against
your rocks, you roar and say: 'Here is learned the use of
words! Here eloquence is acquired. . . .' " [54]

Nor can a civilization rise above the level of its mode of
educating its youth: "For these are the practices that pass
from tutors and teachers, and from nuts and balls and birds,
to governors and kings, and to money and estates and slaves.
These very things pass on, as older years come in their
turn. . . ." [55]

It is the very essence of the *Confessions* that Augustine
embraced the system with his whole heart and soul, learned
all its lessons, and made its pride his own. "Yet foul and
vicious as I was," he recalls, "with overflowing vanity, I took
pride in being refined and cultured." [56] "I was already the
leading student in the school of rhetoric, and in my pride I
rejoiced and I was swollen up with vanity." [57] His father
took it all as something quite normal and natural; not even
his mother grasped the situation. "My parent's . . . only
care was that I should learn to make the finest orations and
become a persuasive speaker." [58] Augustine comes to the
heart of the matter and touches the first principle of educational philosophy when he describes the sacrifices his father,
typical Roman of the *Spätantike*, made to advance his obviously talented son. "But meanwhile," the Bishop quietly
remembers, "this same father took no pains as to how I was
growing up before you, or as to how chaste I was, as long as
I was cultivated in speech, even though I was left a desert,
uncultivated for you, O God, who are the one true and good
Lord of that field which is my heart." [59] In this flashing play
on the senses of cultivation and culture Augustine, the
contemporary witness, exposes the cause of Rome's decline
and fall, a cause much discussed and controverted by his-

torians to the present day; at the same time he lays down
the point of departure for that Christian approach to education, already occupying him as he wrote, which will be
designed in theory and implemented in practice to achieve
for young people a Christian culture or cultivation of mind
and soul. He is indeed the lofty figure who stands at the
world-historical juncture, the "axial period" of Jaspers, at
Toynbee's point of affiliation between the classical civilization and our Western Christendom.

Deficient and hence to that extent evil as social systems
and educational establishments may be, there remains in
them also the positive factor, the element which men concerned with basic positions in the true and the good have
placed and preserved there. In and through this element
Providence still can work. For the same system which Augustine experienced so keenly and evaluated so critically contained also the solid stones which gave him a footing, in the
human sense and aspect of the matter, for his slow and perilous climb out of the condition in which the demoralizing
educational flood had deposited him. The regular curriculum entailed the systematic study of Cicero who was to the
rhetor as Vergil to the grammaticus: "Et usitato iam discendi
ordine perveneram in librum quemdam Ciceronis . . . ex-
hortationem . . . ad philosophiam." [60]

The "Hortensius": Augustine Discovers the Philosophic Ideal

"In the ordinary course of study I came upon a book by
a certain Cicero, . . . This work contains his exhortation
to philosophy and is called *Hortensius*. This book changed
my affections. It turned my prayers to you, Lord, and caused
me to have different purposes and desires. All my vain hopes
forthwith became worthless to me, and with incredible ardor
of heart I desired undying wisdom. I began to rise up, so that
I might return to you. I did not use that book to sharpen my

tongue . . . nor did it impress me by its way of speaking but rather by what it spoke." [61]

How many young people had encountered that book in the curriculum of studies and passed it by without thought? But Augustine had the talent of genius and bore within himself the vestiges of a Catholic conscience. The first and most fundamental impression concerns the entire educational system which used these books for the cultivation of verbal style and oratorical skill without concern for content or attention to truth. Augustine by means of Cicero's book pierces through the prevailing educational philosophy, apparently without help from his *rhetor:* "Nor did it impress me by its way of speaking but rather by what it spoke." We have here the point of departure toward what will become ultimately a philosophy of education which restores and renovates content, giving it its due relationship to form: a truth-centered education, the *doctrina Christiana* proper to the City of God.

"How I burned, O my God, how I burned with desire to fly away from earthly things and upwards to you, and yet I did not know what you would do with me! For with you there is wisdom. Love of wisdom has the name philosophy in Greek, and that book set me on fire for it, . . . that great, and beauteous, and honest name." [62]

It is a true conversion, a conversion to philosophy in the sense not uncommon in antiquity, and at the same time the beginning of that final and full return to the God of Christianity. Hence one day he will attribute even this early insight of his student days to the prayers of his saintly mother.[63]

Conversion to philosophy was a fairly frequent event in the intellectual and spiritual life of antiquity, a unique change in the entire orientation of life. Teaching later on as a *rhetor* at Carthage, Augustine will use philosophy to bring his friend and disciple Alypius to renounce the pleasures of the circus.

"Upon hearing those words he burst forth from that deep pit in which he had willingly plunged himself and wherein he was blinded with its strange pleasures. He shook his mind with a vigorous self-control. All the filth of the circus fell off from him, and he never returned there again." [64] Alypius began attending Augustine's lectures and entered Manicheism thinking to find true wisdom there. But the original episode is a graphic instance of the meaning of conversion to philosophy in classical times.[65]

Although Augustine's "Quest for Wisdom" was an arduous one which occupied many more years, there is practically unanimous agreement that his was a genuine conversion to philosophy at the age of nineteen.[66] "Many, perhaps twelve, of my years had flown by since that nineteenth year when by reading Cicero's *Hortensius* I was aroused to a zeal for wisdom." [67] It is an important fact for us, for it is essential to his thought about the field of education as well as his work in it. "The effect upon him was decisive," writes Boyer. "That reading revealed Augustine to himself. From that time truth appeared to him as the sole object really worthy of human search. He judged vain any hopes which did not terminate in truth. His conversion has begun . . . when he closed the *Hortensius*, he had become a philosopher." [68] "The prominence given to the reading of the *Hortensius*," states O'Meara, "is meant to stress Augustine's awakening to a real interest in truth. . . . Its reading in part provoked, and in part coincided with, the true beginning of philosophy in his mind." [69]

Etienne Gilson, speaking of his own lifetime of scholarship in the history of philosophy, calls it an attempt "to establish the reality of Christian philosophy as an historically knowable fact." [70] St. Augustine, it is generally acknowledged, is the patriarchal figure of this Christian philosophy, indeed in many respects its founder. The reading of the *Hortensius*, then, was a momentous event in the history of Western thought. Was it likewise so in the history and the philosophy of Western education? Or did it perhaps introduce a period in St. Augustine's life in which philosophy absorbed him as a personal preoccupation of the inner world of thought distinct from the external framework in which his life was to unfold?

An initial clue is contained in the fact that Augustine soon after this changed from the career in law to which his parents aspired for him to one in the field of education.[71] "He first of all taught literature in his own town," Possidius tells us, "and then oratory at Carthage, the capital of the Province, and, later still, overseas in Rome and at Milan, where at that time the Emperor, Valentinian the Younger, had established his court." [72] Augustine had made a decision fraught with world-historical consequences, making it as he did at Jasper's "axial period," as we have noted. For civilizations live through the dynamism of their educational systems by which they renew themselves in the minds and hearts of the oncoming young people, and falter and die when they fail to do so. Augustine's decision, accordingly, might well relate to the very meaning of history, that concept which his name has come to evoke, in a manner which merits attention. Could it have been that he forsook the field of law, in which his parents anticipated rich temporal benefits for their brilliant son, for the sake of his new love of wisdom? Might it not have been, furthermore, already, that he entered the field of education out of some obscure sense of mission?

"Augustinus Rhetor"

If purely formal education, neglectful of true content and indifferent to moral substance, had so triumphed by his time in the *Spätantike*, how could Augustine turn to it as his professional field precisely in conjunction with his conversion to philosophy? The final answer will be that he could not: his quest for wisdom eventually drove him out of the schools of rhetoric. But that came years later, after much study and thought and anguish of soul. At first, it seemed the most natural thing to seek wisdom in the field of education, as a dis-

ciple of Cicero.[73] As a matter of fact, there was no other
choice for the philosophical opposition, so to term it with
Eggersdorfer, but to work within the framework of the
rhetorical schools: so complete had the triumph of Isocrates
over Plato long since become.

Cicero himself recognized this, as did Quintilian even
more. It was Cicero who opened the door to education for a
young man like Augustine suddenly zealous for philosophy.
Cicero argues, as Gwynn points out, "that great oratory is impossible without a study of philosophy. That argument is the
culminating point of his educational theory. . . . "[74] When
due reflection is given to the considered judgment of Clark
in his study of Roman education, the intrinsic relationship
of philosophy and the profession of teaching in Augustine's
life emerges into better view.

"It was Cicero's achievement," he writes, "to lift rhetoric
above academic pedantry and narrow professionalism to the
higher level of a genuine humanism. To appreciate his contribution justly it must be seen against the background of
contemporary rhetorical teaching. One will then recognize
the pertinence of the main theme of *De oratore*. In empha-
sizing the importance of having something to say as well as
knowing how to say it, and the desirability of combining the
two main disciplines of the ancient world, rhetoric and philosophy, he was putting his finger on one of the weaknesses
of ancient education. It was unfortunate that his message
was so little heeded." [75]

We need not imagine, therefore, that the traditional opposition between rhetoric and philosophy should have caused
Augustine to avoid rather than embrace the former, or once
having adopted it as his means of livelihood, to have pursued
his love of wisdom in a merely private and personal way after
his return from his day of teaching.[76] He met the *Hortensius*
in his regular studies, and a year later Aristotle's *Categories*
in the same way: it was the *rhetor* who taught philosophy,
however badly, at that time.[77] The drama of Augustine's life
continues to unfold in intrinsic contact with the field of edu-

cation and his zeal for wisdom, it seems likely, actually led him to choose the teaching instead of the legal profession.

A better and deeper insight into the close union of philosophy and education in Augustine's thinking is revealed by another set of facts, those which concern his self-study in the full content of the liberal disciplines omitted or slighted by the rhetorical schools. There could be no better indication of the concrete pedagogical nature of his conversion to philosophy.

Cicero's *Hortensius* contained two fundamental concepts: first, an exhortation to wisdom, to remain dissatisfied until a substantial content of humanizing truth and virtue has been discovered and acquired; secondly, a positive evaluation of the entire circle of the arts, sciences, and disciplines of human culture as the normal preparation for this discovery and acquisition.[78] None should be omitted: the natural sciences, astronomy, music, mathematics in all branches, and logic and the teaching of philosophy itself. Each is important, each contributes in proper order to the philosophical crown of education. The prevailing trend toward neglect of solid content, the drift into mere formalism with nothing but grammar and rhetoric, would undermine civilization and leave it an empty shell. So Cicero; *schola loquax,* Augustine will say one day, when he comes to oppose to it a new concept, *schola nostra.*

Augustine's relationship to these two concepts in the *Hortensius* opens the way to a grasp of the essential nature of his career as a *rhetor.*

In response to the first, the exhortation to wisdom, he turned to the Manichees. He thought indeed of the faith of his boyhood and of his mother and looked cursorily into Scripture. "But it seemed to me unworthy of comparison with the nobility of Cicero's writings. My swelling pride turned away from its humble style. . . . "[79] He joined the Manichees, to his mother's consternation, seduced by their claim to possess all wisdom, all knowledge of natural things, in the heavens and on earth, and a superior insight into the corrupted and unhistorical character of the Christian Scriptures.

It was his response to the second concept which under God finally saved him. Cicero demanded a thorough study of the complete circle of the arts and disciplines, especially mathematics and the natural sciences, and not merely grammar and rhetoric, as the necessary preparation of the intelligence and cultivation of the mind for philosophy. At one stroke the glaring deficiency of the Schools of Rhetoric stood revealed to Augustine. Not even the preparation was properly organized into the 'circle," or, as we have begun to say for a century or so, the curriculum. The entire educational institution of the time was characterized by emptiness. It had become to a large extent devoid of content.

Looking within himself, typical product of the system, Augustine recognized the same deficiency. If philosophical knowledge is the worthwhile end of education, if these slighted or even omitted disciplines are the curricular means, then he must acquire them by himself. He plunged into a program of self-study, "without help of human teaching," as he says, after finishing his formal course.[80] Thus his very return to God is from within the field and process of education, not from a pursuit of philosophy somehow in isolation from his profession. For his study of the real disciplines in the full circle of the classical *paideia* led to the conquest of Manicheism, when he perceived in conversation that Faustus, the touted man of wisdom and famed intellectual light of the sect, was only a grammarian, a man with a flow of words and nothing more.[81] Gradually from that point Augustine acquired intellectual humility as the concomitant of genuine knowledge. Step by step, with the help of Plato's philosophy, he penetrated to a grasp of non-corporeal intelligible being, an insight into the fact that God is a spiritual reality[82] From this point his progress was rapid: he advanced to the Sacred Scriptures, to Christ, to the God of the Catholic Church and of his own mother Monica. It is all within the field of education, indeed part and parcel of his fulfillment of the profession of *rhetor* in the schools of Rome.

What kind of teacher and educator was St. Augustine? The essential features of his professional approach are now clearly visible.[83] As Finaert says, he was "a *rhetor* in the service of truth." [84] Already the fundamental metaphysical concept and point of departure of the future Christian philosopher, the idea of truth, is becoming visible from within his experience of the shortcomings of his own profession.[85] He is a philosopher in his very work of teaching, and an educator because he is a philosopher. His purpose in teaching is virtue and moral substance, truth sought and seen and declared on human fundamentals. In all of this he is the disciple of Cicero and thus indirectly of Plato as opposed to Isocrates and the current of educational theory and practice which he had come to symbolize. Augustine has entered into the deep philosophical and educational issue which both Cicero and Quintilian sought to clarify for the Roman world. "For the one point in which we have our very greatest advantage over the brute creation," writes Cicero, laying down the foundation and point of departure for his educational theory and his humanism, "is that we hold converse with one another and can reproduce our thought in word." [86] He goes on to praise the culture of the word as the very power which has led humanity "out of its brutish existence in the wilderness up to our present condition as men and as citizens." [87] But this culture of the word, the *logos,* must be first and foremost a philosophical cultivation of truth, the inner spiritual form of the word: it must not degenerate into a development of the mere powers of speech and persuasion divorced from the content and substance and truth of knowledge. This basic concept of human excellence runs through Cicero's philosophical and educational works like a golden thread, seeking to bind the Roman world with its native virtue to the best in the Greek heritage of *paideia.*[88] Hence the Latin translation of this rich Greek word: *humanitas.* Augustine made all this his own. As he says himself, with "incredible ardor of heart," and "set on fire for . . . that great, and beauteous, and honest name" of philosophy, he sought wisdom in the field of education.[89] Such a *rhetor* was Augustine, a worthy disciple of Cicero in the *Spätantike* and the bearer of the heritage of *paideia* there in those last days of Rome.

What of the externals of Augustine's career in education? He was unquestionably successful. Sufficient testimony has come from his students on the one hand, and from the sense of loss among the parents when he resigned his post in Milan.[90] On the other hand, there is his entry into the field of publication with the lost work *De pulchro et apto*,[91] and his advancement to Carthage first and then to Rome. His own motive in desiring the chair at Rome gives evidence of the born teacher: he sincerely looked forward to a more studious and academic atmosphere than that which characterized the provincial capital.[92] It is significant that Symmachus, the prefect and most important figure at Rome, famed as the greatest living orator, befriended Augustine and recommended him for the post of *rhetor* at the capital of the Western Empire at Milan. At the same time, it is even more significant that Augustine won this supreme professional honor by victory in public competition. Sometimes his career in education is passed off too lightly, as if he were but another teacher among many. The facts seem to indicate that he was a luminary of the first order who could look forward, on the basis of contemporary analogies, to high appointment within the imperial administration, indeed to positions verging on the supreme power itself.[93] Augustine's references in the *Confessions* to the pull of ambition as well as to the weakness of the flesh may well have had a vivid concreteness which escapes us in reading his work today.

The events which culminated the career of this renowned *rhetor* and led him to resign his chair at Milan are too well known from the *Confessions* to need mention here. Seen from the field of education, the entire process of his conversion, all the zeal for wisdom and the awesome intellectual and moral struggle from beginning to end which he describes in the matchless self-revelation, have a striking unity with his professional career.[94] The internal intellectual insecurity of his mind was one piece with the state of educational philosophy in the schools of rhetoric. Thus the *Confessions* actually form an instructive treatise in the philosophy of education as well as the magnificent personal document admired ever since. It is not too much to say that the love of truth and the zeal for wisdom which fired him since the reading of the *Hortensius* did at last become incompatible with continued professional work in the schools of imperial Rome. In a true sense, one which perhaps explains the alacrity with which he rose above the shudder of horror which ran through the ancient world at Alaric's deed, his resignation from his professional chair marked one of the meanings which attach to that pregnant phrase, the decline and fall of Rome.

Notes from Chapter Two

[1] Erwin R. H. von Kienitz. *Augustinus: Genius des Abendlandes* (Wuppertal: Abendland Verlag, 1947).

[2] See the introduction to the bibliography below for the standard approaches to the immense literature on St. Augustine. Unfortunately the forthcoming fourth volume of Johannes Quasten, *Patrology* (Westminster, Maryland: The Newman Press, 1950), which will be devoted to the great Latin Fathers, has not yet appeared and could not be used for the present study. Reference is made to it for the most up-to-date and comprehensive treatment of texts and studies on St. Augustine, as well as for the summary and evaluation of his works.

[3] The relative dearth of studies on St. Augustine's contact with education is reflected in the general bibliographies. See, for example, Eulogius Nebreda, *Bibliographia Augustiniana* (Roma: Tipogr. Cuore di Maria, 1928), published to anticipate the work done in observance of St. Augustine's fifteenth centenary in 1930: out of 934 titles, only four are listed under the heading "Opera circa paedagogiam divi Augustini," the older works of Ballerini, Buschik, Eggersdorfer, and Popp. There are the two chapters in Edward Kennard Rand, *Founders of the Middle Ages* (Cambridge: Harvard University Press, 1928; Dover edition, 1957), "The New Education," pp. 218-250, and "St. Augustine and Dante," pp. 251-284, with valuable references. Perhaps the best general appreciation of Augustine's historical position and importance as a bishop and an educator is Christopher Dawson's "St. Augustine and His Age," in *A Monument to Saint Augustine: Essays on Some Aspects of His Thought Written in Commemoration of His 15th Centenary* (London: Sheed and Ward, 1930), pp. 11-77. Then there is of course Henri-

Irénée Marrou's monumental *Saint Augustin et la fin de la culture antique* (4th ed.; Paris: Editions E. de Boccard, 1958). In his more popular *St. Augustine and His Influence Through the Ages* (London: Longmans, 1957), Marrou (p. 188) characterizes his earlier work as a study of "the mental formation and equipment of St. Augustine." The relevance of Marrou's treatise is clear; at the same time it is not precisely a study of St. Augustine's contact with the field of education. In his bibliographical orientation (*ibid.*, pp. 187-190), Marrou gives fundamental works dealing with Augustine's life and thought, including the contact with theology, the Church, the theology of history and the political ideas. Education does not appear. Concerning Augustine's influence upon the future, where his educational doctrine and activity would be directly involved, Marrou remarks "The domain to be explored is immense" (*ibid.*, p. 190), and gives no specific works. Cf. the comprehensive study by Pierre Riché, *Education et culture dans l'occident barbare, vi-viii siècles* (Paris: Editions du Seuil, 1962), for an introduction to the nature and magnitude of St. Augustine's influence.

4 We have used Migne, P.L., vols. 32-47, *Opera omnia S. Augustini* for the Latin edition of St. Augustine's works, as the most convenient for purposes of general study. For the critical editions of St. Augustine's works available thus far, cf. Eligius Dekkers, *Clavis Patrum Latinorum* (Steenbrugis: In Abbatia Sancti Petri, 1961). For the *Confessions*, the version which we preferred is *The Confessions of St. Augustine*, translated with an introduction and notes by John K. Ryan (New York: Image Books, 1960).

5 *Vita Sancti Augustini ex eius potissimum scriptis concinnata*, Migne, P.L. 32, 65-578.

6 *Vita S. Aurelii Augustini* auctore Possidio Calamensi Episcopo, Migne, P.L. 32, 33-66. There is a translation with good critical notes by Herbert T. Weiskotten, *Sancti Augustini Vita Scripta a Possidio Episcopo* (Princeton: Princeton University Press, 1919). We have used the more recent and generally available translation by F. R. Hoare, *The Western Fathers* (New York: Sheed and Ward, 1954), pp. 189-244, in the series "Makers of Christendom" edited by Christopher Dawson.

7 Le Nain de Tillemont, *Memoires pour servir à l'histoire ecclésiastique des six premiers siècles* (Paris: C. Robustel, 1693-1712): "Tome treizième qui contient la vie de Saint Augustin," pp. 952, with "Notes et éclaircissements," pp. 953-1048.

8 Carl Bindemann, *Der heilige Augustinus* (3 vols.; Berlin: Verlag von Hermann Schultze, 1844-1855).

9 Jean Poujoulat, *Histoire de saint Augustin: sa vie, ses oeuvres, son siècle, influence de son genie* (3 vols.; Paris: J. Lafitte, 1845).

10 C. Wolfsgruber, *Augustinus* (Paderborn: Schöningh, 1898), pp. xvi and 952.

11 Eugène Portalié, "Augustin (Saint)," in *Dictionnaire de théologie catholique*, I, 2268-2472. English translation by Ralph J. Bastian, *A Guide to the Thought of Saint Augustine* (Chicago: Regnery, 1960), pp. xxvii and 428.

12 *Ibid.*, p. 5.

13 Franz Xavier Eggersdorfer, *Der heilige Augustinus als Pädagoge und seine Bedeutung für die Geschichte der Bildung* (Freiburg: Herdersche Verlagshandlung, 1907). This work has fallen too far out of sight and deserves to receive the continued close attention of Augustinian scholars. While it does not penetrate to a full view of St. Augustine's contact with the field of education, and while it suffers from an excessive dichotomy between Augus-

tine's "philosophical" and "ecclesiastical" periods, perhaps already under the influence of Harnack's views which were to generate the still-continuing Alfaric–Boyer controversy, the fact remains that Eggersdorfer establishes a major aspect of the life of the Bishop of Hippo.

14 Jules Martin, *Saint Augustin* (2d ed., "Les grandes philosophes"; Paris: F. Alcan, 1923). First edition, 1901.

15 For example, "La connaissance," pp. 1-98 including "La formation intellectuelle," pp. 7-21; and in the discussion of St. Augustine's social doctrine, pp. 365-388, the short topic on "Direction des études."

16 Hugh Pope, *Saint Augustine of Hippo: Essays Dealing with His Life and Times and Some Features of His Work* (Westminster, Md.: The Newman Press, 1949), XIX, 408. Cassiciacum is devoted to "philosophical disputations," p. 92; in connection with Augustine's two monasteries, a "school" is not mentioned, p. 111; when the bishops he trained are mentioned, there is no word of a "school," p. 132. The word "education" does not appear in the index.

17 Heinrich Hubert Lesaar, *Saint Augustine* (New York: Benziger, 1931), translated from the German which was dated August 28, 1929.

18 Gustave Bardy, *Saint Augustine: L'homme et l'oeuvre* (Paris: Desclée, 1940). No chapter is devoted to St. Augustine as an educator: the nearest is "Le prédicateur," pp. 213-263. "Education" and "enseignement" do not appear in the index.

19 Vernon J. Bourke, *Augustine's Quest of Wisdom: Life and Philosophy of the Bishop of Hippo* (Milwaukee: Bruce, 1945). In chap. iii, "Master of Rhetoric," pp. 28-47, the author gives an excellent sketch of the external educational framework of Augustine's earlier life, but seems to miss its intrinsic relationship to his quest for wisdom. "Very little is known about his work as a teacher at this time" (p. 28). At "The Retreat at Cassiciacum" (chap. v, pp. 67-80), "Augustine was still teaching Licentius as a private pupil . . ." (p. 70). Then education falls out of sight in the rest of the book: the contact with the field of Catholic education as such does not appear. "Education" is not listed in the index.

20 M. F. Sciacca, *Saint 'Agostino* (Brescia: Morcelliana, 1949). Cf. especially chap. iv, "La verità: ragione e intelletto," pp. 189-243, discussing "il Maestro interiore: il problema dell' insegnamento" and "l'illuminazione e le sue tre forme."

21 Lucien Fabre, *Saint Augustin* (Paris: Hachette, 1951). For the treatment of Cicero's influence, cf. chap. vii, "L'Hortensius," pp. 79-89, to which we shall return below.

22 Paul Simon, *Aurelius Augustinus: Sein geistiges Profil* (Paderborn: Schöningh, 1954).

23 John J. O'Meara, *The Young Augustine: The Growth of St. Augustine's Mind Up to His Conversion* (London: Longmans, Green, 1954).

24 A. Sizoo, *Augustinus: Leven en Werken* (Kampen: J. H. Kok, 1957).

25 In St. Augustine's own references to his life, as well as in the phraseology of Possidius, we believe this fact is borne out by the constant use of the standard terminology, as we know it from Cicero and Quintilian, of the educational institution of classical antiquity. This could well be made the object of a special study. For whatever initial light may be obtained in this manner on St. Augustine as an educator and educational philosopher, we shall cite the Latin from Migne when quoting the translations of the *Confessions, Dialogues,* and Possidius' *Life*—not in full, lest the footnotes become

too burdened, but only the phrases typical of the official world of education in Augustine's day. In this way the very language used might well be seen to manifest a more clear and definite contact of his life and work with the field of education than biographers since Tillemont usually describe.

26 See below, the discussion of the nature of Augustine's activity at Cassiciacum and the purpose of the *Dialogues* which resulted, and Appendix II, "The Controversy on the Conversion of St. Augustine."

27 There is much obscurity on this question. Even one so deeply versed in St. Augustine as H. I. Marrou gives only two works and a passing comment on the matter: "A special place must be given to what we may call his educational works, such as *De catechizandis rudibus,* a little book of elementary religious instruction, or his *De doctrina christiana,* a thesis on Christian education . . ." (cf. his *Saint Augustine and His Influence* . . . , p. 55).

28 We have noted already that a sound and salutary "return to the sources," to the Scriptures, namely, and the liturgy, has characterized the life of the Church in the first half of the twentieth century, indeed since the Pontificate of Pope Leo XIII and his *Providentissimus Deus* (Nov. 18, 1893). This prepares the way for a deeper appreciation of the approach of the Fathers of the Church to Catholic education, an approach which was directly concerned with the Bible and the Liturgy.

29 Possidius, *Vita,* 1; Hoare, *op. cit.,* p. 194.

30 Portalié-Bastian, *op. cit.,* p. 6.

31 Cf. *Conf.,* III, 4.

32 Cf. *Conf.,* VI, 16, Ryan, *op. cit.,* p. 154: ". . . the fear of death and of your judgment to come, which never left my soul through all my changing opinions."

33 *Conf.,* III, 4; Ryan, *op. cit.,* p. 82.

34 Cf. *Conf.,* I, 11.

35 *Conf.,* I, 15; Ryan, *op. cit.,* p. 58.

36 Cf. *Conf.,* I, 11.

37 Possidius, *Life,* I; Hoare, *op. cit.,* p. 194; Migne, P.L. 32, 35: ". . . saecularibus litteris eruditus apprime, omnibus videlicet disciplinis imbutus, quas liberales vocant."

38 H. I. Marrou, *A History of Education in Antiquity* (New York: Sheed and Ward, 1956), XIII.

39 *Ibid.,* XII.

40 *Ibid.,* p. 212.

41 *Ibid.,* p. 265.

42 For the Graeco-Roman educational institution of classical antiquity, there are the two comprehensive and fundamental works of Grasberger and Marrou, cited above. For Roman education in particular, see A. Gwynn, *Roman Education from Cicero to Quintilian* (Oxford: At the Clarendon Press, 1926), a work of first importance in connection with St. Augustine due to its clear portrayal of the philosophic tension regarding quality in education centering about Cicero's lost work, the *Hortensius.* See also A. J. Festugière and Pierre Fabre, *Le monde gréco-romain au temps de nôtre-seigneur* (Paris: Bloud et Gay, 1935), esp. Vol. I, "L'Education," pp. 160-174; Jérome Carcopino, *Daily Life in Ancient Rome* (London: Routledge, 1941), chap. v, "Education and Religion," pp. 101-140. For additional references see Marrou, *Saint Augustin et la fin* . . . , pp. 9-10. Due to the fundamental unity between Greek and Roman education, both in structure and in philosophy, the student of St. Augustine seeking the full educational significance of the

episode in his life connected with Cicero's *Hortensius* demands a study of Greek education in its relation to Greek philosophy. The fundamental work here is Werner Jaeger, *Paideia: The Ideals of Greek Culture* (New York: Oxford University Press, 1944), esp. Vol. III: *The Conflict of Cultural Ideals in the Age of Plato,* together with Marrou's *History,* cited above. See also James Drever, *Greek Education: Its Practice and Principles* (Cambridge: At the University Press, 1912), and Paul Girard, *L'éducation athénienne au Ve et au IVe siècle J.-C.* (Paris: Hachette, 1891). For a comprehensive study of the philosophical conflict in the field of education throughout classical antiquity, see the introductory chapter in Hans von Arnim, *Leben und Werke des Dio von Prusa, mit einer Einleitung: Sophistik, Rhetorik, Philosophie in ihrem Kampf um die Jugendbildung* (Berlin: Weidmannsche Buchhandlung, 1898), pp. 4-114. Speaking of Plato and Isocrates, von Arnim writes: "Die platonische Akademie stand . . . als ein nur durch seinen Lehrplan unterschiedenes Erziehungsinstitut. Nur wenn man sich das klar macht, versteht man die Rivalität der beiden Männer und überhaupt den Rangstreit der Philosophie und der Rhetorik, der hier zuerst entsteht, um dann in mannichfach veränderter Weise die folgenden Jahrhunderte hindurch bis in die römische Zeit hinein fortzudauern" (p. 20). It is this which illuminates the incident of the *Hortensius,* and indeed the entire life of St. Augustine, with a special significance for the field of education.

[43] Apuleius, *Florida,* 20, in Carcopino, *op. cit.,* p. 107. See *Confessions,* I, 13–II, 4, for St. Augustine's description of his student days, where exactly the same structural pattern of the classical educational institution comes to view.

[44] Gwynn, *op. cit.,* p. 247. For the same conclusion, see Marrou, *A History of Education in Antiquity, passim.* It is the merit of Eggersdorfer to have seen the fundamental and philosophical nature of Augustine's contact with classical education. When he entered the system, rhetoric had long since triumphed completely and was in full possession of the field. "Da neben läuft die Opposition der Philosophen her" (*op. cit.,* p. 9): St. Augustine goes over to this philosophical opposition, but in so doing—a point frequently missed—remains an educator, indeed in most consistent fashion, to the end of his life.

[45] Marrou, *A History of Education in Antiquity,* p. 79. Cf. *ibid.,* "Rivalry between Philosophers and Rhetors," pp. 210-212; cf. p. 210: ". . . they were two hostile cultures, and they fiercely disputed each other's right to existence."

[46] *De Oratore,* III, 93: "Iuventus nostra dedisceret paene discendo"; cf. Gwynn, *op. cit.,* p. 113.

[47] Gwynn, *op. cit.,* p. 114.

[48] *Ibid.,* p. 118.

[49] Cf. *Conf.,* I, 9-20; II, 3; 6; 10; III; 1-3.

[50] Eggersdorfer, *op. cit.,* p. 10.

[51] *Conf.,* I, 18; Ryan, *op. cit.,* pp. 60-61.

[52] Cf. Eggersdorfer, *op. cit.,* p. 11.

[53] Cf. J. M. Nielen, "Der letzte antike, der erste moderne Mensch," *Unitas,* LXXVII (1937-1938), 67-72.

[54] *Conf.,* I, 16; Ryan, *op. cit.,* pp. 58-59.

[55] *Ibid.,* I, 19; p. 62.

[56] *Ibid.,* III, I; p. 77.

[57] *Ibid.,* III, 3; p. 80.

58 *Ibid.*, II, 2; p. 67.

59 *Ibid.*, II, 3; p. 67; Migne, P.L. 32, 677: ". . . dummodo essem disertus, vel desertus potius a cultura tua, Deus, qui es unus verus et bonus Dominus agri tui cordis mei."

60 *Conf.*, III, 4; Migne, P.L. 32, 685. For the critically corrected reading *quiusdam Ciceronis* and its interpretation see Maurice Testard, *Saint Augustin et Cicéron*, Vol. I: *Cicéron dans la formation et dans l'oeuvre de Saint Augustine* (Paris: Etudes Augustiniennes, 1958), pp. 11-19, with the references to recent discussion of the point.

61 *Conf.*, III, 4; Ryan, *op. cit.*, p. 81.

62 *Ibid.* For other references of St. Augustine to the impact of the *Hortensius* on him, see *Conf.*, VI, 11; VII, 7; *De beata vita*, IV, 10; *Solil.*, I, 17.

63 Cf. *De ordine*, II, 20.

64 *Conf.*, VI, 7; Ryan, *op. cit.*, p. 143.

65 For conversion to philosophy in general, see Gustave Bardy, *La conversion au Christianisme durant les premiers siècles* (Paris: Aubier, 1949), chap. ii: "La conversion philosophique," pp. 46-89; A. D. Nock, *Conversion* (New York: Oxford University Press, 1933), esp. chap. i: "The Idea of Conversion," pp. 1-16, and chap. xi: "Conversion to Philosophy," pp. 164-186; for St. Augustine in particular, see Marrou, *Saint Augustin et la fin . . .*, "La conversion à la philosophie," pp. 161-186, a lucid chapter remarkable for its success in relating this entire aspect to Augustine's mind and life to the field of education. Cf. also Werner Jaeger, *Humanistische Reden und Vorträge* (Berlin: Walter de Gruyter, 1960), "Die Griechen und das philosophische Lebensideale," pp. 222-239.

66 "Quest for Wisdom": The title of Vernon J. Bourke's work which studies Augustine's life and philosophy in a comprehensive manner from this point of view.

67 *Conf.*, VIII, 7; Ryan, *op. cit.*, pp. 193-194.

68 Charles Boyer, *Christianisme et Néo-platonisme dans la formation de Saint Augustin* (Paris: Gabriel Beauchesne, 1920), pp. 32-33.

69 O'Meara, *op. cit.*, pp. 59-60.

70 Etienne Gilson, *Christianity and Philosophy* (New York: Sheed and Ward, 1939), "Preface," p. viii. This is one approach to the recent controversy, dating from Bréhier's 1928 lectures, "Is There a Christian Philosophy?" Bréhier of course denied the possibility. The fact is, however, that there has been: it stands there as a magnificent historical reality, one of the most striking features on the landscape of the Christian era. Christopher Dawson, forced to enter the lists to defend the very idea of Christian culture, used the same approach in his *The Historic Reality of Christian Culture* (New York: Harper, 1960), a book essential to contemporary application of the Biblical and patristic concept of education. For the same thought expressed in a quite different connection and linguistic world, cf. Adriano Bernareggi in *San Tommaso d'Aquino* (Milano: Vita e Pensiero, 1923), p. 227: "La 'civitas christiana' è stata una felice realtà, corrispondente ad una concezione Cristiana integrale di tutta la vita, in tutti i suoi aspetti."

71 Cf. *Conf.*, III, 3; Ryan, *op. cit.*, p. 80: "Moreover, my studies, which were called honorable, were directed to the practice of law. . . ." Then comes the reading of the *Hortensius* (III, 4), then he describes his association with the Manichees (III, 6-12), and in Book IV law is completely forgotten. Augustine has entered the field of education and has become a professor on the level of higher studies: "In those years I taught the art of rhetoric. . . . (*ibid.*, IV, 2; *op. cit.*, p. 92).

72 Possidius, *Life*, I; Hoare, *op. cit.*, p. 194. Cf. Migne, P.L. 32, 35: "Nam et grammaticam prius in sua civitate, et rhetoricam in Africae capite Carthagine postea docuit. . . ."

73 For this discipleship, see the recent comprehensive study and extensive bibliography of Maurice Testard, *Saint Augustin et Cicéron*, Vol. I: *Cicéron dans la formation et dans l'oeuvre de saint Augustin;* Vol. II: *Répertoire des textes* (Paris: Études augustiniennes, 1958).

74 Gwynne, *op. cit.*, p. 112. For Cicero's teaching on this point see E. W. Sutton and H. Rackham, *Cicero de oratore*, Vols. I-II (Cambridge: Harvard University Press, 1959), esp. Crassus' speech in Book III. See also M. L. Clark, *Rhetoric at Rome: A Historical Survey* (London: Cohen and West, 1953), and Louis de Mondadon, "Saint Augustin, professor," *Études*, 1910, pp. 5-34.

75 Clark, *op. cit.*, pp. 60-61. Cf. Gwynn's summary of Tacitus' *Dialogue:* "In Cicero's day men studied history, philosophy, law, music, geometry, grammar, all the liberal arts: nowadays it is rhetoric, and nothing but rhetoric" (*op. cit.*, p. 243). In the larger sense Cicero's message was to be heeded, but not within the philosophical and social framework of the classical educational institution; this took place in the Schools of Christendom, organized according to the educational thought of Cicero's Christian disciple, Augustine.

76 See P. Courcelle, *Recherches sur les Confessions de saint Augustin* (Paris: E. de Boccard, 1950), p. 60.

77 Cf. *Conf.*, IV, 16; Ryan, *op. cit.*, p. 110.

78 Cf. Eggersdorfer, *op. cit.*, p. 12.

79 *Conf.*, III, 5; Ryan, *op. cit.*, p. 82.

80 *Ibid.*, IV, 16; *op. cit.*, p. 112. Cf. Testard, *op. cit.*, pp. 45-48, "Les études personnelles," with the references for fuller study of the point.

81 Cf. *Conf.*, V, 6-7; Ryan, *op. cit.*, pp. 119-122. "For almost nine years . . . I awaited with intense longing the coming of their Faustus . . . [p. 119]. I saw at once that the man was unskilled in the liberal arts . . . [p. 120]. So [he] who had been a fatal snare to so many men, now began, neither willing it nor knowing it, to loosen the snare in which I was caught" (pp. 121-122).

82 This philosophical break-through to *ipsum esse subsistens* and to the concept of creation *ex nihilo* might well be termed the dawn of Christian Philosophy as such, taking the term to denote the now stronger and more vigorous and luminous activity of healed and restored human reason. See Etienne Gilson, *God and Philosophy* (New Haven: Yale University Press, 1941), esp. pp. 51-62. For St. Augustine's own description of his process of thought on this point, cf. *Conf.*, VII, 8-18; Ryan, *op. cit.*, pp. 168-176. For his earlier inability to rise to the concept of God as a non-material reality, see *Conf.*, IV, 16, 31; V, 10, 19 (". . . for I thought that anything not a body was nothing whatsoever. This was the greatest and almost the sole cause of my inevitable error."); VI, 4, 5; VI, 11, 18; VII, 1, 1 ("I could conceive of no substantial being except such as those I was wont to see with my own eyes."); VII, 20, 26; finally, IX, 10, "The Vision at Ostia," the famous conversation with his mother: the full peace of the Christian philosopher.

83 For the comprehensive study of Augustine's mind, cf. Marrou, *Saint Augustin et la fin . . .* , esp. chap. iv, "Un lettré de la décadence," pp. 85-104, and chap. v, "L'érudition: ses origines," pp. 105-124, for this period of Augustine's life.

84 Cf. J. Finaert, *Saint Augustin rhéteur* (Paris: Les Belles Lettres, 1939),

chap. i, "Un rhéteur au service du vrai," pp. 1-21. There have been those who doubted Augustine's excellence in his field (pp. 1-2), but without justification: "Son talent et ses déclamations lui avaient valu d'éclatants succès" (p. 2).

85 Cf. Charles Boyer, *L'idée de vérité dans la philosophie de saint Augustin* (Paris: Beauchesne, 1921).

86 Cicero, *De oratore*, I, 32; Sutton-Rackham, *op. cit.*, I, 25.

87 *Ibid.*, I, 33; *loc. cit.*

88 Cf. Jaeger, *Paideia*, for a comprehensive treatment of the meaning of this heritage. For a short summary, cf. Otto Willmann, *The Science of Education* (Latrobe: The Archabbey Press, 1930), I, 118-162. It is the concept of the culture of the human arts and disciplines as a preparation for the philosophical and ethical knowledge which characterizes genuine humanism and offers young people the prospect of a genuinely human mode of living.

89 *Conf.*, III, 4; Ryan, *op. cit.*, p. 81. Cf. Testard, *op. cit.*, "L'élan intellectuel du disciple de Cicéron," I, 41-80.

90 Cf. *De cura pro mort. gerend.* for his influence on his student Eulogius who followed his footsteps as the *rhetor* at Carthage; cf. *Conf.*, IX, 2, for the opposition of the parents.

91 Cf. Testard, *op. cit.*, pp. 49-66, "Le De pulchro et apto," for a full report and discussion of what is known concerning St. Augustine's first work. From his own description, *Conf.* IV, 13-15, it is clear that the work bears witness to the philosophical approach in education described above: he stood firmly with Plato against Isocrates.

92 Cf. *Conf.*, V, 8; Ryan, *op. cit.*, p. 122: "The greatest and almost the sole reason was because I had heard that young men studied there in more a peaceful way and were kept quiet by the restraints of a better order and discipline."

93 For *rhetors* in Augustine's time who had received appointments to the highest posts in the imperial administration, cf. John J. O'Meara (trans.), *St. Augustine Against the Academics* (Westminster, Md.: The Newman Press, 1950), pp. 8-9; Finaert, *op. cit.*, p. 2: "Augustin s'était avancé rapidement vers les postes les plus âprement disputés."

94 It seems insufficient, for example, to speak of Augustine's study of Neoplatonism at Milan in the manner of Portalié: ". . . he was carried out of himself and seized by a new passion, a passion for philosophy" (Portalié-Bastian, *op. cit.*, p. 12). This seems incompatible with *Confessions* III, 4 (7-8), and plays directly into the hands of Boissier, Harnack and Alfaric. Augustine's "new" passion is for God, now at last seen to be so purely spiritual reality, not for philosophy. Augustine actually says so himself: "Many, perhaps, twelve, of my years had flown by since that nineteenth year when by reading Cicero's *Hortensius* I was aroused to a zeal for wisdom" (*Conf.*, VIII, 7 (17); Ryan, *op. cit.*, pp. 193-194). It could be conceded that Augustine has a new appreciation for philosophy, or that he has discovered that new thing which he will bequeath enriched to the future, *Christian philosophy* namely, formally as such, with its new healed and healthy natural insight into the fact that God is *ipsum esse subsistens*, creating *ex nihilo sui et subjecti* the *esse* of all other existing realities. This is precisely the insight to which classical philosophy, even at its strongest, could not attain: there was always the dark area of being and of life shrouded by *Moira*.

3

Philosopher
of the Christian
Education of Youth

IF OUR investigation so far has proceeded from the evidence and has adhered to the nature of the case, St. Augustine's interest in education and his professional involvement in the field have been an integral part of his thought, of his innermost moral and spiritual aspiration, indeed of his very personality. Is this all to change with his resignation from his professorial chair in the educational system of imperial Rome? "Soon after this," writes Possidius, "with every fiber of his being he renounced all his ambitions for this world . . . and he duly gave notice to his pupils in oratory that, as he himself had decided to enter God's service, they must find another teacher." [1]

Did Augustine then leave the field of education when he resigned the chair of rhetoric at Milan? It could have been, but it does not necessarily follow. So intense a personality and so powerful and consistent a mind might well have had some deeper unity in his life. If, as we have suggested, he forsook the field of law at nineteen and entered the field of education precisely to seek and to find divine wisdom, then we might well expect some further and perhaps even closer and more profound contact with the field of education after his resignation.

There is no question but that Augustine was characterized by a strong dislike of the schools of rhetoric. He voiced
his views on many occasions after his conversion to the
Church and resignation from his professorship. He speaks of
his decision "to give up my profession of windy rhetoric." [2]
He tells us that it was a "school, from which I am glad that
I had in some measure escaped," [3] and remembers with regret
when he "taught such things for money." [4] Looking back on
his professorship in the schools of Rome, he sees that entire
historic educational system as a mountain barring the way of
human minds to truth and hence to the happiness of intellectual peace: the mountain is nothing else than the approach to education in "those schools": "the proud study of
vain glory." [5] These are his views on what he constantly calls
"those other schools" in the writings which come out of the
period immediately after his conversion and resignation, before his baptism.

Nor did this hostility to the schools of rhetoric decrease
as time went on. The *Confessions* contain a series of critical
evaluations of the other system, frequently expressed in
strong and striking language. Teachers there, he tells us, are
buyers and sellers of literature, itself only poetic fable and
a cloak for error: inane tales contrasting with useful studies.[6]
Closely related to this is the unforgettable passage on the
torrent of human custom, flowing through the educational
system, plied by drunken teachers, to the moral detriment of
mankind.[7] He remembers his work in the schools as that of
a "seducer" [8] and he calls his former position that "chair of
lies." [9]

These strong statements, together with his resignation,
imply perhaps a definite severance of the life and works of
Augustine from the field of education. It becomes plausible
to see him departing into a new professional mode of existence, a convert to "philosophy" at the same time that he
gives his life in the Church. Thus Cassiciacum becomes a "retreat" while he organizes a "monastery" at Thagaste, and
soon enters the busy life of a priest and a bishop, preaching,

administering the sacraments, and conducting a life-long polemic against the heresies of North Africa. These do indeed represent fundamental phases of his activity, and, as we have seen, the life and work of Augustine have come to be portrayed largely in terms of these categories.[10]

Possidius, on the other hand, uses the terminology of the field of education to describe these months and years after the conversion in the garden of Milan. "His next step after being admitted to the sacrament," he writes, "was to return to Africa and his own house and estate, in the company of some fellow-countrymen and friends of his who were joining him in God's service. On arriving there, he settled down there for about three years, selling his property and, with his companions, giving himself to God in a life of fasting, prayer and good works. . . . And what God revealed to his understanding as he reflected and prayed, he taught by sermons to those who were with him and by books to those who were not." [11] Indeed, Possidius continued, Augustine during this period became well known in North Africa: "His good name and his teaching. . . ." [12]

Thus briefly this disciple and companion for forty years sketches that period of Augustine's life prior to his ordination. Taking his words as they stand, there is justification for Eggersdorfer's statement that Augustine "remained a professor after his conversion." [13]

In continuing our inquiry into the contact with the field of education manifested by St. Augustine's life and work after his conversion only an analysis of the evidence can decide first, whether it is a fact, and if so, of what nature and degree.

The School at Cassiciacum

After resigning the chair of rhetoric in Milan, Augustine retired to a villa at Cassiciacum outside of the city, made available to him by a fellow teacher in the schools of Milan. Here he spent the months from autumn, A.D. 386, to Easter, 387, when he was baptized by St. Ambrose.

The first step in investigating whether Augustine actually continued a definite and substantial contact with the field of education is to determine, if possible, how he spent his time at this villa. Was it simply a "retreat"? Was "philosophy" his sole interest? Or a rule and order of religious life? Discussing the "occupation of the saint in the country: the manner in which he educates two young men," Tillemont describes the order of the day and asserts that Augustine "also took some care to instruct his companions in *belles lettres*. For it was to that end that he had them with him." [14] Tillemont also points out that the young people were at the proper age for achieving a love for philosophy and truth: hence Augustine caused them to read Cicero's *Hortensius,* "which produced in them a part of the effect of which the saint desired." [15]

Turning to the works which Augustine wrote during these months at the country villa, we find substantial evidence that Augustine looked upon his occupation as nothing else than the conduct of a school. So important is this point that we shall gather at some length the statements in the *Dialogues* which bear upon this fact.

"I was exhorting and encouraging them," St. Augustine informs us, "to the pursuit of study." [16] There is a systematic method and process of teaching with Augustine definitely in charge, functioning in his professional capacity.[17]

One of the youths, Licentius, is the son of his friend and patron, Romanianus, to whom he dedicated and sent the treatise *Against the Academics* partly for Romanianus' own sake and partly to show him the intellectual development of his son. Thus the *Contra Academicos* becomes in a sense a school report to the father of one of his students. Augustine tells the father that Licentius has made a good beginning in philosophy, but must still have that careful training in the subjects which are prerequisite for philosophy, if his development is to attain the desired end.[18]

Augustine gives the group a definite study plan, and reports the use of Books II, III, and IV of Virgil.[19] A little later on Augustine describes explicitly the purpose of the dialogue

Against the Academics: "This discussion between us has been undertaken to train you and to incite you to cultivate your mind." [20] Thus there is an educational motivation in the dialogue itself, in addition to the plan of the studies and the academic order of the day to which Augustine refers.[21]

The fact that the days in the country at Cassiciacum are devoted to an educational situation is clear, furthermore, in the manner in which Augustine organizes the private time of the group associated with him. It is to be used "for your studies." [22] Noting that Licentius is becoming excessively devoted to poetry, Augustine directs his studies in the manner of a professional teacher, simply commanding him to take up the study of philosophy instead. He admonishes the youth to remember that "our school," the characteristic term which Augustine uses in contrasting his present work with "that other school" from which he is happy to have resigned, is characterized by the use of *"Hortensius* and philosophy." In *nostra schola* the entire circle of studies is introduced, not for its own sake, but to develop the mind for the philosophical crown of academic work.[23] Here again we meet the central current of St. Augustine's life, dating from his first reading of the *Hortensius* when he was nineteen years of age. It is a current that has been growing in strength ever since, as we have seen in discussing his career in the schools of rhetoric. Thus there seems to be not only a relationship but a fundamental identity between Augustine's work in the schools of rhetoric and the activity which is taking place here at the villa outside of Milan.

Further in the same dialogue Augustine gives an implicit instruction on the purpose of their work at Cassiciacum, contrasting "the rhetoric school" with "our school." He is conducting a definite educational enterprise organized to carry on the specific activities and to achieve the purposes of a school. Indeed, he appeals to Cicero to make clear to his group, as well as to his readers (for he has now definitely taken up the pen), what his purpose is at the villa. "We are dealing with the morals and lives of young men," he writes, "with those formation and instruction all your writings are concerned." [24] Again we meet the explicit contact with the ideals of Cicero in Roman education, carrying over now into St. Augustine's new life after his resignation from his post in the educational system of the classical civilization.

The same constantly recurring reference to the nature of the activity taking place at the villa is manifest in the other "philosophical dialogues" of this period. Augustine speaks of "the school work of the boys," "the work of study," tells about "their books," and reports how he instructs them in the way they should study.[25] Again he calls it "our school" [26] and describes his life there as a daily teaching carried on in a philosophical way.[27] Like the true and born teacher, Augustine reports his joy when he notes that his daily work of teaching is visibly effective with the young people.[28] Indeed, Augustine gives us to understand that he hopes for a religious vocation for Licentius,[29] and rejoices that the boy is "becoming a son to me as well"—that final triumph and privilege of the teaching profession.[30]

The fact that Augustine was conducting a school at Cassiciacum emerges from a new direction when he corrects the boys for their display of vainglory, and takes the occasion to explain what the motive for study shall be in "our school," contrasted again with "that school," the educational institution from which he had recently resigned. "Pay me the fee," he says, "be good!" [31] It is impossible to ponder upon these clear statements without the growing conviction that Augustine remained in the field of education after resigning from the schools of rhetoric. He is continuing his educational profession, but now with a new motive on the part of his students and with a new type of fee for his own work as an educator.

It would take us too far afield from our present purpose, which is to establish the fact of an educational activity at Cassiciacum, to cite the second book of the *De ordine* in which St. Augustine explains to his students the order of learning and of teaching, the sequence of studies which characterizes the school which he is now conducting.[32] That it is a regularly recurring instruction Alypius makes clear when he says, "We daily hang upon your teaching." [33] Alypius remarks upon the philosophical character and the philosophical result of this teaching. Augustine with a graceful compliment to his more mature student and friend explains that these explanations of the nature of the "order of studies" are "necessary . . . for the sake of these boys." [34]

"The well-instructed soul," Augustine says further on in the same book, is one which knows and ponders the philosophical truths regarding God and the soul. This is the very essence of a proper order of studies. "I am longing to teach you order. . . . " [35] Augustine promises a further discussion of "these matters," the order of studies to which he has devoted the second book of *De ordine*. He hopes in conclusion that they will decide to follow "that order mentioned by us or perhaps another order more concise and appropriate, but, at any rate, a right order—and will seriously and consistently hold it." [36]

From these statements of Augustine himself, it seems clear that the activity at the villa of Cassiciacum is more than a simple "retreat" in preparation for baptism, and something quite other than a period devoted to pure philosophy, to speculations of a Neoplatonist type.[37] There is concern with philosophy, obviously, but there is the additional fact that the philosophical concern takes place in an educational process, in the actual conduct, in an orderly and systematic manner, in accordance with the educational practices of that time, of a school program functioning daily for the small group. Augustine is still the teacher, precisely as he has been since he entered the profession years before. The change is in the purpose and the motivation, and in the content and order of studies. The motive is "to see God, . . . this beauty—and he will see it who lives well, prays well, studies well." [38]

In the light of St. Augustine's own declarations it becomes clear that the activity at Cassiciacum is a continuation of the "Studium Sapientiae," as Marrou terms his brilliant analysis of Augustine's approach to education.[39] For there is indeed a planned and systematic course of study taking place under Augustine's supervision for this group of young people, all of them catechumens like himself. Furthermore, it is a "study of wisdom" because of the peculiar place and role which is given to philosophy in this school.

Nevertheless, as Zumkeller has pointed out, there is more involved than the mere study of wisdom, in a merely philosophical sense—in the sense, that is, of classical philosophy. To elaborate this point would take us beyond the purpose of the present discussion; we shall return to it later. Zumkeller's study, on the other hand, misses the "school aspect" of Cassiciacum entirely. "With his new-found peace and his freedom to serve God," he writes, ". . . Augustine was also concerned in a special way with the spiritual and moral formation of his students. He liked to hold conversations with them concerning philosophical questions, in which he also included his other friends and even his mother." [40] Zumkeller looks upon the activity at Cassiciacum as purely philosophical in nature, overlooking the specifically educational aspect, not to say foundation, of the life at the villa. "True it is," he writes, "that Cassiciacum is not yet cloister. . . ." He points out, however, that the entire arrangement and order of the day is a preview of the later monasteries founded by Augustine. "Cassiciacum is a genuine pre-school of monastic life for St. Augustine." [41]

These remarks on the part of the scholar who has analyzed so well the religious foundations made by St. Augustine at Thagaste and at Hippo are entirely justified. They point out the additional factor in the reality at Cassiciacum which takes the true nature of the activity at the villa beyond Marrou's concept of a mere philosophical *studium sapientiae*. Actually, what St. Augustine is conducting at Cassiciacum is a preview of the *schola perfectionis*, the "school of perfection," a phrase used to this day in religious communities; but Augustine's use is strict and proper, not metaphorical. This is indeed also the very idea of Catholic education, a "school of perfection" for the Christian young people who frequent it.[42]

There is more involved at Cassiciacum, therefore, than a mere personal tutorship which Augustine owes to his benefactors or some quite minor and incidental instruction. Such a characterization misses the point and fails to grasp the truth of the matter. Augustine was conducting a school at Cassiciacum, an organized and systematic order of studies for young people of an age corresponding to our late high school and early college years. The failure to grasp the truth of this matter causes the *Dialogues of Cassiciacum* to be placed in a false light, one which leads readily to a misapprehension of their nature. The next step in our investigation of St. Augustine's contact with the field of education, therefore, leads us to an analysis of these earliest of St. Augustine's literary works.

"The Dialogues of Cassiciacum"

The months at the villa outside of Milan are distinguished by St. Augustine's four "philosophical dialogues." Controversies regarding their exact nature and significance continue to the present day among Augustinian scholars. Whatever the answer may be, the fact remains that these weeks in the country saw St. Augustine embark upon that career as a writer which has produced the vast body of the *opera omnia sancti Augustini.* These dialogues, *Against the Academics, On the Happy Life, Divine Providence,* and the *Soliloquies,* remain as an abiding monument to these months, spent, as we have seen, in the conduct of what was a school situation containing a definite academic program. While these dialogues are sometimes described as appendages to Augustine's literary works, we believe that they offer the introduction to his entire later life and apostolic activity, and that they contain the key to a full understanding of the nature of his contact with the field of education. We must, therefore, give them special attention.[43]

Are the *Dialogues of Cassiciacum* only exercises in Neoplatonist philosophy? Are they simply philosophy and nothing more, whether that philosophy be Christian or Neoplatonist? What was St. Augustine's purpose in composing them?

"In him (Augustine)," writes Alfaric, "the Christian disappears behind the disciple of Plotinus. If he had died after publishing the *Soliloquies* or the treatise *On the Greatness of the Soul,* he would be remembered only as a convinced Neoplatonist, more or less tinctured with Christianity. Because, however, he later on wrote much on behalf of the Church, and because the evolution which brought him to do so has been overlooked, his first works have been interpreted in the light of the later ones, and it has been believed, falsely, that his Neoplatonism was nothing but the garb of his Catholic faith." [44]

Thus the *Dialogues of Cassiciacum* would not be Christian works at all. A milder view, yet one which rests upon a large concession to Alfaric's position, is stated by Professor O'Meara. These *Dialogues,* according to him, reflect the decision which Augustine made in the garden at Milan "to throw up his profession . . . and devote himself to a life of Christian philosophy." [45]

What, then, are we to say? Did Augustine compose the *Dialogues of Cassiciacum* to allay his own doubts? Certainly his own progress in philosophical insight was one of his motives. "Up to now, in my mind," he writes, "even the question of the soul is uncertain and changeable." [46] On the other hand, this is not Augustine's primary motive. It is difficult to find references to himself and his own advancement through the means of these dialogues while those which manifest his purpose of helping the young people with him and the readers for whom the dialogues were published are plentiful. [47]

Were these dialogues purely and simply philosophy, the product of a mind not yet really converted to Christianity, as Alfaric has maintained? What is the significance of the fact which Boyer has demonstrated so conclusively against Alfaric that the dialogues are the product of a mind already completely convinced of Christianity, and fully in possession of the fundamental tenets of the Catholic Church? [48] It is of basic importance to determine whether the *Dialogues* are the work of a Catholic thinker; we shall gather the main points of evidence.

In the dialogue *Against the Academics* Augustine speaks of Christ as him "to whom I have given myself completely." [49] Later on in the same work Augustine describes his intention to renounce the world, to embark upon the quest for wisdom, fully resolved "in nothing to depart from the authority of Christ." [50] "The Son of God is truly God," he writes in *The Happy Life,* and calls the Catholic Church one and the same with truth and wisdom, and therefore with the happiness of the soul.[51] In the work on *Divine Providence,* Augustine teaches that authority is partly divine, partly human, and explicitly relates the divine authority on earth to the Incarnation.[52] In the *Soliloquies* Augustine manifests a definitely Catholic understanding of the three theological virtues, faith, hope, and charity, stating that they heal the eye of the soul for seeing God.[53] Finally, it might be mentioned that whatever the philosophy is which these philosophical dialogues represent, it is a philosophy which prays for help precisely in philosophical thinking.[54]

We may consider, then, that the case for the Neoplatonism of the *Dialogues of Cassiciacum,* in the sense that the author was not yet actually Catholic in his thinking, may be dismissed as refuted.[55] The fact remains, however, that they are not theological treatises, and that they are couched sufficiently in the terminology and philosophical tools of Neoplatonism to provide a footing for the controversy which has stirred about them for nearly a century. It is necessary, therefore, to take further steps toward the elucidation of their nature.

The first clue is the fact that they were composed at Cassiciacum, which we have seen to be manifestly concerned with formal teaching. Hence it is no surprise to find that they arise out of the teaching process itself which Augustine was conducting at the villa. Significant here is the fact that Augustine repeatedly exercises care to have a stenographer present, so that he is able to publish the works as representing actual discussions which took place at the school he was conducting. Why this? Can it be dismissed as insignificant or incidental? Or did Augustine have some special reason? We touch here the much-discussed question of the historicity of these dialogues, a question vital to the understanding of them, and one which can be answered only after a survey of the evidence.

"I engaged a stenographer . . . and I allowed nothing to be lost." [56] Had Augustine left nothing else than this categorical statement, we should have perhaps all the evidence needed to understand the nature of the *Dialogues*. Nevertheless, there is far more to garner from the *Dialogues* themselves. He tells us a little further on that the group came together "for this purpose," namely, for the stenographic notation of the discussion. Augustine tells us that the discussion was terminated because it became "too dark to write down the record." [57] Apparently a dilemma is rising before us: either Augustine will appear compromised in the *Confessions,* or in these documents.[58] The controversy has revolved around the point that both cannot be historical: either the one or the other. But let us continue with the evidence. St. Augustine states explicitly that the dialogue *Against the Academics* is being recorded for the sake of Licentius' father. "Let us send a record to your father. . . . " [59] He mentions that people will be able to read what his group is saying.[60] "I had once and for all ordered that every word should be written down," Augustine states in *The Happy Life.*[61] Again in the same dialogue Augustine pauses at a particular point to order the stenographer explicitly to write the youth's words down just as he had spoken them.[62]

The dialogue on *Divine Providence* abounds in evidence that a stenographic record was made of discussions which actually took place at Cassiciacum and that the works which we possess today are historical reports of these dialogues. "At that villa," writes St. Augustine, "we used to conduct among ourselves whatever discussions seemed useful. Of course, we used to employ the writing instrument, so that all our discussions would be recorded. . . . The writing instrument was used so that, if it should be decided to make a permanent record of anything we said, there would neither be the need of saying it in another form nor the effort of remembering." [63]

When the young Licentius elaborated some especially telling points, Augustine hastened to have the stenographer write down his "excellent arguments." [64] Indeed, apparently recognizing the solid substance of the discussion which he was leading and guiding, it is here that Augustine begins definitely to plan the dialogue as a published work.[65] On another occasion, awakened during the night, they happened to take up their discussion in darkness. "We garnered into . . . the notebook all the points of our nocturnal discussion," Augustine tells us, reporting on his care that the substance of the philosophical points not be lost.[66] Speaking of his absent friends, Augustine asserts that "they shall read our written records, for we have already arranged not to lose the words spoken on these problems, and to tie together the things that tend to drop out of memory by the bond of writing, so speak, by which they can be retrieved." [67] In fact, Augustine has some wider purpose in mind, for he explicitly states that the publication of the dialogue will fit into some goal, whatever it is, which animates his mind during these weeks and months at Cassiciacum. "When they for whom we are most solicitous," he writes, "will have read these records, if anything will provoke them to disagree, then this disputation of ours will engender other disputations, and the very series of discussions will engraft itself into the order of teaching." [68]

Further evidence that an actual discussion is being recorded by the stenographic technique familiar in classical antiquity is revealed when Augustine finds his students indulging in vainglory, the besetting vice of the schools of rhetoric which he had left behind.[69] The boys insist that the record not be changed. Then Licentius becomes perturbed, realizing that everything they are saying is going to be consigned to writing. After correction by Augustine, the boys see his point: "Let our penalty remain recorded." [70] On another occasion Augustine's mother enters the room where the dialogue is taking place and joins the discussion. At this point, apparently in answer to a perhaps wordless question on the part of the stenographer, Augustine says, "Let record be made of her entrance and her question." [71]

It so happened that Licentius was absent from the group for some days. The life of the school continued, however, and indeed even the recording of these discussions. "Licentius will have to read these points," states St. Augustine, "just the same as those friends of ours who are not living with us." [72] Again, Augustine speaks of "those points which this written record will not permit you to lose." [73] At the end of the dialogue, finally, Augustine states that he has "decided to send these records" to others and to see to their publication: the career of Augustine as a writer has been launched.[74]

The *Soliloquies,* as the title indicates, are discussions between Augustine and his own reason: he preserves the dialogue form in these much-admired unfinished works which are his personal composition during the weeks at Cassiciacum. But he has a published book definitely in mind, linked with whatever his real purpose is in the other *Dialogues.* He has some project in view which he wishes to place before the public for testing and confirmation. "We shall do what we can," he writes, "to have these discussions read by learned and wise men." [75]

In the light of these numerous and categorical statements by Augustine himself, it seems we cannot escape the conclusion that the *Dialogues of Cassiciacum* grew directly out of the educational process, whatever its nature, which Augustine was conducting at the villa. During his entire life St.

Augustine has been seeking wisdom in and through the process of education. Could it be that his school at Cassiciacum, *nostra schola,* was a qualitatively different and higher type of education, deliberately projected now under Catholic auspices? In this case, the *Dialogues of Cassiciacum,* growing as they do directly out of St. Augustine's teaching, indeed reflecting that teaching in a unique way, would be invested immediately with a special significance for the field of education.[76] This is a large topic, one to which we shall return later; for the present we are concerned only with the fact of a continuing contact with the field of education, not with its nature. We leave the pleasant villa in the country outside of Milan, accordingly, to review the factual nature of Augustine's subsequent activities.

The Monastery School at Thagaste

Augustine with his mother, his friends, and his small group of students returns from the villa for the catechumenate in Lent of 387, to complete the formal and institutionalized instruction of the Catholic Church for the reception of the sacrament of baptism. It was a momentous day in the life of the Church of God when St. Ambrose poured the waters of baptism over the brow of Augustine, this famous teacher and educator of late antiquity, the accomplished type of the intellectual of his day. We know little of the thoughts and discussions of the two great Fathers of the Church. Soon we find Augustine on his way back to his home in North Africa, when his mother's illness halted the journey at Ostia, the occasion of the lofty conversations recorded in the *Confessions.*[77]

The death of his holy mother at Ostia caused Augustine to spend an unforeseen additional year in Italy, mostly at Rome, but also at Milan. This proved to be a providential delay, for it provided him with an opportunity to study monasticism, an institution recently taking root in Italy from Egypt, Palestine, and Syria.

The idea of a "school of perfection," in the specific meaning of the phrase which attaches to St. Augustine's life and work, had been maturing since his days at Milan when he was still a professor in the schools of rhetoric.

"Many of us who were friends together," he writes, "discussed among ourselves the turmoils and troubles of man's life and had a common disgust for them. We deliberated about a life of quiet apart from the crowd, and had almost decided upon it. This life of retreat we would arrange for thus: whatever we possessed we would put into a common fund, and out of all these goods, we would establish a single household. . . . The whole would belong to each of us individually, and everything would belong to all of us. We thought that there would be about ten men in this society, some of whom were very rich, especially Romanianus . . . who was extremely interested in this project, and he had great authority in persuading us to it, since his ample wealth much exceeded that of the others. . . . " [78]

St. Augustine states that this project collapsed: "It was completely broken up," he says, "and thrown aside." [79] He notes, however, that God himself had not forgotten even though he and his companions had: "Out of that council you derided our plans," he concludes, "and you prepared your own, according to which you were to give us meat in due season, and to open your hand and fill our souls with blessing." [80]

We have here another indication of that underlying unity and consistency which characterizes the life and thought of St. Augustine. There is a clear connection between this first beginning of his thought on the religious mode of life, and the life which we have noted at Cassiciacum. It is this germ which now takes nourishment from the study of monastic establishments at Rome and Milan, which the founder of Augustinian monasticism will use when he returns to his African homeland.[81]

It was more than a year, therefore, that Augustine and his companions remained in and about Rome, occupied with the further study of this project of a certain definite type of life. Also during these months, as he himself states, he continued his project in authorship, publishing at Rome his books on the moral teaching of the Catholic Church contrasted with that of Manicheism, his treatise *On the Greatness of the Soul,* and his three books *On Free Will.* At last, nearly a year and a half after his baptism, the group sails to North Africa and to Augustine's native city of Thagaste. To outward appearances, a completely new phase of Augustine's life is about to begin. On the other hand, knowing the power of his mind and the consistency of his character as we do, we should be alert to some continuing bond, perhaps so fundamental as to be hidden to first view, between his past and this future life which will occupy so public a position on the stage of our Western history.

St. Possidius tells us explicitly that Augustine returned to his birthplace to establish a monastery.[82] We have here, then, an epoch-making event: Augustine, the educator, the convert to the Catholic Church, founds a monastery. It is not a hermitage for hermits living separately according to the pattern of Egypt. It is a community life, and, in addition, one which manifests from the start St. Augustine's contact with the field of education. It is to be a school of perfection, with "school" understood in the literal sense. Augustine founds a monastery, and at the same time a genuine educational institution. The educational process which is to take place in connection with this institution, however, is entirely rebuilt in purpose, in motivation, and indeed even in its "order of studies." It is an educational institution set up to provide an academic pathway for the mind and the soul to know God and to know itself: *noverim me, noverim Te.*[83] "It is clear that Augustine never conceived a grouping of ascetics," writes Dominguez-del Val, "which would not be at the same time an association of friends consecrated to the intellectual life." [84]

The project of a monastic life for lay intellectuals, of which Augustine first thought before joining the Church, proved to be an idea which grew upon him after his conversion. This project of entering "the service of God" developed in the inner life of his soul, through the life of prayer which we can see so clearly in the *Soliloquies* at Cassiciacum, and grew also through his continued observation of the example of St. Ambrose, who had established a monastery in the outskirts of Milan, and the work of St. Eusebius of Vercelli. Then there were the monastic establishments, including convents for women, which Augustine was able to observe in Rome. The trajectory of St. Augustine's thinking, however, is unified and consistent throughout: from the very beginning while he was still teaching rhetoric at Milan to this foundation at Thagaste he has in mind always "an association of Christian intellectuals." [85]

At this fountainhead of Western monasticism, therefore, we might well be at the fountainhead also of Christian culture and Catholic education. For the "school of perfection" which Augustine established at Thagaste bore within itself a unity which should not be overlooked. The two aspects, "school," namely, and "perfection," can be considered so separately that each appears to represent the whole of St. Augustine. But we know him as a man in quest of wisdom, the integration and synthesis of life and thought: we have here in the process of its educational institutionalization that admirable unity of a complex set of human accomplishments, aspirations, and ideals which will constitute Christian civilization. Christian culture is already in sight, as well as the characteristic trait of the religious life in Western Christendom, its close association with the work of cultivating the mind. It is interesting to note that while Augustine always includes physical work in his program for the life of the group, the emphasis remains on intellectual work coupled with prayer.

Here at Thagaste, then, St. Augustine "settled down for about three years . . . with his companions, giving himself to God in the life of fasting, prayer and good works . . . and what God revealed to his understanding as he reflected and prayed, he taught by sermons to those who were with him and by books to those who were not." [86] These "sermons," as we have noted, cannot be the sermons preached by priests in the pulpit. Possidius is careful to point out that Augustine is a layman in these years, hence we must understand these "sermons" as academic discussions and lectures given, as Possidius explicitly states, "to those who were with him." Thus we have an educational situation, a monastery school; and it seems a justifiable inference to conclude that the basic pattern of the life is precisely that which we can see so clearly from the dialogues of Cassiciacum. In fact, Possidius mentions that his reputation spread over North Africa at this time, and states that the reputation was precisely for "his teaching." [87]

Noteworthy also is Possidius' statement that St. Augustine "taught . . . by books." The apostolate of authorship and publishing continues. He tells us himself that he composed or completed, after returning to Africa, and while living in the newly established monastery at Thagaste, his two books *On Genesis, Against the Manicheans,* and his six books *On Music,* and the treatises *On the Teacher* and *On the True Religion.*[88] To this same period belong the books on the liberal arts which he drafted and outlined but never found time to complete.[89]

With this monastic foundation at Thagaste the conversion of St. Augustine has found its term. The process which began with the reading of the *Hortensius,* which developed in his career as a *rhetor* in the imperial schools, and which climaxed with the resignation at Milan, has been a conversion in the strict sense, a complete change of life over into monasticism. His religious rule contains the program for his own personal way of life.[90] At the same time, it is a *conversio* of his entire person to God which includes the *conversio mentis* as an integral part of the process, by means of a masterful and sweeping program of educational restoration and renewal. The admirably synthetic character of St. Augustine's thought is reflected in his *De magistro,* composed at Thagaste, yet completely consistent with the *Dialogues of Cassiciacum.* After seven chapters of linguistic analysis, establishing the principles of human teaching and learning, Augustine suddenly reveals the educational aspect of all his thought and activity, an aspect which is one thing with his conversion. "Maybe you think," he writes, " . . . that the practical result we are after is but slight or mediocre. . . . But I would have you believe . . . that what we are giving our thoughts to is of no slight or ordinary profit; though, if I say that there is a happy life, and that everlasting, to which I desire that God—that is, Truth itself—may lead us by stages suited to our weak step, I am afraid I shall appear ridiculous for having set out on this great Journey by considering not the realities themselves which are signified, but only the signs. So then, you will pardon me if I play this prelude with you, not to do any play-acting, but to exercise the powers and keenness of our minds and so prepare ourselves not only to bear, but also to love the warmth and light where the blessed life reigns." [91]

Thus St. Augustine's conversion embraces the field of education, just as his quest for wisdom had embraced it in those earlier years when he was a *rhetor* in the schools of Rome. This new contact with education, furthermore, which begins at Cassiciacum and is revealed in the *Dialogues*, continues here at Thagaste. He founded a monastery as the secure way toward the *beata vita*, and includes in it as its chief work the order of learning which leads us, by stages suited to our weak step, up to the God who is truth itself. It is a monastery founded by an educator. It contains a school, *schola nostra*, which exercises the powers and keenness of minds and thus prepares souls to love the warmth and light where the blessed life reigns.

Notes from Chapter Three

1 *Vita*, c. 2; Hoare, *op. cit.*, p. 196; P.L. 32, 36: "Renuntiavit etiam scholasticis, quos rhetoricam docebat, ut sibi magistrum alium providerent, eo quod servire Deo ipse decrevisset."

2 St. Augustine, *Contra Academicos*, I, 1 (3); O'Meara, *St. Augustine Against the Academics*, p. 38.

3 St. Augustine, *De ordine*, I, 9 (27); Robert P. Russell (trans.), "Divine

Providence and the Problem of Evil," in *Writings of St. Augustine,* ed. Ludwig Schopp (New York: Cima Publishing Co., 1948), I, 264.

4 *Contra Academicos,* III, 15 (34); O'Meara, *op. cit.,* p. 138.

5 St. Augustine, *De beata vita,* 1 (3); Ludwig Schopp (trans.), "The Happy Life," in *Writings of St. Augustine,* p. 46. It is an approach to education "so empty and groundless inwardly," continues St. Augustine, "that it submerges and absorbs the conceited through the crackling, fragile ground upon which they presently walk and throws them back into the darkness. . . ." Important perspectives open here upon the relationship between St. Augustine's doctrine on illumination, the purpose and content of Christian philosophy, and the purpose and content of Augustine's program for the Christian education of youth, to which we shall return later.

6 Cf. St. Augustine, *Confessions,* I, 13 (22); Ryan, *op. cit.,* pp. 56-57.

7 *Ibid.,* I, 15-16 (24-26); *op. cit.,* pp. 58-59. P.L. 32, 672-673: "Non omnino per hanc turpitudinem verba ista commodius discuntur; sed per haec verba turpitudo ista confidentius perpetratur. Non accuso verba, quasi vasa electa atque pretiosa; sed vinum erroris quod in eis nobis propinabatur ab ebriis doctoribus: et nisi biberemus, caedebamur. . . . Et tamen ego . . . libenter haec didici, et in eis delectabar miser, et ob hoc bonae spei puer appellabar." Implicit in these words is the program of the *De doctrina christiana* and the motivation of the *Libri disciplinarum:* a new educational approach which will save what is sound and good in the heritage of *paideia, quasi electa atque pretiosa,* but which will screen out resolutely the *vinum erroris* by a fundamental reorganization of both method and content. The *Confessions* seem to urge students of the literary works of St. Augustine to look for a continuing *ex professo* contact with the field of education.

8 *Confessions,* IV, 1 (1); cf. Ryan, *op. cit.,* p. 93.

9 *Ibid.,* IX, 2 (4); *op. cit.,* p. 207.

10 Tillemont, *op. cit.,* p. 81, tells us that St. Augustine "quitte sa profession et retire avec ses amis à la campagne, chez Vereconde." French works on St. Augustine ordinarily designate the period at Cassiciacum as a *retraite*—for example, Boyer, *Christianisme et néoplatonisme* . . . , pp. 148 ff., "Raison de sa retraite." Tillemont discusses the "occupation du Saint à la compagne; manière dont il y élève deux jeunes gents" (*op. cit.,* pp. 84-87), and tells us that he "prénoit aussi quelque soin de les belles lettres. Car c'estoit pour cela qu'il les avoit avec lui" (*ibid.,* p. 86). With these words Tillemont verges closer upon the intrinsic and essential relationship of Cassiciacum to the field of education, the point of the present study, than do most biographers since his time. Yet Augustine's occupation at Cassiciacum appears to be something other than education, which becomes an incidental which later writers frequently omit altogether. It is a "retreat" and comes gradually to be conceived as a fundamental rupture with his erstwhile profession, nothing else than an exercise in Neoplatonism or in the Catholic religious life.

11 Possidius, *Vita,* c. 3; Hoare, *op. cit.,* p. 197. P.L. 32, 36: ". . . et presentes et absentes sermonibus ac libris docebat." Augustine was a layman at this time: these could not have been ecclesiastical sermons; *docebat!* Possidius states (*eodem loco*) that knowledge of Augustine's *bona fama atque doctrina* soon spread over North Africa; this is the reason the congregation at Hippo "seized hold of him," to his surprise, to make him their priest: ". . . iam scientes Catholici sancti Augustini propositum *atque doctrinam,* manu injecta . . . etc." (*ibid.,* c. 4; P.L. 32, 37; emphasis added).

12 Possidius, *Vita,* c. 3; *loc. cit.*

13 Eggersdorfer, *op. cit.*, p. 75: "Wir möchten erwarten, dass sich jetzt Augustin ganz und gar von aller Lehrtätigkeit abgewandt und sich allein seinem Innenleben gewidmet habe. Doch dem ist nicht so; er ist Professor geblieben." This is a fundamental insight which should not be allowed to fall into oblivion; on the contrary, it should be deepened and extended, as we shall see, beyond the positions reached by Eggersdorfer to cover much more of St. Augustine's literary production, more basic aspects of his thought, and an important phase of his care of souls as a priest and a bishop.

14 Tillemont, *op. cit.*, p. 86; see n. 10, above, p. 77.

15 *Ibid.* Tillemont touches here the underlying unity of St. Augustine's thought and life before and after conversion, perceptible from the field of education. It is an insight which Tillemont does not elaborate, and which seems to have been quite generally overlooked.

16 St. Augustine, *Contra Academicos*, I, 1 (4); O'Meara, *St. Augustine Against the Academics*, p. 39.

17 Cf., for example, *ibid.*, I, 4 (11); *op. cit.*, p. 48: "On the following day when we had sat down together, I said: 'Take up what you began yesterday.'" There are many such passing references in the *Dialogues* to a systematic teaching procedure with Augustine not only in charge but in command. He is operating a school, *schola nostra*, in contrast to *schola illa* from which he had resigned.

18 Cf. *ibid.*, II, 3 (8); *op. cit.*, p. 72.

19 *Ibid.*, II, 4 (10); *op. cit.*, p. 74: ". . . studying them . . . seemed to be a suitable occupation at the time."

20 *Ibid.*, II, 7 (17); *op. cit.*, p. 82.

21 Cf. *ibid.*, II, 9 (22), *op. cit.*, pp. 87-88, where Augustine discusses philosophy not in itself but as a *paideia*, a formative influence in the education of youth. "I do not want this discussion," he says with some severity, "to be undertaken merely for the sake of discussing with these young people. . . . We are concerned with life, with morality, with the spirit. . . . I have decided, however, to commit to writing now those points which we have often gone over together both to help the memory, which is an untrustworthy guardian of what one has thought out, and so as to induce those young men to apply themselves to these problems and attempt to approach and deal with them for themselves." This passage seems sufficient, even if we had no others, to place the entire purpose of the *Contra Academicos* in the field of education. Cf. *ibid.*, II, 13 (29), p. 95, where Alypius asks Augustine to explain further the purpose of this investigation into skepticism, and says, "Do not weary of being my teacher."

22 *Ibid.*, III, 1 (1); *op. cit.*, p. 98.

23 Cf. *ibid.*, III, 4 (7); *op. cit.*, p. 105; "But I suggest that you go, if you wish, and drink something and then return to our school, provided the *Hortensius* and philosophy still mean something to you."

24 *Ibid.*, III, 16 (35); *op. cit.*, p. 140.

25 Cf. St. Augustine, *De ordine*, I, 3 (6); Russell, *op. cit.*, p. 244: "I did not let the school work of the boys take me away from myself. . . . Because they were doing so much during the whole day . . . it seemed excessive to me to have them employ any part of the night as well for study. This, indeed, was the instruction they had received from me: that conversation between them should be on some subject aside from their books, and that they should train the mind to be at home with its own thoughts."

26 Cf. *ibid.*, I, 3 (7); *op. cit.*, p. 245.

27 Cf. *ibid.*, I, 3 (9); *op. cit.*, p. 248: "For philosophy . . . as you prove it day by day, is our true and tranquil abode." Augustine rejoices over this insight of Licentius, which takes him from the spirit of *schola illa* and brings him to *schola nostra* (cf. *ibid.*, I, 4 (10).

28 Cf. *ibid.*, *op. cit.*, pp. 248-249.

29 Cf. *ibid.*, I, 5 (13); *op. cit.*, p. 251: "He . . . who daily heareth my lamentations, and whose herald you, I believe, some day will be—and perhaps that 'some day' is not far distant." Augustine apparently was disappointed in this hope for Licentius, but the very statement of it reveals the nature of this activity at Cassiciacum: it was a Catholic school. Cf. *Epist.* 26 written to Licentius about ten years later, and *Epist.* 27 to Paulinus of Nola, asking him to keep an eye on his former student. The born teacher and the apostolate of the classroom: both are manifest at Cassiciacum.

30 *Ibid.*, I, 6 (16); *op. cit.*, p. 254.

31 Cf. *ibid.*, I, 10 (29-30); *op. cit.*, pp. 266-268.

32 Cf. *ibid.*, II, 2 (4-7); *op. cit.*, pp. 276-282; II, 8-10 (25-29); pp. 301-308.

33 *Ibid.*, II, 10 (28); *op. cit.*, p. 305.

34 *Ibid.; op. cit.*, p. 306. From these passages it becomes clear that the very title of this dialogue refers to the field of education, forming with its order of studies an integral part of that larger order which Providence maintains throughout the universe. In human affairs, there will be a close relationship between fidelity to Providence and due care for this specific order of definite studies.

35 *Ibid.*, II, 19 (50); *op. cit.*, p. 327.

36 *Ibid.* (51); *op. cit.*, pp. 328-329. This is to advocate a definite program for a curriculum of studies, which may vary, of course, but must always be "a right order."

37 Father Boyer in his work on Alfaric's thesis to this effect, to which we shall return in Appendix II below, sees indeed that there is a teaching process among the activities at Cassiciacum; it remains incidental, however, instead of furnishing the central insight and the full light upon the character of the *Dialogues* which would have removed all foundation from Alfaric's position (cf. Boyer, *Christianisme et néo-platonisme* . . . , pp. 154-155).

38 St. Augustine, *De ordine*, II, 19 (51); *op. cit.*, p. 328. For an excellent study of the fact that the occupation of St. Augustine at Cassiciacum was the conduct of a school, see Eggersdorfer, "Pädagogische Praxis der ersten Periode," *op. cit.*, pp. 73-96. This is the strongest section of Eggersdorfer's work, establishing positions which later writers have almost entirely overlooked.

39 Cf. Marrou, *St. Augustin et la fin* . . . , deuxième partie, "Studium Sapientiae," pp. 161-327, where St. Augustine's sponsorship of the Ciceronian educational ideal is analyzed in detail: the full circle of the liberal arts and disciplines taught as a preparation for philosophy. One can go a step further, as we shall see, and hold that the *Dialogues of Cassiciacum* are actually treatises which both declare and exemplify this same ideal, but now in terms of Christian philosophy, formally as such.

40 Adolar Zumkeller, *Das Mönchtum des heiligen Augustinus* (Würzburg: Augustinus-Verlag, 1950), p. 34.

41 *Ibid.*, p. 39.

42 It is well known that such is the explicit teaching of Pope Pius XI in *Divini illius magistri*, who insists on a rigorous integration of the entire

teaching, the textbooks and the syllabi in every branch, with the ultimate purpose of Christian life.

43 For the Latin texts, cf. Migne, P.L. 32 and Dekkers, *op. cit.;* we have used the translations of the two recent patristic series, *Ancient Christian Writers* and *Fathers of the Church.*

44 Prosper Alfaric, *L'évolution intellectuelle de saint Augustin,* Vol. I: *Du Manichéisme au Néoplatonisme* (Paris: Émile Nourry, 1918), p. 527.

45 O'Meara, *The Young Augustine,* p. 191. Clearly this view provides no place for a continuing substantial contact with the field of education. Furthermore, for those who do not grant the autonomous reality and validity of Christian philosophy, but conceive of it as this world's contemporary thought-patterns which men of faith simply adopt for use in their own thought and their communication, O'Meara's position becomes difficult to distinguish logically from that of Alfaric.

46 St. Augustine, *De beata vita,* 1 (5); Schopp, *op. cit.,* p. 49.

47 Boyer, *Christianisme et Néo-platonisme . . . ,* pp. 177-181. Boyer points out that Augustine reports the hold of the New Academy upon him as a thing of the past, broken by Ambrose and Sacred Scripture (cf. *De beata vita,* 1 (4); furthermore, both the *De ordine* and the *De beata vita,* completely free of philosophic doubt, were composed before *Contra Academicos,* II-III, the formal refutation of the New Academy. In other words, St. Augustine has some other purpose in mind while composing the *Dialogues of Cassiciacum,* quite different from a personal philosophical need. When this purpose is identified, the question of personal philosophizing will vanish.

48 Boyer, *Christianisme et Néo-platonisme . . . , passim;* cf. Appendix II below, "The Controversy of the Conversion of St. Augustine."

49 St. Augustine, *Contra Academicos,* II, 1 (2); O'Meara, *St. Augustine Against the Academics,* p. 66. See also *ibid.,* II, 1 (1) and II, 2 (5).

50 *Ibid.,* III, 20 (43); *op. cit.,* p. 150.

51 St. Augustine, *De beata vita,* 2 (34); Schopp, *op. cit.,* p. 82.

52 Cf. St. Augustine, *De ordine,* II, 9 (27); Russell, *op. cit.,* p. 304. See also *ibid.,* I, 10 (29); I, 11 (32); II, 5 (16).

53 St. Augustine, *Soliloquia,* I, 7 (14); Thomas F. Gilligan (trans.), "The Soliloquies," in *Writings of Saint Augustine,* p. 361. See also *ibid.,* I, 6 (12); *op. cit.,* p. 359.

54 Cf. *Solil.,* II, 6 (9); *op. cit.,* p. 391.

55 "Le seul fait qu'Augustin ait admis," writes Gilson reviewing Alfaric's book, "dès le début, la creation et l'égalité des personnes divines suffirait à établir qu'il fut immédiatement catholique et non plotinien." Cf. *Revue philosophique,* LXXXVIII (1919), 503. This is close to expressing the full truth of the matter: it is *Christian* philosophy which is involved, an independent, autonomous philosophical position with characteristic doctrines which distinguish it from Neoplatonism. It is wrong to call St. Augustine a Neoplatonist at Cassiciacum, in Alfaric's sense, and inexact to speak of some synthesis of Neoplatonism and Christianity.

56 St. Augustine, *Contra Academicos,* I, 1 (4); O'Meara, *St. Augustine Against the Academics,* p. 39.

57 *Ibid.,* I, 5 (15); *op. cit.,* p. 53.

58 Cf. Appendix II, pp. 347-380 below, for a study of the literature which has grown up in connection with this apparent dilemma.

59 *Ibid.,* I, 9 (25); *op. cit.,* p. 64.

60 *Ibid.,* II, 7 (17); *op. cit.,* p. 83.

61 St. Augustine, *De beata vita,* 2 (15); Schopp, *op. cit.,* p. 63.

62 Cf. *ibid.*, 2 (18); *op. cit.*, p. 66.

63 St. Augustine, *De ordine,* I, 2 (5); Russell, *op. cit.*, pp. 243-244.

64 *Ibid.*, I, 7 (20); *op. cit.*, p. 257.

65 *Ibid.; op. cit.*, p. 258.

66 *Ibid.*, I, 8 (26); *op. cit.*, p. 263.

67 *Ibid.*, I, 9 (27); *op. cit.*, p. 265.

68 *Ibid.* This is a definitely significant reference to the field of education. Augustine apparently has some far larger end in view than these few months and this small group at Cassiciacum.

69 For the general use of shorthand in classical antiquity, see Marrou, *A History of Education . . . ,* pp. 312-313: "Shorthand spread from the civil service and passed into general use. Ausonius had a shorthand secretary to take down his works. The Christian Church began to do the same: the reason why so many of the sermons composed by the Fathers of the Church in the fourth and fifth centuries have come down to us is that shorthand secretaries used to sit in the basilica at the feet of the bishop and take down his words as he delivered his homily during the service." From this viewpoint, Augustine was clearly doing nothing unusual, here in the late fourth century, in recording the philosophical discussions at Cassiciacum. He may have had some special purpose or enterprise in mind. At least there is reason not to press unduly the point that he composes in a purely literary genre, simply imitating Cicero and Plato. The *Dialogues of Cassiciacum* are indeed in that general genre: but only in general, with their own specific differences due to St. Augustine's special purpose and to this developed technique of shorthand.

70 St. Augustine, *De ordine,* I, 10 (29); *op. cit.*, p. 266. See also *ibid.,* (30); *op. cit.*, pp. 268-269.

71 *Ibid.*, I, 11 (31); *op. cit.*, p. 269.

72 *Ibid.*, II, 5 (17); *op. cit.*, p. 293.

73 *Ibid.*, II, 7 (21); *op. cit.*, p. 297.

74 *Ibid.*, II, 20 (54); *op. cit.*, p. 330.

75 St. Augustine, *Solil.*, II, 15 (28); Gilligan, *op. cit.*, p. 414.

76 "Die Krone der erziechlichen Arbeit Augustins," writes Eggersdorfer, *op. cit.*, p. 79, "repräsentieren die Dialoge. Sie schildern uns nicht bloss diese Arbeit, sie sind sie selber." This leads directly to a view of St. Augustine at Cassiciacum, Milan, Rome, and Thagaste which sees him as one of the most successful and best-known educators of his day deliberately shaping in his life and literary program a new theory and practice of education. It would be new, yet characterized by a fundamental consistency with his ideals and practice as a *rhetor:* witness the use of Vergil and of the *Hortensius* at Cassiciacum.

77 Cf. *Confessions,* IX, 8-13 (17-37); Ryan, *op. cit.*, pp. 216-228.

78 *Ibid.*, VI, 14 (24); *op. cit.*, p. 152.

79 *Ibid.*, p. 153.

80 *Ibid.*

81 After his baptism—Easter, 387—"he undoubtedly remained at Milan until the autumn of the year, continuing his works on the immortality of the soul and on music" (Portalié-Bastian, *op. cit.*, p. 19). His delay of a year at Rome until autumn, 388, writes Dominguez-del Val, was "un momento decisivo para el monacato" ("Cultura y formación intelectual en los monasterios agustinianos de Tagaste, Cartago e Hipona," *La Ciudad de Dios,* CLXIX [1956], 426). St. Augustine used the time to study the religious life and, even more important, to live with monks at Milan and Rome. Cf. *De*

moribus Ecclesiae Catholicae, I, 31 and I, 33. From this time Augustine turns definitely toward cenobitism from his earlier leaning to the eremetical life. It is difficult to exaggerate the importance of these developments in St. Augustine for the character of the coming civilization in the West. Cf. Zumkeller, *op. cit.*, pp. 40-45.

82 Cf. Possidius, *Vita*, 3 and 5; Hoare, *op. cit.*, pp. 196-199. "He himself had . . . established a monastery . . . before, when he returned from across the sea to his own home" (p. 198). Migne, P.L. 32, 37: ". . . Monasterium . . . instituit; et cum Dei servis vivere coepit secundum modum et regulam sub sanctis Apostolis constitutam (Act. 4, 32): maxime ut nemo quidquam proprium in illa societate haberet, sed eis essent omnia communia, et distribueretur unicuique sicut opus erat."

83 St. Augustine, *Solil.*, II, 1 (1); Gilligan, *op. cit.*, p. 381: "O God, ever the same; may I know myself, may I know Thee. That is my prayer."

84 Dominguez-del Val, *op. cit.*, p. 427. On the other hand, as Zumkeller points out (*op. cit.*, p. 50), von Kienitz reflects a false understanding of the project when he states that St. Augustine intended to establish "kein eigentliches Kloster, sondern ein Oratorium von frommen Intellektuellen." For the text of St. Augustine's original Rule at Thagaste, and the text of his own supplement for the second foundation at Hippo, see Winfried Hümpfner, "Die Regeln des heiligen Augustinus," in Hans-Urs von Balthaser (ed.), *Die Grossen Ordensregeln* (Einsiedeln: Benziger, 1948), pp. 121-133; for the history of the texts and the spirit of St. Augustine's Rule, see the introductory essay by Hümpfner and Adolar Zumkeller, *ibid.*, pp. 101-119, with references. These documents and studies leave no ground for views such as those of von Kienitz.

85 Dominguez-del Val, *op. cit.*, p. 428.

86 Possidius, *Vita*, c. 3; Hoare, *op. cit.*, p. 197.

87 *Ibid.*

88 St. Augustine, *Retr.*, 10-13; P.L. 32, 599-605.

89 On the *Disciplinarum libri* see *Retr.*, 6; P.L. 32, 591; for the *De diversis quaestionibus octoginta tribus*, which came directly from St. Augustine's work of teaching at Thagaste, and which he gathered into one book and published later, see *ibid.*, c. 26; P.L. 32, 624.

90 Cf. Zumkeller, *op. cit.*, pp. 113 ff.; in general for St. Augustine's participation in the general movement of spiritual reform and renewal in the early Church, see Gerhart B. Ladner, *The Idea of Reform: Its Impact on Christian Thought and Action in the Age of the Fathers* (Cambridge: Harvard University Press, 1959), esp. "St. Augustine's Program of Education and Its Relation to the Ascetic Reform Ideal," pp. 373-377. For an example of the disfiguration of this entire process under the influence of the Alfaric thesis, see Jean-Daniel Burger, *Saint Augustin: Un Père de l'Église* (Neuchâtel: La Baconnière, 1948), p. 105, where Augustine's conversion is seen to be "achieved" at Thagaste, in his discovery at last of Sacred Scripture and of the Church. At the same time, Thagaste is still a philosophical academy chiefly dedicated to Plotinus: Augustine in the *De magistro* teaches Adeodatus prayer, together with the idea of education, because he is carrying on the heritage of Plotinus! "La bonne méthode philosophique fait à la prière une large place" (p. 97).

91 St. Augustine, *De magistro*, 8 (21); Joseph M. Colleran (trans.), *St. Augustine: The Greatness of the Soul, the Teacher* (Westminster, Md.: The Newman Press, 1950), p. 158.

4

Paideia Theou: The Birth of Christian Philosophy

IN VIEW of the positions reached so far, it is necessary to pause, before continuing to the study of St. Augustine's contact with the field of education as a priest and a bishop, in order to document carefully and in detail the nature of his life and work at Cassiciacum. This is of interest for the light it should throw on St. Augustine's integrity in the *Confessions* and on the kind of philosophy which his early works represent.[1] It should be also of definite practical value in uncovering the patristic roots and fundamentals of certain abiding features of the Catholic philosophy of education. We are seeking to learn, furthermore, whether St. Augustine's thought and activity in the villa at Cassiciacum and at the monastery of Thagaste are characterized by a fundamental identity and consistency, or whether it is true that he was undergoing an intellectual evolution from Neoplatonism toward what is termed his ecclesiastical period. In the latter case, Cassiciacum and Thagaste might be poles apart; in the former, St. Augustine is establishing at Thagaste a way of life which satisfies him fully and which he has had in mind for some time. He is building an institution, a "school of perfection," in which wisdom is both sought and possessed. This is the happy life. This seems to be furthermore, precisely the nature of the school at Cassiciacum and the character of St. Augustine's first writings, which he composed at the villa.

St. Augustine gives us our point of departure himself. It is a striking passage in the dialogue on *The Happy Life* where he tells us that he has set up the discussion and arranged for the stenographic record of the teaching process which he is conducting, because the resulting published dialogue has some relationship to "the difficult matter I was undertaking." [2] In other words, St. Augustine is not on a leisurely retreat in the countryside preparing for baptism, but in the intense and consistent manner which his character and personality lead one to expect, he is pursuing a project of some kind and indeed not an easy one. What is this "difficult matter" which Augustine was undertaking at Cassiciacum? Is he still pursuing it at Thagaste? To answer this question, we must go through the evidence in still more detailed fashion, to determine more precisely, if possible, the nature of the *Dialogues of Cassiciacum*.

Qualitative Excellence in Education

Our analysis begins with Augustine's first extant work, the significant dialogue on *The Happy Life* which stands at the head of the vast body of his *Opera omnia*. *The Happy Life* is commonly acknowledged to establish his point of departure in philosophy. St. Augustine builds his philosophy upon an absolute basis in knowledge, which is furnished by our human consciousness of selfhood and of existence: "At least you know you are alive." [3] In other ways as well, this treatise from those weeks at Cassiciacum provides us with the fundamentals of St. Augustine's philosophy, its personal concern, its preoccupation with the life and happiness of each human soul, and with the fundamental relationship of the quest and the possession of truth to this human happiness. All of this is certainly true. The fundamentals of Christian philosophy as a distinctive body and heritage of thought on the human scene can be found in the dialogue on *The Happy Life*. We believe, however, that it does not do full justice to this dialogue to see in it nothing else than a purely philosophical exercise. This is the crux of the matter, and must be analyzed in detail.

The very arrangements made for the dialogue reflect definite purpose, some larger intention. St. Augustine assembles his small group with complete authority, exactly as a full-fledged professional teacher at work, and arranges for the stenographer with a certain air of solemnity which rings through the words of the dialogue itself. Augustine names the members of the group, and takes pains to explain why the two younger boys, not yet finished with their training in grammar, are included in the discussion. "I believed their common sense was needed for the difficult matter I was undertaking." [4] St. Augustine is animated by a definite purpose, a concrete project or plan. This remains an enigma unless the fact is kept in mind that the entire proceeding reflects a teaching process. It is this educational activity which reveals the nature of this difficult undertaking and enables us to understand why he arranged for the stenographic records of these discussions and for their publication which launched him on his new literary career.

Taking his philosophical point of departure from the absolutely certain biological fact that each person is a body and has life, St. Augustine leads his youthful participants to the conclusion that "life belongs only to the soul." [5]

Immediately Augustine leads the group from a discussion of the growth of the body through food to wonder whether the soul has a way of growing. " 'What about the soul?' I asked. 'Is there no food proper to the soul? Or do you think that knowledge is its nutrition?' 'Obviously,' said our mother, 'I believe that the soul is not nourished except by the understanding and knowledge of things.' " [6]

St. Monica, an active participant in the discussion, representing, one might well believe, the voice of the Catholic Church in St. Augustine's artistry, places the entire purpose of the group and of the dialogue on *The Happy Life* squarely in the field of education. The body grows; the "growth" of the soul is not a mere biological development, not a growth in the biological sense. There is an analogous growth of the soul, however, to which definite attention must be paid and careful provision made: this is nothing else than the function of the field of education. This dialogue stands revealed as a truly striking treatise on educational philosophy, which must be read to be appreciated. Excerpts cannot do it justice.

Augustine goes on to guide the discussion toward the understanding that there is a hunger of the soul. This undernourished condition can become so serious that illnesses of the spirit betray it, just as malnutrition of the body eventually makes itself manifest in the appearance of the body. There will be ills of the spirit and of the mind which betray educational impoverishment. When this unhappy condition of the educational establishment prevails, souls are left "hungry and famished." [7] Indeed, he leaves no possible doubt that he is discussing the field of education in one of its most fundamental aspects, namely in the very content of its curriculum. "Then we state correctly," he concludes for his group, "that the souls of people not scientifically trained and unfamiliar with the liberal arts, are, as it were, hungry and famished." [8]

Continuing in the same chapter, Augustine leads the analysis toward an insight into qualitative excellence in educational fare. Here we gain further understanding of the "difficult matter" upon which St. Augustine has embarked. It is the renovation and restitution of the heritage of *paideia*, full in the spirit of Plato and of Cicero in the *Hortensius:* we can see here a consistent continuation of Augustine's thinking and career, made now suddenly efficacious through his conversion to Christ in the garden at Milan. He is still engaged professionally in education, and indeed in a more fundamental way than ever before.

"The quality of this meal," Augustine continues, "I will reveal, if you are hungry." [9] With these words he presents his statement of the intention which he has in mind when composing the works of this period of his life. He is concerned with the quality of the fare of the soul to be provided by a properly organized and implemented educational system. As the skilled educator knows, there must be a desire for learning before learning can take place. "Although this may be too obscure for your understanding at present," St. Augustine tells his students, "you will certainly concede, when the souls of the uneducated are filled, that there are likewise, as for body, two kinds of food for souls: one healthful and beneficial; the other unhealthful and harmful." [10] This is the point of departure of the *Dialogues of Cassiciacum;* it stands at the very beginning of the dialogue which by common consent launches the philosophical career of St. Augustine. Indeed, it can be called rightfully the birthplace of Christian philosophy as such. It is not a birth distinct and separate from the field of education, but an integral part of it, exactly as the philosophy of Plato himself was developed as a renewal and a deepening of the ideals of Greek culture.[11]

Furthermore, it is impossible to ponder upon this passage without reflecting upon St. Augustine's career in the rhetorical schools of classical antiquity. From the time that he became interested in the love of wisdom, the pursuit of philosophy, at his reading of the *Hortensius* when he was nineteen years of age, from his change of profession from law to teaching, Augustine has been in search of wisdom within the field of education. What else can his reference to the two kinds of food for souls, one healthful and beneficial, the other unhealthful and harmful, mean, except that he has in mind a philosophy of education which is able to provide the spirit of man with a criterion for understanding and judging this difference? If these striking passages are read from the viewpoint of the field of education, it seems that Augustine himself states explicitly the true nature of the *Dialogues of Cassiciacum.* It is his word, and not our interpretation, that he is far from a leisurely spiritual retreat, that he is involved in a "difficult undertaking"; it is he who specifies for us exactly what it is. It is the elaboration of an educational food and fare for souls which will be helpful and beneficial, as contrasted with that torrent of human custom bearing souls down to the ocean of immorality and unhappiness, which he experienced so deeply in his personal life.[12] Instead of a contrast between the *Confessions* and the *Dialogues of Cassiciacum*, a most complete harmony and fundamental unity and consistency is readily visible, if this educational purpose and intention is kept in mind.

Let us pursue this fundamental point further. "The quality of this meal, I will reveal," Augustine assures his students, "if you are hungry. For in case I tried to feed you against your will and taste, my undertaking would be in vain and prayers should be said that you would be more desirous for those meals than for the ones of the body. This will be the case if your souls are healthy, for sick souls, as can be seen in a diseased body, refuse their food and spit it out." [13] A certain disposition of soul is necessary in students, if this healthful and solid and substantial education which Augustine is planning is to be found tasteful. Indeed, Augustine, Christian soul that he already is, sees that those responsible for young people must pray for them, that these intellectual and spiritual dispositions prerequisite for sound education be found in their souls. More and more clearly it emerges into view that we have here not a Neoplatonist but a Catholic thinker, devoting his thought to the Christian education of youth.

"By the expression of their features," the dialogue continues, "and by their words of approval, all said they were ready to accept and eat whatever I had prepared." [14] "Then I spoke again: 'We wish to be happy, do we not?' No sooner had I said this, then they agreed, with one voice." [15] Augustine comes in this way to the theme of this particular dialogue, after his general statement of the purpose underlying the fundamental undertaking which he had embarked upon. He did so, we think, in a general way when he read the *Hortensius* at the age of nineteen, but again in a particular

and unbelievably concentrated way after his conversion to
Christ in the garden of Milan. There is not a change in his
life, or a departure from the field of education, but rather
a more intensive search and grasp and possession of wisdom,
still in this same teaching profession.

His thesis is clear: happiness is the health of the soul and
this health of the soul depends upon the fare which the soul
is given. The structure arranged in human affairs to feed the
souls of men is the educational establishment. Thus there
is the closest relationship between the happy life for men and
the kind of education which society plans for them in their
formative years. Augustine's dialogue is designed to make
this point explicit. Happiness depends on knowing what to
desire, and this depends on education. How else can young
people gain this knowledge what to desire? [16] Still leaving
nothing to inference on our part, St. Augustine explicitly
brings Cicero's *Hortensius* into the discussion and holds it up
to his students as the basis upon which his school, *schola
nostra,* is founded. This is the nature of the school at the
villa at Cassiciacum. The classical philosophical heritage of
mankind is directly related to this educational fare of the
soul. Indeed, St. Augustine calls the insight which the *Hortensius* represents "the very stronghold of philosophy," and
congratulates his Catholic mother for her mastery of its essential point. As he explains elsewhere in the *Dialogues,* she
possesses this mastery by virtue of her faith: thus the harmony between the philosophical heritage of man and the
work of the Catholic Church is laid down at the very outset
of this treatise which marks the birthplace of Christian philosophy.

"Behold, not the philosophers," Augustine writes, "but
only people who like to argue, state that all are happy who
live according to their own will. This, of course, is not true,
for, to wish what is not fitting is the worst of wretchedness.
But it is not so deplorable to fail of attaining what we desire
as it is to wish to attain what is not proper. For, greater evil
is brought about through one's wicked will than happiness

through fortune." [17] Here the flashing mind of Augustine moves rapidly from his first positions and point of departure to the very center of educational philosophy—the role of the will, namely, and the question of value theory and value judgment.[18]

"Then Licentius spoke up: 'You must tell us what a person has to wish in order to be happy, and what kind of things he must desire.'" [19] Augustine intends this to indicate what young people naturally desire from their teachers and from the educational system. For it is the educational establishment which is called upon to provide young people with this knowledge on what a person has to wish in order to be happy, and what kind of things he must desire. We have here a basic premise of Christian humanism in education, elaborated as one thing with Christian philosophy. As the dialogue continues, Augustine formally accepts the request of the youthful Licentius, himself about nineteen years of age, that very age when Augustine, as he recalls so well, discovered the love of wisdom by reading Cicero's *Hortensius*. " 'But what preparation should a man make to gain happiness?' I asked," says St. Augustine, continuing from Licentius' question.[20] Augustine stresses constantly the concept of preparation, which is simply the process of education. This preparation of the mind for happiness is identical with the preparation of the mind for seeing the truth, for grasping intelligible, nonmaterial reality, for coming to a real conviction that God exists and for appreciating what it is to be a human soul. This is the recurrent theme of all of the *Dialogues of Cassiciacum;* seen from the vantage point of education, they portray nothing else than the work of the teaching profession. It is the work of the teacher to organize the "order of learning" in such a way that the souls of young people gradually are prepared precisely for this happiness, which is itself nothing else than the possession of God, the truth on divine things and on the greatness of the soul.

In the paragraphs which follow, Augustine leads the group logically past the position of the secularists and materialists of his time directly to God himself. The God whom Augustine teaches in this educational program is the God "eternal and ever-remaining." [21] "This, of course, is so certain," replied Licentius, "that the question is unnecessary." All the others agreed with pious devotion.

"Therefore, I concluded," St. Augustine continues, "whoever possesses God is happy." St. Augustine makes it clear in this fashion that we are in the presence of a group which sees the reality of Almighty God exactly as Augustine himself had come to see that reality through his study of the heritage of classical philosophy and through the gradual dawn of intellectual clarity regarding the spiritual nature of God in the course of his mental development at Milan. There is a fundamental and central consistency here between the chapters of the *Confessions* and these pages of the *Dialogues*.[22] This is a Catholic group and the project is one of Catholic education, involving the knowledge and the love of God. This is the happy life, the possession of God. This is the end of the quest for wisdom, this is what Augustine has found in his conversion, and this is why he is at the villa, under the general supervision of St. Ambrose, preparing for baptism. At the same time, however, his active and penetrating mind is already at work, projecting a "difficult undertaking," a continuation of his profession of teaching in a new program which will lead youthful spirits to God and the soul, and which will make the work of the educator in the fullest sense a service of God.

The Exemplification of Philosophical Method in Teaching

The very beginning of St. Augustine's literary apostolate is a philosophical exercise, but not in the Neoplatonist genre; the dialogue on *The Happy Life* is a philosophical analysis of Christian humanism in education. Philosophy is portrayed as the specifically human activity; St. Augustine presents it as a formative influence on youth, as a method of learning and teaching, and as a discipline with a content in its own right. This is the genuine humanism of the tradition of Catholic education, where humanism is not mere philology but the philosophical study of all the arts and disciplines of human culture, crowned by "the science of wisdom and virtue" itself.[23] From St. Augustine's early work in these treatises on educational philosophy this fundamental concept of Christian humanism in education will enter into the monastery and cathedral schools to become the common intellectual and humanistic patrimony of our civilization.

In this same second chapter of *The Happy Life,* Augustine exemplifies teaching method. Teaching done in such a manner that the youthful mind actually grasps this solid and substantial health-giving fare must be accomplished in a definite way. This teaching is to be a gradual process, Augustine explains, keeping his figure of speech. "For the mind also in its feasts," he tells us, "may go to excess if it indulges too greedily in the meal—in this way it digests poorly, and the consequent discomfort is no less harmful to the health of the mind than is hunger itself. Therefore, if you do not object, we will take up this question tomorrow, when we are hungry again." [24]

Here we have another important insight into Augustine's purpose in the *Dialogues of Cassiciacum.* They exemplify teaching methods. They demonstrate how teaching ought to be done, if this philosophical approach which gives substantial content and health-giving character to the fare of the mind is to be achieved by the teaching profession.[25] If this fundamental principle is borne in mind, the nature, plan, and purpose of all four *Dialogues* become clear. In fact, in several places Augustine explains why he is using a circuitous route to a truth rather than a direct and brief one: always it is this same intention of manifesting how the mind, granted our human condition, must move gradually and laboriously toward insight and understanding in these philosophical fundamentals which he is introducing into the content, process, and method of education.

While this symposium on *The Happy Life* is taking place, Augustine in his teaching procedure and methodology at Cassiciacum also has launched a series of discussions, with careful attention to stenographic reporting, which later will be published as the dialogues *Against the Academics.* He explicitly links the two works, showing that they both form part of this "difficult undertaking" which inspires the general intention in his mind.[26] Without truth, he says, there can be no happiness. The Academics bar the pathway to truth, hence fail to attain to wisdom and therefore lack the secret of the happy life. The total educational situation, in other words, must be based upon a sound philosophical foundation, one which perceives the ability of the human mind to attain truth since it was made for that purpose. Thus the central thesis of the discussions in the *Against the Academics* is directly related to this educational project and undertaking which Augustine unveils so clearly in *The Happy Life.*

On the following day, the discussions concerned Almighty God in Himself, leading toward an insight into the fact that the possession of God is the very essence of wisdom, of truth, and therefore of human happiness.[27] Once again, Augustine brings Cicero's *Hortensius* into his teaching, keeping before us the profound unity and consistency of his entire life since his decision as a young man of nineteen to embrace the teaching profession as the way of his search for wisdom.[28]

This same foundation on the *Hortensius* is visible throughout Chapter IV, the record of "the third day of our discussion." [29] St. Augustine draws the thread of the dialogue together, noting the joy in his youthful students when they come to perceive what he is teaching. "Licentius joyfully exclaimed: 'Verily, no truer or more divine words could have been spoken. For, there is no greater and more pitiable want than the want of wisdom. Whoever does not lack wisdom cannot lack anything.' " [30] Augustine's "difficult undertaking" is succeeding. Several times he records the personal joy of the teacher experiencing his specific reward: these youthful souls are reaching the insight and understanding under his teaching which he wants them to gain. Augustine begins to draw his conclusion. " 'Consequently, the want of the soul is nothing but foolishness,' I said. 'It is the opposite of wisdom as death is the opposite of life, or a happy life is the opposite of a miserable one.' . . . " [31] Skillfully he relates the conclusion to the position established in the introductory chapters: a soul without wisdom is in hunger and misery. It cannot become healthy and happy until it discovers and possesses this indispensable food of the soul, wisdom itself, which it is the function of the teaching profession to provide. In final summary he explains to his students that Christianity is this wisdom and that the Catholic faith provides the soul of man with this happiness.

"We have also heard through divine authority," he tells them, "that the Son of God is nothing but the wisdom of God, and the Son of God is truly God. Thus, everyone having God is happy—a statement already acclaimed by everyone at the beginning of our symposium. But, do you believe that wisdom is different from truth? For it has also been said: 'I am the Truth' (John 14, 6). . . . A certain admonition, flowing from the very fountain of truth, urges us to remember God, to seek Him, and thirst after Him tirelessly. This hidden sun pours into our innermost eyes that beaming light. His is all the truth that we speak, even though, in our anxiety, we hesitate to turn with courage toward this light and to behold it in its entirety, because our eyes, recently opened, are not yet strong enough." [32]

"This, then," St. Augustine concludes, "is the full satisfaction of souls, this is the happy life: To recognize piously and completely the One through whom you are led into the truth, the nature of the truth you enjoy, and the bond that connects you with the supreme measure." [33]

"While all rejoiced and praised God," St. Augustine writes, "Trygetius said: 'How deeply I wish that you would teach us every day with the same measure.' "[34] This is, of course, simply the reaction of a student to his teaching, but at the same time in his edition of the record, it seems probable, St. Augustine intended to convey the thought that youthful souls wish to have this kind of philosophical teaching, this solid and substantial educational fare, as the daily approach to the educational process. Augustine is giving us to understand, furthermore, that this dialogue is not a mere sporadic affair which took place on one occasion only. It is intended to convey to the teaching profession his view on sound methodology.

This first of the philosophical dialogues of St. Augustine and the first work of his literary corpus does indeed manifest the birth of Christian philosophy; at the same time, it seems that to view it as a purely philosophical discussion is to miss its central point: it is at one and the same time a discussion of the renovation and restitution of *paideia,* in theistic terms and under the auspices of Christ, to Whom, as Augustine says, he was resolved to give his entire life. A brief analysis of the other *Dialogues* will corroborate this concept of their nature.

Truth-Centered Education

"I perceive," said Licentius, "that you are doing your best to make us argue the question with one another, and, I am sure, you do so with some good purpose in mind." [35] Augustine indicates here once again the fact that he has a definite project in mind in these philosophical works, namely, to manifest and to exemplify a teaching methodology with young people. When the *Contra Academicos* is viewed in this light it becomes a striking example of the philosophical method of teaching, illustrating how youthful minds should be brought to philosophical insights and understanding as well as to a love for the quest and the grasp of the truth. Throughout these discussions concerning the skeptics of the New Academy, St. Augustine teaches the fundamental position of the classical philosophy deriving from Socrates, Plato, and Aristotle, that truth exists and can be achieved by the human mind. Thus St. Augustine conducts his procedure

95

at Cassiciacum in terms of a truth-centered education. Once again, there is this fundamental unity between Christian philosophy as such, and the Christian education of youth. The role of truth in St. Augustine's philosophy reflects his lifelong connection with the field of education, which exists to teach, a process which is impossible without a truth to be taught.

St. Augustine's very manner reflects the assurance of truth: he authoritatively guides the course of conversation, remaining fully in charge at all times. He begins and ends the discussions, he takes definite positions when the young people are inaccurate or fail to grasp a proposition, and he gives orders as any teacher does at the beginning of a class. "On the following day when we had sat down together, I said: 'Take up what you began yesterday.' " [36] This is the manner and bearing of the professional educator who knows exactly what wealth and treasure he has in hand, and who is animated by the desire to share it with youthful minds.

"But, to be brief, let us now, if you please, close the discussion. Indeed, I think that it is unnecessary for us to delay upon it. We have sufficiently, in view of our purpose, dealt with the matter, one which could be disposed of in a very few words, if I did not wish to put you through an exercise and make a test of your capacity and tastes. This is a real concern of mine. When I decided to do all I could to encourage you in the quest of truth, I started to ask you how much importance you attached to it. But I found you all so intent on this that I do not desire more. . . . And now, let us finish, as I said, this discussion, and, above all, Licentius, let us send a record of it to your father. I have already made him really interested in philosophy. I am only waiting for the good turn of fortune that will admit him to it. He will be better disposed to yearn for these pursuits of ours more ardently when he learns not only by your telling him, but also by reading the record of our debate, that you are thus spending your time with me." [37]

In this passage we have another instance where Augustine

explains the nature of the "difficult undertaking" which has been launched at Cassiciacum, and the educational purpose which he has in mind. The union between philosophy and education at Cassiciacum is precisely that of the *Hortensius* of Cicero, which itself represents the best of the Greek heritage of *paideia*. It appears from these words of St. Augustine that the *Against the Academics* is a school exercise, representing and exemplifying educational methodology in what he is so frequently at pains to call "our school," in contrast with "that other school" from which he is happy to have resigned. It is a school exercise, but it is also Christian philosophy: not Christian philosophy in itself, so to speak, as if it were a mere Neoplatonist exercise, but the work of the Christian philosopher busy with youth in their studies. Augustine has a purpose, as he says, and he is satisfied that it is achieved sufficiently so far. His own statements justify the position that this purpose is in the field of education.

A detailed analysis of all of the relevant passages in the *Contra academicos* would be helpful, but is necessarily replaced by brief references. In Book II, for example, the educational relevance of the discussion is repeatedly manifest. Vergil is used systematically every day as a basic textbook. Licentius becomes more interested in poetry than Augustine desires. He praises philosophy to the young man and brings him to desire a return to the discussions concerning the Academics and their philosophical teachings.[38]

In Book III of the same work, Licentius reaches a critical point. This gives Augustine the occasion he needs to make perfectly clear the nature of his undertaking at Cassiciacum and to show how it relates to his earlier professorship in the schools of the Roman Empire. He solves the crisis by deliberately, forcefully, and authoritatively transferring Licentius from the study of poetry to philosophy.[39] As the crisis with the young man develops, Augustine in his discussions grants that literature belongs "in the circle of those studies by which the mind is developed," but regrets that Licentius is becoming lost in poetry. He sees this as the basic tendency of those

97

other schools, the imperial schools of rhetoric. He himself intends to organize education on a totally different philosophical foundation. The school he is exemplifying is based upon the *Hortensius* and its philosophical approach. After he has made this clear, Augustine finishes the *Against the Academics* by sustained lecture.[40]

Some have seen this departure from discussion into sustained lecture as a defect, somehow, in St. Augustine's artistry, as if he suddenly realized that he could not cope with the Platonic dialogue as a literary genre. This hardly does justice to the stature of Augustine. He is perfectly consistent, viewing the matter from the field of education, in turning at this point to sustained lecture: he is simply carrying out his purpose, which is to exemplify teaching method. He takes pains to explain that "our school" will not dispense with the lecture method entirely, a method which characterizes these other schools, the schools of rhetoric of the Empire. While he does indeed wish to introduce a new turn in methodology, a more philosophical type of teaching, leading to a personal grasp of philosophical insight through the thought-producing and convincing search for truth which he has been exemplifying so far, nevertheless, as he says, there are times when the teaching profession must expound doctrine by sustained exposition.[41] St. Augustine is careful to point out, however, that his school, the philosophy of which he is exemplifying as well as elaborating, will not be motivated as are those other schools in the current of Isocrates by the search for glory and fame; rather, they will be motivated in teacher and in student by the love and quest for truth. This is to sustain the tradition deriving from Plato. His conversion to the Church has not taken him from the teaching profession, or from that fundamental qualitative issue which was central, as we have seen, in the development of the educational establishment of classical antiquity.[42]

With this philosophical position that truth is possible to our cognitive powers, and the pedagogical application of truth as the very meaning and purpose of the educational profession, we leave the dialogue *Against the Academics* and turn briefly to the *De ordine*.

The Order of Studies Leading to God

The disputation *De ordine* supports the pedagogical understanding of the *Dialogues of Cassiciacum* for it exemplifies Augustine's manner of teaching his students the reason for their arduous work in the circle of the sciences. From beginning to end, it is designed to improve the motivation of young people in their studies by relating their academic work to that knowledge of God and the soul which is its immediate end. Thus the *De ordine* is entirely devoted to the field of education. Its purpose is twofold: first, to reveal to the youthful mind the God of Christianity who rules human events by a providential order; secondly, to establish the "order of studies" which prepares youthful minds to perceive this sublime truth, the truth of the Christian God who is the God of providence. This dialogue, therefore, is characterized by a profound unity which sometimes is missed, because it is not seen from the viewpoint of the field of education from which it was written and for which it was intended. Considerations of space do not permit us to cite these passages in full, but we shall at least touch upon the salient points which bring the educational relevance of this fundamental treatise into view.

There are in the first place St. Augustine's instructions to his youthful group on the conduct of their studies.[43] He proves to them day by day in his teaching and its methodology that philosophy is their real purpose and the animating intention of their work together.[44] There are the beautiful passages in which the saint rejoices that the bright and questioning mind of Licentius is turning more and more definitely away from sympathy for the Academics and their skepticism to believe in "order." By this term, as Augustine makes clear, he means nothing else than the fact that his youthful student is becoming a Christian philosopher. He is a theist who understands, with a philosophically cultivated insight and conviction, the providential care of Almighty God over human affairs, rather than an implicit atheist who does not grasp this providential order.

The educational purpose of this first half of the *De ordine* becomes clear when Augustine introduces the second half, turning from the study of God's providential order in itself to an explanation of the kind of education needed by the human mind to appreciate and to discern the reality of that divine order in the universe. This education is itself an integral part of the divine order and must not be neglected. "On the other hand," he writes, "if your weakness—which, because it is not nourished by erudition and training, may perhaps be unable to uphold so great a God—should yield to cleverness or to some sophistic error of men that very fact will show you what strength you must acquire in order to return to Him with added vigor: and at the same time, . . . I wish this disputation of ours to eventuate as something rather elaborate. . . . " [45] Augustine is bringing his young students to see that "so great a God" is not upheld by Christian people without attention to education. He is in the process of developing and forming young persons of genuine Christian culture, able to sustain by Christian philosophy that God whom they know through revelation. This is a point at which one can perceive the special relevance of Augustine's educational doctrine for an age in which Catholic schools are preparing and forming young people to live in an atheistic environment. They too are called upon to "sustain so great a God," in the face of much cleverness and sophistic error; they too need this same "order of studies," consciously arranged, and skilfully taught through sound methodology, in order to achieve the cultivated strength of mind to fulfill their role in the modern world. There is, furthermore, the entire formidable question of the recent rise and spread of this atheism in Christian civilization, a question in which education is involved and which the Augustinian teaching illuminates in a striking way.

There are unforgettable pages where Augustine records his joy that Licentius, his bright philosophical prospect, has forsaken the path of Isocrates and exclusive devotion to poetry for the way of Plato and the *Hortensius*. What he calls "our school" is successful in practice, and he rejoices with the joy which only the teacher knows.[46] Further insight into the nature of the *Dialogues of Cassiciacum* is contained in his explanation of his "undertaking," that project which entails an entire plan for a writing apostolate. Augustine intends to publish these philosophical discussions, which do not take place for their own sake in some Neoplatonist sense; he looks upon the entire series as purposeful in nature, engrafted, as he says, "into the order of teaching." [47] The *Dialogues* are philosophical, indeed, but they have their origin and specific purpose in the field of education. They represent Christian philosophy not in itself but rather at work in the formation of youth.

The method of Christian philosophy is exemplified when Augustine returns constantly to the definition of terms: concepts must be treated accurately and in an orderly manner. "Define order!" he commands, opening a new turn of the discussion.[48] Again he describes the motives which young people are expected to have in "our school," quite different from the schools of rhetoric. St. Augustine's school is imbued with the new type of philosophical thinking which these dialogues contain. They become an entire program of education, in the general tradition of Plato indeed, but now a *paideia Christi*.[49]

To bring this survey of Augustine's statements regarding his "difficult undertaking" and its purpose to a conclusion, he defines it at last as "the duty of teaching them wisdom." [50] When he says that the human memory must be stocked with the branches of learning in order to bring souls to this wisdom, and indeed that this must be a process transpiring "systematically," and that the duty of teaching wisdom can be done in no other way, we encounter a new dimension in the nature of the contact with education which his early writings afford. We shall return to this phase of the investigation later. In conclusion, then, Christian philosophy is equated with wisdom, contrasting with the darkness of unwisdom. Christian philosophy frees souls from this darkness, Augustine states, "by instruction and disputation." [51] This contains a clear reference to that current which we have noted throughout the educational experience of classical antiquity, the opposition between the educational ideals of Plato and those of Isocrates. In fact, in this phrase of Augustine, it is perhaps not going too far to see the two essential aspects of his educational philosophy and its methodology: instruction, one might well believe, refers to the circle of the sciences; disputation, on the other hand, denotes the crown of the order of learning, philosophy itself.

The Program of a Catholic Lay Teacher

An examination could be made in similar detail of the other works of St. Augustine which occupy this period between the activity of the villa, beginning with the publication of *The Happy Life,* and extending through the months at Rome and the years at the monastery in Thagaste, until to his surprise he is enlisted into the Catholic priesthood. Not to burden the present discussion with the details of such an analysis, we shall simply state the general conclusion that they continue the same features and the same approach noted in the *Dialogues of Cassiciacum.*

Possidius is careful to point out that St. Augustine throughout these years is a Catholic layman, both in fact and in his own understanding of himself.[52] The life which he has in mind embraces what he calls God's service, the monastic way of living, and the chief work he intends to do is this "difficult undertaking" in the field of education. His literary apostolate is the direct outgrowth of this project, and even more: it exemplifies his method and is designed to carry his educational thinking to a wider public. Seen in this light, all the works of these years when he was a Catholic layman manifest a striking unity through their direct relation to his educational work and thought. They offer a classic example of the Catholic lay teacher at work with Catholic students, thinking in closest union with the mind of the Church. It is this fundamentally Catholic thinking, this soundness of philosophical approach, which made of his teaching a genuine apostolate and caused it to share in this official work of the Church.

His literary apostolate, then, begins at Cassiciacum in the manner we have seen, with the four *Dialogues*. While at Milan for his baptism, he composed his *De immortalitate animae* and drew up the drafts for his textbooks in the liberal arts, the *Disciplinarum libri*.[53] Three works came from his pen during his unexpected year at Rome: the *De moribus Ecclesiae Catholicae et de moribus Manichaeorum*, the *De quantitate animae* and the *De libero arbitrio*.[54] At Thagaste he published the *De Genesi adversus Manichaeos*, the six books *De musica*, continuing consistently his project with the liberal arts, the *De magistro*, and the *De vera religione*, which significantly enough he had projected since his stay at Cassiciacum.[55] Then there is the *De diversis questionibus octeginta tribus* which St. Augustine collected and published as one book when he was consecrated Bishop of Hippo; he tells us that these miscellaneous short pieces resulted from questions raised by his group at the monastery in Thagaste: the direct result, in other words, of his educational work as a layman. They are placed properly, therefore, in this period of his life.[56] Finally, there are the letters of these years, several of which are directly relevant to the unity of his thought and work which becomes visible from the field of education. In all, therefore, fourteen items in the *opera omnia sancti Augustini* reflect these years between his conversion and his ordination. They form a natural group with a unity of their own. This unity is not fully grasped when these years are understood as a mere "philosophical period," especially when the phrase implies that his conversion was to Neoplatonism instead of Christianity. They are not philosophy pure and

simple, certainly not Neoplatonist works, but also not even
treatises of Christian philosophy formally and exclusively as
such. They represent the same contact with, and concern for,
the Christian education of youth which we have observed
from their beginning in the *Dialogues of Cassiciacum;* all
fourteen works are a monument to the "difficult undertaking" in the field of education which this great educator of
the *Spätantike* has in mind.

The educational reference, for example, is as striking in
the treatise on *The Greatness of the Soul* as it is in *The
Happy Life* or in the *De ordine*.[57] It was at the monastery at
Thagaste, as we know, that Augustine composed his dialogue
on *The Teacher*, a work obviously educational, which discusses the manner in which the teacher leads youthful souls
toward wisdom. Perhaps most striking of all the evidence
which justifies an approach to these early works of St. Augustine from the field of education is the fact that he actually
undertook the composition of a series of textbooks in the
preparatory liberal arts. He intended to exemplify proper
content and methodology in teaching these human studies
which would enable them to fulfill their providential role in
preparing the soul for Christian wisdom, the knowledge of
God and the soul. It is significant that St. Augustine completed the *De musica* at the monastery in Africa. At the end
of his life, furthermore, he reaffirmed this work in the area of
the liberal arts and stated emphatically its importance in his
life-work as a whole.[58]

In the light of these considerations, therefore, it seems
justified to perceive the birth of Christian philosophy in
these fourteen works, in a certain specific way, in connection,
that is, with the proper formation of Christian youth. Christian
philosophy, we have said. By this we mean that the philosophical teachings of these works are definitely not Neoplatonism,
although St. Augustine, of course, consciously uses the terminology and intellectual equipment of Platonism. It is furthermore, we believe, not precisely correct to say with Portalié
that Augustine in these works "has devoted himself to true

philosophy, which he no longer differentiated from Christianity." [59] It seems more exact to say that Augustine differentiated his philosophical thinking definitely and distinctly from Christianity, which he clearly understood to be a revelation coming from the God knowable by human reason. His philosophy, however, is chiefly concerned, as he tells us in his *Soliloquies*, with God and the soul.

The central point of his teaching is the God-given ability of the human mind to rise to this supreme wisdom, this knowledge of God as a spiritual and intelligible reality, and in the light of that knowledge to return to a strong appreciation of the spiritual greatness of the human soul, to see it as a spiritual entity, God's creature, cared for with a special love under the order of Providence. This rise of the human mind to *ipsum esse subsistens*, to the concept of creation from nothing, and to a perception of the providential order with which this supreme spiritual reality governs His creation, is the very heart of Christian philosophy. It is this which we find in the writings of this period, all fourteen of them, the same thinking which comes to view in the *Confessions*.[60]

It is beyond the scope of the present discussion, concerned as it is specifically with the field of education, to go further into the Christian philosophy of St. Augustine.[61] Sufficient for the present is the conclusion which seems to follow directly from the evidence of Augustine's own statements, that the works of this period between the launching of his "difficult undertaking" at Cassiciacum with the publication of *The Happy Life* through the other works extending to his ordination, are all bound together by a common unifying theme. They represent Christian philosophy, indeed, but Christian philosophy as a body of thought developing in and for a renewed and reformed education of youth. Like Plato himself, this Christian Plato is concerned primarily with *paideia*, the proper formation of young people toward true and integral humanity. There is basically only one difference: this is a Christian *paideia* imbued with a philosophy of education which applies the new-born Christian philosophy.

There is no happiness without wisdom, and wisdom cannot be separated from truth, its quest and its possession. In Augustine's view education for young people has no reality or goodness except in terms of this wisdom: not knowledge in itself and by itself, but this wisdom and the love of it which is philosophy. For these reasons, we believe that all the works of these years form a unity which derives from the fact that they spring from one abiding intention in St. Augustine's mind. It is the intention to carry out the "difficult undertaking," under Christian auspices, of the reform, renewal, and fulfillment of the heritage of *paideia*.

Notes from Chapter Four

1 The question concerning the kind of philosophy contained in the early works of St. Augustine has been the object of discussion for nearly a century due to the rise of the interpretation which views the change described in the *Confessions* as a conversion to Neoplatonist philosophy and not to the Catholic faith. Cf. Appendix II, below. According to this interpretation, St. Augustine's intellectual position did not become fully and genuinely Catholic until some time after his baptism, indeed perhaps not until his ordination to the priesthood. It is essential to this interpretation that the philosophical works written at Cassiciacum represent not Christian philosophy but Neoplatonism. It is possible, however, that the *Dialogues of Cassiciacum* are philosophical in nature not because St. Augustine has not yet become converted to the Catholic faith, but because he has a practical reason in mind which involves philosophy in a special way. When the practical purpose is seen to be educational, within the framework of his conversion to the Catholic Church, a helpful vantage point will be gained for judging what kind of philosophy is involved. It is intended in this chapter to document the educational purpose of the *Dialogues of Cassiciacum;* this lays the foundation for the interpretation of them as works of Christian philosophy and not Neoplatonism. We are actually studying the seminal works of St. Augustine's Catholic philosophy of education.

2 St. Augustine, *De beata vita*, 1, 6; Schopp, *op. cit.*, p. 50.

3 *Ibid.*, 2, 7; *op. cit.*, p. 51.

4 *Ibid.*, 1, 6; *op. cit.*, p. 50.

5 *Ibid.*, 2, 7; *op. cit.*, p. 52.

6 *Ibid.*, 2, 8; *op. cit.*, p. 53.

7 *Ibid.; op. cit.*, p. 54.

8 *Ibid.* The relevance of St. Augustine's educational doctrine in our time is plain to see, for the two contemporary centuries just ending have witnessed

the rise of philosophies which belittle the concept of the liberal arts and which have undermined their use in popular education. The consequences are visible over wide areas of contemporary social life. Hence Pope Leo XIII was careful to point out the educational necessity for the restoration of sound philosophy. When philosophy was fundamentally sound, he writes, "the liberal arts flourished as never before or since; but, neglected and almost blotted out, they lay prone since philosophy began to lean to error and join hands with folly" (*Aeterni Patris* [August 4, 1879]; see *The Great Encyclical Letters of Pope Leo XIII* [New York: Benziger, 1903], p. 55). Cardinal Newman was keenly aware of this process which leaves souls "hungry and famished"; "the result on ordinary minds," he writes, "and on the common run of students, is less satisfactory still; they leave their place of education simply dissipated and relaxed by the multiplicity of subjects, which they have never really mastered, and so shallow as not even to know their shallowness" (*The Idea of a University* [New York: Longmans, 1947], p. 132).

9 St. Augustine, *De beata vita,* 2, 9; Schopp, *op. cit.,* p. 55.

10 *Ibid.,* 2, 8; *op. cit.,* p. 55.

11 Cf. Werner Jaeger, *Paideia: The Ideals of Greek Culture, passim,* esp., e.g., "Reform of the Old Paideia," pp. 208-211. Jaeger speaks of "the fundamental paideutic tendency of his [Plato's] philosophy" ("Preface," II, xiv); we believe that St. Augustine, often called the "Christian Plato," built his Christian philosophy with the same "paideutic tendency." This is the precise point which we see in the *Dialogues of Cassiciacum.*

12 Cf. St. Augustine, *Conf.,* I, 16 (25-26); Ryan, *op. cit.,* chap. xvi, "The Influence of Immoral Literature," pp. 58-59. This eloquent passage characterizes the corrupted condition of *paideia,* the educational system of classical antiquity; St. Augustine's works contain a program which, far from discarding the heritage, saves and renews it by applying to *paideia* two healing founts, Christian philosophy and *Doctrina christiana.* Just how he did this is a worthy and practical object of study, for it touches the roots of our Western and Christian culture.

13 St. Augustine, *De beata vita,* 2, 9; Schopp, *op. cit.,* p. 55.

14 *Ibid.*

15 *Ibid.,* 2, 10; *op. cit.,* p. 55.

16 Cf. *ibid.; op cit.,* p. 56.

17 *Ibid.*

18 The treatises *De moribus ecclesiae* and *De libero arbitrio,* composed at Rome later in this period of his life, fall readily and naturally into this perspective.

19 St. Augustine, *De beata vita,* 2, 10; Schopp, *op. cit.,* p. 56.

20 *Ibid.,* 2, 11; *op. cit.,* p. 57.

21 *Ibid.; op. cit.,* p. 58.

22 Cf. in particular *Conf.,* Book VII; Ryan, *op. cit.,* pp. 157-180. This entire book on the immediate preparation for the grace of faith is a striking description of the manner in which St. Augustine's mind penetrated to the characteristic themes of Christian philosophy, which contrast with Neoplatonism, but which the natural soundness of Plato's philosophical tradition as a whole foreshadows and prepares. Cf. in particular chaps. x-xii (16-18); *op. cit.,* pp. 170-172, for the ascent to *ipsum esse subsistens,* to *creatio ex nihilo,* and to the *ordo providentiae,* the birth of Christian philosophy in St. Augustine's mind.

23 *De magistro,* 14 (45); Colleran, *op. cit.,* p. 185: "The science of virtue and wisdom" is included among the subjects taught. That St. Augustine held this view consistently to the end of his life as a bishop is clear from the *Liber retractationum;* cf. I, 6, *De libris disciplinarum.* Cf. *De ordine,* II, chap. v, *passim.*

For a penetrating analysis of the decline of the concept of humanism in education from the philosophical level of the Quattrocento to the merely literary and philological approach of more recent times, see Ernesto Grassi und Thure von Uexküll, *Von Ursprung und Grenzen der Geisteswissenschaften und Naturwissenschaften* (München: Leo Lehnen Verlag, 1950); the authors lament that "wir heute unter humanistische Studien nur noch philologische und literarische Untersuchungen, aber nicht mehr die Erörterung philosophischer Probleme verstehen," and speak of our contemporary need "den Begriff 'humanistische studien' aus den Fesseln und Einshränkungen (zu) befreien, in denen sein eigentliches Wesen vergessen oder verdeckt wurde," and "den Reichtum und die ursprüngliche Weite zurückzugewinnen, die er im Zeitalter des Humanismus besass" (p. 9). This illuminates the precise role of philosophical content and philosophical method in the educational program exemplified in the *Dialogues of Cassiciacum.* To state the full truth of the matter, this relevance of philosophy to humanism in education is a Catholic heritage descending not from the Renaissance but from St. Augustine and the Patristic Age, and is witnessed strikingly in our own day in the recent work published under the patronage of Cardinal Pizzardo, *Filosofia e formazione ecclesiastica* (Città del Vaticano: Tipografia poliglotta Vaticana, 1960).

24 St. Augustine, *De beata vita,* 2 (13); Schopp, *op. cit.,* p. 60.

25 Both Eggersdorfer and Marrou have noticed this fact about the *Dialogues of Cassiciacum,* but St. Augustine's biographers and students of the controversy on his conversion for the most part have paid it little or no attention, perhaps because the point has not been seen in the larger context of St. Augustine's plan and program for education as the unifying theme of his life from his conversion to his ordination. Be that as it may, the testimony of the two scholars on the true nature of the *Dialogues* is unequivocal. "Es sind Niederschriften wirklich gehaltener Gespräche," states Eggersdorfer, "die er mit seinen Schülern geführt hat zu keinem andern Zwecke, als um sie in der bezeichneten Weise zu erzihen" (*op. cit.,* p. 74). "Es scheint ihm von vornherein klar gewesen zu sein, dass der Unterricht einer gewissen Einheit und Konzentration nicht entbehren dürfe. So rückt er die philosophischen Disputationen in den Mittelpunkt und macht ihnen die Lektüre dienstbar" (*ibid.,* p. 79). Cf. also *ibid.,* p. 81, where Eggersdorfer discusses St. Augustine's view (*Contra Academicos,* I, 4), that philosophy is relevant to all levels of education, calling it his *Haupterziehungsgrundsatz,* and linking it with the quest for truth and wisdom which for each young person ought to be the substance of education. Eggersdorfer even anticipates the contemporary ado about critical thinking, showing that St. Augustine had in mind what is actually the only sound approach to this currently popular goal in teaching (cf. *ibid.,* pp. 85-87).

Marrou understands the *Dialogues of Cassiciacum* in relation to the rivalry between literary and philosophical culture visible throughout the century-long history of *paideia.* Cf. *Saint Augustin et la fin . . .,* pp. 169 ff.; 173 ff. Cf. esp. his chap. vi, "Reductio artium ad philosophiam: Exercitatio animi," pp. 299-327, in which Marrou demonstrates clearly that the *Dia-*

logues of Cassiciacum exemplify St. Augustine's method of teaching, a method which recurs, as Marrou shows (pp. 315-327), in the later *De Trinitate*. Noteworthy also is Marrou's comprehensive grasp of the relationship of this *exercitatio animi* in educational method to the entire larger concept and program of moral reform, the catharsis and *purgatio animae*, a relationship which is essential to a proper understanding of St. Augustine's educational apostolate. "Tout cela est encore exercice, gymnastique intellectuelle. Ce n'est pas de ma part une simple hypothèse. Augustin s'est expliqúe de la facon la plus claire . . . [cf. *De magistro*, 8 (21)] . . . ce role pédagogique, pour cet assouplissement de l'esprit" (*ibid.*, p. 308). Marrou even sees a definite plan of composition in the *Dialogues,* reflecting what we might call Augustine's "lesson plan" in approaching the elucidation of a topic with a group of youthful students (cf. *ibid.*, p. 310).

26 St. Augustine, *De beata vita,* 2 (13); Schopp, *op. cit.*, p. 60: " 'Do you think,' I asked, 'that the business we undertook with the Academics is completely finished?' " St. Augustine shows that happiness depends upon wisdom, and that wisdom is one thing with the knowledge of the truth, which in turn is the realm and function of education.

27 Cf. *ibid.*, chap. iii (17-22); *op. cit.*, pp. 64-70.

28 Cf. *ibid.*, 3 (33); *op. cit.*, p. 70; there are numerous references to the *Hortensius* in the *De beata vita,* which seem to indicate that it had been used as a textbook to prepare the group for the type of discussions and conclusions reflected by Augustine's *Dialogue.*

29 Cf. *ibid.*, 4 (23-26); *op. cit.*, pp. 70-84.

30 *Ibid.*, 4 (27); *op. cit.*, p. 76.

31 *Ibid.*, 4 (28); *op. cit.*, p. 76.

32 *Ibid.*, 4 (34-35); *op. cit.*, pp. 82-83. St. Augustine's educational program aims at theistic conviction in intellectually cultivated Catholic youth through the instrumentality of Christian philosophy. We shall return to this theistic orientation of the culture of the human arts and disciplines, a matter of fundamental importance in guarding civilization against the rise and spread of atheism, in chapter IX, below.

33 *Ibid.*, 4 (35); *op. cit.*, p. 83.

34 *Ibid.*, 4 (36); *op. cit.*, p. 84.

35 St. Augustine, *Contra Academicos,* I, 3 (7); O'Meara, *St. Augustine Against the Academics,* p. 42.

36 *Ibid.*, I, 4 (11); *op. cit.*, p. 48.

37 *Ibid.*, I, 9 (25); *op. cit.*, p. 64.

38 Cf. *ibid.*, II, 4 (10); *op. cit.*, p. 74: "After the previous discussion which we have put together in the first book, we held none for almost seven days. We were in the meantime . . . studying . . . the three books of Vergil . . . as it seemed to be a suitable occupation at the time. As a result, Licentius became so enthusiastic for poetry, that I felt compelled to restrain him somewhat. . . . When I, so far as I was able, had praised the light of philosophy, he at length consented to take up again the question concerning the Academics which we had postponed."

39 Cf. *ibid.*, III, 1 (1); *op. cit.*, p. 98: "It was especially for his [Licentius'] sake that I had decided to bring up the topic. It is high time that philosophy should take and hold a greater part in his mind than poetry or any other subject." This *Dialogue* reflects an experienced teacher at work, one animated by a definite philosophy of education. It is simply Christian philosophy, the cultivated knowledge of God and the soul, applied to peda-

gogy, and hence establishing the primacy, among the arts and disciplines of human culture, of "the science of virtue and of wisdom" (*De magistro*, 14 (45)).

40 Cf. *Contra Academicos*, III, 7 (14); *op. cit.*, p. 113: ". . . I would prefer you," Alypius says to Augustine, "to achieve the result you aim at rather by means of an uninterrupted discussion than by this questioning. . . ." The change to sustained lecture at this point is deliberate, part of the educational purpose and not a mere inability on Augustine's part to compose well or to cope with the dialogue as a literary genre.

41 Cf. *ibid.*, III, 7 (15); *op. cit.*, p. 114: There are two methods "to conduct these enquiries": "by question and answer" and "in continuous exposition."

42 Cf. *ibid.*, II, 14 (30); *op. cit.*, p. 134: "For we are not interested in covering ourselves with glory but in the finding of the truth." This attaches the Christian schools of the future directly to the heritage of Plato and Aristotle and deliberately rejects the sophistical educational current deriving from Isocrates which had become so general in the schools of Rome.

43 St. Augustine, *De ordine*, I, 3, (6); Russell, *op. cit.*, p. 244.

44 *Ibid.*, I, 3, (9); *op. cit.*, pp. 247-248. Licentius remarks that St. Augustine admonishes him "to study philosophy rather than to compose poems. . . . For philosophy—as I have begun to believe as you prove it day by day—is our true and tranquil abode." This contains the central point of the present discussion: there is a systematic daily teaching at Cassiciacum which is philosophical in nature, indeed in a new and strong sense, for it is a new and strong philosophy which is involved. It is the birth of Christian philosophy in *ex professo* treatments of its basic themes composed to show their application in a fully christianized *paideia*, a Christian education of youth.

45 *Ibid.*, I, 7 (20); *op. cit.*, pp. 257-358.

46 Cf. *ibid.*, I, 8 (21); *op. cit.*, p. 259: " 'I am suddenly become quite averse to these poetic matters' [Licentius tells Augustine]. 'Something, I know not what, has flashed to me by another light—a far different light. Philosophy, I avow, is more beautiful than Thisbe, than Pyramus. . . .' [and] he gave thanks to Christ." "I heard these words," St. Augustine confides, "—with delight, shall I say? Or, rather what shall I not say? Let each one take it as he will, but my only anxiety is that perhaps my rejoicing was beyond due measure. . . . I, shedding tears, spent much time in prayer." Again the clear fact: Christian philosophy is involved here, coming to birth in the work of a Catholic man engaged upon the Christian education of youth.

47 Cf. *ibid.*, I, 9 (27); *op. cit.*, pp. 264-265.

48 *Ibid.*, I, 10 (28); *op. cit.*, p. 265.

49 Cf. *ibid.*, I, 10 (30); *op. cit.*, p. 268.

50 *Ibid.*, II, 2 (7); *op. cit.*, pp. 280-281: ". . . a wise man needs memory for such things as these, namely, the worthy and necessary branches of learning." This is the preparation for "the duty . . . most insistently demanded of him—the duty of teaching them wisdom." This is Augustine's conception of himself, especially since his decision to join the Catholic Church: He has not left the field of education for philosophy. Christian philosophy, rather, is coming to birth in a work of restored *paideia*, a Catholic education of youth.

51 *Ibid.*, II, 3 (9); *op. cit.*, p. 283: "Since the things which a wise man understands are united with God, then unwisdom is rightly discerned apart from God" (II, 3 (8)). The strong and direct theism of this concept of edu-

cation recurs constantly. The teacher is the "wise man who by instruction and disputation willingly frees us from an evil so great" (II, 3 (9)).

52 Cf. Possidius, *Vita*, 4; Hoare, *op. cit.*, p. 198: "While a layman, as he [St. Augustine] used to tell us, he used to keep away from churches where the bishopric was vacant but only from these." Augustine was a layman dedicated to "God's service," indeed to the pursuit of perfection within the monastic way of life, with no other intention in mind. Within this way of life, he planned to carry out a "difficult undertaking" the reform and re-construction of education by means of new, clear-sighted Christian philosophical thinking as well as by means of the Sacred Scriptures.

53 Cf. St. Augustine, *Retr.*, I, 5-6; P.L. 32, 590-591. "Per idem tempus quo Mediolani fui, baptismum percepturus, etiam Disciplinarum libros conatus sum scribere, . . . huiusmodi studiis . . . per corporalia cupiens ad incorporalia quibusdam quasi passibus certis vel pervenire vel ducere." This recollection of the aged Bishop is invaluable: it bears witness to the fact that Augustine's mind was preoccupied with education throughout this entire period, and in precisely the way we have analyzed in the *Dialogues of Cassiciacum.* He intends to re-think and to re-write the very textbooks of the entire circle of the sciences, to restore and renew them as stepping stones for the youthful mind to intelligible reality, to a cultivated knowledge of God and the soul. He is indeed the Christian Plato, able at last, thanks to the transforming religious power of Christianity, to accomplish and to surpass the aspirations of the human *paideia* at its best.

54 Cf. *Retr.* I, 7-9; P.L. 32, 591-599. These works are as fully imbued with educational thought and reference as the *Dialogues of Cassiciacum.* St. Augustine does not make this explicit in his *Retractationes,* as he of course did for the *Libri disciplinarum.* Perhaps he felt that the nature and intention of these works, written by a noted educator, were well known at the time, as indeed they might have been. In any case, the works themselves bear witness to the same contact with the field of education, now broadened and deepened through his profound reflection on the nature of the soul and its highest powers, which begins in the treatises written at Cassiciacum.

55 Cf. *Retr.*, I, 10-13; P.L. 32, 599-605. For the *De vera religione,* cf. *Contra Academicos,* II, 3 (8); cf. the comment of Professor O'Meara, *Against the Academics,* p. 182, n. 32: "The *De vera religione,* which was either prepared or projected at this stage, but was not published until 389-390. See Augustine's letter to Romanianus, Epist. 15." Again the evidence of a fundamental unity of purpose and intention becomes visible, running through St. Augustine's entire life and all his literary works of his period as a Catholic layman.

56 Cf. *Retr.*, I, 26; P.L. 32, 624: "Sicut interrogabar a fratribus. . . ."

57 This pedagogical nature of the *De quantitate animae* will be analyzed below in connection with St. Augustine's teaching on the culture of the human arts and disciplines and its proper design so that it leads the mind of young people, as the first Vatican Council states, up to God (cf. *Denz.* 1799).

58 Cf. n. 53 above. For the *De musica* in particular, cf. St. Augustine, *Retr.*, I, 11; P.L. 32, 600-602; Book VI of *De musica* was treated by St. Augustine as a separate work, for it explains his general philosophy of theistic method in teaching all the arts and disciplines of human culture. For the *Libri disciplinarum* and the renovation of the teaching of the liberal arts in general, cf. Eggersdorfer, *op. cit.*, pp. 92-94; Marrou, *Saint Augustin et*

la fin . . ., "Les arts liberaux chez saint Augustin," pp. 237-276, and especially "Reductio artium ad philosophiam," pp. 277-298.

59 Portalié-Bastian, *op. cit.,* p. 13.

60 Cf. St. Augustine, *Conf.,* VII (1-27); Ryan, *op. cit.,* pp. 157-180. If
efforts to see St. Augustine as a Neoplatonist in these years could cease at
last, the striking harmony and consistency between the *Confessions* and these
fourteen works, altogether worthy of St. Augustine's stature as a person and
as a thinker, would emerge into clear view.

61 Cf. Etienne Gilson, *The Christian Philosophy of St. Augustine* (New
York: Random House, 1960), with extensive bibliography, pp. 367-383. Augustine's philosophy will be summarized below to relate it with his concept
of right procedure and method in the culture of the human arts and disciplines.

5

The Educational
Apostolate of
the Bishop of Hippo

IN A.D. 391 St. Augustine was ordained to the Catholic
priesthood, in 395 he was consecrated coadjutor to Bishop
Valerius of Hippo, in 396 Bishop Valerius died and Augustine succeeded him as the Bishop of Hippo. St. Augustine
held this office in the Church until his death in 430. Our
purpose here is to sketch the outline of this concluding phase
of the life and work of St. Augustine, carrying forward the
investigation of the question whether there is a continuing
substantial contact with the field of education.

The chief apostolate of the bishop in the Catholic Church
is to teach the truths revealed by Christ. The formation of
souls in Christ is the work of the teacher, who shares this
responsibility with the parents of children. It is pre-emi-
nently the responsibility of the bishop, who holds the official teaching office in the Church of God. Catholic teachers
are co-workers with the bishops. This is especially so with
priest-teachers, who are the close co-workers of the bishop in
his chief apostolate, which is to teach.

Since the Catholic Church, in fact, had received a divine
commission to teach all nations, she emerged out of Palestine
and went into the classical world of antiquity with a mission
in religious education. This new Israel actually embodies

an institution for divine teaching on earth. Essentially, this teaching is the supernatural social heritage of the new chosen people of God, which possesses revealed truth to impart to its own oncoming generation. It is an authoritative teaching from God, not a work of mere human wisdom or a persuasion of mere human words. As this supernatural mission of teaching developed, the additional task of bringing all human wisdom and the natural heritage of human culture under the sway of revealed truth was undertaken and developed by the Church, chiefly through the work of her early bishops. This cultural program entailed the gradual development of the organs and facilities for social and cultural education, growing with the growth of the Church, expanding with the broadening responsibilities of the Church, and reaching a climax in the patristic age. When peace came to the Church, the heritage of the human civilization either had to be cleansed, reformed, and brought into proper relationship and submission to revealed truth, or the Church in her members had to undergo distortion and disfiguration at the hands of the inveterate imperfections and swollen perversities of this human social accumulation. The teaching mission of the Church, therefore, involves not only the heritage of revealed truth, but also its proper relationship to the natural heritage of human culture.

At the climax of this process in the patristic age Augustine, the *rhetor* of Milan, has become a convert to the Catholic Church, and later a priest and a bishop. Will he continue his work as an educator? His ordination to the priesthood and his consecration as the Bishop of Hippo introduce him into this historic mission of teaching and place in his hands the responsibility of the official teacher in the Church of God. He will necessarily be a teacher. But will he be a teacher in some special sense because of his background as an educator, and in particular because of this undertaking in the field of education which can be seen in connection with his life at Cassiciacum and at Thagaste?

The circumstances of St. Augustine's ordination to the Catholic priesthood, as related by Possidius, reveal that he entered the priesthood in a manner which begets the anticipation that he will have some special mission and apostolate in connection with the field of education. "At this time," writes Possidius, "the office of bishop in the Catholic Church at Hippo was held by that holy man Valerius. He was now impelled by the pressing needs of the Church to address his flock and impress upon them the necessity of finding and ordaining a priest for the city. The Catholics were by now aware of the holy Augustine's teaching and way of life and they seized hold of him—he was standing in the congregation quite unconcerned and with no idea of what was going to happen to him. . . . Holding him fast they brought him, as their custom was, to the bishop for ordination, for they were unanimous in asking for this to be done then and there. And while they were demanding this with eager shouts, he was weeping copiously . . . bemoaning the many great dangers to his way of life that he anticipated would come crowding on him if he had to govern and to direct the Church, and that was why he was weeping. But they had their way." [1]

"The Holy Valerius," continues this forthright account, "who had ordained him and was a devout man living in the fear of God, was filled with joy and gave God thanks. He used to tell people how the Lord had heard the prayers he had so often sent up to Him that heaven would send him just such a man as this, who would help to build up the Lord's Church by his invigorating teaching of the word of God." [2]

Reflecting on Augustine's career in the field of education as we know it so far, a career which could not have been unknown to Bishop Valerius, it is not difficult to see what the aged bishop had in mind. Perhaps he foresaw a mission in the Church for this famous and experienced educator.

These circumstances of Augustine's ordination to the priesthood make it clear that he is not necessarily entering into a new life which involves a departure from the field of education. In fact, he happened to be standing in the congregation on that occasion because of an apostolic mission. He had travelled from Thagaste to Hippo at the request of a certain man who wished to discuss with him some matters of the soul and the teaching of the Church. It was fitting that he should have been enlisted into the Catholic priesthood as a result of such a mission. For his new life will not involve an inner break with his professional past, nor a completely different inner orientation. He went to Hippo out of charity toward a soul; Augustine, the teacher, educator and monk at Thagaste, is already the Augustine who is interested in the salvation of souls. In the same way, in his new capacity as shepherd of souls, he will remain an educator because his care for souls will involve teaching in the most direct way. This way will be that of a bishop, who by his office is involved in the work of teaching. The background and professional experience of St. Augustine will enable him to perform this office in an especially fruitful way.

In this fashion, the very ordination of St. Augustine opens possibilities for a continuing contact with the field of education. Coming at this precise juncture of the patristic age, this is a matter of unusual interest and importance. The stage is set in a providential manner precisely for such a specialist in the educational problem both of classical antiquity and of the Catholic Church at that moment of time.

The Priest-Teacher at Hippo

Recognizing the special qualifications of his new priest, Bishop Valerius gave him the full responsibility of Christian doctrine, contrary to custom in Africa at that time, not only in preaching but also in the catechetical school. Thus St. Augustine received an appointment which today would be called that of "superintendent of schools" or "director of catechetics," and was placed in charge of preaching.[3] Augustine was unwilling to assume this responsibility without time for a special preparation, which he formally requested from his Bishop.[4] "I ought to study all His remedies in the Scriptures," St. Augustine writes to his Bishop, "and by praying and reading, so to act that strength sufficient for such perilous duties may be granted to my soul. I did not do this before, because I did not have time, but, as soon as I was ordained, I planned to use all my leisure time in studying the Sacred Scriptures, and I tried to arrange to have leisure for this duty." [5]

St. Augustine entreats his Bishop to give him a period of time for himself in order to prepare himself with a better knowledge of the Bible. "I venture to say," he writes, "that I know and hold with firm faith all that is necessary for my own salvation. But, how am I to make use of this for the salvation of others? . . . How can this be done, except as the Lord Himself says, by asking, seeking, knocking: that is, by praying, reading, weeping? For this purpose, I wanted the brethren to secure for me from your most sincere and venerable charity, a little time, at least until Easter, and this I myself now ask. . . . Take pity on me and grant me as much time as I have asked, for the reason I have asked. . . . Perhaps the Lord . . . will restore me in a shorter time than I have asked, armed with saving knowledge from the Scriptures." [6]

A reply from Bishop Valerius to the newly ordained priest has not been preserved. It is safe to assume, however, that he granted the permission which Augustine requested; indeed, a marked change in Augustine's writings occurs from this point which indicates that he has taken the time for the systematic study of the Scriptures which he desired. Henceforth Augustine is a man of the Bible, as he expects every priest to be.[7] Every priest is a teacher of Scripture, it was Augustine's firm conviction, and hence a familiarity and even complete mastery of it is necessary. This is the first point in the development of St. Augustine's contact with the field of education in his new mode of life: he has been reading parts of the Bible since the beginning of his conversion, but henceforth he is literally filled with Sacred Scripture in a striking new way. The imagery, the language and the teachings of Sacred Scripture suddenly dominate his writings. The disciple of Plato recedes into the background and Augustine becomes more visibly the follower of the apostles and the prophets. References to Sacred Scripture flow from his pen, and he discusses the doctrines of the Church in Scriptural language. An easy familiarity with Sacred Scripture becomes the hallmark of his works.[8] It is difficult to exaggerate the importance of this new fact for the Christian culture of the future. St. Augustine legislates the reading of Sacred Scripture firmly into the life of his monasteries, and thus the *lectio divina* passes into the religious life of the Western world with the development of monasticism; and he places the Bible at the center of his program of studies, as we shall see, and thus the mind of the West will receive its characteristic biblical understanding of universal history.

Returning from his retreat for the study of Scripture, Augustine plunged into the busy life of a Catholic priest in the city of Hippo. "Augustine continued to teach and preach the message of salvation," writes Possidius, "both privately and publicly, in his home and in the Church. He opposed with the fullest confidence the African heresies and especially the Donatists, the Manicheans and the pagans, in carefully finished books and in extempore sermons. The Christians admired him beyond words and were full of his praises. . . . In fact, by God's good gift, the Catholic Church in Africa began to lift its head again after a long period during which it had lain prostrate—led astray, overpowered and oppressed, while the heretics grew strong, especially the re-baptizing Donatist party, which comprised the majority of Africans." [9]

In this summary of a busy life, we read between the lines that this converted educator, now the priest in Hippo, was having a powerful influence which was beginning to be felt over North Africa as a whole. He continued his literary apostolate at the same time. "As for these books and pamphlets of his," Possidius states, "which by the marvelous grace of

God issued from his pen in a constant flow, they were founded upon an abundance of reasoned argument and the authority of Holy Scripture, and the heretics themselves used
to come hurrying with the Catholics with intense eagerness
to hear them read aloud. Those who wished to have what
they heard taken down, and could afford to do so, brought
shorthand writers with them. Thus the splendid teaching
. . . was spread abroad and made known through the length
and breadth of Africa." [10]

The foundation for this type of apostolate is seen in the
monastery which Augustine founded at Hippo, with the permission of his Bishop. For this monastery contained a school.
We must look into this fact in order to see the real and objective character of the continuing contact of Augustine's
priestly life with the field of education. "Once a priest,"
writes Possidius, "it was not long before he established a
monastery within the precincts of the Church and entered
upon a life with the servants of God in accordance with the
method and rule established under the holy Apostles. . . .
He himself had done this before, when he returned from
across the sea to his own home." [11]

The elderly Bishop donated a piece of ground to Augustine for this purpose, and it is safe to assume that the first
nucleus of members were close companions of Augustine
from the monastery at Thagaste. In the absences necessitated
by his priestly duties, the daily life of the community at the
monastery was governed by Possidius, who acted in Augustine's place.

From his first days in the priesthood St. Augustine determined to unite in his own personal living the monastic way
of life of the monastery with the external works of the
priestly apostolate. His monastery began to flourish, attract-
ing members in considerable numbers; soon it became a
training ground for the priesthood of the diocese and for
the bishoprics of neighboring cities. The members of the
monastery were of various ages, and included young people
in the earlier stages of their education. From letters and ser-

mons of St. Augustine, it is clear that the monastery operated a school for young men and had definite and systematic provision for the education of adolescents.[12]

"As divine truth made headway," writes Possidius, "those who had been serving God in the monastery with the holy Augustine, and under his rule, began to be ordained as clergy for the Church at Hippo. The result was to make better known and more evident every day the truth preached by the Catholic Church, the way of life of the holy servants of God, their chastity and their utter poverty. Then, in the Church of peace and unity, there grew up a strong desire for bishops and clergy from the monastery founded by, and flourishing under, this remarkable man. They began to be asked for, and presently what was asked was obtained.[13]

Possidius informs us that no less than ten bishops were supplied to neighboring cities in North Africa by St. Augustine and his monastery-school, "including some of the most important," Possidius says, "in response to requests. These in turn, having come from the religious life, founded fresh monasteries as the Churches of the Lord multiplied; and then, as zeal for the spread of God's work went on growing, they supplied brethren to yet other Churches for promotion to the priesthood." [14] This eyewitness report makes it clear that Augustine in *schola nostra* is not only producing powerful preaching and effective written works himself, but he is actually renewing the Church of God in North Africa through his educational institution. This new school, this Catholic institution of monastic living and learning which he founded and operated, is now becoming a model for other places as well. St. Augustine is conducting a process of spiritual renovation and of Christian progress in and through a work of teaching, and by means of an institution of education.

The fact that the apostolic priest who stands behind this activity is an educator and remains one is clear in his own teaching that the precept of love of neighbor implies the duty of instruction in truth. For if charity demands that we care for the sick and help the poor, Augustine teaches, giving aid to our neighbor in all his bodily needs, how much more must we be concerned with the health and welfare of his soul? The apostolate, therefore, includes the work of teaching: it must provide for souls that health-giving truth which God has made accessible to mankind through his priestly apostolate at one of its highest levels. Catholic education is the therapy of mankind, that cure for the mental and spiritual ills and needs of man which has been provided by the divine teacher and is distributed through the ministry of his own teaching institution, the Church which he sent to teach all nations.[15] It was this view of education which Augustine represented within the Church; he is organizing it in these years after his ordination and bringing it to ever more efficient perfection in his priestly ministry. His priestly work is not confined to the externals of preaching and visitation; he continues his monastic life and the effective direction of his monastery school.

It is from this intellectual foundation and from this academic position that he is able to carry on his demanding literary apostolate. For his works continue to come forth from his pen, as Possidius notes, springing from this very apostolate in the field of education. The body of patristic writings which we know as the *Opera omnia sancti Augustini* continues to grow—not as an independent entity but as the natural outgrowth of his busy life as a priest-teacher. Perhaps the clearest indication of his continuing basic interest and activity in formal education as such is the fact that his treatise *On Catholic Teaching and Learning,* the *De doctrina christiana* published in 397, must have been composed before his consecration as a bishop, during these years of his work as a priest-teacher. Perhaps the fact that it remained incomplete for thirty years is due to his consecration as Bishop of Hippo. Thus this famous treatise becomes his educational testament as a priest-teacher, as it were, which he will complete and confirm in his last years as a bishop.

This review of St. Augustine's contact with education as

a Catholic priest would not be complete if we omitted mention of the catechumenate, for his Bishop placed him in charge of this official and institutionalized preparation of converts for baptism into the Catholic Church. Many of his extant sermons were composed and delivered in connection with his work in this phase of Catholic education.[16] Augustine was familiar with the content and methods of the catechumenate, for he himself had received this course of instructions under one of the most competent of teachers, St. Ambrose, Bishop of Milan. The catechumenate was an institution intended originally and primarily for adult education, developed since the times of the Apostles and long since the standard procedure in the early Church as a whole. The first stage followed upon an application on the part of a prospective convert. Such an applicant was assigned to a priest or deacon as a *rudis*, one uninstructed in the Catholic faith, for initial instruction and probation. These applicants attended the Mass of the Catechumens and studied religion privately under tutorship from their priest.

Each year at the approach of Lent the priests and bishops were wont to urge the people at Mass to enroll their catechumens for baptism. Those responding were formed into a group or class for final and specific instructions during Lent, together with a set of liturgical preparations and functions leading up to Holy Week and baptism on Holy Saturday and Easter Sunday. This group received a special and formal course of instruction from the priests and bishops on the Our Father, the Apostles' Creed, and the moral principles of Christian living. The solemn liturgical functions were interwoven with these regular instructions for the group; vestiges remain in our liturgy to this day, and several courses of instruction and many sermons delivered on these occasions have been preserved in the works of the Fathers of the Church.

It was in such a framework that St. Augustine functioned as the priest in charge of the catechumenate at Hippo.[17] Here he was soon able, using his general educational background and his acquaintanceship with the practices of the Church at Rome and Milan, to bring about certain improvements in the instruction of converts in North Africa.[18]

We can only mention here the treatise which Augustine wrote as a result of his work in this area of the apostolate, the *De catechizandis rudibus*. This model catechectical instruction, which gives Augustine's educational principles and provides two examples of his manner of presenting the content of Christian doctrine, is a rare instance from the early Church of the teaching given to a convert. St. Augustine's method introduces the prospective Christian into an understanding of the Bible, not in detail or in knowledge about its human authorship, but in the historic plan or economy of salvation which extends under the Providence of God, as he says, "from the text: *In the beginning God created heaven and earth,* down to the present period of Church history." [19] St. Augustine explicitly demands a systematic instruction and manifests throughout the treatise his unusual competence and experience as a teacher. This handbook of the Christian teacher and charter of religious and catechetical instruction throughout the centuries to the present, serves to illustrate the continuing contact of Augustine in his priestly ministry with the field of education. St. Augustine will transfer many points from this institution of the early Church which provided Christian instruction to adult converts into his plan and program for the Christian education of young people who are children of Catholic parents. With his synthetic mind, it is to be expected that he would incorporate the essential content and procedures of the catechumenate into their order of studies, leading young people to the same mature and adult understanding of the true religion.

St. Augustine, Bishop of Hippo

St. Augustine was consecrated Bishop of Hippo in A.D. 396, an office which he fulfilled for thirty-four years until his death in 430. This long period of time, in which he functioned as a member of the official teaching body possessing the *charisma veritatis,* saw the educational apostolate of the Church develop toward its full implementation with pedagogical organs. The teaching apostolate exercised in the infancy of the Church could not, of course, possess "schools," for these belonged to the temporal civilization; they prepare young people with all the arts, sciences, and disciplines of human culture for the various human responsibilities of earthly living. Since, however, the Christian holds a twofold citizenship—a citizen of eternity as well as of the earthly city —the teaching mission of the Church by virtue of the very responsibility of the apostolate and the very nature of the Kingship of Christ came to embrace the entire area of human culture. Throughout the patristic age the question of sacred doctrine and secular learning gradually received its answer until by Augustine's time a synthesis was possible and a program for Catholic schools could be drawn.

"As bishop," Possidius tells us, "he preached the message of eternal salvation more insistently and fervently than ever and with greater authority, and no longer in one district only but in others where he went by invitation; and the Church of the Lord blossomed and expanded, briskly and busily." [20] Possidius emphasizes this fact that Augustine appeared frequently in various places of North Africa: "When he happened to have been asked to go and pay a visit, or to instruct or preach to Catholic congregations, as he very often was." [21]

Our question, then, continues the investigation whether there was a substantial contact with the field of education in these thirty-four busy years. There was, of course, the catechumenate; but a genuine "education" in the institutional sense of schools, cultural organs of civilization? Was there the culture of the human arts and disciplines in addition to sacred doctrine, but now in a Christian manner?

It is possible to portray St. Augustine's apostolate as a bishop without bringing into view any particular contact with the field of education. As an example, we might cite Portalié who tells us that St. Augustine soon moved for practical reasons from his monastery to the bishop's residence, and that "his palace became a monastery in which he established the practice of common life with his clerics. . . ." [22] In his discussion of the episcopate, Portalié describes his devoted care of his flock and concentrates on his struggle with the heresies of the day: the Manicheans, the Donatists, and the Pelagians. His last years are taken up with "struggles against Arianism." [23] St. Augustine's activity as a bishop, of course, includes his controversies with these heresies, and his work of preaching and of writing in connection with them. Furthermore, in a work such as that of Portalié, which concentrates on the literary production and doctrinal teaching of St. Augustine, it is doubtless justifiable to portray his life in this manner. The fact remains, however, that an entire dimension of his episcopate is missed, the one in which St. Augustine is visible precisely as an educator.

Similarly deficient is the otherwise meritorious work of Van der Meer on St. Augustine as a shepherd of souls.[24] Bishop Valerius prayed for a teacher, a man experienced in the field of education. It is as an educator that Augustine made perhaps his most lasting contribution to pastoral care, for his educational work was an integral part of his personal care of the souls committed to his charge. There is in addition the fact that through his educational theory and practice he has exercised a continuing pastoral care, transcending the small diocese of Hippo, over countless souls through the coming centuries of Christendom, and indeed to this very day, wherever Catholic schools assist the bishops in their work.

Approaches to the episcopal apostolate of St. Augustine at Hippo which describe the outer framework of his life in this fashion, whether from the viewpoint of doctrine, as Portalié, or from the viewpoint of the holiness and charity of his external ministration to his people, as Van der Meer, have this in common, that they omit the educational foundation of his apostolate. Eventually, therefore, the contact of Augustine as a bishop with the field of education becomes obscure and even disappears from modern memory. The work of producing his literary output and of conducting his pastoral care of souls seems to float free from the concrete educational milieu and institution in which he functioned.

The fact is that the astonishing literary production did not, and could not, so to speak, arise out of thin air; it demands as its adequate explanation some concrete institutionalized basis in the busy reality of Augustine's life.[25]

Possidius, who first published a catalog of the writings of St. Augustine, shows us the view which men had of his literary work while he was yet alive. "As for all that he dictated and published," he states, "and all the debates in the cathedral that were taken down and revised, some were against heretics of various kinds, others were expositions of the canonical books for the instruction of holy sons of the Church, but there are so many that there is hardly a student who has been able to read and get acquainted with them all." [26] It seems to be a fact, although quite often overlooked, that all of this was possible because Augustine functioned as the head of a well-organized school, with a stimulating student body, with a fresh "order of learning" rooted in vigorous Christian thinking and Christian philosophy, with a central core of research assistants, and with one of the finest libraries of the early Church. If this is the case, there was a massive continuing contact with the field of education in St. Augustine's life and work now as a bishop which should not be allowed to drop out of view. This is the case when Augustine is depicted simply as a "preacher," a "controversialist," or a "shepherd of souls." There have been many shepherds of souls and many preachers, but few who have produced a body of writings in the magnitude of St. Augustine, entirely apart from the challenge of scholarship which some of his topics presented. We have but to think of the historical sources for the *City of God!* The problem, therefore, is to understand how this immense crowning work of the Age of the Fathers was produced, not to mention his many other writings; for when full insight is obtained, we will have by that very fact the full answer which we are seeking to the question whether in Augustine's life and work as a bishop there was some substantial and specific continuing contact with the field of education.

St. Augustine's Cathedral School

When he was first consecrated, St. Augustine intended to continue his residence in his monastery in the garden at Hippo. He soon recognized that the responsibilities of the episcopal state were inconsistent with this withdrawal from the public. The very obligations of a bishop toward the numerous pilgrims and travelers caused him to reconsider his plans. He decided to move to the spacious bishop's residence which his predecessors had developed. He determined to retain the essentials of the monastic life, legislating a common life upon his clergy for the future and urging those already with him to join him in his habitual manner of living.[27] "Other companions," writes Zumkeller, "Augustine called out of the earlier monastery at the garden, which continued to function, and proved to be in the future a continuing source of vocations for the clergy of the diocese." [28]

At the same time, it seems that Augustine soon organized a new school in connection with the bishop's residence, as may be seen in Sermon 356, as part of his concern to build a well-educated and deeply formed body of clergy for his Church.[29] The episcopal residence became two things at once, a *monasterium clericorum* and at the same time a school, *schola nostra*. Augustine continues consistently with his past, retaining his contact with the process of education in his new responsibility. In fact, now that he is a bishop, all of his thinking regarding the field of education can be brought to full fruition. It is this fact which we want to clarify, in order to prepare the way for a study of the nature of this program and practice of Christian education which is evolving in the life and work of St. Augustine. In this project of a cathedral school within the framework of a monastic institution operating in connection with the bishop's residence, Augustine had his forerunners: Eusebius of Vercelli, among others, including the incipient monastic life which Augustine had been able to study at Milan and at Rome. "Nevertheless," as Zumkeller says, "Augustine was the first to establish this new institution on a deeper and more permanent foundation." [30] The central idea of Augustine's thinking was to unite the monastic way of life with its discipline in a close yet flexible and practical union with the pastoral care of souls. This was the basis for the improvement of his clergy and the germ from which specialized educational institutions for the formation of young men toward the priesthood were to develop in the future. In all of his educational thinking, St. Augustine has been concerned to provide a complete and integral formation, embracing the intelligence and the will at one and the same time. This ideal, actually at least implicit in his thinking since he entered the field of education after reading the *Hortensius,* has been deepening with the years and finds now its full realization in his work as a bishop. The success of his educational apostolate is demonstrated by the manner in which his fame spread over North Africa, which we have seen, and by the fact that his school produced so many priests and at least ten bishops in his own lifetime. As a matter of fact, Augustine was soon the general superior of approximately twenty similar foundations, all of them monastic in nature under his religious rule of life, but each functioning also as a school and carrying on a process of formal instruction according to his educational thinking. The effectiveness of St. Augustine's educational institution can be studied to this day in the disputations and conferences with the Donatists and other heretics, for the transcripts reveal a high level of theological culture, transcending what the Catholic Church was able to produce in North Africa prior to the educational renewal launched by the Bishop of Hippo. Another insight into the high level of Christian educational culture in Augustine's institution is obtained from the works which he wrote because the *fratres,* as he termed his fellow-monks and younger students, requested them.[31]

It is possible to go considerably beyond these general considerations in clarifying the fact that St. Augustine functioned as a school administrator, operating his own cathedral school at Hippo. The rule of life devised for the first foundation at Thagaste and its supplement for the monastery at Hippo are introduced into the new institution at the bishop's residence, where the life differs from that of the earlier monasteries only in a certain greater freedom of movement to provide for the demands of pastoral care. It is an educational institution which has an order of the day planned to provide an academic framework for learning.[32] Augustine's cathedral school maintained a *scriptorium,* a fully equipped department for transcribing and maintaining manuscripts and for producing and copying books according to the methods of that time. In addition to this important aspect of an institution of learning, Augustine had with him a group of carefully chosen research assistants, above and beyond the teaching staff.[33] This group of specialists assisted the Bishop in his various tasks of research and documentation. Furthermore, as we know, the Bishop of Hippo almost never wrote his works by hand, but dictated with all of the technical help provided by the cultural development of the time, as we have seen in connection with the *Dialogues of Cassiciacum.* His school provided him with this indispensable foundation and implementation for his intellectual and literary apostolate, and even functioned as a printing establishment, as we would say today, from which he sent out his works in answer to requests from St. Jerome, from Paulinus of Nola—indeed, from many quarters of Christendom. In all of this Augustine was not inventing new procedures: he was simply using standard techniques of classical antiquity at his cathedral school in the service of the Church and Christian culture. Here, then, is the practical and material explanation for the unparalleled literary productiveness of the Bishop of Hippo. Without this educational institution with its various organs and its array of personnel, the very physical production of St. Augustine's literary works would be difficult to understand.

In a larger perspective the institution of learning organized by this former *rhetor* at the bishop's residence in Hippo is an integral part of the continuing and developing mission of the Church, a supernatural teaching mission which embraces all human culture in its field of vision. The work of St. Augustine's school represents in an advanced form the concrete process by which the natural heritage of classical antiquity entered into the Church, and by which the arts and disciplines which transmit that heritage to the young generation found a home in Catholic education. From beginning to end, therefore, Augustine remains in contact with the field of education. He is operating a strikingly elaborate educational institution in connection with his bishop's residence and apostolate, the frequently overlooked practical explanation of the other more visible aspects of his life and work. St. Augustine's life as a shepherd of souls, as Van der Meer so well portrays it, was a striking work, worthy of one of the greatest saints of God; by the same token, his intellectual victory over the chief heretical currents of thought in his time, which had gained the upper hand in North Africa when he entered the priesthood, is another monumental achievement. All of this, in addition to the *opera omnia*. Can this be explained sufficiently merely by the extraordinary mind and intellectual genius of Augustine? By his devotion of his life to his studies, his willingness to work into the hours of the night, and his methodical approach to the use of his time? One is inclined to agree with Dominguez-del Val that, humanly speaking, these factors do not appear to account satisfactorily for the immense work which Augustine accomplished in the apostolate on behalf of human science and learning. Without his monastery school, without his skilled staff of research assistants, without his craftsmen and technical facilities for book production, he could not have carried on this apostolate.[34] In his *Soliloquies* Augustine mentions his ideal of gathering together a group of educated men to live a religious life of the intellect and to carry forward the quest for wisdom.[35] Was this not what he had brought at last to full fruition at Hippo, a monastic life which embraced a full-fledged institution of learning? When we see the reality of this truly powerful institution, we can understand how there came to be not only a flow of written works but also a constant procession of fully educated, properly formed Catholic men, entering with renewing and regenerating force into the life of the Catholic Church in North Africa.[36]

The fact that Harnack was able to claim that St. Augustine as a bishop had no library worthy of mention, having so far departed from the field of education and intellectual interests upon becoming a priest and a bishop that he was content with his own writings and a few copies of the Bible, indicates how completely this fundamental aspect of Augustine's life and work can fall out of sight. However, as Altaner has demonstrated, Harnack is "completely false" in his views on this point.[37] "St. Augustine's library," writes Dominguez-del Val, "contained one of the finest collections of all Christian antiquity in both quality and in number."[38]

We have here a special instance of the contact of St. Augustine with the field of education, the fine fruit of his lifetime spent in the teaching profession. He had been over forty years building this library, for it had grown with him and gone with him from place to place: it retained in Hippo that "profane" nucleus which reflects his earlier years as a *rhetor*. The character of this library changed gradually until at Hippo it had become essentially Catholic and ecclesiastical. In this remarkable library, which has been so completely overlooked, we have the mute witness to Augustine's continuing profound contact with the field of education. An analysis of the sources of his literary production would reveal the content of this library, but this mammoth task of scholarship has not yet been undertaken. The fact that this library existed is quite clear to students of St. Augustine. In addition, he speaks of it on several occasions.[39] Possidius tells us that " . . . he made no will, because, as one of God's poor, he had nothing to leave. It was a standing order that the library of the Church and all the books should be carefully preserved for posterity . . . for he left a library of books containing writings by himself and other holy men. It is through these, thanks be to God, that his quality and stature in the Church is known to the world; and in these he will always live among the faithful." [40] These words may well have denoted a reality of a magnitude which escapes us at this distance.

It would take us beyond our present purpose to analyze the present state of scholarship on St. Augustine's library. Suffice it to recall what he had to have available when organizing and composing *The City of God:* the forty-one books on *Antiquities* by Varro, the works of Josephus and Philo, all the standard works of ancient historiography, Sallust, Livy, Tacitus, and the rest, not omitting the Greek authors. Even a cursory reading of the *City of God* demands this and much more. Augustine's library was a complete repository of Graeco-Roman culture, that profane or secular culture of classical antiquity which was in process of entering the Church, purified and restored precisely through the work of patristic educational institutions, of which St. Augustine's is the most fully developed.

Then there were, of course, all the treasures of biblical knowledge, with the various texts and translations, as well as commentaries from various sources extending back to apostolic times. But in addition to this Augustine's library contained a nearly complete collection of all the Greek and Latin Fathers who came before him, providing the physical mechanism for the fact that he is the culmination of the patristic age. Indeed, in his Christian order of studies he puts the Latin Fathers on the curriculum, so to speak, for literary formation in his plan of education. St. Ambrose's works have a preferential position; the works of Tertullian and Cyprian are there, as well as those of Hilary, of his correspondents Paulinus of Nola and St. Jerome, and finally the work of his young Spanish disciple, Orosius.[41]

As his school work and his personal literary apostolate developed, however, St. Augustine was forced to embark upon a careful study of the works of the Greek Fathers, and there is definite factual information that he set about systematically to collect their works. Thus his library at last came to possess the works of Irenaeus, of Origen, Eusebius' *Church History* and *Chronicle,* and many others.[42]

The final and perhaps the most important fact concerning the cathedral school at Hippo was the body of teachers headed by St. Augustine himself. For he never ceased his profession of teaching, even in the busy period of his episcopal ministry, and always attended personally to the intellectual formation of his followers and of his students. As Dominguez-del Val writes, "Augustine continued this teaching apostolate throughout his life as a priest and bishop in a most direct and personal manner." [43]

St. Augustine's teaching methods were twofold: first, exposition of doctrine, as he had been accustomed to carry it out from his entrance into the teaching profession as a youth; secondly, the technique of disputation and discussion, a method especially developed and popular in the *Spätantike.* We have graphic examples, as we have seen, in the *Dialogues of Cassiciacum,* which enable us to see Augustine actually teaching. In his later life he never gave up this technique and, as the Bishop of Hippo, his devotion of time to these teaching techniques was lessened, no doubt, but it never ceased altogether.[44]

There are frequent indications in his works of St. Augustine's direct activity as a teacher, for upon close inspection several are seen to come directly out of his teaching. There are, for example, the *Eighty-three Questions,* and his expositions of Sacred Scripture, especially the commentaries on St. Paul. But above all there is the *ex professo* treatise on Christian teaching and learning, the *De doctrina christiana.* This work is fundamental in the question whether and just how his life as a bishop continued to have a contact with the field of education.

"Ratio Studiorum": The Treatise "De doctrina christiana"

St. Augustine's *De doctrina christiana* has been the object of a recent controversy which bears directly upon the present discussion: we must, therefore, review the facts of the matter.

In his Augustine the Bishop, Van der Meer devotes an extensive space to St. Augustine's preaching.[45] The first chapter of this part, under the title "The Handbook for Preachers," contains a discussion of St. Augustine's *De doctrina christiana*. The title which the Bishop of Hippo placed over his work would be translated today, Van der Meer tells us, approximately as follows: "An Exegetical Handbook with an Introduction to the Biblical Instruction of Christians.[46] "It is a book," continues Van der Meer, "definitely intended for preachers and its assumption is that whoever ascends the pulpit must have a thorough knowledge of Holy Scripture." [47] Van der Meer dismisses the first three books with a sentence and devotes his entire treatment to Book IV. This alone suffices to illustrate how completely he omits St. Augustine's contact with the field of education.[48]

"In many respects this last book is a disappointment," continues Van der Meer. "Yet apart from another book that is rather more detailed, namely, his *Instruction for Beginners,* it contains everything that Augustine wrote on the art of preaching and instruction. However, we do not find here any systematic treatise on spiritual eloquence or on the construction of the Christian homily, but only a number of pieces of very excellent advice, all delightfully expressed, combined with a number of examples designed to serve as models. Finally, there is a sort of legacy of the old school, namely, the division, following Cicero, of the art of speaking into three kinds." [49]

It seems legitimate here to recall the observation made in connection with the controversy on the nature of the *Dialogues of Cassiciacum*. When a modern writer finds one of St. Augustine's works a "disappointment," it may be taken as a preliminary indication that he is perhaps misconceiving its nature and purpose. These controversies on St. Augustine's works are not properly solved by assuming some failure on the part of their author to think clearly or to compose well. In the present instance the source of the difficulty seems once again to be the failure to see St. Augustine's work in the light of his educational profession. Once that is done, there is nothing disappointing in the *De doctrina christiana* as a literary composition; but all four books must be viewed as a unit, exactly as Augustine saw them. How Van der Meer misses the point and omits this contact with the field of education comes to the surface when he comments on St. Augustine's stated intention not to compose another mere textbook of rhetoric, a useful discipline but not indispensable. "A very bold observation," writes Van der Meer, "even though Quintilian had been dead some three hundred years. Indeed, this is another of those occasions on which Augustine, without willing it, brings about a minor educational revolution." [50]

The genesis of such an opinion, that St. Augustine's effect upon the field of education was unintentional, is the excessive compartmentalization of his life: first a *rhetor*, then a "philosopher," then an ecclesiastic, with education considered rather incidental even to the first period described in the *Confessions*. The *De doctrina christiana* is viewed, in conflict with the very words, as a mere adjunct of St. Augustine's sermons, "disappointing," indeed, in relationship to the art of preaching.[51]

This view, however, fails to do justice to the content of

St. Augustine's treatise, and seems to represent simply another instance of the manner in which St. Augustine's contact with the field of education can fall almost completely out of sight. "None of the biographies of St. Augustine which we possess," writes Marrou, "gives a satisfactory presentation of the 'ecclesiastical period.' There is a task to accomplish in this regard, indeed, a formidable one . . . once past the point at which the Confessions terminate their report, the personality of Augustine recedes into a semi-obscurity. . . ." [52]

It is Marrou's merit to have brought the *De doctrina christiana* into a better light, which does justice to its content in itself and to its relationship with the general character of St. Augustine's educational career. "In order to appreciate the real content of Augustinian culture," he writes, "we possess an abundant and varied documentation. Fourteen-fifteenths of the immense literary work of St. Augustine were accomplished during this 'ecclesiastical period.' On the other hand, to come to an understanding of the principles which he held on this subject, we possess the treatise in four books which were devoted expressly to Christian culture, the *De doctrina christiana*, a work long meditated and well ripened in which St. Augustine expounds for us everything essential on the idea of intellectual culture, its place in Christian life, its purpose, its technique, and its methods, which he held at the end of his life." [53]

Marrou perceives that this work contains the very heart and core of St. Augustine's educational philosophy, which cannot be brought into proper relief if it is seen as a simple manual of scriptural hermeneutics or a book on homiletics and preaching for the use of priests. It is Marrou's opinion that St. Augustine treats the problem of education and of Christian culture in its entire general sweep, for both clergy and laity, and develops his treatise as a cultural synthesis from the viewpoint of the priest and bishop concerned with Catholic education as such, with a program of studies for the Christian intellectual.

St. Augustine states that the very essence of Christian formation and Catholic education is the *tractatio Scripturarum:* the Sacred Scriptures, in other words, have been moved to the central position in the educational process previously occupied in classical education by the works of Homer and Vergil. It does not follow, therefore, from the fact of St. Augustine's concern for the study of Sacred Scripture, that it is intended solely for preachers, as a handbook for their homilies in the pulpit, or even exclusively for the educational preparation of the clergy as such.[54] The *De doctrina christiana* rather concerns the entire plan of a Christian education designed to be a "safe way for youth" in contrast with the corruptions of the *paideia* which St. Augustine had experienced as a student and teacher in the educational institutions of imperial Rome.[55] The first three books explain proper methods in the study of the Sacred Scriptures, with rules based on the sciences of grammar and rhetoric for determining the true meaning of revelation. The fourth book is devoted to the principles for teaching the Scriptures to others, and for Christian preaching. In his development of these topics St. Augustine laid the ground plan for theological teaching, in such a fashion that his book became the foundation of Peter Lombard's *Sentences* in the twelfth century, the direct result of the use of his basic plan of teaching for eight centuries in the schools of Christendom. This fact alone should suffice to indicate that the *De doctrina christiana* is a basic treatise in Catholic education and not a mere handbook for preaching.

The content of Book II, a discussion of the arts and disciplines of liberal education in relationship to the Christian culture deriving from the study of the Bible, in our view, justifies the position taken by Marrou. This is actually an exposition of St. Augustine's teaching on the proper manner of introducing the heritage of human and secular learning into the educational work of the Church. Seen in the light of Augustine's entire professional career in the field of education, and seen in the light of the *Dialogues of Cassiciacum*, of the drafts of his textbooks on the liberal arts and of the

De musica, this treatise of St. Augustine takes its place full in the main stream of his life and work as an educator. Understood in this fashion, the *De doctrina christiana* is a beautifully unified composition presenting an order of studies which heals the heritage of *paideia* precisely by taking all of its positive content and relating it to the study of revealed truth in and by means of the Scriptures. In fact, this order of studies is itself the continuation of the quest for wisdom, for God and the good of the soul, a quest which becomes richly fruitful now through the instrumentality of education, for the Divine Truth hidden in the sacred text is unveiled by *doctrina*, the act of teaching, and made the possession of the youthful soul.[56] Teaching, therefore, is a most priestly work, and there is indeed an "Apostolate of the Classroom."

Finally, we must discuss whether Eggersdorfer's view that we have here only a "manual for the instruction of the clergy" is true, or whether St. Augustine's treatise involves the very nature of Catholic education for all members of the Church, whether clergy or laity.[57] In this case again Marrou appears to grasp correctly the nature of the *De doctrina christiana*, when he writes, "It is a strictly 'modern' idea, one which seems to me a stranger to the patristic age, to distinguish between a religious culture reserved to the clergy alone, and a profane culture which would be legitimate for the laity." [58] In support of his statement Marrou cites a sermon of St. Augustine in which he rejects with indignation the hypothesis that the traditional classical culture of the pagan schools is legitimate and proper for the Catholic laity.[59] It is beyond the purpose of the present discussion to analyze in detail the nature of the educational teaching of the *De doctrina christiana*. For the present, we may take it as established that there is more involved in this treatise on Christian teaching and learning than those authors perceive who omit the contact with the field of education in their exposition of St. Augustine's life and work. Seen in the light of St. Augustine's career as a *rhetor* and of his philosophical writings, the *De doctrina christiana* becomes a consistent continuation of his educational thought and activity in his life as a priest and a bishop. It is this fact, rather than a description of the content, which is our present purpose.

Father of the Church, Teacher of Christendom

St. Augustine's school, operated in connection with his bishop's office and cathedral at Hippo, became the model, as we have seen, for a group of similar institutions in North Africa which he was able to see as the fruit of his apostolate as he neared the end of his life. But this is not the end of his institutional influence. From North Africa the basic idea of Augustine's concept of the episcopal apostolate in the field of education was transferred to the mainland of Europe, to the episcopal centers of Italy, Spain, and Gaul, so that his influence passed into the structural formation of Western civilization. St. Augustine's contact with education is not limited to the philosophical and pedagogical doctrines found in his writings; there is also the massive institutional and structural influence upon the schools of the future which actually shaped and formed our Western Christendom. He has made monasticism intellectual in its core and purpose, and has linked study with the care of souls. He fashioned the model according to which, in the times of the formation of Christendom, future educators and school administrators developed the monastery and cathedral schools. Out of these schools, as time went on, the idea of the university, unique in the Western world, was gradually to mature and to receive in due time its proper institutional and juridical form. St. Augustine's apostolate, taken as a whole, occupies a seminal position, both in philosophy and in practice, in the entire development of Western education.

When old age had come upon him, St. Augustine had been prevailed upon to pass his literary works under review. In A.D. 426, therefore, thirty years a bishop, we find him producing that unique work, his *Libri retractationum*, which gives us his own listing of his writings and the inestimable benefit of his own considered judgment upon them.

In the course of this systematic and chronological examination he came upon the *De doctrina christiana*, unfinished at Book III, Chapter XXV, where he had set it aside thirty years before. On the basis of our consideration thus far, we can see how this might have happened. The book had been sufficiently completed in his days as a priest to explain the proper manner of arranging and conducting the order of studies in his Catholic school. Perhaps interrupted by his consecration, it had served during these many years in its unfinished form as a guide for his staff of teachers.

What will he do with it now? Disclaim it? Leave it as it is with a few words of explanation and correction, and continue the *Retractationes*? It is a significant fact that he broke off his review of his other works, in order to complete this treatise on Christian teaching and learning.[60] St. Augustine indicates by his action both the importance which he attaches to the *De doctrina christiana* and the consistency with which he has worked in the field of education throughout his life. He not only reaffirms in a most positive manner his earlier views on the proper order of studies in Catholic education, but now in his old age he completes the book by adding the treatise on the proper manner of teaching Sacred Scripture in the classroom and especially of preaching the word of God in the pulpit, the highest use to which Catholic education will be put. We possess in the *De doctrina christiana*, therefore, the fruit of his mature reflection, confirmed by the full authority of his personal review as a bishop. This reveals the deeply fundamental nature of St. Augustine's contact with the field of education, reaffirmed in strongest terms by this action at the end of his life.

In his review of his earlier works, finally, it is important to note that he repeats his original doctrine on the position of philosophy in the order of studies. There is no question of the fact that he reasserted as an elderly bishop the substance of his earlier treatises on the arts and disciplines of human culture.[61] It is basically wrong, therefore, to look upon him as abandoning, after he becomes a priest and a bishop, that program of education which we have seen him establish at Cassiciacum and explain in his so-called philosophical works. The contrary is the case: he reaffirms this earlier work in strongest terms in this review of his literary production three years before his death, and bears witness, if we pay close attention to his words, to the fundamental consistency which is perceptible in his entire life when it is viewed from the field of education. This is what we should expect of so great a man and so powerful a mind. It corroborates once more the view that in resigning his professorship at Milan he did not in any sense of the word depart from the field of education. The truth is rather to the contrary: he entered more deeply into it than ever with a vast program of regeneration and renewal which was to receive its crown and completion in his priestly work as a shepherd of souls.

Notes from Chapter Five

1 Possidius, *Vita*, c. 4; Hoare, *op. cit.*, pp. 197-198; P.L. 32, 37: ". . . iam scientes catholici sancti Augustini propositum et doctrinam," etc.

2 *Ibid.*, c. 5; *op. cit.*, p. 199; P.L. 32, 37: "Deo gratias agebat, suas exauditas a Domino fuisse preces, ut sibi divinitus homo concederetur talis, qui posset verbo Dei et doctrina salubri Ecclesiam Domini aedificare." The word "doctrina" in these passages seems to have its usual and proper active sense; the Bishop of Hippo prayed for a man skilled in teaching, a man who could cope with the educational problem of a somewhat backward Catholic group hard pressed intellectually by the Donatists and the Manicheans, in addition to the continuing pagan opposition.

3 Cf. Possidius, *Vita*, c. 4; Hoare, *op. cit.*, p. 199; P.L., 32, 37: "Et eidem presbytero potestatem dedit coram se in ecclesia Evangelium praedicandi, ac frequentissime tractandi; contra usum quidem et consuetudinem Africanarum Ecclesiarum. . . ."

4 Cf. *Epist.* 21.

5 *Ibid.;* Sister Wilfred Parsons (trans.), *Saint Augustine, Letters,* I (1-82) (New York: Fathers of the Church, 1951), 49.

6 *Ibid.; op. cit.*, p. 51.

7 Cf. *De doctrina christiana*, IV, 4 (6).

8 Cf. on this point Zumkeller, *Das Mönchtum* . . ., p. 59, and esp. Marrou, *Saint Augustin et la fin* . . ., pp. 387-503, for a comprehensive view of

the place and role which the Bible came to have in St. Augustine's program of education.

9 Possidius, *Vita*, c. 7; Hoare, *op. cit.*, p. 201.

10 *Ibid.; op. cit.*, pp. 201-202.

11 *Ibid.*, c. 5; *op. cit.*, p. 198.

12 Cf. Dominguez-del Val, *op. cit.*, pp. 429-430.

13 Possidius, *Vita*, c. 11; Hoare, *op. cit.*, pp. 205-206.

14 *Ibid.; op. cit.*, p. 206.

15 Cf. *De moribus ecclesiae catholicae*, I, 26 (48) to I, 28 (56); P.L. 32, 1331-1334. Taking his point of departure from St. Paul, "Dilectio proximi malum non operatur" (Rom. 13:10), St. Augustine gives his definition of man and immediately relates the field of education to it. "Homo igitur, ut homini apparet, anima rationalis et mortali atque terreno utens corpore. Partim ergo corpori, partim vero animae hominis benefacit, qui proximum diligit. Ad corpus quod pertinent, medicina nominata est; ad animam autem, disciplina" (*ibid.*, I, 27 (52)). Father Roland-Gosselin in his translation (*La morale chrétienne* [Paris: Desclée, 1949], p. 213) rightly uses the word "education": "Ce qui regarde le bien du corps on l'appelle médicine, le bien de l'âme éducation." After considering in terms of medicine all the corporal works of mercy, St. Augustine turns to education as a merciful saving and healing remedy for the soul. "As far as education is concerned," he writes, "which restores health to man's very soul, without which bodily health means nothing, we have a most difficult subject to grasp and elucidate" (*De moribus* . . ., I, 28 (55)). Always St. Augustine's concern with the field of education recurs, and in a way which shows his profound professional competence in the field. "Nevertheless," he continues, "this idea of education which we are discussing at present, that it is the medicine of the soul, contains two components, as we can judge from the Scriptures themselves, discipline, namely, and instruction. Discipline is brought about through fear, and instruction through love, love, I say, of the person whom one is helping by means of education" (*ibid.*, I, 28 (56)). Cf. Marrou, *Saint Augustin et la fin* . . ., p. 383, to whom we owe this reference, for a synthetic paragraph summarizing these pages of St. Augustine which reveal the very heart of his apostolate of the classroom and the very idea of Catholic education. "Il proclame nettement que le précepte de l'amour du prochain implique le devoir d'instruire nos frères dans la vérité: car si la charité nous demande . . . de soulager notre prochain dans son corps, combien plus ne devons-nous pas nous préoccuper de la santé de leurs âmes, leur offrir cette vérité salutaire que Dieu lui-même a rendue accessible à l'homme par les saints Ecritures." Perspectives of widest bearing and deepest significance open out in this fashion upon the educational apostolate of the Catholic Church, with its forming of minds and wills to the objective, divine, and biblical view of individual and social life. This is preventive medicine and the therapy of mankind, in terms of the concept which V. E. Frankl has in mind in his secular apostolate, so to speak, of psychotherapy by radio. Cf. Viktor E. Frankl, *Pathologie des Zeitgeistes* (Wien: Franz Deuticke, 1955). In an age beset with mental illness, the conditions are maturing for a new appreciation of the medicinal role of Catholic education for the human spirit, so acutely perceived by St. Augustine. Noteworthy also is the fact that this apostolic and most priestly insight is contained in a work written at Rome immediately after his baptism: a Catholic lay teacher's understanding, therefore, of the idea of Catholic education.

16 Cf. Eggersdorfer, *op. cit.*, pp. 155-168, with the references, for a discussion concerning the particular sermons which belong to this category. Cf. also F. Van der Meer, *Augustinus der Seelsorger: Leben und Wirken eines Kirchenvaters* (Köln: Verlag J. P. Bachem, 1958), "Christwerden," pp. 365-405, and "Die Katechese für die Neulinge," pp. 472-486. Cf. the English translation, *Augustine the Bishop* (London: Sheed and Ward, 1961), pp. 347-387; 453-467.

17 For a comprehensive treatment of this phase of St. Augustine's priestly apostolate, see the concluding part of Eggersdorfer's work, *op. cit.*, "Drittes Problem: Katechumenat, Katechese und Katechet," pp. 153-200, still unsurpassed. General studies include Johann Mayer, *Geschichte des Katechumenates und der Katechese* (Kempten: Josef Kafl, 1868); A. G. Weiss, *Die altkirchliche Pädagogik dargestellt in Katechumenat und Katechese der ersten sechs Jahrhunderte* (Freiburg: Herder, 1869); Chan. Hezard, *Histoire du Catéchisme depuis la naissance de l'église jusqu'au nos jours* (Paris: Victor-Retaux, 1900), a collection of short sketches of the work of the best-known teachers of Christian Doctrine: for St. Augustine, cf. chap. xiii, "Catéchismes de s. Augustin, de s. Fulgence, et der Ferrand diacre," pp. 52-57, a title which indicates the nature and limitation of the work. Not to be overlooked is Gerhard von Zeschwitz, *Der Katechumenat, oder die Kirchliche Erziehung nach Theorie und Geschichte: Ein Handbuch für Seelsorger und Pädagogen* (Leipzig: J. C. Hinrichs'sche Buchhandlung, 1863), a Lutheran tome ponderous with excellent scholarship on the origin of the concept and practice of catechesis in the Greek-speaking early Church. Extensive summaries of earlier scholarship on the catechetical institution are contained in the French *dictionnaires:* H. Leclercq, "Catéchèse-catéchisme-catéchumène," *D.A.C.L.*, II, 2530-2579; P. de Puniet, "Catéchuménat," *D.A.C.L.*, II, 2579-2621; E. Mangenot, "Catéchisme," *D.T.C.*, II, 1895-1968; and the two articles by G. Bareille, "Catéchèse," *D.T.C.*, II, 1877-1895, and "Catéchuménat," *ibid.*, pp. 1968-1987. Important monographs, which help to illustrate the central fact that St. Augustine's final program of education is built upon an already traditional educational institution and heritage, include B. Capelle, "L'introduction du catéchuménat à Rome," *Recherches de théologie ancienne et médiévale*, V (1933), 129-154; Pierre Biard, "Histoire du salut au coeur de la catéchèse," *Catéchèse*, I (1960), 11-20, and Jean Daniélou, "La catéchèse dans la tradition patristique," *Catéchèse*, I (1960), 21-34. Cf. the articles by G. Bardy, "L'église et l'enseignement pendant les trois premiers siècles," *Revue des sc. relig.*, XII (1932), 1-28, and his series "L'enseignement religieuse aux premiers siècles," *Rev. Apol.*, LXVI (1938), 641-655 and LXVII (1938), 5-18; also Gerard S. Sloyan, "Religious Education: From Early Christianity to Medieval Times, in *Shaping the Christian Message* (New York: Macmillan, 1958), pp. 3-37. Much relevant material and suggestive references are to be found in Jean Daniélou, *Sacramentum futuri* (Paris: Beauchesne, 1950), especially in the "Introduction," pp. x-xvi. For the indispensable and often-neglected background in the education carried on by the Jewish people, cf. Nathan Morris, *The Jewish School* (London: Eyre and Spottiswoode, 1937), and an unpublished work of Herman Mueller, "A Critical Analysis of the Jewish Educational Philosophy in Relationship to the Epistles of St. Paul" (Washington: The Catholic University of America, 1961), which draws upon the Talmud, Josephus, and Philo. On St. Augustine in particular, in addition to Eggersdorfer, cf. the recent work of Bonaventura Parodi, *La catechesi di sant'Am-*

brogio: Studio di pedagogia pastorale (Genova: Scuola SS. Vergine di Pompei, 1957); Benedictus Busch, *De initiatione christiana secundum doctrinam sancti Augustini* (Roma: Typis polyglottis vaticanis, 1939); R. G. Bandas, *Catechetics in the New Testament* (Milwaukee: Bruce, 1935), "Appendix: St. Augustine's Catechetical Method," pp. 119-132; L. Allievi, "Catechesi primitiva," *Scuola cattolica*, 1942, pp. 21-36; and Louis A. Rongione, "Saint Augustine, The Catechist," *Journal of Religious Instruction*, XV (1945), 461-469. In general, cf. J. A. Jungmann, *Katechetik* (Wien: Verlag Herder, 1953): "Eine zusammenfassende Darstellung der Geschichte der Katechese bis in die Gegenwart, die dem heutigan Stand unserer Kenntnisse entspräche, ist nicht vorhanden" (p. 5).

[18] The bishops of North Africa invited the priest of Hippo to explain his work to them, from which the *De fide et symbolo* has resulted. Cf. *Retr.*, I, 17: "Per idem tempus coram episcopis hoc mihi iubentibus, qui plenarium totius Africae concilium Hippone Regio habebant, de fide et symbolo presbyter disputavi. Quam disputationem, nonnullis eorum qui nos familiarius diligebant studiosissime instantibus, in librum contuli." For the details regarding these improvements in religious education, introduced by St. Augustine, largely reflecting practices at Rome and Milan, cf. Eggersdorfer, *op. cit.*, pp. 156-164.

[19] St. Augustine, *De catechizandis rudibus*, 3 (5); Joseph P. Christopher (trans.), *The First Catechetical Instruction* (Westminster, Md.: The Newman Bookshop, 1946), p. 18.

[20] Possidius, *Vita*, c. 9; Hoare, *op. cit.*, p. 203.

[21] *Ibid.*, c. 12; *op. cit.*, p. 206.

[22] Portalié-Bastian, *op. cit.*, p. 22.

[23] Cf. *ibid.*, pp. 22-36.

[24] Cf. Van der Meer, *op. cit.* Van der Meer's attractive presentation is a wondrously detailed mosaic, as he himself calls it, quarried by means of a loving familiarity with St. Augustine's writings. For the most part it does justice to the somewhat neglected period, precisely the life of the canonized saint, which follows upon the years described in the *Confessions*. At the same time, there is again the almost standard omission of the field of education, with hardly a reference beyond the two chapters on catechesis cited above. Van der Meer himself has qualms whether these tiny stones really fell by themselves into an adequate picture of Augustine. But he trusts so: "Ich habe nicht einmal den Versuch gemacht," he acknowledges, "eine Synthese anzustreben. Aber vielleicht ist eine lesbare Darstellung in manchen Fällen die beste Synthese und bilden die vielen kleinen Steinchen doch ein gutes Mosaik aus dem fünften Jahrhundert . . . eine Geschichtsschreibung, die nichts anderes sein will als die ausführliche und getreue Wiedergabe vieler kleiner Einzelheiten" (p. 17). This he has indeed accomplished and in a truly beautiful book for which Augustinian scholarship can only be grateful. The fact remains, however, that the mosaic should delineate St. Augustine sharply in all his specific stature and greatness, and not come rather flatly and simply, as Van der Meer puts it, "out of the fifth century." We believe it is this massive contact with the field of education, locating Augustine as it does at the unique juncture and point of affiliation of these two rather final civilizations, which lifts his figure above a vague chance pattern in the fine details gathered by Van der Meer to bold prominence on the landscape of universal history. Were Van der Meer to recast his many small stones upon the underlying framework of St. Augustine's footing and activity

in the field of education, he would be verging upon the definitive portrait of this Bishop, Father, and Saint of the Catholic Church.

25 The places where St. Augustine mentions the extreme pressure on his time are numerous and striking, more than modern in their strangely calm tone. Cf., for example, *Epist.*, 33, 1, "inter arctissimas occupationes"; 261, 1 "pauculae temporum stillae"; 110, 5, "Vix mihi paucissimae guttae temporis stillantur"; 237, 1, "Occupatissimus et aliorum curorum molibus vallatus et obstrictus." They seem to be the reflective observations of a man who almost coldly has made himself this inhumanly busy by deliberately uniting with his episcopal administration and pastoral care of souls a teaching and writing apostolate of first magnitude: *De Trinitate, De Civitate Dei!* If he did not have a full-fledged intellectual institution at hand, it seems he could not have accomplished his mission or have become the man we know, the controversialist, the preacher, the author of the *opera omnia sancti Augustini;* that he had such an institution, as we shall see, there is every reason to believe.

26 Possidius, *Vita,* c. 18; Hoare, *op. cit.,* p. 217.

27 Zumkeller, *op. cit.,* p. 70; cf. *Epist.,* 60.

28 Cf. Zumkeller, *op. cit.,* p. 71: "In seiner Sorge um einen guten Klerus scheint Augustin in Hippo auch frühzeitig eine eigene Schule für die künftigen Kleriker errichtet zu haben. Hier sollten junge Leute für den heiligen Dienst erzogen und geschult werden." Cf. also *Serm.,* 355, 2.

29 *Serm.,* 356.

30 Zumkeller, *op. cit.,* p. 78.

31 Cf. Dominguez-del Val, *op. cit.,* p. 434, for the references which show that a large number of St. Augustine's works were composed *petentibus fratribus.* "La Ciencia de estos Monjes doctos no es sino la consecuencia de una instruccion intelectual recibida en los monasterios del Obispo de Hipona" (p. 435).

32 Cf. *De opere monachorum,* 17: "Horae quibus ad erudiendum animum vacatur." Cf. Dominguez-del Val, *op. cit.,* p. 436, for the schedule of time for class and study in St. Augustine's rules which St. Benedict was to incorporate unchanged into Benedictine monasticism. The intellectual labor of the monks of the West and the monastery schools of the future make manifest the powerful influence of Augustine upon the formation of Christendom.

33 Cf. Dominguez-del Val, *op. cit.,* p. 437: ". . . y un grupo de letrados que le recogian material cientifico."

34 Cf. Dominguez-del Val, *op. cit.,* p. 440.

35 Cf. *Solil.,* I, 12 (20); Gilligan, *op. cit.,* 369-370: "But I ask you (Reason), why do you want the men you love to live or to dwell in your company? So that we can all, (Augustine answers), at the same time and in unity of heart seek our souls and God. In this way the one who first makes the discovery easily leads the others thither without any toil. Suppose they do not want to seek such things? (Reason asks.) I will induce them to want to. (Reason fears there will be instances when he will fail in this; would Augustine then prefer that they not be with him? He grants this freely.) Therefore, you desire their life or their company, not for its own account, but for the discovery of wisdom?" Augustine is clear and definite. "I agree entirely," he concludes. This passage from the *Dialogues of Cassiciacum* illuminates anew that strong intellectual consistency which characterizes the thought and educational career of St. Augustine. From this position in the *Soliloquy* there is a direct line back to the youth reading the *Hortensius* and forsaking law for educa-

tion, and an equally direct line forward to this bishop's intellectual institution at Hippo.

36 Cf. Dominguez-del Val, *op. cit.*, p. 440: ". . . este monasterio era un foco de cultura y letras ambicionado por todas las iglesias de Africa."

37 Berthold Altaner, "Die Bibliothek des heiligen Augustinus," *Theologische Revue*, XLIV (1948), 73-78. As Altaner points out, it would take years of concentrated critical analysis to determine from Augustine's works the detailed list of library materials which he had to have at hand. But we have already a general knowledge of the matter. "Jedenfalls ist es gewiss [against Harnack's assertion] dass die Bibliothek des hl. Augustinus ein der bedeutendsten Büchersammlungen des christlichen Altertums gewesen ist" (p. 76). Harnack's interpretation of Possidius is "vollständig falsch" (p. 73). Altaner rightfully deplores that Harnack's prestige has caused his erroneous and derogatory view to be copied into standard treatises of library science (cf. p. 73).

38 Dominguez-del Val, *op. cit.*, p. 445.

39 Cf. *Epist.*, 231; *De haeresibus*, 88.

40 Possidius, *Vita*, c. 31; Hoare, *op. cit.*, p. 243.

41 Cf., for example, *Epist.*, 31, 8; 295, 3.

42 Cf. Pierre Courcelle, *Les lettres grecques en Occident de Macrobe à Cassiodore* (Paris: E. de Boccard, 1948), "Saint Augustin et l'Hellénisme en Afrique," pp. 137-209, in particular "Augustin et la patristique Grecque," pp. 183-194. Courcelle maintains that St. Augustine mastered the Greek language in connection with his literary and educational apostolate at Hippo, no longer leaning upon translations: ". . . mais à la fin de sa vie, il n'a plus même besoin de ce secours et lit des oeuvres grecques de toutes sortes à livre ouvert" (p. 182). "L'étude de la culture ecclésiastique grecque d'Augustin confirmera ce résultat" (p. 183). For Augustine's successful efforts to obtain the Greek originals of Eusebius' *History* and *Chronicle*, cf. *ibid.*, p. 187. St. Augustine is indeed difficult to encompass. All of this indicates a careful scholar and the life of a man who has reserved a considerable portion of his time for active teaching and research. It seems to demand, furthermore, an elaborate and even powerful physical institution of learning. Who shall say what it was that the Vandals snuffed out?

43 Dominguez-del Val, *op. cit.*, p. 441.

44 Cf., for example, *Epist.*, 101, 1: Possidius himself had St. Augustine as a teacher. "You will find," Augustine writes, "no small part of me in him [Possidius] . . . He has been nourished by my efforts with the bread of the Lord, not by those studies which are called liberal by those slaves of all sorts of passions." Augustine is writing in answer to a request from a fellow-bishop for his *De musica* and uses the occasion to contrast once more *nostra schola* with "those other schools."

45 Cf. Van der Meer, *op. cit.*, Part III, pp. 405-467.

46 *Ibid.*, p. 405. Much closer to the truth is Professor Ladner, *The Idea of Reform*, p. 373, when he describes St. Augustine's *De doctrina christiana* with the phrase "the concept of Christian teaching and learning"; closest of all, however, is St. Thomas Aquinas in his opening question of the *Summa*, "De sacra doctrina, quid sit et ad quae se extendat," where "doctrina" denotes the field of education in the comprehensive sense of the living act of teaching together with the full range of content taught. On this correct understanding of the word "doctrina," cf. the study of G. F. Van Ackeren, *Sacra Doctrina* (Rome: Officium libri catholici, 1952).

47 Van der Meer, *op. cit.*, p. 405.

48 *Ibid.*, "The first three books discuss the value of this most helpful of sciences and explain the rules for interpreting the various meanings of Scripture, particularly in its nuptials and allegorical meanings." This dismisses St. Augustine's entire program of Christian learning and misses the unity which characterizes his life as a whole—especially the unity manifested by the pedagogical doctrine of Augustine's earlier works as a layman and this program of studies which reflects his educational work as a priest and bishop.

49 *Ibid.*

50 *Ibid.*, p. 424. This position conflicts directly with the entire body of evidence for the contact of Augustine's life and literary work with the field of education—a contact which began when he changed from law to the teaching profession as a young man and proceeded most purposefully as his life went on. The inadequacy of Van der Meer's position is made fully visible by comparing it, for example, with the work of Finaert, *op. cit.*, esp. pp. 98-101, where the valid sense is clarified in which St. Augustine "remained all his life a *rhetor*." St. Augustine did not disparage this discipline in itself and in its proper place, but provided for it a secure position on his order of studies. This can be discerned properly only by including the field of education in his life and work, not by omitting it; when this is done, there does indeed emerge into view a genuine "revolution"—in fact, a large one, not a small one, and qualitatively different from the negative one Van der Meer seems to have in mind. "With these words the liveliest speaker of the old school impatiently throws overboard all the useless antique ballast that cluttered up this subject" (p. 406). Cutting through the rhetoric of this statement, one must say that it is not true wihout qualification, and conflicts as it stands with Book II of the *De doctrina christiana* itself.

51 For a list of the authors who represent the older view that the *De doctrina christiana* is simply a manuel of instruction for the clergy in relation to the work of the pulpit, cf. Dominguez-del Val, *op. cit.*, p. 449. We do not deny this aspect of St. Augustine's work, and of his intention in composing it; but we believe this does not suffice to explain the work as a whole. Furthermore, this view seems to imply that it was a manual for self-instruction, whereas St. Augustine looked upon the preparation for Christian life and work in general, and priestly work in particular, as a systematic process in the field of education with a definite order of studies.

52 Marrou, *Saint Augustin et la fin* . . . , p. 333, n. 1.

53 *Ibid.*, pp. 331-332.

54 Perhaps we are prone today to misconceive St. Augustine's concept of education in this fashion because we have become gradually accustomed to a different theory and practice of the curriculum than he had in mind, and have lost to a considerable extent his way of thinking about the place and role of the Bible in *doctrina*, the act, process, and content of teaching.

55 Cf. *Confessions*, I, 15 (24); Ryan, *op. cit.*, p. 58. We have mentioned several times the relevance of this "safe way in which children should walk" to St. Augustine's earlier works. It is even more relevant to this work which he, now an aged and experienced bishop, bequeathed to the Catholic world as his final word on the relationship between education and the care of souls.

56 The alternative is to view Book II as a "problem" which is solved by assuming some deficiency in the author: it crept into his composition as a verbose disgression, perhaps, reflecting his inability to compose well or to

sustain a consistent and logical line of thought. Hence his work is felt to be a disappointment. In the case of lesser but more contemporary authors such assumptions are seldom ventured; when the author is St. Augustine, they are even less likely to be objectively valid, for the fact remains that he is one of the truly great minds of human history. Here even Eggersdorfer (*op. cit.,* p. 127) fails to perceive adequately the unity and consistency of St. Augustine's work, for he weakly states that Book II is "similar" to the *De ordine,* and that "perhaps it was remembered" as the *De doctrina christiana* was composed. This indicates how Eggersdorfer, although grasping the educational significance of Augustine's earlier works, fails to rise to a comprehensive view of St. Augustine's full and conscious contact with the field of education consistently throughout his entire life and career whether a professor in the schools of Rome or a bishop at Hippo.

57 Cf. Eggersdorfer, *op. cit.,* p. 140, following Gaston Boissier, *La fin du paganisme* (Paris: Hachette, 1891), I, 243. Perhaps one can detect here an early effect of the general view of Augustine's life and work which was to become the Alfaric thesis. At least, however, Eggersdorfer sees clearly that the author of the *De doctrina christiana* "nicht bloss ein Lehrbuch der Hermeneutic darbieten wollte, sondern das er sich die ganzen Bildung des Geistlichen, die ihm gleichbedeutend war mit der 'christlichen Bildung' überhaupt, in ihrem vollen Umkreis zu beschreiben" (*ibid.,* p. 145). This last is an unsupported assertion, and seems untenable in view of Professor Marrou's work. Certainly the Bishop of Hippo had the education of priests much in mind; it does not follow that this was the extent of Catholic education in his thinking.

58 Marrou, *Saint Augustin et la fin . . . ,* p. 383.

59 Cf. *ibid.,* n. 3.

60 Book III, chaps. xxv-xxxvii, and Book IV date from A.D. 426.

61 Cf. *Retr.,* I, 6: "Per idem tempus quo Mediolani fui baptismum percepturus, etaim disciplinarum libros conatus sum scribere. . . . Sed earum solum de grammatica librum absolvere potui, quem postea de armario nostro perdidi, et De musica sex volumina, quantum attinet ad eamdem partem, quae rhythmus vocatur. . . . De aliis vero quinque disciplinis illic similiter inchoatis, de dialectica, de rhetorica, de geometrica, de arithmetica, de philosophia, sola principia remanserunt, quae tamen ipsa perdidimus, sed haberi ab aliquibus existimo." It is difficult to exaggerate the significance of this reassertion of his earlier work in these measured words of the elderly Bishop. The seven liberal arts are to be taught as a complete circle of content, and they are to contain philosophy itself. This latter point is perhaps the most significant of all, both from the viewpoint of the consistency of St. Augustine's quest of wisdom within the field of education since he was a youth of nineteen, and in relation to the qualitative nature of the regeneration and renewal of *paideia* which he handed forward to the schools of Christendom.

6

The Culture of
the Human Arts
and Disciplines

U P TO this point the present study has been concerned
primarily to establish the fact of St. Augustine's life-
long contact with the field of education. While much information regarding the nature of this contact has been uncov-
ered in the process, we have nevertheless left the consideration
of the qualitative character of St. Augustine's educational
philosophy to one side.

Turning now to consider the nature of St. Augustine's
philosophy of education, we are in a position to analyze it as
the direct application of his Christian philosophy in his
teaching profession and priestly apostolate. For St. Augustine, a philosophy of education is not an entity distinct from
philosophy as such; it is simply philosophy at work in the
formation of youth toward the ideal expressed in its philosophical anthropology. Christian philosophy from its very
inception in the patristic age has been in and of the school.
The venerable term "scholasticism," sometimes used in op-
probrium, is actually a title of honor, especially when seen
from the viewpoint of St. Augustine's use of this Christian
philosophy to introduce soundness and meaning into education.

It should be noted that the synthesis on St. Augustine's

philosophy of education which we are seeking is a view of the teaching profession which remains stable in its essentials throughout his entire life. His earlier published works, directly related to the proper culture of the human arts and disciplines, as we have seen, represent the maturation of his quest for wisdom within the field of education since entering it at the age of nineteen; and the reaffirmation of the fundamental educational positions of these earlier works is one of his last and most significant actions as an aged bishop of the Catholic Church.

The Rise of the Mind to Intelligible Reality

A central theme of the *Confessions* of St. Augustine is his earlier inability to conceive of God as a spiritual reality. "I did not know how to think of him," he writes, "except as a vast corporeal mass, for I thought that anything not a body was nothing whatsoever. This was the greatest and almost the sole cause of my inevitable error." [1]

It was the turning point of his life when he broke through, with the help of the school of Plato, to the personal discovery of the concept of spiritual reality. For the day came at last when Augustine's mind "in a flash of its trembling sight came to that which is. Then indeed I clearly saw your 'invisible things, understood by the things which are made.' " [2] This flash of insight brings us immediately to the very center of St. Augustine's philosophical thinking, for it is a vision accomplished not by the bodily eyes but by the inner eye of the human spirit. This initial insight, when it is elaborated with all its implications, will become St. Augustine's Christian philosophy. [3]

In the dialogue *Against the Academics* St. Augustine gives the first extant account of his conversion, describing how the slow fire which had been burning in him since the age of nineteen when he read the *Hortensius* was suddenly turned into an incredibly great conflagration when he came upon the book which taught him a better insight into the philosophy of Plato and his school.[4] Here he discovered the intelligible reality of God, *ipsum esse subsistens*. Fearing that Christianity might be opposed to his discovery, he hastened to reread the Scriptures, especially St. Paul. This discovery and knowledge of God, Source and Creator of all existing reality, is the origin of Christian philosophy; and in St. Augustine's own life, it was the beginning of his conversion and of his creaturely service of the one true God.[5]

Christian philosophy, then, brings to the human spirit this immeasurable benefit, a knowledge of the Supreme Being. This hidden God is "presented to our view—as it were, through shining clouds." [6] This is "the true and inscrutable God, Who is perhaps—but only rarely perceived by intelligence, and is never perceived by any sense." [7] Christian philosophy is this purified human knowledge which rises to God and brings to the human soul an insight into divine things. Truth, the central concept of St. Augustine's thought, is to be found only in this orientation.

It is apparent that Christian philosophy breaks through to ground never attained by Greek thought. Earlier thinkers were unable to rise to the living God of creation and providence.[8] Such, then, is "that philosophy to which I call you." [9] It is a philosophical knowledge of God which provides an understanding that there is a providential care over the universe and mankind. This results from the new view of God as *ipsum esse subsistens*, the Creator of all things, and hence the Lord of creation who governs what he has made. Finally, St. Augustine concludes, "by the very fact that He truly *is*, He is always present." [10]

All of this is "Christian philosophy," a universe of insight and understanding and a point of departure for further thought which the classical philosophy of the Greeks did not achieve. St. Augustine speaks of it as "the one system of really true philosophy . . . not of this world, but of the other, intelligible world." [11] "Our sacred mysteries," he says, speaking of the Catholic faith, "justly detest a philosophy of this world." [12] St. Augustine emphasizes this fact that there are two kinds of philosophy, and that "the philosophy of this world" is to be avoided by Christians.[13] This Christian philosophy is "a certain exalted branch of learning." [14] It is a divine science which holds its propositions more clearly than the science of mathematics grasps its object.[15]

This rise to the knowledge of God opens a series of insights which are not "progress by addition," but which rather reflect a deepening understanding of the object known and the extension of its light to a wider range of objects.[16] Included among these objects is the soul itself. For the mind returns to understand itself after this rise to intelligible reality. It achieves a new insight into truth, begins to recognize a light different from this earthly and material light, and perceives gradually the fact of an inner eye of its mind, different from the eyes of the flesh. This puts the human spirit on the path which leads to an understanding of itself as a person.[17] All of this leads into the very heart of Christian philosophy, into a universe of thought and understanding which makes of this Christian philosophy a definite entity distinct and unique among the philosophies erected by man, a philosophy which has had its own reality and history across the centuries since St. Augustine.

In his *Soliloquies,* however, St. Augustine indicates to us what the first step is toward these other insights which are consequent upon the rise of Christian philosophy to this elevated knowledge of God. "Therefore you love life," he writes, "not for the sake of living, but for the sake of knowing ... there will then remain an inquiry concerning understanding." [18] It is understanding and knowledge which brings happiness to the human spirit, and thus the happy life is one which this Christian philosophy prepares.[19]

Two Kinds of Knowledge

The rise of the mind to the intelligible reality of God, therefore, provides the springboard for a return to the self, and for a new and more clear realization of what this is within man which enables him to rise to the intelligible order. In his treatise on *The Greatness of the Soul,* St. Augustine devotes five chapters to a discussion of the distinction between sensation and knowledge, taking the brute animals as the point of departure for his analysis.[20] The brute animals do not possess knowledge and reason, St. Augustine concludes, but man possesses a mental sight as the direct consequence of what the mind is able to do. "Thus, reason is in a sense mental sight," he writes, "while reasoning would be reason's search, that is, the moving of that sight over the objects that are to be seen. Hence, the function of the latter is to search, that of the former, to see. And so, when that sight of the mind which we call reason, is directed upon some object and sees it, that is called knowledge." [21]

Brute animals have sensation, Augustine continues, not genuine knowledge. "The soul of brute animals is more closely bound to the body . . . the human soul, however, because the instruments it uses, reason and knowledge—and it is these we are concerned with now—are far superior to the senses, makes itself independent, as far as it can, of the body. . . . " [22] St. Augustine presses the discussion on to its conclusion: "The brute animals have sensation but they do not have knowledge . . . the difference between brute animals and man [is] that to have sensation and to have knowledge are to have two different things." [23]

This fundamental understanding concerning man, consequent upon his rise to intelligible reality and *ipsum esse subsistens,* recurs again and again in the philosophical writings of St. Augustine. "Nothing else ranks me above the brute animal except the fact that I am a rational animal," he writes in the *De ordine.*[24] In the *Soliloquies* he develops an elaborate description of the difference between the image and the concept in human knowledge, showing that the latter is best illustrated through the work of mathematics, which is the natural means for the human mind to advance to the concept of higher truth.[25] "To perceive by the senses is one thing," he writes in still another place, "but to know is something else. Wherefore, if we know anything, I think it is contained in the intellect alone, and by it alone can it be grasped." [26] It is this intellectual knowledge which rises to God, not the knowledge of the senses: again and again St. Augustine returns to this understanding of man which is consequent upon the rise to Almighty God. The two kinds of knowledge are described in terms of two kinds of light. "The star of wisdom does not appear as easily to our minds as does the light of our eyes." [27] There are two kinds of knowledge, in other words, one in the order of that possessed also by the brute animals, and the other of a higher order which distinguishes man alone.

It is one thing to see this fact concerning human knowledge, and another thing to explain it.[28] The explanation of the fact is the central problem of the causality of knowledge. Christian philosophy attacks the problem of this explanation not by denying the fact but by admitting it as seen. Locke, Hume, and their school, on the other hand, turn their faces away from the facts about human knowledge and seek causes why we are deceived into thinking that we have this different and higher kind of knowledge. In St. Augustine's thinking the causality of knowledge is not adequately explained by calling it simply the product of environmental impression. If this were the case, we would have no knowledge distinct from that of the brute animals. But his point of departure in his doctrine on man is the fundamental fact that we do have this qualitatively distinct knowledge. Hence the quest for the cause of knowledge is at one and the same time the elaboration of a philosophical concept of man.[29]

The question of the causality of knowledge brings us up against two categorically opposed positions. The first places the entire and adequate cause of all human knowledge in impressions from the environment; the other recognizes the necessity of an active agent in man if the facts concerning human knowledge are to be explained rather than distorted or denied. The classical Greeks perceived the truth of the matter regarding man and his knowledge, although in a somewhat fitful light, and without the vigor and strength of St. Augustine's perception of the reality.[30] Augustine's vision of the matter is strengthened by that healing influence which comes to the human mind from Christianity, taking the best in Greek thought to a new level of perfection. For St. Augustine perceives with a new clarity that man is simply a thing, as indeed the Lockean tradition asserts, if his knowledge is conceived as simply the product of environmental impression. "John Locke," writes Professor Allport, "assumed . . . the intellect itself was a passive thing acquiring content and structure only through the impact of sensation and the criss-cross of associations, much as a pan of sweet dough acquires tracings through the impress of a cookie cutter." [31]

These strong and clear observations regarding the philosophical facts of human knowledge do not precede the rise of the mind to incorporeal reality, but rather result from it. This ascent of the mind, however, is not spontaneous but must be prepared by sound education, by the diligent work of the teaching profession. This is the unique place and irreplaceable role of the liberal arts, especially the quadrivium. But this is a later insight into educational reality born of these basic positions of Christian philosophy; the next step after the recognition of these two kinds of knowledge is the advance to the idea of truth, the central concept of St. Augustine's Christian philosophy.

The Idea of Truth

The concept of truth is so central in St. Augustine's thought that it is justly called the very soul and inspiration of his philosophy. Truth for St. Augustine is nothing else than that wisdom which the reading of the *Hortensius* caused him to love when he was a youth of nineteen; it was the quest for this wisdom which led him from the schools of rhetoric into the Catholic Church. Christian philosophy, he states, is a doctrine concerning God and the soul. "I desire to know God and the soul," he writes in the *Soliloquies,* "Nothing more? . . . Absolutely nothing." [32]

Later on, Augustine relates truth to this constant object of his thought. "Do you say with certainty that you desire to know the soul and God? That is my only desire. . . . Nothing else? . . . Absolutely nothing. . . . What? Do you not want to know truth? . . . As if I could know these except through its means!" [33] Truth, therefore, is the means for coming to a knowledge of God and the soul, and the quest for wisdom is one thing with the pathway of the human mind to the truth on God and the soul. "Oh, God, ever the same; may I know myself, may I know Thee. That is my prayer." This is the famous *Noverim me, noverim Te* which is the very definition of Augustine's quest for truth and wisdom.[34]

In the *Soliloquies,* then, we meet the elevated concept of God which Christian philosophy bestows upon the soul, this God "Who from nothing has created this world . . . Who does not cause evil." [35] This is the God who is Truth itself. "I call upon Thee, O God the Truth, in Whom and through Whom all those things are true which are true." [36] From a consideration of things that are true, Augustine comes to the conclusion that the true is "that which exists." [37] Thus from the things that are true the quest converges on Truth itself.[38] "Nothing is true without truth," he concludes; "nothing is true which is not made true by truth." [39]

This is the central theme of St. Augustine's philosophical thought, this identification of the intelligible world, to which the human mind rises in its knowledge of God, with God Himself, the truth which gives this human knowledge its substance and reality, the ultimate ground and explanation by virtue of which it *is* intelligible.

"Even if the whole world should fall in ruins," St. Augustine says of a mathematical relation, "that ratio will always necessarily be." [40] This power of the human mind to perceive intelligible reality in the relationships of mathematics is fundamental in St. Augustine's thinking, and of direct importance for his philosophy of education and his teaching on the causality of knowledge. This insight into the central position of truth as the means whereby the mind rises to a knowledge of God, and then returns to an understanding of itself, is the basic difference between Augustine's Christian philosophy and the Neoplatonism which he has left behind, even while continuing to use its concepts and philosophical instruments. Truth has replaced the transcendent One of Plotinus, a truth standing at the center of all reality, identified with God himself, *ipsum esse subsistens*. It is a living truth which not only is discovered by the human mind, but which is heard speaking by the human mind, speaking in divine revelation. This Christian philosophy, therefore, has a new source of supernal light and strength to use as a great mirror, as it were, in which it can see its naturally perceived positions and propositions more clearly.

"We know the truth," writes Father Boyer; "this is the fact on which the philosophy of St. Augustine is founded." [41] "The idea of truth in the philosophy of St. Augustine," he states, "explains many questions besides that of certitude. The existence and nature of God, the problems of creation and providence, the explanation of human knowledge, the study of the soul, the principles of morality, in a word, the entire Augustinian philosophy in its own characteristic aspects, appears to us as if suspended from this notion of truth." [42]

The Light and Eye of the Mind

There are two kinds of knowledge. The second is incomparably higher than the first, the intellectual knowledge which lifts the human spirit into contact with this intelligible or divine order. This is the world of necessary truths, which the mind perceives first in mathematical relationships, and then goes on to perceive in the truths which pertain to God. This order of objective truth to which intellectual knowledge admits the human spirit is a fact. The cause of this fact is therefore the cause of knowledge. But before St. Augustine takes us to an explanation of the causality, there is a further step in his observation and philosophical description of the fact of human knowledge. This is his description of intellectual knowledge in terms of an inner light proper to what he calls the eye of the mind. With this we enter the border region between fact and explanation, the famous theory of illumination which is so characteristic of St. Augustine's philosophical doctrine.[43]

"Intellectual knowledge," writes Thonnard, "is an immediate participation in the light of the subsistent truth. . . . This theory of illumination has for its unique purpose the explanation of the fundamental fact that we possess the truth. . . . For when he examines the possible role of sensation in explaining this fact, St. Augustine finds it insufficient. Hence he calls upon a necessary intervention of God, which on the other hand does not suppress the proper role of the human intelligence in its knowledge." [44]

The proper principle for interpreting St. Augustine's teaching on the inner eye of the mind is contained in the *City of God:* "Though his nature has no need of either heaven or earth," St. Augustine writes, "God fills them both with his presence and his power. Yet, the Creator of every nature has so ordained that each of his creatures is permitted to have and to exercise powers of its own." [45]

Let us then review some of the more striking passages in St. Augustine which speak of the human power to know truth, and of the truth which the human mind knows, in terms of the inner eye of the mind and its light. This light somehow reflects God himself, the eternal truth, illuminating the human mind which otherwise could not see at all. Clearly, we are coming closer to the question of the causality of knowledge.

"There is a certain unspeakable and unincomprehensible light of minds," writes St. Augustine. "Our common light may teach us, as far as is possible, how that light operates." [46]

This is the central question in the causation of knowledge, and it is the central question of educational theory and practice. As we shall see, St. Augustine does not separate the two considerations.

Continuing in his soliloquy with his own reason, St. Augustine teaches explicitly his doctrine of the eye of the mind. "Reason, which is speaking with you," he writes, "pledges to make God known to your mind just as the sun is shown to the eyes. The senses of the soul are, as it were, the mind's own eyes; those things, moreover, which are most certain in the sciences are like the things which the sun shines upon that they may be seen—such as the earth and all things earthly: But it is God Himself Who does the illuminating. Yet, I—reason—am in minds as the act of looking is in the eyes." [47]

St. Augustine goes on to point out that the health of this inner eye is the work of the three theological virtues—faith, hope, and charity—which heal and strengthen the eye of the soul for seeing God. "The mind is like healthy eyes when it is cleansed of every taint of the body, that is, detached and purged of the desires for earthly things—which it obtains, at first, only by faith." [48]

"Reason is the gaze of the soul," St. Augustine continues, "but, since it does not follow that everyone who gazes at an object sees it, correct and perfect gaze, of the kind which is followed by vision, is called virtue; for, virtue is correct and perfect reason. . . . This vision itself is the understanding which is in the soul, brought forth by the one who understands and that which is understood—just as in the eyes, what is called seeing consists of the sense itself and the thing sensed, either of which being withdrawn, nothing can be seen." [49]

St. Augustine calls the human intelligence "the head and eye of the soul." [50] "There is an immutable truth embracing all things that are true," he writes in the same treatise, "a truth you cannot call yours, or mine, or any man's, but which is present to all and gives itself alike to all who discern the things that are immutably true, as a light which in some miraculous way is both secret and yet open to all." [51]

We may conclude this survey of St. Augustine's teaching on the eye of the mind, and that light by which it sees and understands, by observing that it is a light which is not of this world, not of the material order. It is a participation in God himself, whom Augustine addresses in the *Soliloquies* as Intelligible Light: "Oh God, Intelligible Light, in Whom and by Whom and through Whom all those things which have intelligible light, have their intelligible light." [52] It is clear from this passage that the intelligible light in the direct object of our understanding is not God himself, but a participation in the divine light.[53]

So far, we have been observing in a philosophical manner with St. Augustine, not explaining; describing in the best way human language can, not analyzing the underlying causes and distinguishing the various more ultimate factors behind the reality observed and described. At the same time, we are verging on the perception of the most important cause and factor in the entire process of knowledge—namely, God himself. Father Boyer's summary on the inner eye and its light provides an exact conclusion on the teaching we have reviewed thus far. "If the relationship of creatures to God," he writes, "is so close that it constitutes their very being, what inter-penetration should one expect to discover between the subsistent Truth on the one hand, and the human intelligence whose very nature is to know the truth, on the other hand? St. Augustine perhaps perceived no truth more strongly than this one which states the dependence of the human spirit in relationship to the Supernal Light. This is the center of his philosophy." [54]

We cannot leave this topic without touching upon the manner in which St. Augustine turns his teaching on this central doctrine of truth toward the field of education. He calls philosophy itself a light illuminating the human mind: "I . . . praised the light of philosophy," he tells us, describing his effort to dislodge his pupil Licentius from his inordinate love of Vergil.[55] In another dialogue of the same period, Augustine reports his happiness as a teacher when he perceived that his gifted student had come to the vision of a "far different light," the light of philosophy, namely, not poetry.[56] On another occasion, discussing the lack of wisdom, Augustine teaches his group of students that it is a darkness of mind, and not a positive doctrine held by the intellect, whereas philosophy in opposition to it is the light of the mind.[57] Again St. Augustine speaks of the *catharsis* or purification which the human mind must undergo, forsaking the things of sense entirely in order to fly from our native darkness to that light: this is the light of the instructed and educated state.[58] This becomes more explicit when he tells us that this light of the mind "glows in a certain measure in the liberal arts," where it awakens the soul to new life so that "it is not content until . . . it beholds in all its breadth and fullness the whole countenance of truth." [59]

With this fundamental statement we are in a position to state a preliminary conclusion. St. Augustine's doctrine on the causation of knowledge involves Almighty God on the one hand and the field of education with its liberal arts on the other hand. Christian philosophy, with its knowledge of God and the soul, will have much to say regarding the theory and practice of education.

The Theocentrism of Christian Philosophy

Up to this point the reality of human knowledge has been observed in a philosophical manner; we are now in a position to turn to its explanation. The reality has been the fact of a second and higher kind of knowledge, different from sensation, perceived as a by-product, as it were, of the ascent of the mind to God, the eternal, intelligible, incorporeal truth, Truth itself. This new further insight is expressed as the recognition that there exists in man an inner eye with its own proper kind of light, by which so great an object is known. This is all in the realm of philosophical observation, insight, penetration, initial understanding of the nature of things.

Turning to consider the explanation of so great a fact about the human mind, we come to inquire into the causality of this knowledge. How can it be? What is its process, its "mechanism"?

The first step in investigating this causality is to recognize the central position which Christian philosophy accords to the Supreme Being. Just as it is the mark of Christian philosophy to rise to *ipsum esse subsistens,* and to perceive the fact that he creates all existing reality out of nothing, so it is the merit of this philosophy to recognize the action of the First Cause in the universe which he has created. This action is nothing else than his divine government which we call providence, which reaches its apex in that special providence described by the Bible, placing an economy of salvation in human history.

Throughout St. Augustine's philosophy, accordingly, the action of the First Cause predominates in his view of the explanation of things, and receives frank and open recognition.[60]

Some have thought that St. Augustine provides no place for secondary causes, simply because he perceives and recognizes so clearly the operation of the First Cause in the order of truth and our knowledge of it. That there are secondary causes in this order of learning, however, is clear from the teaching which we have noted already, that philosophy is itself a light, a factor which *causes* knowledge, which *illumines* the soul. "I . . . praised the light of philosophy." [61] This is in contrast with the lesser arts and disciplines, which are preparatory in Augustine's teaching, not educational ends in themselves. The curriculum, St. Augustine states, is composed of "the branches of learning—and among these it is proper to count the study of wisdom itself." [62] We have here, then, a direct statement on the causality of knowledge. There is the activity of the First Cause, the eternal Truth itself, illuminating the intelligence with a participation in its supernal light. It is through this illumination that our mind understands whatever it understands beyond the order of sense imagery. At the same time, St. Augustine provides explicitly for the instrumentality of the liberal arts. These are human disciplines, administered by the teaching profession. They prepare for philosophy. They, together with philosophy, are the instrumental causes of knowledge, for they enlighten the mind, they cause its illumination, especially the real disciplines of the quadrivium which raise the intelligence into direct contact with the intelligible character of reality and dispose it for the still brighter light which is philosophy itself. This is true humanism in education, for it sees the mathematical and scientific disciplines in an orientation toward God and the soul.

The purpose of teaching, St. Augustine points out in his treatise *On the Teacher,* is to bring the knowledge of truth to minds and to build up in them "confidence in evident truth." [63] With this distinction between the activity of the First Cause in the order of understanding and intelligibility and the role of the teaching profession with its arts and tools which provide the instrumental causality of knowledge, we can see the fundamental identity which St. Thomas perceived between his own teaching and the position of St. Augustine. Christ is indeed the interior teacher, the Eternal Truth that teaches internally; and at the same time place is provided for all the arts and disciplines of human culture.[64]

"Teachers do not claim, do they," St. Augustine asks, laying his finger on the very idea of human education and stating the very definition of the curriculum, "that their own thoughts are perceived and grasped by the pupils, but rather the branches of learning that they think they transmit by speaking? For who would be so absurdly curious as to send his child to school to learn what the teacher thinks? But when they have explained, by means of words, all those subjects which they profess to teach, and even the science of virtue and of wisdom, then those who are called pupils consider within themselves whether what has been said is true. This they do by gazing attentively at that interior truth, so far as they are able. Then it is that they learn." [65]

Clearly, what we call the curriculum is an objective educational reality, an order of studies and of learning which transcends the subjective thoughts and experiences not only of the learners but also of the teachers. This is the case precisely because the curriculum is an ordered pedagogical participation in truth itself.

Truth: The Central Concern of Education

The *Soliloquies* of St. Augustine are usually considered to be purely philosophical in nature, even if an educational relevance is granted in the other philosophical dialogues. The fact is, however, that the *Soliloquies* themselves, if analyzed closely, are educational treatises. Having arrived at truth itself through the analysis of things that are true, St. Augustine proceeds upon an explicit study of truth as established in the branches of learning. Thus he brings truth-centered education to the center of the stage. [66]

In the passage on the fact that there is a "certain unspeakable and incomprehensible light of minds," cited above, St. Augustine goes on to relate this light explicitly to the work of the teaching profession in the field of education. [67] This light is so elevated and so bright, he points out, that human beings actually need training in order to see it, to have the strength to gaze upon it.

"They are, therefore," he writes, teaching by illustration, "first to be trained. . . . First, they should be shown some things which do not shine with their own light, but which may be seen only by means of light, such as a garment or a wall or something of that kind. . . . It is through these things that, each one according to his strength growing more proficient, either through all the steps or leaving out some of them, sooner or later he will behold the sun without flinching and with immense delight. Some such thing is what the best teachers do for those who are most desirous of wisdom, but who, though they see, do not see clearly. For it is the duty of good education to arrive at wisdom by means of a definite order; without order this is a matter of chance hardly to be relied upon." [68]

This is the central thesis of St. Augustine's educational doctrine, the identical doctrine which is to be found in the *De ordine*. It is significant to find it stated here full in the center of the philosophical *Soliloquies*. It is the educational character of the *Dialogues of Cassiciacum* which comes repeatedly to light, this time in the *Soliloquies* themselves.[69]

St. Augustine concludes his *Soliloquies* by an explicit analysis of the relationship of truth to the arts and disciplines which constitute the field of education. It is the responsibility and the privilege of the teaching profession to bring the on-coming generation to a knowledge of the truth concerning God and the soul. It does this by a gradual preparation of youthful spirits for this higher insight and understanding. This gradual process and the artistry needed to bring it about is the characteristic benefit conferred by the teaching profession. It does this by means of the arts, sciences, and disciplines which prepare the mind for philosophical knowledge and understanding, for this knowledge of God and its reflection upon the nature and the greatness of the soul.

In Chapter XVIII, Augustine teaches the distinction between the image and the concept by the use of the science of geometry, indicating what the teachers of that discipline have at hand for young people. "Who, indeed," he writes, "is so mentally blind as not to see that those which are taught in geometry abide in truth or the truth abides in them?" [70] Youthful intelligence can be brought to understand the eternal truth in these objects of geometry. The mind of youth is prepared in this manner for that ascent to God which is the essence of philosophical knowledge.

"What you seek," St. Augustine continues, "is something

which can be seen only by one who is most pure, and you are poorly trained for the vision of such a thing. We have labored for no other purpose in these digressions but your own training, so that you may be capable of seeing this." [71] Once again the educational purpose of the *Dialogues of Cassiciacum* is stated explicitly, and the role of the quadrivium in lifting the youthful mind to intelligible reality is explicitly affirmed. "Those who are well trained in the liberal arts," St. Augustine emphasizes, "are like this. . . . They are not content and they cannot contain themselves until they behold in all its breadth and fullness the whole countenance of Truth, whose splendor already glows in a certain measure in those arts." [72]

It is fully in accord with the mind of St. Augustine to call this a truth-centered education, because it recognizes a participation of the eternal Truth in the pedagogical arts and disciplines. Such an education enkindles the light gradually in the youthful soul and directs it in a basic orientation of life toward the Supreme Being, toward "beholding in all its breadth and fullness the whole countenance of Truth."

In the same passage St. Augustine points out explicitly that it is mathematical knowledge which enables the mind to perceive gradually more clearly the fact that we possess concepts and insights which are distinct from the sensory image. "These things will be treated with greater care and subtlety," he promises, "when we begin to discuss the understanding and . . . to explain in detail, as far as we are able, all that concerns the life of the soul." [73]

To summarize, there is in general a twofold causality of knowledge. The first is due to the action of the First Cause, God himself, the Eternal Truth, the Intelligible Light, who endows certain of his creatures as a part of His creative activity with a participation in the selfsame light. It is by this endowment that intelligent creatures have their power of understanding, their ability to rise to a knowledge of their Creator, and to return to a comprehension of their own spiritual nature. This is nothing else than that knowledge of God and the soul which is the essence of Christian philosophy, the goal of St. Augustine's philosophical thinking.

When St. Augustine links this doctrine with the secondary causes, the instruments of learning, we come to the secondary causality of knowledge. These instruments, the arts and disciplines of human culture, contain in themselves reflections of the selfsame Eternal Truth. Thus they are fitted for preparing the soul, for illuminating the soul, for bringing the spirit of man to the knowledge of God—provided they are taught and learned in the right way.[74] This is the privilege and the responsibility of the teaching profession, the key factor in determining whether theism or atheism shall prevail among men. St. Augustine's philosophy of education, the application of his philosophy of God and the soul to the education of youth, is linked closely with the orientation of social living to God and abiding values. It is directly connected with the formation and the continued life of Western civilization and with a deeper understanding of the rise and spread of contemporary atheism.

St. Augustine grasped the present condition of human nature with great clarity and saw with keen perception that faith in God on earth depends, among other things, upon genuine education. "To philosophy pertains a two-fold question," he writes, "the first treats of the soul; the second, of God. The first makes us know ourselves; the second, our origin. The former is more delightful to us; the latter, more precious. The former makes us fit for a happy life; the latter renders us happy. The first is for beginners; the latter, for the well-instructed. This is the order of wisdom's branches of study by which one becomes competent to grasp the order of things . . . and the very Author of the universe. . . ."[75]

St. Augustine, in other words, stresses the concern of Christian philosophy with God and the soul and relates that concern explicitly to the field of education: "This is the order of wisdom's branches of study." To see the full sweep of his educational doctrine and to perceive better its relationship to the spiritual and social welfare of mankind, we must turn to his view of the present condition of human nature and the providential order in education which is a significant part of the divine plan to alleviate this condition.

The Human Condition

Contemporary thought has a characteristic bent to dwell upon the details of what it loves to call "the human situation." This is another reason for a harmony, frequently noted, between St. Augustine's manner of thinking and the problems and questions of our own times. For he too was concerned with questions of the human soul, its origin, its future duration, its greatness, and its qualities.

Fundamental in St. Augustine's thinking is the fact that the human situation is to be an organism alive and breathing in this material cosmos. The human condition is first of all an organic one. To be a man is to be an organism; not just any organism, however, but one entitatively equipped to "become" and to "be" a person.

It is the human condition, furthermore, to be immersed in matter to such a degree that action as a person is encumbered. Through this immersion in matter the light of the mind is dim and the eye of the soul is weak. Here Augustine habitually describes the human condition in the imagery of the soul as imprisoned in matter, living in chains in the darkness of Plato's cave.[76]

This material condition of life is natural to man. It is part of being an organism, a *Lebewesen*. Man is an "anima-l," a piece of "animated matter," in this respect exactly like the lower organisms. Augustine saw all of this clearly, and it is in no sense a modern discovery. The only question is the "greatness" of the animating principle.[77] Our human matter is a bodily complex of physical elements, chemical properties, and organic functions, but it is also and most certainly animated in some special way, indeed, in a great and striking way. It is a piece of matter, consequently, which is pre-eminent in worth and dignity. Just how great the soul is was a constant preoccupation of St. Augustine's thought, and a wealth of doctrine on the point has remained one of the most significant characteristics of Christian philosophy ever since.[78]

The problem of the human situation, therefore, is that seen so clearly by Plato and discussed so lucidly by St. Augustine, the problem of liberating the soul of man from this immersion and imprisonment which encumbers it in the conditions of matter. This human situation is perceptible in any system of philosophy, whether that of Plato, of Aristotle, of Thomas Aquinas, or of the moderns. It is a common fact of general human observation and not the endpoint of a philosophical investigation. All men observe the fact. It is the duty of philosophy to clarify and explain it, and to point out the means for meeting this human condition.

According to the mind of St. Augustine, a providential means or "order" is at hand for mankind, an integral part of the divine plan for man in this task and challenge of coping with this fundamental element in the human situation. It is nothing else than the culture of the human arts and disciplines of which the Vatican Council speaks, nothing else than the field of education and the work of the teaching profession. It cannot be left to chance, as St. Augustine points out, nor can it be done in an arbitrary order. The order must be rooted in truth; hence it will have a certain definite structure. Men must use this order if they are to free themselves from the material conditions which establish the human problem: either this, or find themselves unable to cope with the human situation. "Aut illo ordine," he writes, "aut nullo modo." [79]

The fundamental importance of the field of education for human welfare comes clearly into view in this teaching of St. Augustine. Liberal education receives its new and full Christian sense: "The truth shall make you free." Indeed, the study of St. Augustine's educational teaching provides the broad background in our civilization for perceiving the importance and the bearing of the teaching of the Vatican Council regarding the cultivation of the human arts and disciplines.

It would be wrong to think that St. Augustine makes education indispensable for a knowledge of divine things, as if to condemn the uneducated to separation from God. He makes his teaching clear in the case of his own mother. What he calls the "soul" of the human arts and disciplines can be grasped by uneducated persons of good will who listen with docility, for they have within themselves the same light of the mind and eye of the soul as those more fortunate ones who have had the opportunity to cultivate that light and eye through education.[80] This is the office of religion in society: it brings through faith the essential benefits of wisdom to all men, even apart from the specialized opportunities and talents for higher education. St. Augustine returns to this point in his *De musica*, where he discusses the relation of education to the needs of Christian souls.[81] Such souls, he states, can "fly past" these arts and disciplines of human culture. They go directly, by means of their faith, to God and a perception of divine things. He hastens to point out, however, that education is needed for Christian leadership in society; it has its own place and importance in the providential order, its own role and function to perform. Christians, therefore, do not disdain education. They value it. At the same time they recognize that simple souls and those who through some turn of providence have not had educational opportunity come by faith to the same God, the God of wisdom, the God who is the cause of the light in the eye of the mind which education cultivates.

The Objective Educational Reality and Its Order

Seen in the light of these considerations, St. Augustine's *De ordine* assumes a special importance. It is actually a treatise on the philosophy of the curriculum, establishing the concept of "order" first in the universe then in the order of studies by which the mind rises to a contemplation of this same God and his providence. It is a work perhaps even more fundamental to the philosophy of education than the *De doctrina christiana*, which presupposes its underlying positions and relates sacred doctrine to this basic and providential academic order. It is difficult to understand Book II of the *De doctrina christiana* unless the educational philosophy of this earlier work is kept in mind.

When the *De ordine* is approached from the field of education, Augustine's pedagogical intention becomes clear. His purpose is to accomplish a synthesis within the soul, giving it peace, health, and happiness.[82] "Believe me, then," St. Augustine asserts at the outset, "you will attain to these things when you will have given to learning, by which the mind, heretofore in no way fitted for a divine planting, is cleared and cultivated. Now these discourses . . . especially if you will have the good will to cooperate and make yourself a part of this very order of which I am writing to you, sufficiently show you what is the nature of all this clearing and planting, and what mode of procedure it demands, and what it is that reason promises to those who study and are good. . . ." [83]

This, it seems clear, can mean nothing else than the intention to discuss the culture of the human arts and disciplines as a means of cultivating the soul to rise to a knowledge of God and Providence, and to attain that peace and happiness which such a properly organized and implemented education confers upon the human spirit. Augustine's purpose is educational: by his own statement, the *De ordine* is a treatise on the philosophy of the curriculum and indeed on the very idea of human education.[84] Discussing the order of causes in the universe, he leads the mind to perceive an objective and extramental educational reality, which also contains "a fixed order of causes." [85] In this fixed order of causes he places the circle of the arts and disciplines of human culture, as a preparation for this philosophical knowledge of God and the soul.[86] He states explicitly the nature of the "difficult undertaking," which characterized the years after his conversion, the project, namely, of organizing the theory and the practice of a new type of school. This new program of education will produce genuinely educated men; men, namely, who possess God, Truth itself and Wisdom, and therefore have the means of the happy life. All the writings of this first period of Augustine's Catholic life as a layman are summarized in this basic concept.[87] It is important, therefore, in order to bring into stronger relief the educational philosophy of this treatise *De ordine,* to analyze its essential teachings on the culture of the human arts and disciplines.

The Philosophy of the Curriculum

St. Augustine agrees with Plato that the denial of a Providence over mankind is tantamount to atheism. The first part of the *De ordine* discusses this providential order in the universe and in human affairs. It is, indeed, the very essence of wisdom to recognize this providential care for us, and thus to live with hope and confidence under so great a God. The teaching profession has "the duty of teaching them wisdom" that young people may perceive this providential order.[88] As his exposition develops, however, Augustine makes it clear that the teaching profession cannot attain this crowning achievement of its work unless the memory of the young people has been stocked by the branches of learning. The educational system must be organized "systematically" to fulfill this duty.[89]

In other words, Augustine lays down as a first principle of educational philosophy the fact that there is a definite, orderly structure and process of education. Unless this structure and process is both understood and kept in good repair, it will become impossible for the teaching profession to fulfill this "duty of teaching them wisdom," the pleasant duty of liberating the souls of young people "by instruction and disputation." [90]

St. Augustine goes on to stress the central core of his educational teaching: knowledge of God is dependent upon this order of learning. The entire social question of atheism and theism among men hinges on this point. What he so constantly calls "our school" contrasts with "those other schools" most basically by this fact that it is an order of means leading to this knowledge of God and the soul. This is exactly the object of knowledge which Augustine has laid down as the goal of Christian philosophy. If the arts, sciences, and disciplines of human culture are taught and learned in the right way, to borrow the phrase of the first Vatican Council; in other words, if the educational system is characterized by sound philosophy of the curriculum, then it will contribute to social welfare and bring personal happiness, the happy life, to mankind.[91] St. Augustine's program, therefore, is a vast project in the philosophy of education involving the regeneration and renovation of the heritage of *paideia*.

St. Augustine, experienced educator that he is, is fully aware of the fact that it is no easy task to teach a knowledge of God and the order of his providence to young people. "When I was explaining this," he tells us, " and repeating it again and again to him. . . ." [92] Augustine at this point asserts that his teaching program is retarded and hindered by a lack of suitable preparation in the minds and souls of his selected group of youthful students. At this juncture his treatise turns from the order of providence in the universe as a whole to the order of studies necessary to prepare youthful souls for a discernment of God and his providential care. We are at the very crux of an education to sustain a living and vivid knowledge of God among men on earth. Seen from this vantage point, the *De ordine* is characterized by an elevated insight into the providential order which governs the development of the human mind as a part of the total providential plan and design of the universe. Seen from the viewpoint of the field of education this treatise does not so much lack unity as manifest a most striking and profound plan of composition entirely worthy of its author.

St. Augustine, therefore, turns to a discussion of that order of studies which will provide a suitable preparation for the perception of these elevated truths of theism, the distinguishing mark of the cultivated Christian soul.[93] The remainder of the treatise elaborates this fundamental educational doctrine. Divine science, he tells us (and it is nothing else than Christian philosophy, that first philosophy which in the Aristotelian tradition is also called metaphysics), is related directly to the philosophy of the curriculum. This Christian philosophy, Augustine continues, demands a twofold preparation, and therefore imposes a twofold obligation upon the educator. The first is a moral preparation, to which he devotes Chapter VIII, a description of the atmosphere which ought to characterize a Catholic institution of learning, devoted as it is to this elevated knowledge of God and the soul.[94] The second preparation is nothing else than the order of studies organized as an objective, extramental structure of education.[95] "It remains for me," he says, introducing this pedagogical discussion, "to declare how instruction is to be imparted to the studious youths who have resolved to live in the manner described." [96]

A little further on St. Augustine's friend Alypius defines the "difficult undertaking" which is under way at Cassiciacum as a teaching which "inflames with . . . zeal for that life," the life, namely, of the service of this Supreme Being and providential orderer of the universe. Then Alypius expresses the desire that "all men were already arrived at that manner of life . . . so that what is so marvelous to hear, might, by universal example, be likewise easy to practice." [97] This is the aspiration of the Christian soul, living in a depraved society, who recognizes how much easier Christian life would be were it sustained by the example of society as a whole in a Christian social order. This is a remarkable anticipation of the coming Christian society of Christendom, and its providential benefit for souls, defined in advance. It is this concept of Christendom which this very philosophy of education, under elaboration in the thought of St. Augustine will help to form, to realize, through the Christian educational practice of the coming centuries.

That the new procedure in education is successful Augustine makes clear when he reports that the young students with him are suddenly manifesting "such antagonism to worldly pleasures" that he can hardly believe it himself. His *paideia* is strikingly effective: it is offering these young people precisely that safe way, that *tuta via* which he missed when he was their age. *Schola nostra* contrasts sharply with *schola illa* from which Augustine recently has resigned.

This philosophical knowledge toward which his students are moving in the order of studies concerns God and the soul; it is prerequisite for avoiding error about the soul and God. "Anyone who does not know these matters," he writes, "and yet wishes to question and dispute about even his own soul—let alone investigating about the most high God . . . such a one will fall into every possible error. . . . But then, whoever has grasped the meaning of simple and intelligible numbers will readily understand these matters. . . . Anyone of good talents . . . if he be eagerly devoted to study and if he follow the above-mentioned order of studies in so far as is required, will certainly comprehend such numbers." [98]

This is the explicit statement of St. Augustine's educational thesis: there is a definite order of studies, giving an indispensable place to mathematics, astronomy, and the natural sciences, which leads *per corporalia ad incorporalia*, upward toward a definite body of philosophical knowledge. This in turn is prerequisite for human insight and understanding on God and the soul. It is this educational doctrine which looms into new relevance and importance in the contemporary atheistic age, when the culture of the human arts and disciplines is faltering in its mission of leading the minds of the young to God.

We shall return below to this fundamental and indispensable place of the quadrivium, the disciplines of mathematics and the natural sciences. St. Augustine is explicit: all the liberal studies, the real disciplines as well as the formal, must be included and properly organized into an order of learning, as a preparation for philosophical understanding and insight regarding God and the soul. Again we perceive the deep unity which characterizes his life since he read the *Hortensius* as a youth. "So," he writes, "any investigation concerning these and similar matters is to be made according to that order, or not at all." [99]

The Ordering of Studies Toward God

In the following chapter of his *De ordine*, St. Augustine defines this order of studies, from mathematics to logic and thence to philosophy itself understood as the "divine science," that first philosophy which raises the mind to the immaterial reality of God, to a discernment of his providential order in the universe and to his special care for his spiritual creature, the human soul. "This is the order of wisdom's branches of study," he writes, in the passage already cited.[100] Holding fast to this order, he continues, the soul, "now devoted to philosophy at first introspects itself." [101] Here the interwoven character of Augustine's philosophy and of his understanding of education becomes more clearly manifest than ever. The knowledge of the soul is a priceless benefit which results gradually from this education, if it is properly organized to lead the mind up to God. Human beings will not understand themselves properly, they will lack a sufficient insight into their own spiritual nature and reality, if education is not planned according to this providential order of studies and method of teaching in them. If it is so organized, however, then the faculty of reason will come to understand itself by the very exercise of its own power to analyze and synthesize the objects of learning.[102]

"By some kind of inner and hidden activity of mine," St. Augustine explains, "I am able to analyze and synthesize the things that ought to be learned; and this faculty of mine

is called reason. . . . Both in analyzing and in synthesizing
it is oneness that I seek, it is oneness that I love. But when
I analyze, I seek a homogeneous unit; when I synthesize, I
look for an integral unit." [103]

Such, then, is the nature and function of intelligence, and
at the same time the nature and function of properly organized education, manifesting a conformity to the providential
order of things in its very order of studies. "The well-instructed soul," Augustine tells us, "grasps and ponders these
truths of God and the soul." [104] In other words, it is a sound
education which counteracts that natural tendency in man,
given his present condition and situation, to fall into a skepticism for simple dullness and lack of knowledge regarding
the things of God, his providential order, and the nature and
capacities and responsibilities of the human soul.[105]

"To see God . . . this beauty—and he will see it who
lives well, prays well, studies well!" These words of St. Augustine lay down the purpose and the means of the Christian
education of youth. This is the synthetic summary and definition of the nature of his contact with the field of education.[106] The immeasurable benefit of such an education will
be a Christian discernment of God and his providential care
for mankind, which leads directly to the properly Christian
resignation to providence, a disposition of the soul ready to
accept the revelation of Jesus Christ. This is "order," in
its deepest meaning, and leads directly to that entire concept
of *metanoia*, that conversion and reform of life which is so
central in the message of the Gospel and in the work of the
Church. St. Augustine's contact with the field of education,
accordingly, is a *paideia Theou* which reorganizes, restores,
and renews the field and institution of formal education so
that it may participate fully in the apostolate of the Church.
This is the climax of the work of the Age of the Fathers, this
is the educational key to the birth and the formation and the
development and the flowering of a Christian culture on
earth. It is, furthermore, the proper background for understanding those significant words of the first Vatican Council

on the culture of the human arts and disciplines as stepping-stones to God, if they are taught and learned in the right way.[107]

St. Augustine promises further discussion of "these matters," that is, the right order of studies, if his youthful students decide "as I earnestly advise and hope," to follow "that order mentioned by us, or perhaps another order more concise and appropriate—but at any rate, a right order, and will seriously and consistently hold it." [108] He is concerned with the philosophy of education, and indeed not exclusively in general and theoretical terms, but also with the practical matters of the philosophy of the curriculum. He is concerned with the branches of learning, with the liberal arts—all of them—the quadrivium as well as the trivium. They are "shrines of truth," as he calls them, and they relate directly to his Christian philosophy of God and soul, that sharp-eyed philosophy which has accorded the primacy to truth and wisdom as the sole course or curriculum open to mankind toward the happy life.

The culture of the human arts and disciplines, therefore, presupposes the existence of an objective educational reality, a structure laid out as a path for youth to follow. We today have come to call it the curriculum, a word which either denotes this objective structure of arts, sciences, and disciplines, or gravitates gradually toward subjective re-definitions and educational meaninglessness. In earlier times this same educational reality was called the circle of the sciences or the cycle of the liberal arts. Whatever it be called, the essential factor in sound pedagogical thinking, as St. Augustine saw, is to recognize it as the objective reality and structure of education, an order which is itself a part of the general providential order and care of God over mankind. This order of studies is a gradual preparatory path which leads the oncoming generation to wisdom concerning God and the soul. This sound education represents the regeneration and renovation of the heritage of *paideia*, the undertaking to which St. Augustine devoted his life and professional career. This theistic orientation in the culture of the human arts and disciplines constitutes in turn one of the abiding positions in educational thought and practice which St. Augustine bequeathed to the schools of Christendom and to sound human education today.

Notes from Chapter Six

1 *Conf.*, V, 10 (19); Ryan, *op. cit.*, p. 127. The implication of a direct connection between materialistic thinking and moral corruption on earth is evident.

2 *Ibid.*, VII, 17 (23); *op. cit.*, p. 176. This, of course, is not to deny the fact that actual grace was at work at the same time within his soul.

3 For general surveys of St. Augustine's philosophical thought, see Gilson, *The Christian Philosophy of Saint Augustine*, the English translation of the work which has become the classic in its field, his *Introduction à l'étude de saint Augustin* (Paris: Vrin, 1943); F. Cayré, *Initiation à la philosophie de saint Augustin* (Paris: Desclée, 1947); F.-J. Thonnard, *Précis d'histoire de la philosophie* (Paris: Desclée, 1952), pp. 198-257, a masterly short synthesis. For the abiding character of St. Augustine's philosophy in his later life as a bishop, a point of special importance for the study of his contact with the field of education, see P. Monnot, "Essai de synthèse philosophique d'après le XIe livre de la Cité de Dieu," *Archives de philosophie*, VII (1930), 142-185; also on the same topic, Maurice Blondel, "L'unité originale et la pensée permanente de la doctrine philosophique de saint Augustin," *Revue de métaphysique et de morale*, 1930, pp. 424 ff. The older study by Jules Martin, *Saint Augustin*, in the series "Les grandes philosophes," remains valuable, especially Livre I, "La connaissance," pp. 1-97, and Livre II, "Dieu," pp. 92-263. Finally, there is the recent comprehensive three-volume work of M. F. Sciacca, *Sant' Agostino*, with good synthetic discussions of truth, the interior teacher, and the various forms of illumination.

4 Cf. *Contra Academicos*, II, 2 (5-6); O'Meara, *St. Augustine Against the Academics*, pp. 69-71; ". . . untouched by that great fire which was to consume us, we thought that the slow fire with which we burned was the greatest. But . . . certain books [of Platonism] . . . stirred up an incredible conflagration—incredible, Romanianus, incredible, and perhaps beyond even what you would believe of me—what more shall I say?—beyond even what I would believe of myself" (*ibid.*, p. 69). The birth of Christian philosophy in this lucidly expressed intellectual grasp of the concept of *ipsum esse subsistens* was indeed a powerful and memorable event in the history of human thought.

5 Cf. *ibid.*, II, 1 (2); *op. cit.*, p. 67, where St. Augustine speaks of "Him to whom I have given myself completely"; he expects confidently that the same philosophical discovery will bring his friend Romanianus, to whom the *Contra Academicos* is dedicated, into the true religion (see *ibid.*, II, 7 (18); *op. cit.*, p. 83). The *De vera religione*, projected at this same time and for the same friend, is thus seen to be directly related to the *Dialogues of Cassiciacum* and illustrates anew the unity of the Christian life and thought and published works of St. Augustine prior to his ordination.

6 *Ibid.*, I, 1 (3); *op. cit.*, p. 38.

7 *Ibid.*, I, 8 (22); *op. cit.*, p. 59.

8 In his dialogue *De ordine*, I, 4 (10), St. Augustine makes it clear that his school at Cassiciacum was teaching this new philosophy. "Philosophy, . . . as you prove it day by day," one of his youthful students remarks, "is our true and tranquil abode." It is "a divine thing, which begins to reveal itself to me, and on it I am much intent." St. Augustine affirms this as the purpose he has in mind to achieve by the instrumentality of this content and method of teaching; he wishes to beget in their minds a desire for order, namely, to bring them to a better understanding of the providential order which governs the universe and human affairs. This is the educational application of the new philosophical grasp of the Supreme Being, which touches the inner life of the human spirit and its happiness with its insight into *creatio ex nihilo* and into the providential government of all creation. In fact, St. Augustine states that this doctrine on the providential order which the mind can discern after perceiving this strong new view of the Supreme Being "is the very heart of philosophy" (*De ordine*, I, 5 (13).

9 *Contra Academicos*, I, 1 (1); O'Meara, *St. Augustine Against the Academics*, p. 36.

10 *De ordine*, II, 2 (6).

11 *Contra Academicos*, III, 19 (42); O'Meara, *St. Augustine Against the Academics*, p. 149.

12 *Ibid.*

13 Cf. *De ordine*, I, 11 (32); Russell, *op. cit.*, p. 271.

14 *Contra Academicos*, II, 3 (9); O'Meara, *St. Augustine Against the Academics*, p. 74.

15 Cf. *De ordine*, II, 7 (24); Russell, *op. cit.*, pp. 300-301. Cf. also *Solil.*, I, 5 (11) for the same teaching that Christian philosophy provides man with a knowledge of God which is qualitatively superior to the certitudes of mathematics.

16 For this distinction of the two kinds and modes of progress in knowledge, cf. Jacques Maritain, *A Preface to Metaphysics* (London: Sheed and Ward, 1948), pp. 2-16.

17 For an introduction to the concept of person in St. Augustine's thought, with references, see Paul Henry, *St. Augustine on Personality* (New York: Macmillan, 1960); also Johannes Stelzenberger, *Conscientia bei Augustinus* (Paderborn: Schöningh, 1959), and the fundamental chapter of Charles Norris Cochrane, *Christianity and Classical Culture* (New York: Oxford University Press, 1944), "Nostra Philosophia: The Discovery of Personality," pp. 399-445.

18 *Solil.*, II, 1 (1); Gilligan, *op. cit.*, p. 384.

19 The close relationship of St. Augustine's philosophy to education is indicated clearly by this designation of his thought as "an inquiry concerning human understanding," a relationship which recalls immediately the works of Locke and Hume and John Dewey's *How We Think*. Philosophies which inquire into our manner of knowing, thinking, and understanding are inevitably philosophies of education.

20 Cf. St. Augustine, *De quantitate animae*, c. 28-32; Colleran, *op. cit.*, pp. 81-98.

21 *Ibid.*, 27 (53); *op. cit.*, p. 79.

22 *Ibid.*, 28 (54); *op. cit.*, p. 81.

23 *Ibid.*, 29 (56); *op. cit.*, p. 83.

24 St. Augustine, *De ordine*, II, 19 (49).

25 St. Augustine, *Solil.*, II, 18-20.

26 St. Augustine, *De ordine*, II, 2 (5).

27 *Contra Academicos*, II, 1 (1).

28 In the case of St. Augustine, who stands at the fountainhead of Christian philosophy, and hence of the philosophical understanding of the causality of knowledge which characterizes Catholic education, it is important to distinguish between the philosophical vision of a reality and the philosophical explanation of the reality perceived. It is one thing for a philosophy to see a reality, to grasp its facts, to penetrate, if only by initial perhaps surprised and even enraptured intuition, to the nature of things; it is another thing to explain these things seen by an explanation which proceeds in a philosophical way, in terms of principles which lie hidden under the level of phenomena. In St. Augustine's philosophical teaching there is a striking discovery and strong statement of the reality of human knowledge, which presents a clearer vision of the fact than classical philosophy had been able to achieve. For the full elaboration of the philosophical explanation, much more time and thought was needed. C. Vansteenkiste brings this point out appositely, as a general consideration in connection with St. Augustine's philosophical thought in his article, "Il posto del Tomismo nella storia del pensiero medioevale," *Aquinas*, III (1960), 314-315: "To St. Augustine belongs the imperishable credit of having founded the entire body of Latin Christian philosophy. He pointed out the way of close collaboration between faith and reason, sketched the first synthesis of all the major problems, gave the exact basic answer to numerous questions, and coined a terminology of which various elements are still alive fifteen centuries later. . . . He gave a magistral practical solution to the fundamental problem of the union of faith and reason: these two bodies of human knowledge penetrate each other with neither opposition nor distorting effect. . . . There is only *one* Christian wisdom. But Augustine does not elaborate the theory of this solution, and hence does not distinguish clearly between the two areas of knowledge. This lack of accurate distinction is perceptible in his treatment of many other problems, as well, in the teaching on the virtues, for example, and in the doctrine on knowledge—the famed question of the divine illumination. . . . The internal tendency proper to Augustinian philosophy as such . . . is therefore a natural tendency toward further perfectioning, even toward the restatement of certain points and the completion of others. Hence it is also perfectly natural that the Christian genius of St. Bonaventure and of St. Thomas sought to respond to this appeal in Augustinian thought. It is in these later Doctors, therefore, that the imperishable elements in St. Augustine's system are to be sought."

29 It is at this juncture regarding the nature, genesis, and elaboration of knowledge that educational philosophy becomes directly dependent upon philosophical anthropology. Cf. Jacques Maritain, *An Introduction to Philosophy* (London: Longmans, 1930), p. 159: " . . . at any rate for us men, the first and most important of philosophic problems . . . is concerned with the nature of the intellect itself and of our ideas, that is to say, with the instrument by which all our knowledge is obtained; and the solution propounded by different philosophers dominates their entire system."

30 Plato and Aristotle, of course, understood best the qualitative difference of the human mode of being from that of the brute animals, as a result of their keen perceptiveness regarding human knowledge. For Aristotle's conscious opposition to the other view of human knowledge, cf. Cochrane, *op. cit.*, pp. 469-474.

31 Gordon W. Allport, *Becoming: Basic Considerations for a Psychology of Personality* (New Haven: Yale University Press, 1960), p. 7.

32 *Solil.*, I, 2 (7); Gilligan, *op. cit.*, p. 350.

33 *Ibid.*, I, 15 (27); *op. cit.*, p. 377.

34 *Ibid.*, II, 1 (1); *op. cit.*, p. 381.

35 *Ibid.*, I, 1 (1); *op. cit.*, p. 344.

36 *Ibid.*, I, 1 (3); *op. cit.*, p. 345.

37 *Ibid.*, II, 5 (8); *op. cit.*, p. 390.

38 Cf. *ibid.*, II, chaps. vii-x; *op. cit.*, pp. 395-402.

39 *Ibid.*, II, 15 (28) and II, 17 (31); *op. cit.*, pp. 413 and 418.

40 *De ordine*, II, 19 (50).

41 Boyer, *L'idée de vérité* . . . , p. 12.

42 *Ibid.*, p. 2.

43 For St. Augustine's theory of intellectual knowledge, there are the general expositions of his philosophical doctrine, especially Gilson, *The Christian Philosophy of Saint Augustine*, chap. v, "The Fifth Step—Rational Knowledge," pp. 66-111; Cayré, *Initiation à la philosophie de saint Augustine*, chap. viii, "Explication du monde intérieur, l'illumination," pp. 209-243; Martin, *Saint Augustin*, Book I, "La Connaissance," pp. 1-97; Thonnard, *Prècis d'histoire de la philosophie*, pp. 198-257, an excellent treatment, especially pp. 231-237, "L'intellection—Role de Dieu . . . Role de l'intelligence"; for *ex professo* discussions, cf. Régis Jolivet, *Dieu soleil des esprits ou la doctrine augustinienne de l'illumination* (Paris: Desclée, 1934); F. Cayré, *Dieu présent dans la vie de l'esprit* (Paris: Desclée, 1951); Martin Grabmann, *Die Grundgedanken des heiligen Augustinus über Seele und Gott* (Köln: J. P. Bachem, 1929); Johannes Hessen, *Augustinus Metaphysik der Erkenntnis* (Leiden: E. J. Brill, 1960, 2 Aufl.; 1st ed., 1916); for a synthetic survey, cf. Jacques Maritain, *The Degrees of Knowledge* (New York: Scribner's, 1959), chap. vii, "Augustinian Wisdom," pp. 291-309; for a recent factual report with complete bibliography cf. C. E. Schuetzinger, *The German Controversy on Saint Augustine's Illumination Theory* (New York: Pageant Press, 1960); for a convenient and carefully chosen collection of the pertinent texts of St. Augustine, cf. L. Keeler, *Sancti Augustini doctrina de cognitione* (Roma: Pont. Univ. Gregoriana, 1933). Much relevant material presented in a different orientation and larger framework is to be found in Michael Frickel, *Deus totus ubique simul: Untersuchungen zur allgemeinen Gottesgegenwart* (Freiburg: Verlag Herder, 1956) and in Stanislaus J. Grabowski, *The All-Present God: A Study in St. Augustine* (St. Louis: Herder, 1954).

44 Thonnard, *op. cit.*, p. 231.

45 *De civitate Dei*, VII, 30.

46 *Solil.*, I, 13 (23); Gilligan, *op. cit.*, p. 373. Cf. *De Trin.*, XII, 15 (24): ". . . the intellectual mind is so formed in its nature as to see those things . . . by a sort of incorporeal light of a unique kind."

47 *Solil.*, I, 6 (12); Gilligan, *op. cit.*, p. 358.

48 *Ibid.*; *op. cit.*, p. 359.

49 *Ibid.*, I, 6 (13); *op. cit.*, p. 360.

50 *De libero arbitrio*, II, 5 (11).

51 *Ibid.*, II, 12 (33).

52 *Solil.*, I, 1 (3); Gilligan, *op. cit.*, p. 345.

53 Cf. Charles Boyer, S.J., *Essais sur la doctrine de saint Augustin* (Paris: Beauchesne, 1932), chap. vi, "La philosophie augustinienne ignore-t-elle l'abstraction?" pp. 166-183, where it is clearly established that St. Augustine

viewed the light of the human mind as a created participation in the Supernal Light.

54 Boyer, *L'idée de vérité*, p. 156; see chap. iv, "La vérité illuminatrice," pp. 156-220, for a full discussion of St. Augustine's teaching on the point.

55 *Contra Academicos*, II, 3 (10).

56 Cf. *De ordine*, I, 8 (21).

57 Cf. *ibid.*, II, 3 (10).

58 Cf. *Solil.* I, 14 (24); Gilligan, *op. cit.*, p. 375.

59 *Ibid.*, II, 20 (35); *op. cit.*, p. 423.

60 Observable here is striking contrast with certain recent philosophical tendencies, on their tortuous path away from the insights and positions of Christian philosophy and from St. Augustine. Modern philosophical thought ends on this path at an outright denial of the First Cause, perceiving nothing but secondary causes, and indeed at its final stage, only proximate ones. At this final stage philosophy announces its identity with the natural sciences, for example, Reichenbach in his *Rise of Scientific Philosophy*. The entire current descending from Comte, Mill, and Spencer, to Dewey and the Neo-Positivists in our own time, is characterized by this blindness. It is a philosophy, St. Augustine would say, which has lost its eyesight and lies *in articulo mortis*.

61 *Contra Academicos*, II, 3 (10), already cited.

62 *Solil.*, II, 17 (31); Gilligan, *op. cit.*, p. 417.

63 *De magistro*, 10 (31).

64 Cf. *ibid.*, 10 (38); Colleran, *op. cit.*, p. 177: "Regarding, however, all those things which we understand, it is not a speaker who utters sounds exteriorly whom we consult, but it is truth that presides within, over the mind itself; though it may have been words that prompted us to make such consultation. And He who is consulted, He who is said to *dwell in the inner man* (Eph. 3, 14-17), He it is who teaches—Christ—that is, *the unchangeable Power of God and everlasting Wisdom* (I Cor. 1, 23 ff.)."

65 *Ibid.*, 14 (45); *op. cit.*, p. 185.

66 Cf. *Solil.*, II, chaps. xi-xx; Gilligan, *op. cit.*, pp. 402-426. This concluding portion is actually the logical climax of the *Soliloquies* as a whole, and is devoted entirely to a study of truth, contained and enshrined for young people in the branches of learning.

67 Cf. *ibid.*, I, 13 (23); *op. cit.*, p. 373.

68 *Ibid.; op. cit.*, p. 374.

69 It is noteworthy that the Rousseau-Dewey current of thought in contemporary times clashes directly with the philosophy of the curriculum contained in St. Augustine's teaching. This current leads to a re-definition of the idea of human education which devalues or even dissolves entirely the objective structure and order of education constituted by the systematic array of arts and disciplines elaborated by mankind as instruments suitable for the cultivation of the human mind, indeed for leading the mind to God, if the teaching is done in the right way (cf. *Denz.* 1799).

70 *Solil.*, II, 18 (32); Gilligan, *op. cit.*, p. 420.

71 *Ibid.*, II, 20 (34); *op. cit.*, p. 422.

72 *Ibid.*, II, 20 (35); *op. cit.*, p. 423.

73 *Ibid.*, II, 20 (36); *op. cit.*, p. 425. Unfortunately for the field of education, St. Augustine was unable to carry out this intention, and the *Soliloquies*, as he himself stated have remained an unfinished work. However, this only serves to emphasize the educational relevance of the *De immortalitate*

animae, the *De libero arbitrio,* the *De quantitate animae,* and, of course, the *De magistro.* These treatises all manifest the unifying theme of this educator's life which we have analyzed in detail above, and they illustrate specifically the "difficult undertaking" which he began at Cassiciacum and continued at Thagaste until to his surprise he was enlisted into the Catholic priesthood.

74 Cf. I Vatican Council (*Denz.* 1799): ". . . si rite pertractentur."

75 St. Augustine, *De ordine,* II, 18 (47); Russell, *op. cit.,* p. 324. This explicit relationship of the *De ordine* to the field of education is frequently overlooked. The very title of Russell's translation, *Divine Providence and the Problem of Evil,* seems to reflect this fact. In the "Introduction," the translator views the discussion of the branches of study as a mere *example* of order drawn from a familiar field, missing entirely the intrinsic pedagogical relationship of these studies to the preparation of youthful minds to discern the providential order of the universe. The educational significance of St. Augustine's treatise becomes lost and indeed the very unity of his plan of composition is missed. Cf. *ibid.,* pp. 231-232. Augustine's work is without doubt a discussion of "Divine Providence and the Problem of Evil"; but, like the other writings of St. Augustine's earlier period, it is also something more. This educational content and bearing of St. Augustine's "philosophical" works ought to be given due recognition for several reasons, including the fact that the question is involved whether he composes well.

76 Cf. Plato, *The Republic,* Book VII.

77 This question is the point of the two philosophical works written at Milan and Rome immediately after the *Dialogues of Cassiciacum,* the *De immortalitate animae* and the *De quantitate animae;* these treatises are as explicitly concerned with the field of education as the *De ordine.*

78 There is an extensive literature on St. Augustine's concept of the union of the body and the soul. It is beyond our present scope to develop the detailed explanation of St. Augustine's doctrine on this point. Cf. *De Trinitate,* XII, 12 (17-18-19). In general, his teaching cannot be expected to have the exactitude and clarity, for example, of that of St. Bonaventure or St. Thomas Aquinas, coming after many centuries of Christian thought launched by St. Augustine himself. With St. Augustine, Christian philosophy is at its origin, using the tools at hand, and needing more time to articulate its explanations of the realities it sees.

79 *De ordine,* II, 17 (46); cf. Russell, *op. cit.,* p. 323.

80 Cf. *ibid.,* II, chaps. xvi-xvii; *op. cit.,* pp. 320-323. St. Monica "has a mental grasp of the faith . . . through the sacred mysteries." "But you," her son tells her, "grasp the almost heavenly power and nature of grammar, and with so much discernment that you seem to have taken hold of its very soul, and to have left its body for the eloquent. And, of course, I could say this also about the other studies of this kind" (*ibid.,* p. 322). In this tribute to his unlettered Catholic mother, St. Augustine also states in a striking way the nature of the liberal studies and their function and peculiar importance in human affairs. Education ought to be of one cut with the wisdom she possesses by her religion; otherwise, leadership in human society, which it is the office of education to prepare and to provide, will not be clear-sighted on fundamental issues of personal happiness and social welfare on earth.

81 Cf. *De musica,* Book VI.

82 Cf. *De ordine,* I, 2 (3); Russell; *op. cit.,* p. 242.

83 *Ibid.,* I, 2 (4); *op. cit.,* p. 242.

84 St. Augustine makes several similar sweeping declarations of his educational purpose during the course of the *De ordine;* for other instances, cf. Russell, *op. cit.,* pp. 250, 257, 261, 282, 291, 292, 300, and 324.

85 *De ordine,* I, 4 (11); Russell, *op. cit.,* p. 250.

86 Cf. *ibid.,* I, 7 (20); *op. cit.,* p. 257.

87 Cf. *ibid.,* I, 8 (21-26); *op. cit.,* pp. 259-263.

88 Cf. *ibid.,* II, 2 (7); *op. cit.,* p. 281. "Can the wise man," he asks, ". . . shirk the duty . . . of teaching them wisdom? And when he is doing that, in order to teach properly and to be himself less unfitted, he frequently prepares something which he will deliver and discuss systematically." Thus Augustine brings his students to see the nature of teaching, and to recognize that "a wise man's store is conserved by memory." This enables him to expound the heritage of the human arts and disciplines as "the well-trained servant" of the teaching profession, its well-stocked memory. This servant functions under the authority of the teacher, and "not by his own reasoning, so to speak, but because the supreme law and supreme order has prearranged it." The teacher also serves, and functions in a larger framework than his own opinion, a framework which is social and which derives from God's providential plan. St. Augustine is not expounding "pure philosophy," teaching wisdom merely by philosophical publications; he has in mind the field of education, the rightly ordered structure and heritage, providential in nature, of the arts, disciplines, and sciences of the teaching profession.

89 *Ibid.*

90 *Ibid.,* II, 3 (9); *op. cit.,* p. 383.

91 The strong consistency of St. Augustine's thought is everywhere apparent in his educational doctrine. The agreement with the *De beata vita,* the first of the *Dialogues of Cassiciacum* and the first work in the *Opera omnia sancti Augustini,* is immediately apparent. Cf. the discussion above, and especially *De beata vita,* 2 (7-16), in particular the description of knowledge as the nutrition of the soul; "the souls of people not scientifically trained and unfamiliar with the liberal arts are, as it were, hungry and famished." When such passages are compared with Augustine's teaching on the relationship of these educational arts to the brightness of the mind's eye in discerning the things of God and the soul, the fundamental nature of his project for the renewal and restoration of the heritage of *paideia* comes strikingly into view, and much light is thrown upon the rise and spread of modern atheism.

92 *De ordine,* II, 7 (23); Russell, *op. cit.,* p. 300.

93 At Book II, chap. vii.

94 Described in *De ordine,* II, 8 (25); Russell, *op. cit.,* pp. 301-302: "Accordingly, this science imposes a twofold order of procedure on those who desire to know it, of which order one part pertains to the regulating of life, and the other pertains to the directing of studies." This is the *tuta via,* the Christian education of youth, which he mentions in the *Confessions:* "I learned many useful things," he says of his youth in those other schools, demoralized and devoid of content, ". . . but they could have been learned from things that were not vain. This last is the safe way in which children should walk" (Ryan, *op. cit.,* p. 58). The vivid experience of this other education as a student and a *rhetor,* and his "difficult undertaking" (*De beata vita,* 1 (6)) in the field of education which began at his conversion and continued until death, constitutes the profound unity of his entire life. This undertaking, we continue to note, is nothing else than the thorough reform

of education to provide this safe way in which the children of men, especially the children of baptized men, should walk. Thus it enters into the life of St. Augustine, the priest and bishop, as an integral part of his care of souls and his apostolate as an episcopal teacher in the Church.

[95] Cf. the remainder of the *De ordine*, II, chaps. ix to xx.

[96] *Ibid.*, II, 9 (26); Russell, *op. cit.*, p. 303.

[97] *Ibid.*, II, 10 (28); *op. cit.*, p. 305.

[98] *Ibid.*, II, 16 (44); *op. cit.*, p. 321.

[99] *Ibid.*, II, 17 (46); *op. cit.*, p. 323. There is an evident, striking, and perhaps fateful contrast between the teaching of Plato, Cicero, and St. Augustine on the proper instruments of human culture and that of the late Professor Dewey, together with the Cardinal Principles Report of 1918, which became common doctrine in the ensuing forty years.

[100] Cf. *ibid.*, II, 18 (48); *op. cit.*, p. 324.

[101] *Ibid.*

[102] Cf. *ibid.; op. cit.*, p. 325.

[103] *Ibid.*

[104] *Ibid.*, II, 19 (50); *op. cit.*, p. 327.

[105] Cf. Theodor Haecker, *Was ist der Mensch* (Leipzig: Jakob Hegner, 1935), p. 123: "Der Mensch ist ja der niederste Geist, seine Existenz als Geist ist gefährdet, in ihm kann der Geist *wunderbarerweise* in Zweifel gezogen werden, wozu freilich auch wieder ein Minimum von Geist gehört; wer *kann* denn Zweifeln, ausser dem Geiste?" This is indeed the human situation, to use the worn-out phrase once more, and this is the reason why mankind depends upon a sound education in order to maintain on earth and in society an effective knowledge of God and the soul.

[106] Cf. *De ordine*, II, 19 (51); Russell, *op. cit.*, p. 328.

[107] Cf. Conc. Vaticanum, Sess. III (24 Aprilis, 1870), where it is stated that the Catholic Church always has promoted the "humanarum artium et disciplinarum cultura"; "fatetur immo, eas, quemadmodum a *Deo scientiarum Domino* (I Reg. 2, 3) profectae sunt, ita, si rite pertractentur, ad Deum iuvante eius gratia perducere" (*Denz.* 1799).

[108] *De ordine*, II, 19 (51); Russell, *op. cit.*, p. 329.

Christian Doctrine:
The Renewal of
Sacred History

WHILE we . . . thus recur to Greece and Athens with pleasure and affection," writes Cardinal Newman in one of his finest passages, "and recognize in that famous land the source and the school of intellectual culture, it would be strange indeed if we forgot to look further south also, and there to bow before a more glorious luminary, and a more sacred oracle of truth, and the source of another sort of knowledge, high and supernatural, which is seated in Palestine. Jerusalem is the fountain-head of religious knowledge, as Athens is of secular. In the ancient world we see two centers of illumination, acting independently of each other, each with its own movement, and at first apparently without any promise of convergence." [1] These words suggest the unfinished state of this study of St. Augustine's philosophy of education at the present point, and what the remainder of his work will be. For the Bishop of Hippo more than any other brought this higher wisdom to play in the education of youth, and indeed in a manner which made Newman's convergence an actual fact in Western education.

Perhaps the most fundamental as well as the most strikingly visible difference between the *paideia* of classical antiquity and the Christian education of youth in Western civilization is the fact that "religion," which was not a course of study in the former, was added in the latter to the arts and sciences as a separate and distinct academic discipline, and indeed placed firmly in the central position as the queen of the sciences. Not only was religion taught but all the other arts and disciplines of the order or curriculum of studies were taught in its light. St. Augustine is the key figure in this development. The manner in which the study of sacred doctrine was added to the order of studies introduces the second phase of St. Augustine's philosophy of education and describes the crowning achievement of his theory and practice of education.[2]

So far, indeed, we have considered only St. Augustine's plan for the Christian education of youth. Due to his lifelong quest for wisdom, he has seen to it that the finest flower of the natural heritage of mankind has been gathered and saved in his plan for Christian culture.[3] The quadrivium has been restored, and philosophy itself, the science of wisdom and virtue, has been incorporated in the order of studies which is being arranged for Catholic youth. A question remains concerning the trivium. In this area of the cultivation of the word, both internal and spoken, St. Augustine finds the objectionable features in the condition of the schools of antiquity from which he has resigned. His work in this aspect of the course of studies presupposes the general background sketched above in Chapter I, concerning the gradual elimination of sacred history and the consequent secularization of the classical *paideia*. The trivium has gradually declined into a cultivation of a purely externalized word, cultivated emptily, without substantial content, and indeed imbued with an indifference to truth, with a corruption and a conversion to created things.[4] These vestiges of primitive revelation and the broken remnants of sacred doctrine and sacred history are completely unable to provide for the spiritual and moral welfare of youth. The great question in the regeneration and renewal of education and of human culture, therefore, is the question whether God has spoken. In his conversion to the Catholic Church, Augustine has found the answer to this question, and his life-work will be the introduction of this answer into his professional work as a teacher and educator. It will provide the complete cleansing and healing of the educational and cultural heritage of mankind. Not only had the quadrivium been omitted by the schools of rhetoric, but the trivium had become swollen with pride and immorality, and empty of purpose and content. Its grammar was nothing but Vergil and the poets; its rhetoric was nothing but Cicero and the skepticism of the New Academy; and logic had declined into mere sophism. The restoration of the quadrivium and the addition of philosophy to it, it was clear to Augustine, could not solve the entire problem constituted by the secularization of the *paideia*. The trivium likewise must undergo its regeneration and renewal, for it touches the very heart of human personal and social welfare: its object is the study of man, the principles by which he lives, the meaning and the examples of his past, and the very nature which he possesses, which it is his responsibility to cultivate through the culture of the *logos*, the word.[5]

The project which St. Augustine has in mind for education, the "difficult undertaking" which he is projecting since his conversion to the Catholic faith, involves two means to renovate the heritage of *paideia*. The first is Christian philosophy, a new and clear perception of natural wisdom, which purges and restores the entire circle of the arts and disciplines of human culture. The second is Christian Doctrine, a new body of truth which has a special bearing upon the field of education. Throughout his life, as he says in his *Retractationes*, he progressed intellectually, even though, as Gilson points out, he did not change his fundamental principles. His view of philosophy, its place and its importance in education, he retained to the end of his life. The place of sacred doctrine, however, and the manner in which it is to be organized into the order of studies, is a matter upon which he developed insight and power as he lived his Catholic years, until he came to the educational synthesis contained in *De doctrina christiana*, his books on the Scriptures, the *quaestiones* concerning them, and his major theological works such as the *De Trinitate* and *The City of God*.

But a question arises immediately. Is not the culture of the human arts and disciplines sufficient to lead the soul to God? Should not this universe, and the study of it as an ordered cosmos, be sufficient to bring the youthful mind to the knowledge of the Creator? In his conversion to the Catholic faith, St. Augustine perceived the answer to such educational questions by an intuitive grasp which remained with him throughout his life. Such an answer in educational matters was indeed precisely the approach of the Neoplatonists. For St. Augustine, however, this was simply intellectual pride, foredoomed to disaster because it misconceived the actual condition of human nature. Human beings are indeed enslaved in the darkness of Plato's cave, but it will take more than the culture of the human arts and disciplines, more even than a renovated and restored human *paideia*, to liberate the soul of man. St. Augustine realizes more fully and realistically the nature of this imprisonment, and the impotence of man to free himself. Men are in a far more sorry condition than Plato knew.

"What is it that presses upon us, and keeps us from seeing?" Augustine asks; "Is it not our iniquity? Sometimes dust or smoke or perhaps a passing illness affects and presses upon the bodily eye, and keeps us from seeing this earthly light. . . . So with the stained heart: shall you lift it up to God? Must it not first be healed so that you may see? Is one not found proud when he says: first I shall see, and then I shall believe? . . . Whence is it that he does not see? The cause is the multitude of sins which obscures the eye. . . . Let the iniquities therefore be removed, and let the sins be forgiven. Let the weight be lifted from the eye, and let that be healed which is weak . . . for all this there must be used the stinging precept as a medicine." [6]

This is the key to St. Augustine's further thinking and

planning for Christian education: his clear perception of the condition of human nature left by original sin. "We have been born blind from Adam, and thus we have need of the illumination which comes to us from Christ." [7]

The Christian vision of man does indeed see him imprisoned in a dark cave. "We find ourselves in this life as night birds, when they are brought out to see the light . . . and not being able to see, the doctor applies medicines, the following medicines: Thou shalt not steal, Thou shalt not bear false witness, Thou should not commit adultery, Thou shalt not defraud. . . . " [8] Already from the beginning of his life and thought as a Catholic, Augustine sees that Sacred Scripture is the new light from God which restores and heals and brightens the inner eye of the human mind in its present condition. "Now, however, when we are still in the darknesses of this mortality, we walk according to the light of the Scripture. Be your own judge," he urges, "and do not find pleasure in yourself. What you find in yourself justly displeasing, castigate, emend and correct. Holy Scripture is a mirror for you. This mirror has a brilliance which never deceives, a brightness which never flatters, never a chooser of persons. Your mirror does not deceive; do not desire to deceive yourself. Be your own judge, become sad over your uncleanness, so that going away sad over your condition, you may return corrected and beautiful in form." [9]

As the light of the sun is constantly present to the blind man, although he is completely oblivious of it, so with wisdom. Divine truth and wisdom are constantly present to the mind of man, but unless the blindness of the inner eye is healed, this light will never be perceived or even known. The blindness is a moral blindness; the absence of God is not physical, but a moral one. It is a darkness which affects the mind of man because of sin. "Let the mind and heart be cleansed in order that it may see God. . . . The dust and the smoke of the inner eye are human sins and iniquities. Remove all those things from that inner eye, and you will see the wisdom which is present everywhere: because God is wisdom itself. Thus the Scripture says, Blessed are the clean of heart, for they shall see God" (Matthew 5:8).[10]

This brings St. Augustine to consider that the cleansing of the human heart and inner eye is the work of the Catholic faith. "By faith let the hearts of men be cleansed," he writes, "for the sake of these inner eyes of the mind, whose blindness is not to understand, so that they may be opened, and gradually see more and more strongly and clearly." [11] Commenting on Philip's question concerning the Father, St. Augustine notes that the Apostle did not have that healthy inner eye as yet whereby man comes to know the Father. The sharp edge of the mind had not yet been restored. This restoration, this healing of the inner eye for this perception, must take place through an anointing by faith. "Walk in the way of faith, that you may come to see." [12]

"Our entire concern in this life, brethren," continues St. Augustine, "is to heal the eye of the heart, in order that God may be known. It is for this that the sacred mysteries are celebrated; for this the sermons of God are preached; for this the moral exhortations of the Church take place, by which we are urged to correct the carnal concupiscences and our way of living, being conformed and renouncing, not by word alone but by a changed life, the ways of this world. Indeed it is with this that the entire Divine and Holy Scripture is concerned, that there be purged within us that which hinders us from the knowledge of God." The inner eye of the mind is hindered from the light just as the bodily eyes common to us and the lower animals are impeded. "Thus the eye of the heart is likewise disturbed and affected, and averts itself from the light of justice, and neither dares look at it nor is able to do so." [13]

In his conversion to the Catholic faith, therefore, St. Augustine sees the problem of the education of mankind in the light of this religious renewal and purgation of the heart and of the inner eye of the mind. Eternal wisdom, the quest for which has occupied his life, is this light which the unpurged condition of the soul prevents a man from seeing.[14]

Our inner eyes are sick. The sickness must be cured, if human knowledge is to be regenerated and renewed. The instrument of knowledge within us must be healed.[15] He sees the field of education as a part of the work of the "grace of the Christians," upon the "mass of perdition from Adam." [16] Catholic education, *doctrina christiana,* both in its theory and in its practical organization of the order of studies, will go hand in hand with this Christian conversion and renewal of the inner nature of man by grace. It will be a teaching that corresponds to that process, and indeed participates in it.

The Reality and the Concept of Sacred History

The idea of conversion was brought graphically upon the consciousness of the neophyte in the liturgy of the early Church by the physical turning of those about to be baptized from the west, from the pomps of the devil, toward the east, toward the light, toward God who is the light, toward the Lord who is our illumination.[17] St. Augustine saw all of these things, during his preparation for baptism and at the ceremony in Milan, in the light of his educated grasp of the human situation in antiquity. Member of the teaching profession as he was, he perceived the true religion as the efficacious education of mankind. It possesses and embodies authority, and the humble submission to this authority in the Catholic faith teaches the human mind the divine plan of conversion, of reform, of regeneration and renewal.[18] His own personal conversion, later to be described in the *Confessions,* is experienced by him as part of this great historic turn of mankind to God in the Catholic Church.

The central fact in this conversion is the figure of Jesus Christ. St. Augustine's conversion is the victory of Christ in his mind and soul. "In the night of this world, my brethren," he writes, "let us pay close attention to prophecy: for our Lord willed in humility to come to our weakness and to the inner darknesses and to the night of our heart. He came as a man . . . to be contemned and rejected by the Jews, but to be honored and received by us. . . . He came in such a fashion, therefore, to fulfill his office of offering light by giving testimony. For what need would there have been that John as a light should have given testimony concerning the day, if the day itself could have been perceived properly by our weakness? But we could not: thus he took upon himself our weakness, and through weakness healed our weakness . . . ; of his own body he made a medicine for the inner light of our minds. Because therefore the Lord came in this fashion, and because we are still in the night of this world, it is necessary for us to hear the prophecies: for it is by means of the prophecies that we convince the pagans who contradict Christ. Who is Christ, asks a pagan? We answer to him "He is the one whom the prophets foretold." St. Augustine proceeds to summarize the major predictions of the prophets concerning the Messiah, and sketches the manner in which all prophecy converges upon the figure of Christ. "Hear the prophets," he calls, "O men of death!" [19]

From the beginning of his conversion and during the weeks at Cassiciacum, St. Augustine was projecting mentally the two works published later which describe his view of the way in which the mind perceives the Providential work of God in history, culminating in the Incarnation, and spreading over the world in the Catholic Church. These are the treatises *De vera religione,* and *On the Advantage of Believing.* In these luminous pages Augustine lays bare the work of the Christian mind, of Christian philosophy, in coming to a new understanding of the historic life of mankind and of the divine revelation which that history contains. "This is, believe me," he writes, "the healthiest authority; this is the first way of uplifting our souls from their dwelling on earth; this is conversion to the true God from the love of this world. It is authority alone that moves fools to hasten on to wisdom. . . . For, if the Providence of God does not preside over human affairs, there is no point in busying oneself about religion." [20]

This is the point at which Christian philosophy meets

the religion which has been revealed by God. Christian philosophy rises to its new and distinct knowledge of God and the soul, perceives the fact of creation, and discerns a providential order in the things which God is making. In this providential care for mankind, somewhere, somehow, there must be a true religion. "Some, I know not what, inner conscience exhorts all better souls, both publicly and privately as it were, that God is to be sought and served. We must not give up hope that God has established some authority, on which, if we rely, just as on a sure step, we will be raised up to God." [21] St. Augustine is describing the process by which his own mind came to discern the reality and the truth of the Catholic Church. "And since it is not easy to recognize God through reason, as has been said, it was necessary to present certain miracles to the very eyes (which fools use much more readily, than they do their minds), so that, moved by authority, men's lives and habits might first be purged, and thus become amenable to the acceptance of reason. Since, then, it had to be that man be imitated, and yet that hope be not placed in him, what could have been done more indulgently and generously by divine providence than that the very wisdom of God, pure, eternal, unchangeable, to whom we needs must cling, should deign to take upon himself manhood? . . . Thus he won our love by his wondrous birth and his miracles, and he banished fear by his death and resurrection." [22]

Recurring constantly in the works of St. Augustine like a vein of pure gold, again and again in his commentaries on the Psalms, in his sermons, in his exegetical treatises, and in most formal fashion in his treatise on *The City of God,* is his perception of the two-fold divine seal upon the authority of the Catholic Church. The first is the fact of prophecy among the Jews, and its fulfillment in Jesus Christ; the second is the efficacious progress of the Catholic Church, spread over the whole world as the most evident fact of his times. "This is the work of Divine Providence," he writes, "achieved through the prophecies of the prophets, through the humanity and teaching of Christ, through the journeys of the apostles, through the sufferings, the crosses, the blood and death of the martyrs, through the admirable lives of the saints, and in all these, at opportune times, through miracles worthy of such great deeds and virtues." [23] Indeed, the second of these two basic arguments stands independently and has its own convincing power. "Even if no testimonies concerning Christ and the Church had occurred in advance," writes St. Augustine, "ought not the unexpected illumination of the human race by divine brightness move everyone to believe, when we behold false gods abandoned; their images everywhere dashed to pieces; their temples razed or converted to other uses; so many vain rites rooted out from the most inveterate human traditions; and the one true God called upon by all classes of people?" [24]

St. Augustine came in this way to the feet of Christ and offered himself for baptism. "When, then, we see so much help on God's part, so much progress and such fruit, shall we hesitate to bury ourselves in the bosom of that Church? For starting from the apostolic chair down through successions of bishops, even out to the open confession of all mankind, it has possessed the crown of authority." [25] This, then, is the way in which divine authority makes itself known to the mind of his human creatures, this is the place where the authority is located, and here is the voice which it uses to speak. Man, with his darkened and wounded inner eye of the spirit, cannot come to God, cannot rise to wisdom by himself. "But this is now our concern—that we be able to be wise, that is, to cling to the truth. Surely, the sordid soul cannot do this. And the sordidness of the soul, to sum it up briefly, is love of anything whatever save the soul and God; insofar as anyone is more completely freed from these vices, he will the more easily gaze on truth. . . . And for a man that cannot see the truth, authority is at hand to make him fit for this, and to allow him to purge himself." [26] This is St. Augustine's view of conversion. It is the great contemporary fact and reality visible in the history of mankind in general in his times, and realized by the grace of God in his own personal life. This is Christian conversion: at one and the same time an intellectual illumination of the mind and a moral cleansing of the human will, a regeneration and renewal of the whole soul of man.

From the viewpoint of his powerful intelligence, the conversion of St. Augustine brought him a vision of universal history which occupied his mind's eye from that point through all his works to the end of his life. It is the vision of the whole world turning to God in the Catholic Church of Jesus Christ. It is very nearly the theme of all his preaching and the thesis of his exegetical and theological works.

This *universal* or Catholic Church, not local like the heresies and the schisms, is the conversion of all mankind to God. It belongs not to a race or a nation, but to man as such. This immense Church is literally the converted state of mankind to God. The Church for St. Augustine is the whole earth.[27] "The whole earth has become the chorus of Christ." [28] The sixth age in the historic life of mankind on this planet is that of rebirth and reform by means of the Gospel: this process elevates the Catholic Church as the spiritual sovereign over all nations.[29] St. Augustine notes that the rule of Christ extends in his Church even over the barbarians never conquered by Rome, and in his view of mankind only a few nations remain outside the Church.[30]

In St. Augustine's spiritual insight, this world-wide fact of the Catholic Church is not only itself a fulfillment of prophecy, but the guarantee to men in the present that the prophecies still unfulfilled will take place in the future. "If the things had not come to pass which have been foretold," he writes, "we would despair that they would ever take place; if however all things which have been foretold concerning the Church are already visibly fulfilled before us, as even the eyes of the blind can see, why therefore should we have any doubt concerning the future fulfillment of the remaining prophecies? When it was stated that the Church of Christ was going to extend over the entire earth, the statement was made by only a few, and it was ridiculed by the multitude. But now that very thing is fulfilled, which was predicted so long ago: the Church has been extended throughout the whole earth. . . . Christ has come from the seed of Abraham, and all nations of the earth are now, even already, blessed in Christ. Schisms and heresies of the future were predicted: we see them now as present facts. The persecutions were predicted: they are now facts of history, having been accomplished by the governments addicted to the idols. . . . The seed of blood has been scattered, and the harvest of the Church has risen from it. . . . It was even foretold in the past that the very idols themselves were going to be overthrown by the name of Christ: for we also find this written in the Scriptures. It was only a few years ago that Christians read this prophecy, and did not see it as a fact. . . . Now in our times, however, even this has been fulfilled and stands as a fact before our eyes. All things, therefore, which have been predicted in the past concerning the Church, we now see fulfilled. Only the day of judgment remains. Shall we think that it will not also be fulfilled?" [31]

St. Augustine's consciousness of the world-wide extent of the Church comes to the fore constantly in his works against the Donatist schism. "It has been evangelized to us that the Church in future time will extend throughout the entire earth. This was foretold in the Law, in the prophets, in the psalms, and indeed Christ our Lord himself testified to it, for he foretold that his Church would begin from Jerusalem and extend out through all the nations . . . until it reached the whole earth. The facts of history have fulfilled these words . . . , for the Church is still growing in the whole earth, and henceforward to the end of the world it will be gathering also the nations that remain. . . ." [32]

In his mind's eye, always quick to grasp the past ages of mankind as well as the present world-wide condition of the human family, St. Augustine continually perceives the concept of historical succession. "The Church is the body of this

Head [Christ the Lord], a body which is not confined to this one place, but which is both in this place and in every place throughout the whole earth; nor is it a Church confined to this one time, but rather a Church which reaches from Abel up to those who are going to born at the end of time . . . , the entire People of the Saints who form one single city." [33]

St. Augustine's Christian philosophy, as we noted in the preceding chapter, has penetrated to the concept of God as the pure spirit who is the God of creation, bringing order and plan into his works. It is this Providential order which St. Augustine marks in the vision which his mind's eye perceives of human life on earth. "All these things, therefore, which are made by the divine artistry, manifest a certain unity in themselves and form an order." [34] It is precisely the authority of the Catholic Church, and the religious knowledge which it brings to the human mind, which enables the inner eye to perceive this unity of the historic life of man and the providential order in the succession of human affairs. "In following this religion," he writes in the treatise which reveals the original religious thinking of his conversion, "our chief concern is with the prophetic history of the dispensation of divine providence in time—what God has done for the salvation of the human race, renewing and restoring it unto eternal life." [35] From the very beginning, in other words, the Catholic religion presses upon the reflecting mind as a fact of history; it is the means whereby the providential care and order and succession become known.[36] This providential order, seen by the eye of religious faith as a fact in the succession of human things, is the very foundation of the religious mind and of the religious approach to human existence. "That God may be feared," St. Augustine writes, "one must become persuaded that all things are ruled by divine providence; for it is not by the various reasons, which a person is able to explore, which causes the mind to perceive the beauty of virtue, but also the examples, whether more recent ones if there are any, or those which come to the mind from history, and those especially which divine providence itself, either in the Old or in the New Testament, has set up for us through the supreme authority of religion." [37] Here St. Augustine implies a teaching of this providential order or "sacred history," and his fundamental grasp of the principles of education as such comes to light. For the very idea of human education is contained in this concept of an uplifting moral instruction that proceeds not only by means of reasons and principles, but also by means of examples provided for the human mind by history, and indeed, in the present providential order, by the sacred history of the Bible. This is the root principle of St. Augustine's approach to Christian Doctrine, and the direct antithesis of Voltaire and the pedagogy of historical atheism during the last two centuries.

St. Augustine's conversion to the Church, therefore, which is simultaneously a conversion to Jesus Christ, brought with it a powerful illumination of his mind which enabled him to grasp the present state of mankind throughout the world as one of striking conversion to God in the Catholic Church, and to see the historic state of mankind as a providential order, a succession of human times and conditions and social states, proceeding in orderly fashion toward this world-wide conversion which is the dominant intellectual experience of his life. From the viewpoint of his educational theory and practice, it is important to grasp these roots of his understanding of universal history, and to recognize that it is an illumination of the mind which comes from divine faith.

"Faith opens the way for the intelligence," St. Augustine writes, "and unbelief closes it. Who would not be moved toward divine faith by the great order of historical facts from the beginning of time, and the very connection of the times, whereby past events testify to our present times, and the things which happened long ago confirm what we see recently, and what we see recently in turn confirms the things of earlier times? One man is chosen from the Chaldeans, endowed with faithful piety, to whom the divine promises after the long series of the centuries are being now fulfilled, and it was foretold that all nations would be blessed in his seed. (Genesis 12:2). . . . This nation, growing stronger, is brought forth from the slavery of Egypt . . . , then, with sin likewise growing . . . it is carried forward to the time of the Incarnation and manifestation of Christ." [38]

The entire Old Testament and all of its institutions, St. Augustine points out, state clearly the coming fact of the Incarnation of God in the flesh, Christ, the Word of God, the Son of God. "At last Christ actually came: there is fulfilled in his origin, in his life, in his teachings, in his deeds, in his sufferings, in his death, in his resurrection, and in his ascension, all the prophecies of the Prophets. He sends the Holy Spirit (Acts 2:2). . . . The preaching of godliness and of the true religion is accompanied by fitting signs and miracles. The violent attacks of infidelity are aroused against his creatures, . . . yet the peoples are converted with a wonderful ease, . . . while at the same time persecutions increase . . . and great talent and men of highest education come into the Church. The infidelity of the Jews and the conversion of the Gentiles—all is foretold, and now stand fulfilled before our eyes. . . . In the face of this panorama, what mind desirous of eternity, and moved by the brevity of this earthly life, would offer further objection to this culmination and this overwhelming light of the divine authority?" [39]

In various places of his works, especially in the sermons, the commentaries on the psalms, and in his *De vera religione*, St. Augustine returns repeatedly to this fundamental historical insight and illumination which his conversion entailed. It is the reality of sacred history which marks St. Augustine's mind, the providential order or succession of things in human history, leading up to this vast contemporary conversion of the world to Christ in the Catholic Church which he was experiencing and in which he personally was participating.[40]

The reality of sacred history is followed by the concept of sacred history in St. Augustine's intelligence; it is this concept which will be of fundamental importance in the program of Christian education which he will elaborate, for it will involve the Sacred Scriptures.

For the Scriptures play a central role in this insight into human history which fills the mind of Augustine. "God is faithful," he writes, "who made himself our debtor; not by accepting anything from us, but by promising us great blessings. Promise, however, was not enough. He even chose to be bound by writing, creating for us a kind of bond for his promises. So that when he began to fulfill his promises, we might contemplate in Scripture the order of their accomplishment." [41] It is the Scriptures, therefore, which make this reality of sacred history visible to the human mind; the Bible is the divine instrument for bringing the concept of sacred history to birth among men. This mighty vision of human history which St. Augustine's synthetic mind compresses in the unforgettable image of the murmur between two silences, of the torrent springing from the sudden rains of spring, is a reality which he has learned to see from his study of the Sacred Scriptures. [42]

Since this point is so fundamental in the theory and practice of Christian education, let us conclude these reflections on the conversion of the whole earth to God in the Church of Christ, and on the order or providential succession of things in human affairs which have brought this wonder to pass, by reflecting upon the explicit manner in which St. Augustine relates human history and human affairs to the pages of Sacred Scripture. "My brief word of counsel to you," he writes to Faustus the Manichean, ". . . is this, that if you acknowledge the supreme authority of the Scriptures, you should also recognize that authority, which from the time of Christ himself, through the ministry of his apostles and through a regular succession of bishops in the sees of the apostles has come down to our own day, safely conserved and made illustrious throughout the whole world." [43] The authority of the Scriptures, in other words, which illuminate the mind with this insight into the providential order of human history, is one thing with the authority of the Church. The two form one single divine authority which has been spread over the whole earth by the world-wide victory of the Church. Even more frequently than he speaks of the Church, St. Augustine refers to these Sacred Scriptures which the Church carries as instruments for teaching this renovating grasp of things. "You recall," he writes, "that since there is one Word of God spread out in all the Scriptures, and as through the many voices of the saints the one Divine Word sounds forth, the same Word which was in the beginning with God, not having a variety of syllables there, because it does not have a succession of times; nor should it be wondered at on our part, when this same Word descended on account of our weakness, that it would be manifested in a series of sounds. . . ." [44] Thus St. Augustine perceives the Word of God as coming to man in the Scriptures, gradually, across the centuries: wisdom itself has come toward us and we toward it, in a joyful encounter.[45]

Finally, this world-wide victory of the Church which wears the very crown of divine authority makes manifest to us the self-same authority which places the Scriptures in our hands and imposes them upon our minds. "This authority," St. Augustine says, speaking of the Holy Scriptures, "God has first of all placed in his Church." [46] The Scriptures are the Scriptures because this divine authority of the Church has proclaimed them to be the Word of God. "The Scriptures are those which the Church receives and holds." [47] This is St. Augustine's well-known doctrine of the canonicity: "I would not believe the Gospel," he states in a famous passage, "unless the authority of the Catholic Church moved me to do so." [48] Speaking of St. John's epistle, he writes, "This epistle is canonical; it is read throughout all nations; it has edified the whole world. In it you are told by the Spirit of God, that God is love. Now if you dare, go against God, and refuse to love your brother." [49] In this brief passage St. Augustine's entire doctrine concerning the Sacred Scriptures is summarized: the Bible is divinely inspired, for the Holy Spirit speaks through it and in it; and it is read throughout the whole world, because the Catholic Church, victorious in the whole world, retains and accepts it as a divine writing. Thus the Bible comes to the hands of Christians with the Catholic faith and through the Catholic authority, and they perceive its divine character by means of the light and authority of divine faith.[50]

Viewing all these things synthetically, as Augustine was wont to do, we see that his conversion involved a bright illumination of the human scene, world-wide in present extent, and reaching backwards through the corridors of time to a perception of the orderly sequence of things which led to Christ and his Church. It is a history of God's humility and condescension toward mankind which the Sacred Scriptures make known to us as a fact. This is the very basis of the teaching of religious knowledge; it contains the foundation of religious education. "It is good that those who are not yet able to rise to a knowledge of spiritual and external things, should be nourished by the faith of temporal history, which the wisdom of God elaborated for our salvation, in whom is salvation for all who believe. That moved by authority, we might obey his precepts, and thus cleansed and purged, and rooted in charity, we might begin to run with the saints, no longer as children in milk, but as growing to stronger food, comprehending the length and the depth and the breadth and the heighth. . . ." [51] Thus the fact and reality of sacred history brings to mind in these Christian times an illumination which is a powerful impetus for carrying out this moral cleansing and for embarking upon the way of divine charity.

In this way the inner eye of the intelligence, weak and half blind, is healed by the Divine Scriptures. The Scriptures, like parchment unrolled, are as a second heaven spread over mankind, through the world-wide victory and teaching mission of the Catholic Church, efficaciously leading the mind and soul of man up to the things of God.

St. Augustine's Attitude Toward Sacred Scripture

The conversion of St. Augustine can be viewed under several aspects. It is, first of all, the personal return to Jesus Christ. This entails finding him in the Catholic Church. This, in turn, means that St. Augustine joined that great march of persons in classical antiquity from paganism to Christ which produced the social victory of the Church on the face of universal history. Since the authority of the Church holds the Scriptures in hand and gives them to the minds of these human spirits turning to God, conversion also means the discovery of the Bible. Finally, since it is intellectual pride which obscures the perception of the Bible as it really is by the inner eye of the intelligence, the conversion of St. Augustine, like the conversion of this multitude as a whole, was a passage from pride to intellectual humility.[52] Etienne Gilson is completely correct in viewing the conversion of St. Augustine as a discovery of humility.[53] This discovery of intellectual humility is one thing with his personal discovery of the Bible. In his quest for wisdom, as we recall, the reading of Cicero's *Hortensius* when he was nineteen years of age was a turning point: it left him with an undying thirst for truth. Looking for it first in the Bible, his literary pride at the time kept him from making the discovery, and he turned to the Manicheans instead, with their superficial rationalism. This attitude of proud disdain of the Sacred Scriptures lasted through the years in which he suffered his deepening fall into moral helplessness. Intellectually considered, St. Ambrose's preaching, which restored to St. Augustine the concept of the intellectual integrity of the Divine Scriptures, was the basic factor in his return to life. Then follow the scene in the garden, with its reading of St. Paul, the discovery of Christ Incarnate in the Gospels, the birth of a new attitude of spirit, humble and receptive toward

God, and a new perceptiveness regarding the truth and beauty of the Scriptures. The proper place has come, then, to analyze more in detail St. Augustine's teaching concerning the Bible.

St. Augustine's submission to the divine authority of the Church, his acceptance by divine faith of the Incarnation of the Son of God, the birth, the life and the redeeming death of Jesus Christ, and his intellectual submission to the Sacred Scriptures, are all one spiritual insight, one luminous intelligible light which constitutes the intellectual side of St. Augustine's conversion. His point of departure as a Catholic thinker, therefore, is the Sacred Scripture: its truth and inerrancy, the fact that it is eternity inserting itself into time, even as the Incarnation itself. "I said: 'Lord, is not this your Scripture true, since you who are true and you, Truth itself, have set it forth? . . . To this you answer me that you are my God, and with a mighty voice you speak to your servant in his interior ear and break through my deafness, and cry out: 'O man, true it is that what my Scripture says, I myself say. Yet that Scripture speaks in time, but time does not affect my Word, because that Word exists along with me in equal eternity.' " [54] The last three books of the *Confessions*, as a matter of fact, are nothing else than St. Augustine's confession of dogmatic faith in the inspiration and divinity of the Bible, and his expression of this faith in his whole-hearted submission to the Scriptures. He concludes his *Confessions* with the books on the Bible and Genesis, revealing his personal reaction to the Word of God; after his conversion the Sacred Scriptures are his light and the supreme pleasure of his intellectual life.[55] This intellectual life is dominated by his grasp of sacred history, which is his characteristic view of reality: a perception of the historical development of the human family, in terms of the Sacred Scripture.[56]

As St. Augustine's apostolate of the pen unfolds, it will become apparent to all down to the present day that the Scriptures occupy the central position in his intellectual life: the works of St. Augustine increasingly devote themselves to the exegesis of Sacred Scripture, to the defense of the Scriptures against heretical misunderstanding, to positive questions of a theological nature concerning various aspects of the Scriptures: and finally there is the total grasp of the meaning of the ordered succession of the two Testaments in *The City of God*. The doctrine of St. Augustine on Sacred Scripture rests upon two doctrinal facts which underlie all of his writings, and which are the constant presupposition of his preaching and teaching. They are the fact that the Scriptures are *canonical*, namely, that we have them because of the authority of the Catholic Church proposing them to mankind as inspired. The second doctrinal fact is the *inspiration* of the Sacred Scriptures, the fact that God himself is their author.[57]

The fact of inspiration as an article of belief in the works of St. Augustine is manifested by the formulas which he uses to quote the Bible. He calls it "the Word of God," "the Divine Words," "the Divine Sermon," "the Works of God," "the Holy Books," "the Divine Scripture," and "Holy Scripture." Again he calls the Scriptures the "Divine Authorities," the "Writings of God," the "Letters of God," the "Divine Testimonies," and the "Prophetical Letters." [58] He explains that St. Paul uses expressions such as "Isaias said," or "It is written," and so on, because he is speaking of "that Scripture in which the authority of God is present." Such expressions in the Bible itself "show us that in this Scripture God himself is speaking." He points out that St. Paul goes so far as to use the words Scripture and God interchangeably, "because the Scripture is from God." "Thus," concludes St. Augustine, "the apostolic authority attests to us by these manners of speaking that the Scriptures come to us from God who is good and true." [59]

This, then, is the basic teaching of St. Augustine concerning the Bible: it is inspired by God, and hence has God himself as its author. He states that it is God himself "who both inspired the Sacred Scriptures, and created this visible cosmos." [60] "Each of the two Scriptures [the Old and the New Testaments] form one writing, because it was written by the one Spirit of Truth which inspires it." [61] He summarizes his teaching in his book on Catholic education: "Our sacred writers, whose writings are divinely inspired, constitute for us the canon of Scriptures proposed to us by the salvific authority." [62]

St. Augustine, therefore, accepts the Sacred Scriptures with a faith which he calls "simple and certain," an integral part of the Catholic faith which constitutes the very substance of his conversion to God and his inner purification from the false love of this world. From this point forward, the inerrancy of the Sacred Scriptures is his guiding rule in their interpretation, an inerrancy which results directly from this divine inspiration and authorship. This faith in the Scriptures is prior to all study of the difficulties proposed by heresy or unbelief, as we shall see when we come to the academic use of the Scriptures in St. Augustine's educational program. In his preaching to his people, he makes this point perfectly clear. "You may say what you wish, they tell us, but we maintain that we discover that your Gospels disagree with each other in their assertions concerning Christ, and therefore they cannot be true when they are in this dissidence. By showing these difficulties and disagreements, the objectors go on, we rightly reject your faith, else you who accept the faith must show us the concordancy and agreement of the Scriptures. What kind of disagreement will you demonstrate, we ask? An open one, they reply to us, to which no one can take exception. . . . Pay close attention, dearly beloved, [St. Augustine warns his hearers] and see how rightly for our salvation the apostle cautions us, saying: Therefore you have received Christ Jesus our Lord . . ., confirmed in the faith. We must firmly abide, therefore, in this simple and certain faith, so that Christ himself may open to us his faithful what in itself is hidden and full of difficulties. Because, just as the same apostle says, in him are hidden all the treasures of wisdom and knowledge. These things are not hidden in the Scriptures in order to promote denials, but so that we may be challenged to seek in faith. This is the usefulness of this aspect of the Scriptures. Honor in the Scripture, therefore, what you do not yet understand; and honor it so much the more, as you perceive it more deeply veiled to the understanding. . . ." [63]

"The Scripture cannot lie," states St. Augustine categorically.[64] The eternal life toward which we look forward comes to us through the remission of our sins. As long as our sins remain, we are in a state of enmity and alienation toward God, which is the result of our own evil. This is because "Scripture does not lie," when it tells us that our sins separate us from God.[65] The truth of the Sacred Scriptures is constantly connected by St. Augustine with the moral truth of the inner state of the soul, and always the germ of the future work, *The City of God*, arising from these two inner states of man, is perceptible in his preaching and teaching.

"I have learned," St. Augustine states, laying down the basic principle of approach to the study of the Scriptures, "to bring this reverential fear to the canonical Books alone and to pay them this respect: I most firmly believe that their human authors were absolutely free of error in writing them. If I find a passage which appears to be contrary to the truth, I know immediately that either the copyists have made a slip of the pen, or that the translators have not expressed the original properly, or that I myself simply do not understand." [66] In St. Augustine's view of things, the composition of these Sacred Scriptures is itself a part of the providence of God which governs the order of the centuries and which has constituted the authority of the Church.

"What are we therefore to understand," he writes in his book on the harmony of the Gospels, "except that these things were done under the hidden direction of the Providence of God, by which the minds of the evangelists were governed? . . . The memory of the sacred writer is itself directed by the Holy Spirit. . . . Thus the Lord himself determined that such and such be written. . . . All our holy prophets, therefore, manifest a wonderful assent among each other, because they are spoken by the one and same

Spirit. . . . And hence without hesitation or doubt everything is to be accepted which the Holy Spirit spoke through them. . . . This is therefore especially to be understood concerning the holy prophets, and especially to be taught, that we should receive the books of all of them as one single book, in which no fundamental disunity or disagreement is to be found, and in which a greater consistency of truth is present, than we grant in the books composed even by the most learned of men. Hence whatever argument unbelievers or unlearned men seek from this source of disagreement or inconsistency, as if to show the disharmony of the holy Gospels, ought to be taken by the faithful and learned men as an opportunity to show the unity of the Sacred Scriptures, even including the prophets of the Old Testament." [67]

The two Testaments convey one intelligible message to the mind of man; this unity of the two Testaments provides the fundamental succession in human affairs, the New Testament succeeding the Old, which gives St. Augustine the basis for the understanding of history which he will teach in his educational program.[68]

The Catechetical Teaching of the Bible

St. Augustine learned all of this, humanly speaking, from his spiritual father, St. Ambrose. His preaching and his catechetical instructions at Milan revealed this intelligible world of Christianity to the mind of Augustine: the reality and the concept of sacred history, and the luminous inner conviction, indeed one of divine faith itself, that the canonical Scriptures are the very word of God incarnate in human speech. Above all, however, he learned that the Catholic Church, now extended over the whole earth, is "crowned with divine authority." It teaches these truths and presents the Sacred Scriptures as the authorized representative and spokesman of God on earth. St. Augustine learned all these things, as all adult converts at that time learned them, in the teaching which the Church carried on in the catechumenate. St. Augustine's brief reference to his own baptismal instruction makes the point explicitly. He returned from Cassiciacum to Milan for the course of instructions, to consider "the depths of your counsel concerning the salvation of mankind." [69]

St. Augustine's baptism is in the fullest sense the beginning of a new life for him, the new life of grace, and a new life of apostolic work in the service of God on earth. "As a foundation of the edifice, we must place first the divine testimonies," he writes in *The City of God*, in a fundamental statement of position which governs all his thought and work.[70] The Sacred Scriptures, which he receives with his Catholic faith, are his guide and often even the fount which he uses in elaborating his vision of human development. The cast of St. Augustine's mind and thought during his entire life after his conversion will be increasingly that of the Bible. St. Augustine's quest for truth, kindled when he was a youth by Cicero's *Hortensius*, has led him to baptism into the Catholic Church and to wholehearted acceptance of the Catholic faith. This love of truth continues to dominate his life and governs his future thought and work as a Catholic. Finding the Catholic Church everywhere through the victory of the martyrs, he encounters the Bible likewise distributed everywhere and daily entering more deeply into the knowledge and the awareness of the people. This universal teaching authority of the Church, implemented by means of the Sacred Scriptures, is the striking new intellectual fact which his conversion entails. Augustine, the imperial *rhetor*, the great philosophic mind, has become the man of faith: his mind bends in that humility which he prizes henceforth, and he receives the Bible as the very word of God. "One is your teacher." [71] The word of God incarnate in human speech, preserved in the Sacred Scriptures of the Catholic Church, teaches a great central message and lesson: the fact and the reality of the Incarnate Word of God in the flesh, in the birth, life, and redeeming death of Christ. This is the substance of the teaching of the catechumenate which St. Augustine received from St. Ambrose. After becoming a priest himself, as we have seen, his bishop assigned him responsibility for the institution of the catechumenate at Hippo. This period of St. Augustine's apostolate has bequeathed the treatise on catechetics, *The First Catechetical Instruction*, a priceless document of the patristic age which summarizes the theory and illustrates the practice in this program of Christian teaching.[72] In order to elucidate properly the place of the Bible in that original catechetical teaching and the academic program which St. Augustine is elaborating, the contents of the treatise must be analyzed.

St. Augustine's catechetical treatise is divided into two parts: the first discusses the theory of catechetical teaching, and the second illustrates the practice. Both exemplify the manner in which the Sacred Scriptures, with their message of God's providential plan and of his own Incarnation and Redemption, manifest his love for men and motivate the love of God in return.

The first part, on the theory, falls into three discussions. The first explains the method of teaching, the narration of Sacred Scripture, actually an explanation of the use of the Bible in teaching various types of prospective converts. "You have asked me, Brother Deogratias," writes St. Augustine, "to write something to you on the instructing of candidates for the catechumenate that may be of use to you. For you tell me that at Carthage, where you are a deacon, those who are to be grounded in the rudiments of the Christian faith are often brought to you. . . ." [73] "Therefore, we shall discuss, as God shall suggest to us, first the method to be followed in the narration—as I understand is your desire; then the duty of admonition and exhortation, and lastly the means by which the cheerfulness in question is to be secured." [74]

"The narration is complete," continues St. Augustine, "when the beginner is first instructed from the text: *In the beginning God created heaven and earth*, down to the present period of Church history." [75] This does not mean, of course, that the catechist repeats verbatim the whole of the Bible, or even attempts to relate in his own words all that is contained in these books; as St. Augustine points out, "neither time serves nor any need calls." "But we ought to present all the matter in a general and comprehensive summary," he states, "choosing certain of the more remarkable facts . . . and by dwelling somewhat upon them to untie, so to speak, and spread them out to view, and offer them to the minds of our readers to examine and admire. But the remaining details we should weave into our narrative in a rapid survey." [76]

The important essential in presenting the reality and the content of sacred history, the order of God's Providence toward us, is to take the occasion to teach God's love for us, and to clarify the bearing of his love upon our present times of the Church and upon our own personal life in return. "In all things, indeed," he writes, "it not only behooves us to keep in view the goal of the precept, which is charity from a pure heart, and a good conscience, and an unfeigned faith —a standard to which we should make all that we say refer; but towards it we should also move and direct the attention of him for whose instruction we are speaking. And, in truth, for no other reason were all the things that we read in the Holy Scriptures written before our Lord's coming than to announce his coming and to prefigure the Church to be, that is to say, the people of God throughout all nations, which Church is his body. . . ." [77]

Everything turns, as St. Augustine points out, upon teaching the cause of this advent of Christ, namely, God's intention to convince us of his love for us. He gave his Son to us in this providential course of events because he loved me. The teaching has become personal, for this human individual. This becomes the motive for the love of God, that divine charity which is the purpose of law. The Christian religion is constantly concerned with this human return of divine love: charity is the purpose of the law and its plenitude. St. Augustine gives attention to teaching the motives of love, and lifts his prospective convert from his knowledge of human love to the love of God. [78] Continuing his teaching of the Bible St. Augustine shows that the spirit and motive and purpose of the Christian religion, and of the catechetical instruction, is divine charity. Christ came at the end of the ages that man might know how much God loves him, and thus begin to glow with divine love in return. The two Testaments are entirely concerned with this central fact, the advent of Christ in divine mercy and love. The Old Testament foreshadows, announces, and prepares the advent of Christ; the New Testament narrates Christ present and brings us to the love of him and to the imitation and the following of him. All of this takes place under the disposition of Divine Providence, to manifest the divine humility and to cure in its root the source of human evil and sin, namely, our spiritual pride.[79] "With this love, then," concludes St. Augustine, "set before you as an end to which you may refer all that you say, so give all your instructions that he to whom you speak by hearing may believe, and by believing may hope, and by hoping may love."

With this St. Augustine turns to the second topic of his theoretical discussion, the teaching of the moral law, and to the various questions and problems of practical Christian living. All of this, too, "must be taught by the testimonies of the Divine Books." ". . . We must instruct him fully by the evidences from the Sacred Books." [81] From beginning to end, therefore, this catechetical teaching is rooted in the Bible, conducted in the light of the basic understanding of the Bible as a succession of the two Testaments, illuminated by the motive of God himself in placing this salvific order of events in his creation. The Sacred Scriptures are the very instrument of the teaching, both for the historical narration of the economy of salvation and for the practices of Christian living. These precepts of Christian living, as St. Augustine calls them, are entirely directed toward the living of a sacramental and liturgical life, for the practical end and purpose of this catechetical instruction is to induce the candidate to active participation in the sacraments.[82]

The lengthiest portion of St. Augustine's theoretical dis-

cussion concerns the question of joyfulness in catechizing.[83]
This is actually the question of a vital teaching of religion,
a *doctrina* which the recipient will perceive as something
attractive and close to personal living. Here St. Augustine
discusses the discrepancy between our language and the flashing intuitiveness of the spirit which our language serves. Far
from solving this human problem in the way of modern vitalists and existentialists, he insists upon a systematic teaching
adapted to the person concerned, and looks to the life of
prayer in the teacher and catechist as the ultimate solution
to the vexing problem of a vital teaching. "But our chief
concern," he writes, "is what means we should adopt to in-
sure that the catechizer enjoys his work: for the more he is
able to do so, the more agreeable will he prove. And a directive indeed for this is ready at hand. For if in the case of
material wealth *God loves a cheerful giver*, how much more
in that of spiritual? But that the catechist may have this
cheerfulness in the hour of need depends on the mercy of
him who has given these commandments." [84] It is clear that
St. Augustine settles the problem of a vital teaching by the
inner life of prayer on the part of the teacher, who will thus
merit to receive this grace at the hour of need when he is at
his teaching. These principles of St. Augustine will be analyzed in greater detail in Chapter X below, in connection with
his relevance for contemporary problems in religious education.[85]

The practice of catechesis, Chapters XVI to XXVII of St.
Augustine's treatise, offer a direct insight into the concrete
manner of instructing used by the early Church. Again these
illustrations which St. Augustine gives of his own theory
make graphic the biblical nature of this catechetical teaching. After an introductory discussion with the prospective
convert on his motives for entering the Church, and the admonition to see to it that he desire nothing from the Church
except eternal life, St. Augustine gives his model instruction.
He begins with God himself, the true beginning, with the
creation and fall of mankind, and with the problem of evil

with its resulting division among men which furnishes the roots of two cities on this earth.

"And we ought not to be disturbed," St. Augustine tells his convert, "that many consent to the devil, and few follow God; for the grain, too, in comparison with the chaff, yields a much smaller amount. . . . Nor must we think that the devil has conquered because he has drawn away many with him only to be overcome, they with him, but by a few. Thus there are two cities, one of the wicked, the other of the just, which endure from the beginning of the human race even to the end of time, which are now intermingled in body, but separated in will, and which, moreover, are to be separated in body also on the day of judgment." [86] This passage, which contains the theme of St. Augustine's *City of God,* still fifteen years in the future, shows definitely that this type of basic historical understanding and underlying concept of sacred history was a part of the teaching in the catechumenate. It is important to note that St. Augustine's concept of history and his *City of God* itself grow out of this biblical teaching in the institution of the catechumenate. This is the root of a sound relationship between the catechetical instruction of the early Church and the academic teaching of the Bible which we are about to consider.

As a matter of fact, St. Augustine illustrates the manner in which he elaborates sacred history so that the prospective convert may come to that grasp of the providential order of things which is the mark of the believer in God. "So five ages of the world are ended," he writes. "Of these the first is from the beginning of the human race, that is from Adam, who was the first man to be made, to Noe, who built the ark in the time of the flood. . . . " [87] St. Augustine continues with his example of catechesis, showing that there is a great advent of universal history, under divine providence, by which all things, all men and all nations, have moved in a great march from the beginning of time toward that fullness of time in which God sent his own Son. In this way he brings his convert to understand who Christ was, and prepares him to learn of his earthly life with a proper interior disposition of soul.[88] The catechesis of the catechumenate was a teaching which used God's own book, the Holy Bible, in forming the mind and will of the convert; Sacred Scripture is the instrument of a teaching which participates in the conversion of the soul to God, which instructs in the providential order of sacred history, and which by that very fact results in the imitation and following of Christ. It remains to consider this same teaching in the academic program of Christian youth in *schola nostra,* that new program of education which the fertile mind of Augustine has been projecting since his resignation from the chair of rhetoric at Milan.

The Academic Teaching of the Bible

In the study of the educational apostolate of the Bishop of Hippo, it was noted that Augustine as a newly ordained Catholic priest received responsibility for the catechumenate, and that he at the same time continued his project, begun at Cassiciacum and Thagaste, for a regenerated and renewed educational theory and process. This is the concern of his treatise *De doctrina christiana.* It is appropriate at this point to sketch these fundamentals of Catholic education more in detail, especially from the viewpoint of the academic teaching of religion, and from that of the renewal of the academic discipline of history.

The important fundamental position here is the fact that St. Augustine continued the basic structure and features of the catechumenate in his plan for the order of academic studies in his school for Christian youth. In the academic program of Christian studies there will be the same primacy of the Bible, and it will be taught as the vision of the panorama of universal history which is God's own view of the life of the human family. The entire teaching will converge upon the person of Jesus Christ, making more clear who he is, and bringing the Incarnation into its proper position as the central teaching of Christianity and the climax of the historic life of mankind. From the Incarnation, the light of faith will make clear what the rightful and factual place of Christ is in the temporal life and development of mankind. This shifts the perspective of universal history from pagan categories of understanding, and regenerates and renews it as a sacred history in the most literal sense of the word. Secondly, there results from this centrality of the Incarnation the direct authority of Jesus Christ over the human way of life, over the moral and social order. The practical result in this academic teaching projected by St. Augustine for the school is identical with that which is the aim of the catechumenate. It is the imitation and the following of Christ, which is nothing else than a personal conversion to the last things and a renovation of personal living according to him who is the model and pattern and paradigm.[89]

When the teaching of Christian doctrine is programmed for the academic order of studies, in other words, it does not change that Christian essence which it possesses in the catechumenate. The academic situation, organized in this fashion, is simply a better opportunity for a more profound and spiritually effective apostolate of teaching. The classroom, far from hindering catechesis, enhances it in a most positive manner through the more intense study of the Sacred Scriptures which it makes possible. The essential content and the motivating purposes remain exactly the same in the catechumenate for adult converts and in the school for Christian youth. It is St. Augustine's greatest achievement in the field of education that he knew how to transfer the basic structure and heritage of teaching in the catechumenate to the order of studies which he is projecting for the Catholic school, *schola nostra,* as contrasted with that other institution of the pagan past, *schola illa.*

The Catholic Church up to this time had no definite system of schools for children and youth. The reception of adult converts, naturally enough, had occupied the apostolate. The life of St. Augustine, however, unfolds at that precise point where the reception of adults begins to recede and the educational problem of children whose parents have been Catholics all their lives becomes a primary apostolic concern of the Church.[90] Much thought had been given to the problem of a suitable education for youth, and St. Augustine entered into a patristic heritage in this regard. It was left to him, however, to elaborate fully and consistently this program for the Christian education of youth, this *tuta via* which youth should walk. St. Augustine's life and work occurred at the precise time when this earlier thought on the educational problem could be completed. The conversion of the social order as such was giving the Church the social means and strength to conduct schools, and to care for the Christian formation of the children coming from an adult population already largely Catholic.

From his conversion and his first work at Cassiciacum and through his monastery school at Thagaste, St. Augustine has been planning an education of youth which would be carried on as a service of God. The labor of scholarship and of teaching is the fitting work of the monastic life, which he conceives as a community of intellectuals converted and devoted to God. Since this conversion to God takes place in the Catholic Church which carries in hand the testimonials of God, the Sacred Scriptures, this intellectual life will concentrate as a matter of course upon the Bible. This will effect a deeper and more educated grasp of the Word of God: the entire heritage of art and science in the cultivation of the word will now be brought to bear upon the study of the Divine Scriptures, with a power and intellectual devotion hitherto given to Homer and other pagan classics. Thus grammar, rhetoric and dialectic, the disciplines of the word, keeping intact their substantial nature and procedures, will turn to a new object, the Bible, which replaces Homer and the authors as the center of academic interest. Out of this will flow the treatises on exegesis and the *quaestiones* concerning particular difficulties or points of sacred doctrine which need more copious and systematic elaboration.[91] This academic program, amounting to a regeneration and renewal of the trivuum, the disciplines of the word, offers an immediate insight into the genesis of many works in St. Augustine's *Opera omnia.*

The study of the arts and disciplines of human culture takes place now under the light of revelation, the *lumen sub quo* which gives unity and synthesis to the entire order of studies. This light is the word of God, coming, speaking educationally and from the viewpoint of the pedagogical formation of the mind, from the Sacred Scriptures. The human arts, sciences and disciplines are invested in this way with a new purpose and a new interior soul: their basic substance and structure indeed remain the same and they continue to serve the needs and the progress of civilized life in earthly society. But it is to be a cultural life carried on by the *conversi,* and the social order which they build will be a Christian social order, theocentric, turned to God. There must be, therefore, an education which prepares the young people for the social life which men like Augustine already can envision, a social life embracing the whole world in the new universe of Christ. For it rests upon a new philosophy and theology of culture, a new wisdom which sees the arts and sciences themselves regenerated and renewed, shaping, forming and fashioning young people who perceive their earthly callings in this light which has come to man in the Incarnation of the Word. This is the meaning of St. Augustine's discussion of the arts and sciences of human culture in the *De doctrina christiana.*[92]

How this Christian formation of young people for this new Christian cultural mission in earthly social living is to be accomplished, is the very substance of the treatise *De doctrina christiana.* It is an active teaching, a formation and education of Christian young people, and not mere instruction for immediate practical ends. It is a teaching of the Bible as a new discipline on their curriculum or order of studies; it is likewise a teaching of all of the other arts and sciences and disciplines of human culture, which form the order of studies, in the light of the Bible. The treatise *De doctrina christiana* in a sense is the most fundamental of all of the works of St. Augustine, the one which illuminates the rest and offers an insight into the pedagogical thought and institution which made his other works possible. The essential portion of this treatise had been finished when Augustine was still a priest; apparently due to the pressure of work, he left its last book unfinished for nearly thirty years. We have noted already that he came upon it during the writing of his *Retractationes,* and considered it so important for the full explanation of his thought that he halted his review to complete it. For he had in mind to show that Christian teaching receives the ancient heritage of rhetoric and transmutes it, changing and adapting it to the needs of Christian leadership, especially that of the priests being prepared to stand before the people with the Word of God.

Book I of the *De doctrina christiana* lays down the fundamental principles of St. Augustine's philosophy of Catholic education. This purpose is clearly academic: the work is directed primarily at the preparation of teachers. "I am undertaking," he writes, "to transmit these principles. . . ." [93] He speaks of "those devoted to the study of this subject," namely, that of "expounding Scripture," and "disclosing the mysteries of the Sacred Writings to others." He speaks of "the principles which we are trying to propose" and his exposition of "certain rules"; and the work as a whole is characterized as "this undertaking of mine which is intended to be useful." [94] He who ponders St. Augustine's own concept of his treatise will recognize that it lays down the guidelines for religious education and adds a new discipline to the cycle of the arts and sciences of culture. The book presupposes the Sacred Scriptures as an object of study, forming the subject of a new discipline; its goal is to develop an independent ability to read and to study the Scriptures with spiritual profit. "The entire treatment of the Scriptures is based upon two factors," he writes; "the method of discovering what we are to understand and the method of teaching what has been understood." [95] From the very beginning, therefore, far more is involved than a mere "handbook for preachers." These are the fundamentals of the field of education, conceived from the viewpoint of Christianity and Sacred Doctrine. St. Augustine lays down these fundamentals in Book I, analyzing Catholic education as an integral part of that light from on high which cleanses and purifies the soul, and which quenches its thirst for wisdom and happiness. It is clear from St. Augustine's discussion of cultural goods that he is projecting the methodology of an academic discipline that provides the mind with a standard of values for use in the pursuits of Christian culture. This is a far more comprehensive approach than the catechesis of the catechumenate. Throughout Book I, he presents as the basic principle of his philosophy of education the fact that the knowledge imparted by teaching serves to illuminate the goods desired, and thus the rational choices, and hence the habits, which establish the character of the educand: a Christian philosophy of culture emerges from his analysis of education.[96] The goods of culture and civilization, which provide the temporal substance of earthly life, are not to be loved for their own sake but used in the light of the Christian regeneration of the soul and the resulting holy newness of purpose in life.[97] In matchless chapters St. Augustine shows that the educator must present Almighty God to the youthful souls as changeless and living wisdom, the supreme good and value which alone can be sought and enjoyed for its own sake. On choosing inferior things, St. Augustine points out that the educator must develop keenness of mind in his students, for he is in competition always with the dulling influence of the carnal shadows and the bad habits which pull men back from their native country.[98] He describes the work of the Catholic educator as a catharsis which cleanses the mind and soul and participates, by means of the teaching, in the very innermost work of the Church, the renovation and salvation of souls. "The mind must be cleansed," he writes, "in order that it may be able to look upon that light and cling to it when it has seen it." "This cleansing," he continues, "is a sort of traveling or sailing to our native country." [99] This is the process of the Christian education and formation of youth. God is everywhere, hence going to him is not locomotion, but a movement of the spirit "by a holy desire and lofty morals." [100] Catholic education is a catharsis, a recollection of the abiding presence of God. The moral gulf between human creatures and God which prevents awareness of the divine light is gradually bridged over by this process of illumination and purification which is the very essence of education.

"We would not be able to do this," St. Augustine points out, "unless he came incarnate to show us the way to live according to human nature." [101] This, then, is Christian humanism in education, entirely centered upon the Incarnation, deriving its inner transforming power from the Word Incarnate and holding up the Incarnate God as the original model, pattern and paradigm of all human perfection. Space does not permit the citation of these truly fundamental passages in which St. Augustine speaks of the power of the Incarnation to effect "a healthy and pure interior eye" through its effective regeneration and renewal of the process of education. It is Christian humanism in the concrete, teaching the Christian attitude toward the body, counseling an ascetism according to reason, and implementing that *metanoia* which is the calling of the Christian.[102]

"So also in this life we must keep in mind that the carnal appetite is to be changed for the better and is not to resist the spirit with its inordinate inclinations." [103] Book I of the *De doctrina christiana,* accordingly, lays down the principles of Christian humanism in education; it comes to close grips with the practical problems of the educator who wishes to participate in the regeneration and renewal of mankind which is the central apostolate of the Church. "Man must be instructed, therefore," Augustine writes, "about the manner of loving, that is how he should love himself so that he may help himself . . . how to love his body . . . to take care of it reasonably and wisely." [104] "Now," concludes St. Augustine, laying down the function of the Christian teacher, "he lives a just and holy life who appraises things with an unprejudiced mind. He is a person who has a well-regulated love, and neither loves what he ought not, nor fails to love what he should." [105] With this basic principle for the formation of sound value judgments in concrete and practical living, by means of a teaching which proceeds in accordance with truth and wisdom, St. Augustine takes up in Book II, as we have seen, the place, the role and the function of the arts and disciplines of human culture in his program of Christian education.

When the Sacred Books form the basic object of study, as they do in St. Augustine's program, it is of first necessity to approach them with the proper attitude: this is to avoid pride, and "to become gentle through piety." [106] "After those two steps of fear and piety, we come to the third step, that of knowledge, which I have now begun to discuss. Everyone devoted to the study of the Holy Scriptures trains himself in this." [107] This is an education which is not distinct from the spiritual life; rather, it is an integral part of the growth of the soul in wisdom and in holiness. When the pursuit of knowledge is carried on with the Bible as the basic text and as the light under which the study proceeds, the educational process itself becomes a part of the conversion of the soul to God and assists the advance of the young person up the steps that lead to wisdom. "Such a child of God," concludes St. Augustine, "mounts to wisdom, the last and seventh step, and this he fully enjoys with perfect calm and serenity. For, 'the fear of the Lord is the beginning of wisdom.' From that fear until we arrive even at wisdom, it is through these steps that we make our way." [108]

St. Augustine devotes his second book of the *De doctrina christiana* to a detailed analysis of this third step which is knowledge. The beginning is the knowledge of Christian Doctrine itself. It is here that St. Augustine adds the new discipline of "Christian Doctrine" or "religion" to the order of studies to be pursued by young people. He lists the canon of Sacred Scripture as forming the basic object of study.[109]

"In all these books," he writes, "those who fear God and are meek in their devotion seek the will of God. The first care of this task and endeavor, as I have said, is to know these books. Although we may not yet understand them, nevertheless, by reading them we can either memorize them or become somewhat acquainted with them. . . . The more anyone learns about these, the more capable of discernment he is. For, among those things which have been clearly expressed in the Scriptures, we discover all those which involve faith and the rules of living, namely hope and charity, of which I treated in the previous book. Then, after a certain intimacy with the language of the Holy Scriptures has been achieved, we should begin to uncover and examine thoroughly those passages which are obscure, and allowing some proofs of incontestable texts to remove the uncertainty from doubtful passages." [110]

The teaching of Christian Doctrine, of faith, of hope, and of charity, an intellectual doctrine which relates directly and immediately to personal living is summarized in this lucid passage. This will be the *sacra pagina,* the Sacred Page which will be the crowning academic discipline in the schools of Christendom. From this approach to teaching will come forth the commentaries upon the Sacred Scriptures elaborated in the schools of the future, the glossaries and exegetical works, as well as the gradual accumulation of doctrinal questions considered by generations of Christian teachers. In due time, many centuries later, these *quaestiones* will be gathered together and put in order to form the mighty synthesis of St. Thomas Aquinas.

Beginning with Book II, Chapter 17, St. Augustine embarks upon the analysis of the teaching of the arts and disciplines of human culture, in the light of this revealed doctrine contained in Sacred Scripture. For the order of studies in this system of education will include the study of the Sacred Page of the Bible on the one hand, and the arts and sciences and disciplines which enshrine the cultural heritage of the human past on the other. To pursue the teaching of St. Augustine on each of the arts and sciences would lead beyond the purpose of the present discussion. We shall concentrate upon the discipline of history, which is affected more directly and substantially than any of the other components of the curriculum. All of them are subjected in these chapters of St. Augustine's treatise to a rigorous examination, to provide a schooling for the entire panorama of social living, such as a renewal of daily life on earth demands. This presupposes an intensive and systematic academic teaching of the young people, which goes into the details of earthly things, but always from the viewpoint of the divine light which has broken upon mankind in revelation and which is taught by means of the Sacred Scriptures.

"That science called history," St. Augustine writes, "is the discipline which teaches us about the order of past events. This is a very important help to us," he points out, for "through it we are aided in understanding the Sacred Books." [111] St. Augustine relates this science called history to the life of Christ, and points out the usefulness of Eusebius' chronology which links the history of the pagan peoples to the "literature of the Hebrew nation." [112]

When St. Augustine came to the Catholic Church and made his act of acceptance of the Catholic faith, he came by that very act to a new understanding of human history, and saw in a new light, at a glance of his inner eye, the entire life of mankind. This brings him to his new definition of the science of history; it grows out of sacred history and, in fact, constitutes that restoration and regeneration and renewal of sacred history which Christian doctrine teaches. "Further," he writes, "when the past arrangements of men are recounted in historical narration, we must not consider history itself among those human institutions. For, things which have now passed away and cannot be revoked must be considered to be in the order of time, whose creator and administrator is God. It is one thing to relate what has been done, but another to teach what should be done. History reports honestly and profitably what has been accomplished." [113]

It is difficult to exaggerate the importance of these principles which St. Augustine lays down for his new program of education. In addition to the discipline of Christian Doctrine, the "sacred page," which is added, as we have seen, these measures concerning history itself as a science amount to the addition of it to the curriculum in a new way. For hitherto history in the pagan schools has existed in a broken state, simply providing examples and illustrations for the work of the grammarian and the rhetorician. From this time forward, however, history will begin to have an independent status on the curriculum, which it will maintain throughout the entire life of the Christian civilization to come. "Despite the vast amount written on Augustine's philosophy of history," writes Professor Green, "little notice has been given to a well-defined instruction in history devised by him and widely adopted in the schools of later days." [114]

"The novelty of the scheme," continues Professor Green, "appears in two aspects: as against the casual instruction of history given in pagan schools, there was opposed a well-defined outline of world history based on the Bible; and as against the Jewish and Christian notion of six thousand years of history (with no natural division into ages), there was opposed the plan of six ages, clearly defined by important crises of Bible history. As priest and bishop, Augustine found his pattern useful for instructing beginners in Christian doctrine. It not only provided a convenient plan of Bible history, but left room for the continuation of history till the end of the world. The student was not to think of a sharp break at the close of the apostolic age, but was rather shown the continued revelation of God's hand in the progress of the Church. . . . History and revelation merge into one symmetrical pattern, in which the believer has his own stable place, fixed in the eternity of God's beneficent purpose." [115]

The Catholic faith brings with it a unique new view of world history. St. Augustine was the first Christian thinker fully to realize this fact. The first element in this Christian view of earthly reality and of human life and destiny, is the fact that certain striking works of God stand in the world history of the human family as real events. These works of God, which Sacred Scripture calls the *mirabilia Dei,* the "wonderful works of God," are real and genuine events, facts established by documentary evidence. These events took place in this world history of the human family on this planet. They are not part of a different "history," called "sacred," a history conceived somehow as running distinct and separate from another history called "profane." [116]

The Incarnation is the chief and the central of these wonderful works of God. The Gospel proclaims and explains the good news concerning this series of events, which Almighty God has intervened to place in the life of the human family. These events constitute the divine plan or economy of salvation, which the Gospel proclaims. This is the very essence of the catechesis of the catechumenate. In St. Augustine's program for the Christian education of youth, this same economy of salvation is worked into the center of the order of studies, through the position given to the Bible, as we have noted, and through the regeneration and renewal of the science of history, which his program establishes.

Thus "religion" or "Christine Doctrine" as a component of the curriculum is sacred history; and it holds the primacy of position among all the other arts and sciences and disciplines of what we call today the curriculum. It not only holds the primacy of position physically, as the most important of the studies, but it furnishes the light under which the discipline of history is restored, returning substance to it, and erecting it upon a chronology which gives it definite meaning. This meaning results from its linear purposiveness in regard to its center and goal, the Incarnation of Jesus Christ and the Redemption accomplished on the Cross.

It is clear that St. Augustine's treatise *De doctrina Chris-*

tiana, containing the program for a new Christian education of youth, is one tapestry with his earlier works which describe his conversion to the Catholic faith. For it is his acceptance of the divine authority of the Catholic Church, presenting with equal divine authority the Divine Scriptures to the mind of man, which has brought him to this view of the historic life of the human family, and to this renovation of the order of studies which teaches these facts and perspectives. The Bible is basic from every point of view in this program of education and order of studies. This renovation and renewal of sacred history and the science of history depends upon a certain view of the Bible as a body of religious and historical truth at one and the same time, capable of establishing the genuine religious education intended by God, if it is approached and taught in the right way.

"By rashly asserting something which the author did not intend," writes St. Augustine, "one frequently runs into other passages which he cannot reconcile to that interpretation. If he agrees that these latter are true and definite, then the opinion which he had formed concerning the former cannot be true, and it happens, in some way or other, that by loving his own opinion he begins to be more vexed at Scripture than at himself. If he allows this error to creep in, he will be utterly destroyed by it. 'For we walk by faith and not by sight' (2 Corinthians 5:7). Faith will totter, if the authority of Sacred Scripture wavers. Indeed, even charity itself grows weak, if faith totters. If anyone falls from faith, it is inevitable that he also falls from charity. For he cannot love what he does not believe exists. But, if he both believes and loves, by leading a good life and by obeying the commandments of good morals, he gives himself reason to hope that he may arrive at that which he loves. And so 'there abide faith, hope and charity, these three' (1 Corinthians 13:1 ff.), which all knowledge and all prophecy serve." [117]

St. Augustine, in other words, in accepting the Bible as containing the religious teaching of God to mankind, accepts it also as a valid knowledge of history, containing fundamental information concerning the historic life of mankind. This vigorous assertion of the historical character and validity of the Divine Scriptures is essential to St. Augustine's program of education, for it affects and governs the manner in which the discipline of history ought to be taught.

The Bible and the New History

From the beginning to the end of his Christian intellectual life, St. Augustine defended with an unequalled lucidity and power the historicity of Sacred Scripture. He rejected vigorously the very thought of a distinction between the religious teaching of the Bible and the factual character of its historical narrative. This fundamental acceptance of the historicity of the Scriptures, so basic for his grasp of the contours of universal history, we can but touch upon by way of illustration.

Of first and basic importance is the historicity of the book of Genesis, for it describes the factual events with which the life of mankind upon this planet begins. The Sacred Scriptures, in other words, recount a history which is not the mere local and isolated memory of the Hebrews as one of the natural peoples; on the contrary, with divine light and power, the beginnings of the human family as such are announced to modern man through the Catholic faith in the Bible. The view of universal history which St. Augustine receives with the Catholic faith depends upon the fact that it takes the mind to the absolute beginning of all peoples, transcending the natural historical memory of any one people, including even the Hebrews.[118]

Let a few examples of St. Augustine's thought concerning the book of Genesis illustrate his mind. He begins his treatise with the question whether "all things are to be understood only figuratively, or whether they are to be asserted and defended according to the reality of historical events?" [119] His own answer, exemplified by his entire mode of treatment, is

230

perfectly clear. "The narration in these books of Genesis," he writes, "is not in the literary kind of figurative speech, as in the Canticle of Canticles, but it is entirely a narrative of historical realities, as in the Books of Kings and others of this type." [120]

In an earlier work on the book of Genesis, St. Augustine writes that "this entire passage is first to be discussed according to history, then according to prophecy. The facts are narrated according to history, but they also predict future things in a prophetic way." [121] "Thus it is written," he states in the later treatise on Genesis, "because thus it took place." [122] Speaking of the tree of life in the midst of paradise, St. Augustine states that it must be diligently considered, lest the mind succumb to the temptation to treat it all as an allegory, believing that those trees were not really present, but only a meaning signified by the trees. Citing Proverbs 3:18, he points out that there is indeed an eternal Jerusalem in heaven, but that there is also a real city on this earth which signifies that other and heavenly one. Sarah and Agar, he points out, also signify the two Testaments, and they existed nevertheless, prior to their signification, as two definite women of this earth. "All such things signified something other than they were in themselves, but nevertheless they also existed in real and bodily fashion themselves." [123]

Speaking of the manner in which Almighty God creates all things at once and nevertheless distributes his works through the six days of the Scriptural narrative, St. Augustine finds no difficulty in the matter. "Because both this Scripture which narrates the works of God through these days which are cited, and that other Scripture which states that he made all things simultaneously, are both veracious and true; and each Scripture is one and the same, because it was written with one and the same Spirit of Truth as the source of inspiration." [124]

In the other books of the Old Testament St. Augustine clearly distinguishes between the poetic writings and the historical narratives. "The statements of the psalmist," writes Costello in summary, "whether historical or predictive, are true. However, in as much as he is a poet, he enjoys privileges in handling his historical themes, not enjoyed by a historian. 'For psalmody is not bound by the law which governs the narrator and writer of history.' But apart from this remark St. Augustine does not engage in any discussion of poetry as a literary type." [125] Speaking of the Books of Kings, St. Augustine writes, "Those things took place and they were written down in the manner in which they took place, and thus we are reading them today." [126] Again speaking of events in the Books of Kings, he says: "And this is most true, because it took place, and what took place was written down. . . . Thus I believe in these written statements . . . and the writing in the Books of Kings, where all things were recorded for us which pertain to the historical deeds of David. . . ." [127]

St. Augustine's sense of the historical veracity and reliability of the Sacred Scriptures reaches its climax in his treatment of the Gospels. As a matter of fact, his work on the harmony of the four evangelists is from beginning to end a testimony to his consistent doctrine on the historical character of the Gospels. "Although we hold that Lazarus was really raised from the dead according to the Gospel history," he writes, "and we hold it with full faith; nevertheless I do not doubt that there is some allegorical significance in this event. For when things are seen to have allegorical meaning, the historical event does not change its character or lose its reliability." [128]

"If reason," he says in summary, "however acute it may be, is found contradicting the authority of the Divine Scriptures, it deceives by a semblance of truth, for in that case it cannot be true. On the other hand, if against the most manifest and reliable testimony of reason, anything be set up claiming to have the authority of the Holy Scriptures, he who does this, does it through misapprehension of what he has read, and is setting up against the truth, not the real meaning of Scripture, which he has failed to discover, but an opinion of his own. He alleges, not what he found in the Scriptures, but what he found in himself as their interpreter." [129]

It is in this fashion that St. Augustine's conversion to the Catholic faith brought him a luminous new view of the universal history of the human family. The authority of the Church which presents the authority of the Divine Scriptures to the mind, by that very fact illuminates the mind with historical understanding. "We, being sustained by divine authority in this history of our religion," he writes, "have no doubt that whatever is opposed to it is most false." [130] This is his final position, from which he develops with complete consistency that understanding of the historical life of mankind on earth for which he is justly and permanently famous. It is this conversion of the Catholic Church and therefore to the divine character of the Sacred Scriptures, including their historical reliability and veracity, which gives him the foundation for his philosophy and theology of history.

St. Augustine's conversion to the Catholic Church has been a conversion to the Bible, and, educator that he is, he proceeds to recast the entire educational program in terms of the Bible. Homer is replaced by the Sacred Scriptures, by the literature of the new Israel of God, the new people that issues forth from the Incarnation. The Catholic faith includes the Sacred Scriptures. They are one with it; and they are historical in character. From this basic foundation in his intellectual life, St. Augustine elaborates his theology of history. He is ready, both intellectually and academically, for the supreme test of the early Church which called upon him to produce the treatise on *The City of God*.

The discipline of history, as a consequence, has undergone a complete regeneration and renewal as a component of the order or curriculum of studies. It is the central academic discipline from the viewpoint of humanism, for it possesses a special nature and pedagogical significance. St. Augustine's philosophy of God and the soul, with its intense desire to know God, incarnate now, as the Catholic faith teaches, is the very foundation of the happy life. His knowledge of himself as a redeemed soul follows directly, a knowledge which is full of faith and which results in a cleansed and purified personal life in hope and in charity.

Thus it is the Incarnation, of which we are apprised in the books of the Old and the New Testaments, which is the center of St. Augustine's quest and discovery of wisdom, and of his program for education. Speaking in his treatise *On the Trinity* of the atheists who perceive the same facts and historical personages of sacred history in the same way as the faithful, but are unable to conceive of them as witnesses sent by God, St. Augustine comes to the very heart of the new historical knowledge which the Catholic faith and the Bible have bestowed upon his intellectual life. Such persons do not discern "what God is, and what it is to be sent from God." [131] It seems clear that the luminous power of St. Augustine's mind grasped the relationship between a sound educational program which leads the mind to intelligent conviction regarding God and the soul, and the propagation of the Catholic faith on a successful, socially widespread scale. His treatise *De vera religione,* conceived at the outset of his Catholic educational thinking and planning, presents a religious message which depends for its discernment and acceptance upon a proper order of studies and plan of the curriculum for cultivating minds to know "what God is and what it is to be sent from God." The God to whom Christian philosophy rises is not only *ipsum esse subsistens;* he is a personal God who exercises an order of providence over his creation. His human creatures, therefore, reflecting upon their own nature and condition, might well expect some message from him, delivered by witnesses sent by him to speak in his name. Immediately the Bible looms up for consideration in educational planning, and the fundamentals of St. Augustine's theology of history come into view. Catholic education, Christian doctrine, *doctrina christiana,* these are indeed the regeneration and renewal of sacred history, an approach to education which overcomes the secularized condition of the trivuum in the schools of pagan antiquity from which Augustine had resigned. It is a "holy teaching," a *doctrina sacra,* as St. Thomas Aquinas terms it, which extends to the very fundamentals of knowledge concerning the historic life of the human family.

Sacred History and Secular History in The City of God

Christian doctrine, the intellectual life and activity of St. Augustine's cathedral school, was faced with a sudden challenge and opportunity when the Eternal City fell in A.D. 410 to sack and pillage by Alaric the Goth. Sacred doctrine and its subsidiary, the new history, are called upon to face the last storm of pagan intellectual opposition. Christian doctrine rises with the pen of St. Augustine to the final victory, the climax of the patristic age, in the treatise on *The City of God* which crowns and completes the historic work of the Christian apologists.

The pagan intellectual world raises the question whether the conversion of the Roman *orbis* to Christ has been a good thing.[132] Is not the misfortune of the City which is the Head of the World due precisely to this abandonment of the historic worship of the gods? It is this conversion of the whole world to Christ in the Catholic Church which is to blame! The gods are angry, for the meaning and direction of human history have gone awry!

Prepared for his lifetime of work in the pagan schools and his twenty-five years in Christian doctrine, St. Augustine possesses the scholarly materials, the erudition, the philosophical training of mind and the mastery of Sacred Scripture to cope with the challenge. This mighty work, the culminating intellectual achievement of the patristic age, is the answer. The first ten books refute in final fashion the claims of the pagan religion which descend from man's historic past; the last twelve books contain St. Augustine's own positive view of the historical life and development of the human family, rooted in the Bible, and pointing forward to the times of the Church, precisely the Providential plan for the social welfare of mankind.

Rejecting the three philosophies of history current in his day, the cyclism of the Graeco-Roman pagans, the Christian progressivism of Eusebius, who saw in the Roman Empire the social embodiment of the City of God, and the millenarism of the heretical sects, Augustine broke new ground in what is actually a comprehensive treatise on the Catholic Church as the earthly embodiment of the City of God. Seeing the Church militant and the Church triumphant as a spiritual unity, he vindicates the conversion of mankind to the Church as one thing with the fulfillment of the divine plan in the Incarnation, as one thing therefore with conversion to the one true God. Thus he vindicates the catechetical proclamation of the good news and completes the work of the apologists, presenting a powerful new synthesis of historical understanding based directly upon the Bible.

"The body of our Head is the Church," he states, "not the Church which is in this particular place or that, but the Church which extends through the entire circuit of the earth. Nor is it a Church limited to this time or that time, but it is the Church which reaches from Abel through the course of all the centuries to those who are going to be born and who believe in Christ at the end of the world: it is the entire people of the saints who form one city. This city is the body of Christ, and Christ himself is its Head. There are to be found the angels, who are our fellow citizens; but because we are on our way of laboring in our pilgrimage, while they are already in the eternal city awaiting our advent: for this reason letters have been sent to us from that heavenly city to accompany our pilgrimage: these letters are the Scriptures, which exhort us to the good life. What do I say, that letters have been sent to us? There is still more: the King himself has descended, and has been made for us our way in our pilgrimage, so that walking in him, we may neither lose our way nor fall by the wayside. Such then is the whole Christ whom we know, whole and entire together with the Church, he however who is our Head alone having been born of the Virgin, the Head of the Church, the mediator between God and men, Christ Jesus our Lord. . . . " [133]

This vision of the past life of mankind is a completely different view of history than that which the pagans have possessed. In this synthetic over-view of all the centuries, St. Augustine is using and completing the chronological work of the apologists, especially the *Chronicles* of Eusebius which St. Jerome recently had translated.[134] It is nothing else than the conquest of time for Christ, time as understood and experienced by men, time as remembered and anticipated. This is the conquest of the mind of antiquity, with the final defeat of that other understanding of time which the pagans were voicing in their alarm at the fall of Rome. Augustine's treatise elaborating this Christian view of the human family represents the final triumph which the victory of the martyrs had prepared, the final triumph of the mind of the Church over the pagan intellectual life of antiquity.[135]

This introduces a question of central interest for the educator, that of the place which the so-called discipline of secular history is to have in this type of historical understanding. We have seen that St. Augustine restores the place of the discipline of history on the order of studies, a new, separate and distinct place which it did not have in the classical *paideia*. It would be a mistake, however, to think that he conceives this discipline which he adds to the order or curriculum of studies as the modern secularist views it. For St. Augustine, the discipline of history is not distinct from sacred history, embodying a contrary wisdom, but rather a science subordinate to the study of the Sacred Page, the course in Christian Doctrine.

St. Augustine recognizes in explicit terms the reality of history as a science and academic discipline. It is the factual narrative which describes *res gestas,* the events which have in fact taken place. He sees the world of reality in two orders, the eternal and the temporal, and places the essence of the temporal order in contingency, the proper matter of history.[136]

The meaning of this temporal order and succession cannot be deduced philosophically, but can only be learned from God himself, who sends his spokesmen, the Prophets, as his witnesses to this meaning of the temporal succession. Mankind, therefore, is completely dependent upon the revelation coming from God for an understanding of this development of human life on earth; it is for this reason that letters worthy of faith have been sent from the Heavenly Father, that mankind might have this knowledge of his own origin, progress, and destiny.[137]

In a basic passage, St. Augustine places the Sacred Scriptures themselves within the orbit of scientific history. The prologue of St. John, he writes, does not descend to human history until it reports that the Word was made flesh and dwelt amongst us. "This even took place in the temporal order," he notes, "and thus pertains to science, the science which is made up of historical knowledge." [138] Thus history is one of the separate disciplines, and the benefit of its knowledge extends also to those documents which constitute the Bible.[139]

With this, St. Augustine introduces his most basic distinction and position in the intellectual order, that between science and wisdom. This historical science, which functions as an academic discipline exactly as it always had in its human way, even when its object is the Bible itself, is understood by a wisdom which illuminates the human mind from the Sacred Scriptures themselves.[140]

Reason tires and faints by the way in its effort to discern divine things: it has a natural tendency to return to its familiar darknesses and its addiction to the temporal order in and for itself. In his love and mercy, therefore, the Heavenly Father offers the way of authority to the human mind, the providential way traced by God and inserted in the very historic life of the human family. This is the separation of

Abraham, the bond of the Law of Moses, the message of the prophets, the Incarnation of the Word, the witness of the apostles and the martyrs, and now at last the conversion of the whole world of gentile nations to the one holy Catholic and Apostolic Church.[141] This is the historical order or way which God himself has inserted into his creation, and documented for us by the letters which he has sent to us from heaven, to which we are obliged to submit our small human reasonings.[142]

Seen in this light, then, there are not two histories, one secular or profane, and the other sacred or religious. There is one religious teaching, one *doctrina sacra, doctrina christiana,* which embraces the entire meaning of the historic life of mankind as a whole. Thus all history shares in the nature of the sacred, and becomes a means of religious education, ministering to a better understanding of the divine economy of salvation. Here the new discipline arises which is at home in the Christian school, of which the pagan past had never heard: this is St. Augustine's basic contribution to educational theory and practice, the provision of a place for this new academic entity and the elaboration of its content and method. It is not "history" in the old secular or profane sense, that dead thing resurrected by the modern secularist, but a *doctrina sacra,* a *Christian Doctrine,* which sees all things in the light of the wisdom from above, implanting the providential economy of salvation in the life of mankind on earth. This order of events in the objective life of mankind, according to St. Augustine, ought to be reflected in the order or curriculum of studies which prepares young people with these understandings upon which their Christian living is based.

"This is the vision of universal history," writes Amari, "which St. Augustine derives from St. Paul and the Fathers who went before him. It is the story of the economy of salvation. Sacred Scripture is a history, but also more than a history, understood as a mere narrative of events or chronicle. In this sacred history, the narrative of events is secondary, a means, a vehicle for conveying a conception of wisdom and a body of doctrine. Creation, the fall, the Old Testament, these are facts located in time, but they carry with them great religious truths, the dogmas of the Catholic religion, and many other secondary and spiritual truths. God has hidden his truths in these human and earthly facts, in order to make them accessible to all men." [143] St. Augustine never ceases to marvel at this divine humility, this wonderful way in which the divine being condescends to approach close to the human family in the mercy and love of the Christian religion.[144]

The God of reason, in other words, known by Christian philosophy, speaks in human history through the Prophets, through Christ himself in person, and through the Apostles. This divine revelation to man comes to us through the faith of the Catholic Church in which we are instructed chiefly by the Divine Scriptures. Wisdom comes to mankind in this way, a light, an illumination which is the faith itself, taught and ministered by the Sacred Scriptures. Wisdom, as St. Augustine puts it, comes joyfully to meet us in our way of pilgrimage toward that supernal city which lies in the future.[145]

Human history is not a mere chronicle or catalog of facts, nor a purely human science or body of knowledge: the facts of history are meaningfully illuminated by the divine light which comes from above. The science of history receives its completion in the Christian wisdom which understands and orders the events which constitute the historic life of mankind. In his discussion of the relationship between science and wisdom St. Augustine lays down the basic principles for teaching history in the right way, as the first Vatican Council put it, so that this discipline too may make its contribution to the ascent of the youthful mind to God.[146] This leads to wisdom, as St. Augustine says, "by passing through the order of disciplines by which the soul is cultivated." [147] This is the very definition of education and the true philosophy of the curriculum. Thus, as Amari points out, the study of sacred history centers upon Christ Incarnate: "the temporal history of Christ, which participates in the nature of science or knowledge, serves and prepares for the wisdom of the soul." [148]

In this way, the new discipline, this *Christian Doctrine* which embraces sacred history and what the world calls secular history in the unified grasp of wisdom, ministers to the good of the soul and serves directly the cause of Christian living and the salvation of souls. It is an academic teaching of religion which preserves the catechetical purposes of the catechumenate, and indeed continues the catechesis in the full and original apostolic sense. It is this approach which St. Augustine bequeathed to the Christian schools and scholars of the future: an academic teaching of an intellectual discipline which is simultaneously a catechetical apostolate of the classroom, in and through the very teaching.[149]

St. Augustine's treatise on *The City of God* contains a striking example that illustrates the right way of accomplishing this type of teaching. It is contained in Book XVIII, which relates the profane history of the city of this world to the sacred history of God, in a pattern of historical treatment which stands abidingly as a model for Christian Doctrine. In this mighty synthesis of the histories of the two cities into one view of God's providential care over the entire life of mankind, St. Augustine weaves the events of the great empires of antiquity into their relationship with the life of the Chosen People, showing the events of pre-Christian times as a providential preparation for the Incarnation. The synthetic unity of the history of the two cities centers upon Christ himself, who becomes clearly visible as the Lord of history, the center and king of all the ages. After the coming of Christ, recorded in the Gospels, St. Augustine concludes the life of the Church to his own day very briefly, for in his perception of things the Church had as yet very little history. He was living, as we have noted, in a present experience of the conversion of antiquity to Christ in his Church. He sketches the life of the Church from the Apostles to his own day in one brief chapter.[150] His principles, however, are clear: they are exactly as he states them in his treatise on the *First Catecheti-cal Instruction,* a graphic instance of the manner in which the heritage of the catechumenate with its catechesis of the good news has passed into the order of studies and into the new discipline of *Christian Doctrine* which he is adding to the circle of the sciences and disciplines that constitute the order of studies in *schola nostra.* This forms the "safe way" for Christian young people to walk.

The last twelve books of *The City of God* contain the classic statement of the Christian view of history. It is bibli-cal from beginning to end. The discussion of human origins (Books XI–XIV) is rooted directly in the Scriptures, and manifests the way in which St. Augustine sees the Book of Genesis as a description of the absolute beginnings of man-kind as a whole. The progress of mankind, Books XV–XVII, is again a biblical panorama in the manner outlined above. The last four books, XIX–XXII, discuss the deserved desti-nies of the two cities, the future events, the last things which are still to come. "St. Augustine's systemization of secular or profane history by means of sacred history," writes Padovani, "proceeds by narrating the panorama of universal history, the history of both the city of God and the city of the world, so that the mind sees a transcendent and synthetic unity of over-view." [151] There is, in other words, only one history, the providential course of human events which prepares for the coming of Christ, and which has as its outcome this present conversion and restoration and regeneration of mankind in the Church. "The hidden meaning of secular history," writes Padovani, "is to be found in sacred history." [152]

The restoration of sacred history which St. Augustine's educational work completes is actually the application of Christian humanism to educational theory and practice. Sa-cred history, linear and purposive, directed to God the Fa-ther, reflects the humanism of Christians which likewise is linear and purposive, directed toward the Father in imitation of the life of Christ. *Doctrina christiana* is simultaneously a religious and a cultural teaching *ad patrem:* this is the renewal of sacred history and of earthly culture, genuine Christian humanism in education. Christian Doctrine is the renewal of sacred history, one may say, the convergence of the studies of polite literature and liberal science, of Athens which is the source and the school of intellectual culture, and of Jerusalem, the source of another sort of knowledge, high and supernatural.

"Hitherto they came from separate sources," to continue the luminous words of Cardinal Newman, "and performed separate works. Each leaves an heir and successor in the West, and that heir is one and the same. The grace stored in Jerusalem, and the gifts which radiate from Athens, are made over and concentrated in Rome. This is true as a matter of history. Rome has inherited both sacred and profane learning; she has perpetuated and dispensed the traditions of Moses and David in the supernatural order, and of Homer and Aristotle in the natural. To separate those distinct teachings, human and divine, which meet in Rome, is to retrograde; it is to rebuild the Jewish Temple and to plant anew the groves of Academus." [153]

Notes From Chapter Seven

[1] J. H. Newman, *The Idea of a University* (New York: Longmans, 1947), p. 230.

[2] Cf. Grasberger, *op. cit.*, III, 532: "It must be borne in mind that there was in antiquity no so-called instruction in religion, either among the Greeks or the Romans. This is to be found for the first time in the centuries after Christ, when 'religion' was added as a fourth school discipline to the three basic subjects of elementary instruction, reading, namely, and writing and arithmetic." Cf. also Paul Girard, *L'education athénienne au V⁰ et au IV⁰ siècle avant J-C* (Paris: Hachette, 1891), p. 253: "Il n'existait pas à Athènes d'enseignement religieux au sens ou nous l'entendons. C'est une conception toute moderne que celle d'une religion formant une science à part. La religion grecque n'avait pas ce caractère: elle était intimement mêlée à la vie et s'y offrait à chaque instant sous les aspects les plus variés. . . ." In one sense, the classical *paideia* was a religious education, as we have noted in chap. i; in another sense it became gradually so secularized that it no longer taught either religious truth or sacred history, even in the garbled form of the myths. The loss of this common human heritage from primitive times inflicted a mortal wound upon man's civilizing effort in the recent 6000 years. It is here that the meaning of the Christian era as the regeneration

and renewal of human culture emerges into full view, and it is against this background that the social significance of St. Augustine's educational work for mankind as a whole becomes sharply visible. For it was the very essence of his pedagogical thinking that religious truth should be taught on each level of education in order to form the educated Christian, the man of Christian moral character and intellectual culture. Cf. Marrou, *Saint Augustin et la fin . . . , passim,* esp. pp. 387-414, "La formation de l'intellectuel chrétien."

3 Cf. E. K. Rand, *Founders of the Middle Ages* (Cambridge: Harvard University Press, 1928; Dover Edition, 1957), p. 228: "In his *De doctrina christiana* he explicitly recognizes the value of the arts as a precursor of the higher studies of divinity; he recommends that the learner begin the difficult programme early, and pursue it vigorously and steadily. Now this is precisely the plan of Plato and Cicero, a curriculum of two parts, an introduction and a fulfillment. For Plato and Cicero the crown of such a course is philosophy. So is it with St. Augustine, save that it is Christian philosophy, that is theology. . . . In his *Retractationes* . . . he makes no changes in the programme of Christian education as he had announced it in his *De doctrina christiana.*"

4 Cf. *Confessions,* Books I-III, esp. I, 16, "The Influence of Immoral Literature"; Ryan, *op. cit.,* pp. 58-59. For the role and importance of the cultivation of the word, the *logos,* in classical education, cf. H. I. Marrou, *A History of Education in Antiquity* (New York: Sheed and Ward, 1956), "Rhetoric," pp. 194-205; "Learning to speak properly meant learning to think properly, and even to live properly. . . . It was the one means for handing on everything that made man man, the whole cultural heritage that distinguished civilized men from barbarians" (p. 196). Marrou's work conveys this inner essence and form of classical education in masterful fashion; cf. also pp. 117, 148, 173-175, 218, 223, 239, 265, 312, 413. We have noted already St. Augustine's positive evaluation of this human heritage of grammar and rhetoric, and the insufficiency of Van der Meer's observations in their regard.

5 St. Augustine's philosophy of history and of culture is an immense body of doctrine which is difficult to master when it is approached in itself, as it stands in the *Opera omnia* of the great Father of the Church. When it is approached genetically, however, as it developed in his life and thought and writing, and as he gradually enlarged upon his plan for the regeneration and renewal of the educational system, a valuable avenue of approach opens to the understanding of his historical and social doctrine. The present chapter sketches the manner in which Augustine himself came upon his philosophy and theology of history and carried it into his educational work, and from this work and institution into the monumental classic which summarizes and concludes the entire patristic age, the treatise on *The City of God.* This itself has a certain practical pedagogical value, in that it illuminates the way which young Catholic students ought to follow, to this day, in grasping the Providential order of things which is the central meaning of the life of the human family on earth.

6 *Enarr. in ps.,* 39, 21; P.L. 36, 447.

7 *In Joannis Ev.,* Tract. 34, 9; P.L. 35, 1655: "Et nos de Adam caeci nati sumus, et illo illuminante opus habemus." Cf. Tract. 34, *passim,* St. Augustine's commentary on "Ego sum lux mundi"; this is the efficacious Christian fulfillment of the catharsis and illumination to which Plato aspired and with him all the best in the heritage of human civilization.

8 *Ibid., Tract.* 18, 11; P.L. 35, 1542-3. Cf. *Enarr. in ps.,* 72, 7; P.L. 36, 919: "Sed quemadmodum sol, oculos puros, sanos, vegetos fortes habebit, tranquillus apparet, in oculos autem lippos quasi tela aspera jaculatur; intuentem illum vegetat, hunc excruciat, non mutatus, sed mutatum: sic cum coeperis esse perversus, et tibi Deus perversus videbitur; tu mutatus es, non ille."

9 *Serm.,* 49, 3; P.L. 38, 321: " . . . nunc autem adhuc tenebras mortalitatis huius circumferimus, et ad lucernam Scripturae ambulamus." Cf. *ibid.,* col. 322: "Iudica te ipsum, noli tibi placere. Quod tibi in te merito displicet, castiga, emenda, corrige. Scriptura Sancta sit tibi tanquam speculum. Speculum hoc habet splendorem non mendacem, splendorem non adulantem, nullius personam amantem. . . . Non te fallit speculum, tu te noli fallere. Iudica de te, contristare de tua foeditate; ut cum abieris et discesseris tristis, foedus, correctus possis redire formosus." This is the very idea of human education, the charter of the religion teacher in high school and college, and the concrete basis of an academic teaching which is at the same time a formative and catechetical apostolate of the classroom. This is the practical bearing of the academic teaching of the Bible which, as we shall see, is the fundamental stroke of St. Augustine in implementing the theory and practice of *doctrina christiana.*

10 *In Joannis Ev.,* Tract. I, 19; P.L. 35, 1388. Cf. *Serm.,* 53, 10; P.L. 38, 368: "Si ergo desideramus videre Deum, oculus iste unde mundabitur? . . . Mundat cor fides Dei, mundum cor videt Deum."

11 *Enarr. in ps.,* 118, *Serm.,* 18, 3: " . . . fide corda mundantur." In St. Augustine's thought, faith, the Scriptures, and Jesus Christ, the Incarnate Mediator, are all one. Cf. *Contra Faustum,* 16, 9: "Moyses omne quod scripsit, de Christo est." "Tutta la Sacra Scrittura," writes J. Amari, "Antico e Nuovo Testamento, non contiene che Gesù Cristo" (cf. *Il concetto di storia in sant'Agostino* [Romae: Ex tipis piae societatis a S. Paulo apostolo, 1951], p. 129). Also the general conclusion of M. Pontet, *L'exegèse de S. Augustin prédicateur* (Paris: Aubier, 1945), p. 179: "Sens spirituel et sens du Christ sont à peu près synonymes chez les Pères." This will be an academic teaching which will be at the same time a Christocentric apostolate of the classroom.

12 *Serm.,* 88, 4; P.L. 38, 541.

13 *Ibid.*

14 *Ibid.,* col. 542: "Lux illa est aeterna sapientia." Cf. *Serm.* 88, 6, *totum:* "Studium morale de mundando cordis oculo."

15 Cf. Pontet, *op. cit.,* p. 112: "Il faut guérir en nous l'instrument de la connaissance."

16 Cf. *Serm.,* 26, *passim;* P.L. 38, 177-178. Cf. Pontet, *op. cit.,* pp. 111-114. For the entire concept of a pedagogical *catharsis ad videndum,* cf. the treatise *De agone christiano liber unus;* P.L. 40, 289-310; e.g. 13 (14), col. 299: "Errat autem quisquis putat veritatem se posse cognoscere, cum adhuc nequiter vivat. Nequitia est autem mundum istum diligere. . . . Talis vita non potest puram illam et sinceram et incommutabilem videre veritatem, et inhaerere illi, et in aeternum iam non moveri. Itaque priusquam mens nostra purgetur, debemus credere quod intelligere nondum valemus. . . ." And St. Augustine cites Isa. 7:9: Except you believe, you shall not understand.

17 Cf. F. Van der Meer, *Augustine the Bishop* (London: Sheed and Ward, 1961), p. 364. For a vivid and scholarly reconstruction of the meaning and practice of baptism in the patristic age, cf. his chap. xii, "Becoming a Christian," pp. 347-387. "Above everything else," writes Van der Meer in cogent summary, "the Christians knew that the essence of Christianity was nothing

less than a completely new life in the Lord Jesus Christ, a complete moral turn-about, a true conversion, for the new life in Christ killed the old life of our corrupted nature, the old darkness could no longer assert itself against the new, all-penetrating light" (p. 347). Augustine the Bishop and Augustine the Educator are one single powerful mind seizing upon the pedagogical institution of mankind and reforming it to participate in this conversion of all things human to God in the Church of his Incarnate Son. This makes of teaching a catechesis and of education an apostolate of the classroom.

18 Cf. the two treatises projected at Cassiciacum for his friends Romanianus and Honoratus, *De vera religione* and *De utilitate credendi*. "A few years ago, my dear Romanianus," he writes in the former (7, 12-13), "I promised to write down for you my sentiments concerning true religion. . . . In following this religion our chief concern is with the prophetic history of the dispensation of divine providence in time—what God has done for the salvation of the human race, renewing and restoring it unto eternal life" (trans. of J. H. S. Burleigh).

19 *In Joan Ev.*, Tract. 35, 6; P.L. 35, 1660. Cf. nos. 7-8, col. 1660-1661, for the concept of Biblical prophecy converging upon Christ, and the conclusion in the words of St. Peter (1 Peter 1:17-19). "Prophetas audi," says St. Augustine, "O homo mortue" (col. 1661). This will be the theme of *The City of God* and the basic plan of instruction in both the catechumenate and the academic classroom.

20 *De utilitate credendi*, 16 (34); cf. Luanne Meagher (trans.), "The Advantage of Believing," in *Writings of St. Augustine*, II, 436.

21 *Ibid.; op. cit.*, p. 437.

22 *Ibid.*, 15 (33); *op. cit.*, pp. 435-436.

23 *Ibid.*, 17 (35); *op. cit.*, pp. 439-440.

24 *De fide rerum quae non videntur*, 7 (10); R. J. Deferrari and M. F. McDonald (trans.), "On Faith in Things Unseen," in *Writings of St. Augustine*, II, 467.

25 *De utilitate credendi*, 17 (35); *op. cit.*, p. 440.

26 *Ibid.*, 16 (34); *op. cit.*, p. 437.

27 *Enarr. in ps.*, 21, 2 (26): "Ecclesia totus orbis est." In this perception Augustine simply follows the footsteps of the Early Church as a whole. "Hesterni sumus," Tertullian writes in the famous passage of the *Apology* (37, 4), "et orbem iam et vestra omnia implevimus. . . ." Indeed, it is of the very essence of the Christian era as such, as the Canon of the Mass, prayed by all times and places, bears witness: "In primis, quae tibi offerimus pro Ecclesia tua sancta catholica: quam pacificare, custodire, adunare et regere digneris toto orbe terrarum. . . ."

28 *Enarr. in ps.*, 149, 7: "Chorus Christi iam totus mundus est."

29 Cf. *In Joannis Ev.*, Tract. 9, 6; P.L. 35, 1461; " . . . sexta inde usque ad finem saeculi . . . sexta illa aetate manifestatur per Evangelium reformatio mentis nostrae, secundum imaginem eius qui creavit nos (col. 3, 10)."

30 Cf. *Enarr. in ps.*, 95, 2; *Epist.*, 197; *Epist.*, 199; *In Epist. Joannis*, 2, 2 ("few nations remain"); *De natura et gratia*, 2 ("paucissimae").

31 *Serm.*, 22, 4; P.L. 38, 151.

32 *De unit. ecclesiae* (*Epist. contra Donat.*); P.L. 43, 415. Cf. *ibid.*, col. 391-392: "Quaestio certe inter nos versatur, Ubi sit Ecclesiae; utrum apud nos, an apud illos. Quae utique una est, quam majores nostri Catholicam nominarunt, ut ex ipso nomine ostenderent, quia per totum est."

33 *Enarr. in ps.*, 90, *Serm.*, 2, 1.

34 *De Trin.*, VI, 10 (12): "Haec igitur omnia, quae arte divina facta sunt, et unitatem quamdam in se ostendunt, et speciem et ordinem."

35 *De vera religione*, 7, 13, already cited.

36 Cf. *ibid.*, 39, 72; also 22, 42-43, where St. Augustine discusses the two obstacles, metaphysical and moral, which frequently hinder the eye of the human mind from perceiving this inherently luminous and imposing order of things in human history. Cf. *De ordine*, II, 19 (51); *De div. qq.*, 83, 27; *De musica*, VI, 11 (30); *Epist.*, 138, 1 (5), "Universi saeculi pulchritudo . . . velut magnum carmen." In *De civitate Dei*, XII, 4, St. Augustine makes it clear that the divine gift of faith is necessary for perceiving this *ordo* in the historic life of mankind: "Cedendo ac succedendo" the "pulchritudo temporum" forms an "ordo transeuntium": "Cuius ordinis decus . . . rectissime credenda praecipitur providentia Conditoris. . . ."

37 *De div. quaest.*, 83, 36, (1).

38 *Epist.*, 137, 4 (15-16); P.L. 33, 522.

39 *Ibid.*, col. 523-524.

40 The *Enarrationes in psalmos,* actually sermons preached at Carthage which contain already in germ the mighty treatise *De civitate Dei,* are literally filled with this vision of the world-wide conversion to God in the Catholic Church. Cf., in addition to those cited above, *In ps.,* 18, *Serm.,* 2, 10; *In ps.,* 34, *Serm.,* 2, 10; *In ps.,* 37, 6; *In ps.,* 56, 1; *In ps.,* 62, 2; *In ps.,* 147, 19. Cf. *Serm.,* 51, 4; *Serm.,* 267, 4. Babylon also is everywhere, of course, but as a dead debris, not the germs of life: and it is receding! *In ps.,* 44, 2: "Residui pagani, . . . templa deserta." Cf. Van der Meer, *op. cit.,* "The Pagans," pp. 29-45, "a dwindling minority." The fact of the Catholic Church as a sudden illumination visible in the whole world, *in toto orbe terrarum,* is the constant intellectual background of all of St. Augustine's preaching and writing, and it is the fundamental theme of his *De civitate Dei.* No phrase appears more frequently in his pages than "toto orbe terrarum," used of the Church which is rapidly unifying all the natural peoples which have grown up in history into the new supernatural unity of the Catholic faith. For a masterly documentation of this point, cf. Pontet, *op. cit.,* chapitre septième, "Les Enarrationes in psalmos: Structure de l'Église," pp. 387-418; for the locale at Carthage, "l'homme ruiné," and Augustine's firm conviction of the coming victory of Christ over the immorality of the great city, cf. *ibid.,* pp. 73-79.

41 *Enarr. in ps.*, 109, 1; P.L. 37, 1445.

42 Cf. *De Scriptura Sacra speculum,* "Praefatio," P.L. 34, 887-889. For the philosophy of history implied by these basic insights of Augustine, cf. Alberto Vecchi, "Il concetto di filosofia e il problema del corso storico nel 'De vera religione' di S. Agostino," *Actes du XV*ᵉᵐᵉ *Congrès Internationale de Philosophie,* XIV (1953), 282-291. For the preparation among St. Augustine's predecessors, cf. Jean Daniélou, "Saint Irénée et les origines de la théologie de l'histoire," *Recherches de science religieuse,* XXXIV (1947), 227-231; "A l'occasion de ces controverses [with the Gnostics and Marcion], les auteurs chrétiennes sont amenés à définir l'attitude de l'Église à l'égard de la Loi ancienne et à poser les fondements à la fois de l'exégèse et de la théologie chrétienne de l'histoire" (p. 228). For comprehensive general treatments of the point, cf. A. Quacquarelli, *La concezione della Storia nei Padri prima di S. Agostino* (Roma: E. S. R., 1955), and Pietro Chiocchetta, *Teologia della storia* (Roma: Editrice Studium, 1953). Cf. also Gerhart B. Ladner, *The Idea*

of Reform: Its Impact on Christian Thought and Action in the Age of the Fathers (Cambridge: Harvard University Press, 1959), "St. Augustine's Program of Education and Its Relation to the Ascetic Reform Ideal," pp. 373-377.

43 *Contra Faustum*, 33, 9; P.L. 42, 517-518.

44 *Enarr. in ps.*, 103, *Serm.*, 4, 1; P.L. 37, 1378.

45 Cf. *De lib. arb.*, II, 17 (45): ". . . sentit sapientiam in via se sibi ostendere hilariter."

46 *Enarr. in ps.*, 103, 8; P.L. 37, 1341.

47 *Contra Faustum*, 23, 9; P.L. 42, 471: "Ipsae [the canonical Scriptures] sunt enim quas recipit et tenet Ecclesia." Cf. *De util. cred.*, 6, 13; P.L. 42, 74.

48 *Contra Epis. Man.*, 5, 6; P.L. 42, 176: "Ego vero Evangelio non crederem nisi me Catholicae Ecclesiae commoveret auctoritas" (Costello's translation).

49 *In epis. Joannis tractatus*, 7, 5; P.L. 35, 2031.

50 Cf. *Enarr. in ps.*, 144, 17; P.L. 37, 1180: ". . . transcurrunt ista saecula cedentibus succedentibusque mortalibus; Scriptura Dei manere debuit, ut quoddam chirographum Dei, quod omnes transeuntes legerent, et viam promissionis eius tenerent. Et quanta sunt quae reddidit ex isto chirographo? Dubitant homines credere illi de resurrectione mortuorum et de futuro saeculo, quod solum iam reddendum restat. . . . Ibi in chirographo meo lege omnia quae promisi, deduc mecum rationem: certe vel computando quae reddidi, potes me credere redditurum esse quod debeo. In ipso chirographo habes promissum unicum Filium, cui non peperci (Rom. 8, 32): iam computa in redditis. Lege chirographum. . . ." Cf. *Contra Faustum*, 22, 65; P.L. 42, 440-441: "Inaniter igitur Faustus, in se ipsum potius dente sacrilego saeviens, Sanctam Scripturam, quam totus iam mundus merito veneratur, accusat. . . ."

51 *Enarr. in ps.*, 8, 5: ". . . ut auctoritate commotus. . . ."

52 Cf. *Epist.*, 118, 22: "Christiana disciplina est prima humilitas, secunda humilitas, tertia humilitas." Pride was the besetting sin of the Platonists, for it kept them from seeing the fact of the Incarnation. Van der Meer (*op. cit.*), with accurate insight, chose for his fly-leaf St. Augustine's exclamation, *Serm.*, 162, 6: "God has humbled himself—and still man is proud!" Cf. *Serm.*, 51, 5 (6): "Loquor vobis, aliquando deceptus, cum primo puer ad Divinas Scripturas ante vellem afferre acumen discutiendi, quam pietate quaerendi: ego ipse contra me perversis moribus claudebam ianuam Domini mei. . . . Superbus enim audebam quaerere, quod nisi humilis non potest invenire."

53 Cf. E. Gilson, *The Christian Philosophy of Saint Augustine* (New York: Random House, 1960), p. 227: "Reduced to its abstract form, Augustine's experience (of conversion) may be said to amount to a discovery of humility. Errors of understanding are bound up with the corruption of the heart through pride, and man only finds the truth which brings happiness by subjecting his intellect to faith and his will to grace, in humility."

54 *Conf.*, XIII, 29 (44); Ryan, *op. cit.*, p. 364.

55 Cf. J. M. Le Blond, *Les conversions de saint Augustin* (Paris: Aubier, 1950), pp. 276 ff.: Conf., XI, 2 (2) contains St. Augustine's submission to Sacred Scripture as the direct result of the gift of the Catholic faith; Books XII and XIII reveal his personal answer to the Word of God, "désormais sa lumière et son plaisir souverain" (p. 276), the completion of his Christian philosophy by the dynamism of duration moving toward a future already

illumined by the Sacred Scriptures. Father Le Blond (p. 316) cites P. Lands-berg, "La conversion de s. Augustin," *Vie spirituelle* (1936): "Nous lui devons la division même de notre livre et l'intuition de l'unité des Confessions." It is the merit of Le Blond that he brings into full view the role of Sacred Scripture in Augustine's conversion and subsequent thinking, and the place and the importance of the last three books of the *Confessions* in the work as a whole. Too often these chapters are considered an unfortunate appendage due to some imagined defect in St. Augustine's plan of composition.

56 Cf. *Conf.*, XIII, 34 (49); Ryan, *op. cit.*, pp. 367-378.

57 For studies of St. Augustine's doctrine on Sacred Scripture, cf. H. J. Vogels, "Die heilige Schrift bei Augustinus," in Grabmann-Mausbach (eds.), *Aurelius Augustinus* (Köln: Verlag J. P. Bachem, 1930), pp. 411-421; C. J. Costello, O.M.I., *St. Augustine's Doctrine on the Inspiration and Canonicity of Scripture* (Washington: Catholic University Press, 1930); H. J. Vogels, *St. Augustins Schrift De consensu Evangelistarum* (Freiburg: Herdersche Ver-lagshandlung, 1908), in particular pp. 64-81. "Der Inspirationsbegriff Augus-tins"; C. Douvais, "St. Augustin et la Bible," *Revue Biblique*, II (1893), 62-81, and "St. Augustin Defenseur de la Bible," *ibid.* (1894), 110-135, 410-432; for a brief conspectus of the history of the interpretation of Genesis, cf. H. Schumacher, "The Historical Value of Genesis, Chapter II," *Homiletic and Pastoral Review*, XXIII (1923), 579-587, 699-706, 803-810, 917-924 (di-rectly on St. Augustine and his literal understanding of the Biblical narra-tive), 1027-1033, 1138-1144; C. Dorsch, "SS. Augustinus und Hieronymus über die Wahrheit der biblischen Geschichte," *Zeitschrift für Katholische Theologie* (1811), pp. 421-448, 601-661; A. Colunga, "S. Augustin expositor de las profecias en la Ciudad de Dios," *Ciudad de Dios* (número extraord.), Vol. CLXVII, 1954; A. D. R. Polman, *The Word of God According to St. Augustine* (Grand Rapids, Mich.: Eerdmans, 1961), the helpful work of a professor at the John Calvin Academy, Kampen, Holland, first published in Dutch, 1955; for a general survey, cf. Spadafora-Romeo-Frangipane, *Il Libro Sacro* (Padova: Edizioni Messaggero, 1958), I, 333-351, "Storia della esegesi." In general, there is a paucity of literature on St. Augustine and the Bible. Vogels (*op. cit.*, *apud* Grabmann-Mausbach, p. 411), writing in 1930, de-clares that Augustine's importance for Scriptural study has been somewhat overlooked in the attention given to his brilliant philosophical talent and theological accomplishments. "Angesichts des Reichtums der Augustinuslitera-tur bleibt jedenfalls der Umstand bezeichnend, dass bis heute nur eine einzige selbständige Schrift vorliegt, die sich mit dem Exegeten beschäftigt. . . ." and he refers to H. M. Clausen, *Aurelius Augustinus Hipponensis sacrae scripturae interpres* (Hauniae: 1827). "Der Stellung," concludes Vogels, "welche die Bibel in der Theologie des grossen Kirchenvaters einnimmt, will das nicht recht entsprechen" (p. 411). Polman, writing in 1955 (*op. cit.*, pp. 39-40), mentions the same paucity. The work of Pontet, already cited, while outstanding, is a specialized study. Polman acknowledges his de-pendence on the work of Costello, which remains the fundamental study of St. Augustine's doctrine on canonicity and inspiration.

58 Cf. Costello, *op. cit.*, pp. 4 ff., for a listing from various works of St. Augustine.

59 Cf. *Contra adv. Legis et Proph.*, II, 4 (13); P.L. 42, 646: "Ea Scriptura, intelligitur, in qua est auctoritas Dei." St. Paul uses such phrases, "Ostendens utique in eadem Scriptura Deum loqui." "His atque huiusmodi attestationi-bus Dei boni et veri esse Scripturas illas . . . apostolica commendat auc-

toritas." Cf. *De Civitate Dei*, XVIII, 41: The fact of the inspiration of the
Divine Scriptures is accepted *toto orbe terrarum*, bringing a unity and
harmony of minds where the philosophers could build only a confused
Babylon; St. Augustine simply receives this universal fact and teaching of
Divine Truth, "divinis vocibus . . . , non argumentationum concertationibus
inculcata."

60 *De Trin.*, Proem.; P.L. 42, 845.

61 *De Gen. ad litt.*, IV, 34 (53); P.L. 34, 319. Cf. *De civitate Dei*, XV, 8:
"Nunc autem defendenda mihi videtur historia, ne sit Scriptura incredi-
bilis. . . ."

62 *De doctrina christiana*, IV, 6 (9); P.L. 34, 92: "Auctores nostri, quorum
scripta divinitus inspirata canonem nobis saluberrima auctoritate fecerunt."

63 *Serm.*, 51, 4 (5); P.L. 38, 336. St. Augustine cites Colossians, esp. 2:6-7
and 3:16, his point of departure in all of his works defending the Bible,
which culminate in his treatises on Genesis and on the concordance of the
four Gospels.

64 *Serm.*, 257, 2; P.L. 38, 1194: "Melius ego mendax ero, quam mentiatur
Scriptura quae dicit, *Omnis homo mendax*. Si enim ego verax, Scriptura
mendax erit. Sed quia Scriptura mendax esse non potest, ego mendax ero . . .
Scriptura (enim) Dei est."

65 *Serm.*, 71, 12 (19); P.L. 38, 454: "Peccatis enim manentibus, manent
quodam modo inimicitiae adversus Deum, et ab illo alienatio . . . quoniam
non mentitur Scriptura, dicens, *Peccata vestra separant inter vos et Deum*
(Isa. 59:2)."

66 *Epist.*, 82, 1 (3); P.L. 33, 277.

67 *De cons. Evv.*, III, 7 (30); P.L. 34, 1175-76.

68 The inerrancy of the Bible as a whole establishes the unity of the
two Testaments, and hence, by virtue of their succession in historical time,
the theology of history. Cf. *De cons. Evv.*, I, 35 (54); P.L. 34, 1070: "Hoc
magnum et inenarrabile sacramentum, hoc regnum et sacerdotium antiquis
per prophetiam revelabatur, posteris autem per Evangelium praedicatur";
and *passim*.

69 *Conf.*, IX, 6 (14); Ryan, *op. cit.*, p. 214. Cf. Courcelle, *op. cit.*, p. 216,
who concludes that St. Augustine was prepared for baptism by the homilies
of St. Ambrose on Isaiah's prophecy and St. Luke's Gospel: the divine economy of salvation history, in other words, which will become the characteristic
subject of Augustine's work as a Father of the Church and as an educator.

70 *De civitate Dei*, XX, 1: "In aedificii fundamento prius ponere testi-
monia divina debemus." From the viewpoint of the Christian educator, this
states the basic principle in curriculum construction.

71 *De magistro*, 14 (46).

72 For the translation of *De catechizandis rudibus* by J. P. Christopher,
in the series "Ancient Christian Writers," and for the literature on the catechumenate, cf. chap. v, above, pp. 143-144.

73 *De catech. rudibus*, 1 (1); J. P. Christopher (trans.), *St. Augustine:
The First Catechetical Instruction* ("Ancient Christian Writers," No. 2;
Westminster, Md.: The Newman Bookshop, 1946), p. 13. For the unabridged
edition of Msgr. Christopher's introduction and notes, cf. *Patristic Studies*,
Vol. VIII (Washington: The Catholic University of America, 1926).

74 *Ibid.*, 2 (4); Christopher, *op. cit.*, pp. 17-18.

75 *Ibid.*, 3 (5); *op. cit.*, p. 18.

76 *Ibid.*

77 *Ibid.*, 3 (6); *op. cit.*, p. 19.

78 Cf. *ibid.*, 4 (7-8); *op. cit.*, pp. 21-24.

79 Cf. *ibid.*, 4: ". . . maxime propterea Christus advenit, ut cognosceret homo quantum eum diligat Deus, et ideo cognosceret, ut in eius dilectionem, a quo prior dilectus est, inardesceret . . . ; omnisque Scriptura divina, quae ante scripta est, ad praenunciandum adventum Domini scripta est, et quidquid postea mandatum est litteris et divina auctoritate firmatum, Christum narrat, et dilectionem monet. . . . Magna est enim miseria superbus homo: sed maior misericordia humilis Deus. Hac ergo dilectione tibi tamquam fine proposita, quo referas omnia quae dicis, quidquid narras ita narra, ut ille, cui loqueris, audiendo credat, credendo speret, sperando amet." This sampling of St. Augustine's pedagogical doctrine indicates the way in which the academic teaching of "religion" will be at one and the same time a genuine catechesis, an apostolate of the classroom.

80 *Ibid.*, 4 (8); *op. cit.*, p. 24.

81 *Ibid.*, 7 (11); *op. cit.*, p. 29.

82 *Ibid.*, 8 (12); *op. cit.*, p. 30: "When an educated person comes who already has considerable knowledge of our Scriptures and our literature," he is to be considered "already equipped" and is "now only to be made a partaker in the sacraments."

83 *Ibid.*, cc. 8-15 inclusive; *op. cit.*, pp. 30-51.

84 *Ibid.*, 2 (4); *op. cit.*, p. 17.

85 Cf. chap. x, below, pp. 324-325.

86 *Ibid.*, 19 (31); *op. cit.*, p. 61.

87 *Ibid.*, 22 (39); *op. cit.*, p. 70.

88 Cf. *ibid.*, 22 (39-40); *op. cit.*, pp. 70-72. For the Christocentric character of this biblical catechesis, cf. M. Comeau, "Le Christ, chemin et terme de l'ascension spirituelle d'après saint Augustin," *Recherches de science religieuse*, XL (1952), 80-89. For the place of Christ in the religious preaching and teaching of St. Augustine in general, cf. Pontet, *op. cit.*, *passim*.

89 Cf. *De doctrina christiana*, Prologue, 6-9; John J. Gavigan (trans.), "Christian Instruction," in *Writings of Saint Augustine*, IV (New York: Cima Publishing Co., 1947), 22-25. St. Augustine stresses the necessity of a human teaching with the Bible as a "textbook," for God uses the human educational system, part and parcel of the providential order of human affairs, for imparting his Word to men. This completes and fulfills the eminence of teaching, to use Gilson's phrase. Holy Scripture becomes in this way a discipline added to the cycle of the human arts and sciences; the entire treatise *De doctrina christiana* presupposes that a new subject, a divine science, "religion," as we term it, has been added to the circle of learning. Since this Sacred Book is entirely concerned with him who is the divine image and model of human perfection (Colossians 2), the move which St. Augustine is making renews that original idea of education common to all humanity and especially visible among the primitive peoples of the earth. Cf. Mircea Eliade, *Cosmos and History* (New York: Harper Torchbooks, 1959); also his *Birth and Rebirth: The Religious Meanings of Initiation in Human Culture* (New York: Harper, 1958), Introduction, p. x: "Every primitive society possesses a consistent body of mythical traditions, a 'conception of the world,' . . . gradually revealed to the novice in the course of his initiation. . . . This 'sacred history'—mythology—is exemplary, paradigmatic: not only does it relate how things came to be; it also lays the foundation for all human behavior and all social and cultural institutions." These generalizations from contemporary

social anthropology open perspectives for the proper understanding of Augustine's program of academic religious education and furnish the background for its significance in the regeneration and renewal of human culture, as such, which is the temporal meaning of the Christian era.

90 Cf. Gerard L. Ellspermann, O.S.B., *The Attitude of the Early Christian Latin Writers toward Pagan Literature and Learning* (Washington: Catholic University Press, 1949), "The Early Christians and Education," pp. 1-13, with the literature indicated, especially the study of G. Bardy: "L'église et l'enseignement pendant les trois premiers siècles," *Revue des sciences religieuses*, XII (1932), 1-28. Cf. also H.-I. Marrou, *A History of Education in Antiquity* (New York: Sheed and Ward, 1956), p. 330: "In the fourth century, however, there appeared a type of Christian school that was wholly devoted to religion and had none of the features of the old classical school; already medieval and not classical in its inspiration, it remained for a long time peculiar to its own environment and had little outside influence. This was the monastic school." That St. Augustine's program is not entirely encompassed in these words will be clear when the teaching of *De doctrina christiana* on the arts and disciplines of human culture is considered. For a comprehensive general summary to the time of St. Augustine, cf. Marrou's chap. ix, "Christianity and Classical Education," pp. 314-329.

91 For the role of the *quaestio* in this academic life and practice, which leads directly from St. Augustine to the *Summa theologica* of St. Thomas Aquinas, cf. E. Bertola, "La 'Quaestio' nella storia del pensiero medievale: Epoca patristica e carolingia," *Aquinas*, V (1962), 230-248, and the earlier studies to which Prof. Bertola makes reference.

92 Cf. *De doctrina christiana*, II, cc. 17-42; Gavigan, *op. cit.*, pp. 86-116, in which St. Augustine discusses this "gold of the Egyptians," how it is to be "cleansed from pride" (c. 41), and what the usefulness of each of the inherited educational disciplines is for Christians. Nothing positive is rejected: it is an authentic and genuine Christian humanism in education.

93 *De doctrina christiana*, prologue, 1; Gavigan, *op. cit.*, p. 19.

94 *Ibid.*, 8-9; *op. cit.*, pp. 23-25.

95 *Ibid.*, I, 1 (1); *op. cit.*, p. 27.

96 Cf. *ibid.*, I, 3 (3); *op. cit.*, p. 29.

97 Cf. *ibid.*, I, 4-5; *op. cit.*, pp. 29-31: "We must use this world," he writes, "and not enjoy it, so that the 'invisible attributes' of God may be clearly seen, 'being understood through the things that are made,' that is, that through what is corporeal and temporal we may comprehend the eternal and spiritual" (p. 30). This is precisely the theocentric program which his earlier works contain, as we saw in chap. vi, "The Culture of the Human Arts and Disciplines," pp. 149-179, above. Augustine's educational program has not undergone a substantial change in his ordination and consecration; it is deepened and made more practically efficacious through the revealed light which transfigures it in the *De doctrina christiana*, but it remains an authentic humanism, authentic by virtue of its openness to God, and human in its balanced approach to all the arts and disciplines of human culture. "Ne quid nimis. . . ." (*De doctrina christiana*, II, 39 (58)).

98 Cf. *ibid.*, I, 9; *op. cit.*, p. 34.

99 *Ibid.*, I, 10; *op. cit.*, p. 34.

100 *Ibid.*

101 *Ibid.*, I, 11; *op. cit.*, pp. 34-35.

102 Cf. *ibid.*, I, cc. 12-30; *op. cit.*, pp. 35-51.

103 *Ibid.*, I, 24 (25); *op. cit.*, p. 45.

104 *Ibid.*, I, 25 (26); *op. cit.*, pp. 45-46.

105 *Ibid.*, I, 27 (28); *op. cit.*, p. 47.

106 *Ibid.*, II, 7 (9); *op. cit.*, p. 67.

107 *Ibid.*, II, 7 (10); *op. cit.*, p. 67.

108 *Ibid.*, II, 7 (11); *op. cit.*, p. 69.

109 *Ibid.*, II, 8 (13); *op. cit.*, p. 70.

110 *Ibid.*, II, 9 (14); *op. cit.*, pp. 71-72.

111 *Ibid.*, II, 28 (42); *op. cit.*, p. 98.

112 *Ibid.*, II, 28 (43); *op. cit.*, p. 99.

113 *Ibid.*, II, 28 (44); *op. cit.*, pp. 99-100.

114 William M. Green, "Augustine on the Teaching of History," *University of California Publications in Classical Philology*, XII (1944), 315.

115 *Ibid.*, pp. 324-325.

116 Cf. Pierre Ranwez, S.J., "Religious and Profane Education," *Lumen Vitae*, VI (1951), 453: "Perhaps a mistake has been made in the separating of secular history from Bible History or Church History; the sacred and the profane have not run parallel lines. All history is sacred, and it is for the teacher to show its significance to his pupils."

117 *De doctrina christiana*, I, 37 (41); Gavigan, *op. cit.*, p. 58.

118 For the resistance of modern unbelief to this view of historical origins, cf. for example Adolf Bauer, *Ursprung und Fortwirken der christlichen Weltchronik* (Graz: Leuschner und Lubenskly, 1910), a work which resents the universalization of Genesis in the Western tradition. "Die im Alten Testament enthaltene sagenhafte Urgeschichte des israelitischen Volkes galt daher den Juden als authentische Darstellung der Anfänge der Menschheitsgeschichte überhaupt" (p. 10). Christianity adopted this Jewish teaching, which accordingly became general in the West with the ascendancy of the Church. For Bauer, this is the chief thing to be deplored in the Christian era; his witness to the fact, however, becomes all the more significant a half-century later in post-modern times.

119 *De gen. ad litt.*, I, 1 (1-2); P.L. 34, 247; "Quaeritur utrum omnia secundum figurarum tantummodo intellectum accipiantur, an etiam secundum fidem rerum gestarum asserenda et defendenda sint." His answer states that the Bible in general is a *narratio rerum factarum*, with allegory confined to writings like the Canticle of Canticles.

120 *De gen. ad litt.*, VIII, 1 (2); P.L. 34, 272: "Narratio in his libris [Genesis] non genere locutionis figuratarum rerum est, sicut in Cantico Canticorum, sed omnino gestarum, sicut in Regnorum libris et hujuscemodi."

121 *De gen. c. man.*, II, 2 (3); P.L. 34, 197.

122 *De gen. ad litt.*, VIII, 3 (6); P.L. 34, 374: "Sic enim scriptum est, quia sic factum est."

123 *Ibid.*: ". . . diligentius considerandum est, ne cogat in allegoriam, ut non ista ligna fuerunt, sed aliud aliquid nomine ligni significet."

124 *De gen. ad litt.*, IV, 34 (53); P.L. 34, 319: ". . . et utraque (Scriptura) una est, quia uno Spiritu Veritatis inspirante conscripta est."

125 Costello, *op. cit.*, p. 56; cf. St. Augustine, *Enarr. in ps.* 104, 27; P.L. 37, 1400: "Libera enim est laudatio a lege narrantis et texentis historiam."

126 *Enarr. in ps.*, 59, 1; P.L. 36, 714: "Facta sunt ista, et quemadmodum facta sunt ita ibi conscripta sunt, ita leguntur."

127 *Ibid.*, 33, 2; P.L. 36, 300: "Et verissimum est, quia contigit, et quod contigit scriptum est . . .; sic credo."

128 *De div. qq. 83,* 65; P.L. 40, 59: "Neque cum res factae allegorizantur, gestae rei fidem amittunt."

129 *Epist.,* 143, 7; P.L. 33, 588 (Costello's translation).

130 *De civitate Dei,* XVII, 40: "Non enim parvus auctor est in historia Varro, qui hoc prodidit, quod a litterarum etiam divinarum veritate non dissonat. . . . Nam et ipsa historicorum inter se dissonantia copiam nobis praebet, ut ei potius credere debeamus, qui divinae, quam tenemus, non repugnat historiae. Porro autem cives impiae civitatis . . . cui potius credere debeant, non inveniunt. Nos vero in nostrae religionis historia, fulti auctoritate divina, quidquid ei resistit, non dubitamus esse falsissimum, quomodolibet sese habeant caetera in saecularibus litteris; quae seu vera seu falsa sint, nihil momenti afferunt, quo recte beateque vivamus." This is the completion, on the intellectual plane of historical understanding, of the victory of the Martyrs over the ancient paganism.

131 *De Trin.,* XIII, 1 (2).

132 In the two contemporary centuries ending in our time secularism has raised an analagous question regarding the Christian religion, and has resolutely opposed Christian Doctrine in the schools and resisted its rightful position on the curriculum of studies. All social progress, secularism has believed, results from the separation of religion and social living and from the departure of Western man from his historic religious institution. These considerations, to which we shall return in the concluding chapters, serve to illuminate the abiding validity of *The City of God* and the contemporary relevance of St. Augustine's pedagogical doctrine for the Christian education of youth.

133 *Enarr in ps.,* 90, *Serm.,* 2, 1; P.L. 37, 1159. Note St. Augustine's central reference to 1 Tim. 2:5: "For there is one God, and one Mediator between God and men, himself man, Christ Jesus, who gave himself a ransom for all, bearing witness in his own time." St. Augustine is indeed "The Second Paul"; his Christian Doctrine and his new history in the schools are the pedagogical application of the theology of St. Paul.

134 Cf. chap. i, above, for this intellectual background and preparation for the *De civitate Dei.* St. Augustine composed his *City of God* with Eusebius' work open before him: "Nam sicut scribunt qui chronicam historiam persecuti sunt . . ." (*De civitate Dei,* VI, 6). The reference is to the work of Eusebius and St. Jerome.

135 Cf. the accurate and graphic passage of Van der Meer, *op. cit.,* pp. 361-362: "Easter eve had begun, the most joyful vigil of Christendom . . ., the feast of a multitude that could not be numbered. We can scarcely imagine the festive excitement and the joy. . . . It was something even more intense and exalted than our modern Christmas midnight Mass . . . for the Church folk of those times [the Christian mysteries] were the celebration of a mighty victory." This is the religious and social atmosphere whence Augustine's *City of God* proceeded, and it is the note, still to be heard in the *Allejuia* of the Easter vigil, which animated *doctrina christiana* in his school. This is the point of primary importance in the Christian education of youth today: the courageous and joyful consciousness of victory over modern secularism and atheism, both in the supervision of the curriculum and in classroom teaching.

136 Cf. Amari, *op. cit.,* esp. "Parte prima: L'oggetto della storia," pp. 15-44. History is a narration of facts which have actually taken place, the *res gestae.* Cf. *De ordine,* II, 12 (37); *De doctrina christiana,* II, 28 (44): *De*

gen. at litt., VIII, 1 (2) (". . . historiam, id est, rerum proprie gestarum narrationem"). From his earliest "philosophical" works to his theological treatises and commentaries on Scripture, Augustine is always perfectly consistent: history deals with the *res gestae,* seen as a complex of contingent facts, not in chaos, but in an order of succession in time. Cf. *De Trin.,* IV, 16 (21): "De contexto saeculorum ordine. . . ."

137 Cf. *De Trin.,* XIV, 8 (11) and XIII (1). Philosophical reasoning by itself cannot discern the order by which the succession of things in human history proceeds. The human intellect can know the natures of things, but not this order among them in human history, for it is a contingent thing known to God alone. Hence a "philosophy of history," in last analysis, must be a philosophy which has ears to hear what the witnesses sent by God have to say concerning the order which he places in his creation. It can escape the condition of an arbitrary construct imposed upon the factually given, and reflect the real order of events, only if it is willing to hear: to learn, in humble docility, from the theology of history.

138 *De Trin.,* XIII, 1 (2).

139 Cf. Amari, *op. cit.,* pp. 61 and 68.

140 For St. Augustine's *ex professo* discussion of "science" and "wisdom," cf. *De Trinitate,* Books XII, XIII, and XIV. For studies of this absolutely fundamental principle for understanding *doctrina christiana,* St. Augustine's educational philosophy, cf. Etienne Gilson, *The Christian Philosophy of Saint Augustine* (New York: Random House, 1960), pp. 115-126, and H.-I. Marrou, *Saint Augustin et la fin de la culture antique* (Paris: Éditions E. de Boccard, 1958), "Cadres généraux de la culture chrétienne," pp. 357-385, and "La formation de l'intellectuel chrétien," pp. 387-413, where the role of the Bible in St. Augustine's *doctrina christiana* is admirably appreciated. For the bearing of "science" and "wisdom" precisely upon secular and sacred history, the fundamental treatise is Amari, *op. cit.,* a doctoral dissertation accomplished under P. Leturia, S.J., at the Gregorian University in Rome. Cf. esp. "La storia come scienza," pp. 47-103; "La storia come sapienza," pp. 107-200, with the discussions of the use of "la scienza storica" in sacred history and church history, and the sapiential mode of teaching, "La sapienza della storia," pp. 119-133.

141 Cf. Amari, *op. cit.,* p. 93: "Questa 'regalis via liberandae animae' tracciata dalla Provvidenza all'umanità, è la storia della religione cristiana. E la visione storica della salute che Agostino attinge dalla tradizione, S. Paolo e i padri. La Sacra Scrittura è una storia, ma qualcosa di più di una storia, intesa come racconto di avvenimenti, come cronaca. In questa storia sacra il racconto è secondario, esso è mezzo, veicolo di una concezione, di una dottrina. La creazione, la caduta, l'antica alleanza sono dei fatti situati nel tempo, ma portano in seno grandi verità religiose, dogmi e altre verità secondari e spirituali. Dio ha nascosta queste verità in fatti, perchè siano accessibili a tutti. Questa accondiscendenza divina è rilevata con parole espressive da S. Agostino." It would be difficult to state more accurately the meaning of *doctrina christiana* in the mind of St. Augustine, or the method and goal of the modern teacher of religion in a classroom simultaneously academic and catechetical.

142 This is the very heart of St. Augustine's preaching, teaching, and writing; cf. *De moribus Ecclesiae Catholicae,* 7, 11-12; *De vera religione,* 7; 13; 25; 46; *De util. credendi,* 8, 20; 16, 34; *De civitate Dei,* X, 32: "Haec est religio, quae universalem continet viam animae liberandae. . . . Haec est

enim quodam modo regalis via, quae una ducit ad regnum . . . aeternitatis firmitate securum." Providence has built this economy of salvation into the very life of mankind on earth; therefore the Christian religion is historical in a unique sense. It *is* history, and the very temporal order, since it contains and manifests this divine and sacred history, is the well-spring of divine faith.

143 Amari, *op. cit.*, p. 93; original text in n. 141, above.

144 By viewing the matter superficially or within the categories of the positivist and secularist concept of "history," it is possible to misconceive such a course in Christian Doctrine for high school or college religion as a mere "social science project" or even as a program which puts religion in second place. When the life of mankind on earth, however, is seen in terms of St. Augustine's "science" and "wisdom," no such misapprehension of the economy of salvation and the teaching of it in the schools is possible. Cf., for example, the statement of Pierre Ranwez, S.J., cited above, p. 253, n. 116.

145 Cf. *De lib arb.*, II, 17, (45).

146 Cf. *De Trinitate*, XII, 3 (3); XII, 4 (4); XII, 13 (21), passages which complement Book I of *De doctrina christiana*, the philosophy of culture which grounds the Christian education of youth by a teaching on the use and the enjoyment of the temporal and external goods and values. For the teaching of Vatican Council I on the point, cf. *Denz.* 1799: all the arts and disciplines of human culture lead the soul to God, *si rite pertractentur*. This proviso is the crux of the matter. Among these arts and disciplines, history is the most crucial, for if it is not taught in the right way, youth will not be able to see properly the divine economy of salvation. *Doctrina christiana* can maintain its full integrity and spiritual effectiveness only when it pays due attention to these fundamentals and principles of the order or curriculum of studies.

147 *De Trinitate*, XII, 14 (23); cf. *ibid.*, XII, 15 (25).

148 Amari, *op. cit.*, p. 125.

149 It is important to note that *doctrina*, in the language of St. Augustine, has both an active and a passive sense. It is not only the "doctrine" which is taught; it is also the act of teaching by which the soul of the learner is actively illuminated through the work of the teacher. Cf. Gerald F. Van Ackeren, S.J., *Sacra Doctrina: The Subject of the First Question of the Summa Theologica of St. Thomas Aquinas* (Rome: Catholic Book Agency, 1952), esp. pp. 51-52; 64-75; and the "Letter of Introduction" by Yves M.-J. Congar, O.P., pp. 13-18.

150 Cf. *De civitate Dei*, XVIII, 50.

151 U. A. Padovani, "La città di Dio di S. Agostino: teologia e non filosofia della storia," *Rivista di filosofia neoscolastica*, XXIII (Suppl., 1931), 241.

152 *Ibid.*, p. 249.

153 Newman, *op. cit.*, p. 231.

8

St. Augustine and the Schools of Christendom

THE educational accomplishment of St. Augustine sealed the victory of the Church of the martyrs and the apologists over the ancient paganism and completed the conversion of the classical civilization, embodying the natural heritage of mankind, to Christ. His principles and fundamentals of education offered to the schools of the future a lucidly-conceived program for the Christian formation of youth. It entailed on the one hand a regeneration of the arts and disciplines of human culture, including the restoration of the sciences which study the natural cosmos; and on the other it was a renewal of sacred history which brought to the very center of the educative process the image of the invisible God, the firstborn of every creature, the perfect model of human perfection to be imitated and followed.[1] It held out the promise, therefore, of a new type of cultural progress based upon truth in the cultivation of the word and upon the systematic inclusion of the natural and mathematical sciences on the order or curriculum of studies; and at the same time it was designed to enable young people to conceive and to plan their earthly living in terms of the sacred.

This is a new pattern of education, even though it incorporates the positive values of the classical culture. Turning from educational theory to administrative practice, St. Augustine's program is seen to blueprint schools of a new type which will be the seedbed of the Christian social order of the centuries to come.[2]

For the approach to education contained in the pedagogical writings of St. Augustine became the pattern and program for organizing the schools of the new Western civilization which was formed after the decline and fall of Rome. It was a program of teaching centered upon the Bible, as the earlier educational institution of the classical civilization had centered upon Homer. The Bible itself presents the framework of universal history, beginning with the creation of the universe and of man and ending in the vision of the final end of history seen by St. John in the Apocalypse. The earliest preaching and teaching of the Christian religion was accomplished on this historical framework of the Bible, as St. Peter's first sermons in the *Acts of the Apostles* bear witness. The continuation and development of this Christian teaching, carried out by the Fathers of the Church, was at the same time a development of this biblical framework of historical understanding. Eusebius and St. Jerome are the culminating figures in the gradual elaboration of a Christian chronology of world history. It was St. Augustine who completed their work by organizing a plan and program of education, a *doctrina christiana,* to embody this biblical framework of history and historical understanding in the textbooks and syllabi, indeed in the entire structure, curriculum and approach to teaching, in both content and methodology. This is the *tuta via* in the order of learning, the Christian education of youth which St. Augustine missed so keenly when he was a student.[3]

In this way, the Bible has become in St. Augustine's hands the center of the educational process, replacing Homer, the core-book of classical antiquity. This heals and restores the teaching of sacred history to young people. This makes education once more a true initiation of youth into the divine economy for human living and plan for human happiness, and accomplishes the reform of the heritage of education to its pristine state. *Doctrina christiana* is the *paideia Theou* for the children of the new Israel of God.

St. Augustine's work, therefore, not only elaborates a body of historical understanding, but also launches a vast program of Christian teaching which became part and parcel of the formation of the new civilization on earth called Western Christendom.[4] Indeed, it would not be too much to say that this new order of studies deriving from St. Augustine is one of the essential factors in the apostolate of the Church which provided the creative dynamism in the formation of Western civilization. It is beyond the scope of the present study to trace the influence of St. Augustine's philosophy of education on the thought of Cassiodorus, St. Isidore of Seville, Alcuin or Rhaban Maur, or to describe the manner in which his concept of the order of studies was realized in the schools of Christendom.[5] The most fundamental feature of this Augustinian influence was the place and function of the Bible in this Christian education of youth, and the closely-related content of basic historical understanding which was taught. In other words, the Christian view of mankind as a historic process and whole was taught in two chief ways: in connection with the teaching of Christian doctrine or "religion"; and in connection with the teaching of "history" as a distinct academic discipline. We shall sketch a synthetic survey of this fundamental feature of Western education and culture, and the pedagogical impact made upon it by the recent rise of the secularized philosophy of history.

The New Christian Historiography

The point of departure in this program of teaching which incorporated the historical understanding characteristic of Christianity appears in the figure of St. Augustine's disciple, Orosius, the young Spanish priest who came to study under the famed Bishop of Hippo while he was engaged on the composition of *The City of God*. St. Augustine, recognizing the talents of the younger man, commissioned him to compose a textbook of universal history on a chronological plan to supplement the vast theological work upon which he was engaged. Orosius continued his journey to Palestine for consultation with St. Jerome, returning a year later to the school and library at Hippo. Here he composed the *Seven Books of History Against the Pagans*, which carries out St. Augustine's assignment and is dedicated to him.[6]

Orosius' work represents the authentic Christian attitude toward history, as Lacroix points out, in that it not only sees history as a general development of mankind under God's providence, but also places the concrete divine economy of salvation in this history as the focal point of its meaning.[7] The Incarnation is the center. The chronology of world history is seen in relationship to the coming of Christ. With Orosius, therefore, the mind of Western man prepares for the relocation of historical reckoning, actually worked out less than a century later, to our present system of dating from the Incarnation of Christ the Lord.[8]

It is difficult to over-estimate the influence of Orosius' work, organizing for teaching purposes, as it does, the *Chronicles* of Eusebius and St. Jerome and *The City of God* of St. Augustine. Until the twelfth century it was the standard textbook of history in the schools of Christendom and the vehicle by which Augustinian historical thought passed to the new world of culture which was under formation in the Christian West.[9] Later teachers and writers, such as Gregory of Tours, Isidore of Seville and the Venerable Bede in England, depend upon St. Augustine and Orosius, and represent in their various works of teaching and historical writing this basic view of the meaning and direction of universal history. In fact, King Alfred the Great translated and adapted Orosius' work into the Saxon language, a striking indication of the penetration of Christian thinking in the area of historical understanding to the common man throughout the Western world.

Throughout the centuries of the formation of Christendom, therefore, this basic pattern of teaching and historical understanding came to characterize the mind of the West. These textbooks and treatises on history were one with the Bible; indeed, they owed their popularity as tools of teaching throughout the rising Western world to the fact that they fitted the "completely biblical mentality" of the teachers in the schools of Christendom.[10] Whether they are minor chronicles of a small abbey, the rude annals of a semi-barbarous kingdom, or extensive works embracing universal history as a whole, the principle remains the same: always they are fitted into the larger biblical framework and illuminated with the light of revealed truth. Historical understanding and interpretation, in other words, are in harmony with the Bible: the educational work of the Fathers of the Church in the regeneration and renewal of history as an academic discipline has borne its fruit. A Christian perception and concept of human history has risen and is becoming universal in the West.[11]

It would lead beyond the present purpose to report on the numerous works of historiography which were produced in these earlier centuries of Western civilization; Otto, Bishop of Freising, and his major treatise on universal history, *The Two Cities*, must stand for them all. This new textbook brought the chronology of the development of mankind down to the threshold of the thirteenth century, supplanted Orosius' work, and became the standard instrument of historical teaching throughout the high middle ages. While it was an original and a personal work of Otto, it also embodies in its own way the same Augustinian and biblical view of history which characterizes the teaching in the schools of Christendom. "Otto did not merely take over," writes Professor Mierow in the introduction to his translation of the work; "he independently worked up anew the philosophy of

history of the middle ages which Augustine had founded. . . .
Everything is judged and explained according to its place
in the divine plan of salvation." [12]

Sacra Pagina: Christian Doctrine in the Schools

These treatises on history implement an academic discipline which occupied a position on the higher levels of education, and which found its characteristic function in the
preparation of teachers for the lower levels of the Christian
educational system, for the apostolate of Christian Doctrine
as such. This introduces the second way in which the biblical
understanding of universal history was taught and the Christian concept of human origins, human life and human destiny was formed. It was the direct use of the Bible itself as
the basic instrument for teaching Christian doctrine in the
schools of Christendom. For Christian doctrine was taught
according to the biblical plan elaborated by St. Augustine.
The teaching was done, for the most part, from the sacred
text itself: it consisted of a lecturing, a *praelectio,* directly
from the sacred pages. Thus it came to be called "teaching *in
sacra pagina,*" and the teachers authorized for this apostolate
were known as *magistri in sacra pagina.*[13] It is apparent that
this manner of teaching the sacred truths of Christianity
brought with it a typical historical understanding, that understanding which the Catholic faith teaches to mankind and
which is reflected in the very structure and organization of
the books of the Bible.

The teaching in the schools of Christendom developed
with the very growth of those schools and of the civilization
which they represented and nourished. This corresponding
development in the formulation and the teaching of Christian Doctrine is the theological movement of the twelfth
and the thirteenth centuries, with the famous lights of the
schools of the period typified by Peter Lombard and St.
Thomas Aquinas. Here again, we see the same biblical historical understanding which has characterized Christian

teaching since the times of the Fathers. "The plan of the celebrated work of Peter Lombard," writes Van Steenberghen, "the *Sentences*, is inspired directly by the *De doctrina christiana*; now, one knows well the unique place which the *Sentences* occupied in the history of theology during the Middle Ages." [14] In other words, the basic Augustinian approach to Christian teaching was continuing in these brilliantly developed forms of the twelfth and thirteenth centuries. Indeed, the teaching continued to be based directly on the Bible itself, and the *magister in sacra pagina* continued his position as the official teacher of Christian doctrine.

In the summation of Christian doctrine for the higher levels of education accomplished by St. Thomas Aquinas, there is the same rooting of the teaching in the sacred history of the Bible.[15] In fact, St. Thomas introduces his *Summa* by a question on "holy teaching," *sacra doctrina* in the active sense, and makes it clear that this teaching is directly related to Sacred Scripture. "Scripture . . . is the book written by God Himself," writes Father Van Ackeren, "for instructing His children in the knowledge of salvation. It is the sacred writing of this instruction: *sacra scriptura huius doctrinae* (*Summa Theologica* 1, 1, Introduction). It is the first and most fundamental book upon which all the other books of sacred instruction depend." [16] These observations receive additional meaning from the fact that St. Thomas was a *magister in sacra pagina* for seventeen years, teaching daily directly from the text of the Bible itself, fully and completely in the historic pattern of teaching on the lower levels of study in those Christian times.[17]

Thus we have in this teaching a profound unity of historical understanding, with no clashing history courses set against the religion courses, reflecting an understanding of human development and purpose and destiny alien or even opposed to that revealed by God in the Bible. All history is taught upon a Christian chronology and the general content of history is taught upon a biblical framework, under the light of the Catholic faith, and in relation to the content of the Bible, as the basic instrument for the teaching of sacred doctrine.

This pattern of historical understanding and teaching continues as the standard procedure in education to the threshold of contemporary times. In 1681 Bossuet published his *Discours sur L'histoire universelle*, a major treatise on Christian doctrine and on universal history and again one which came from the activity of teaching. For the Bishop of Meaux composed his work for the Crown Prince of France and his companions, with whose Christian education he had been charged. We have here, therefore, once again the close relationship between historical understanding and the Christian formation of youth. It would lead too far afield to analyze the details of the plan and content of Bossuet's masterpiece; it is sufficient to note that it continues the tradition of Orosius and Otto of Freising. Bossuet's work is a new presentation of human development adapted to his own time and responsibilities, but one which at the same time incorporates the biblical understanding deriving from the Fathers of the Church and in particular from St. Augustine.[18]

The point which is of present concern does not involve the details of this historical understanding, but the fact of its striking unity in the schools of Christendom over so many centuries. Since St. Augustine, from one end of Christendom to the other, the schools on the various levels of education have been teaching this new understanding of the historical life of the human family which is rooted in the Bible and which conveys the revelation of God. For over a thousand years this Catholic view of the historical development of the human family has been taught as a fundamental element in the educational method of Christian culture.

This teaching always begins with the great themes of the Old Testament, and presents the choice of the Hebrew people as the central fact in the development of the economy of salvation. It is this choice of Israel which emphasizes the fact that the entire course of universal history, the life of all the peoples and nations of ancient times, proceeded as a majestic providential advent, marching as an *ordo saecolorum* toward the fullness of time, as God prepared mankind for the coming of the promised Redeemer. In this teaching of universal history in the schools of Christendom, there is no question about the divinity of Christ and his Incarnation by which the Word was made flesh and dwelt amongst us. Without hesitation this sacred mystery is placed at the center of world history as the most important event in the historical life of the human family. Each oncoming generation, accordingly, received an integrated understanding of the life of man on earth, with Christ in the central position of King and Lord of history, issuing his call to each one to take up the way of Christian living.

"The Incarnation is the supreme interest of mankind," writes Hilaire Belloc, "the one essential question in human history which must always be answered by a 'yes' or 'no': and according to that answer our whole view, not only of human society on earth, but upon the very nature and destiny of man, depends." [19]

Writing in the organ of UNESCO, the contemporary Polish Catholic scholar, Oscar Halecki, has placed the same issue squarely before his fellow-historians. "The history of Christendom," he writes, "cannot be separated from the study of the universal problems which have been raised by the appearance of Christ and by the preaching of his gospel which he wanted to reach all peoples of the globe. . . . For the Christian, or, to put it more plainly, for those who believe in the divinity of Christ, the mystery of the Incarnation is the great turning point of all history, dividing its course into two parts whose distinction is more important than any other question of periodization. . . . Was Christ God incarnate who this time directly and decisively interfered with human destiny, or just one more human spiritual leader of unquestioned virtue? This is an alternative to which every serious historian must take a definite position. . . . Even today every cultivated mind has to take a personal attitude with regard to the carpenter from Nazareth, an attitude on which one's whole outlook on the world and its history depends." [20]

From St. Augustine to Bossuet, then, there has been in the schools of Christendom a magnificent panorama of religious and historical teaching. It has unified the mind of Western man into a Christian and biblical pattern of historical understanding.[21] This teaching is itself considered to be a work of God, for it is carried on by the Church, which is the body of Christ. It is an understanding of mankind, our corporate origin, the pattern of our development, and our corporate destiny to come, which is embodied in the wisdom of the Church, imparted by the Sacred Magisterium, the teaching office of the Church, and elaborated in all the various works of historiography and of doctrinal teaching on each of the levels of education in the schools which depended upon ecclesiastical authority. Part and parcel, therefore, with this teaching of historical understanding, was the conviction that this same history was actually being made by the embodiment of spiritual knowledge and wisdom on earth, in the Catholic Church. For the Church, center and bearer of the meaning of human history, was universally understood to be the body of Christ and the extension of the Incarnation.

He who ponders in his mind's eye this vast panorama of educational work and accomplishment which formed and transmitted and enlarged our ancestral heritage cannot but wonder anew at the greatness of Augustine of Hippo, truly, to use the title of Von Kienitz' study, "The Genius of the West." Augustine is so because he organized and implemented the order of studies, the curriculum, to lead the youthful soul not only to the God of reason but also to the Lord of history, the incarnate God of Christianity. It is a curriculum which teaches young people the Christian and biblical view of the human family, that they might find in it their own personal goals, their personal principles for living and their personal models and paradigms of human perfection.

This is to restore and to renew the very idea of human education. The inner core of this educational program and process is nothing else than St. Augustine's *doctrina christiana;* and it embodies his plan for the regeneration and renewal of human culture. "Woe to you, O torrent of men's ways!", he had cried in anguish; "Who will stand up against you? How long will it be until you are dried up? How long will you sweep the sons of Eve down into that mighty and hideous ocean. . . ?" [22] Augustine himself is the one who stood up against this human social flood with his new program of Christian schooling, the fountainhead of a renewed and purified river of human social order and custom.

For Augustine's philosophy of education is the conversion of the educational institution of civilized man as such. It reflects his own conversion to the authority of the Catholic Church, to the Bible, and hence to a new perception of the meaning and direction of the historic life of mankind. It is the educational counterpart of the conversion of mankind to God in his Church, as Augustine perceived and experienced it in his own lifetime, launched now with new impetus and social effectiveness into the future. The Christian era is this regeneration and renewal, Western civilization is its social expression, and this theory and system for the Christian education of youth is its process. It is simply an academic teaching of the Incarnation of the Son of God, using the Sacred Book as its primary instrument, consistently applied through the length and breadth of the order of studies. Its name is *doctrina christiana.* Its content is historical theism.

Bayle: The Negative Preparation of Historical Atheism

The relationship of St. Augustine to the schools of Christendom, with their teaching of the biblical understanding of the historic life of mankind on earth which characterizes Western man, would be insufficiently surveyed were we to omit the rise and spread of modern secularism and atheism. Nor in such a case could the continuing relevance of Augustine's philosophy of education and order of the curriculum be brought properly into focus. Our purpose here is to analyze historical atheism as a fact and as a concept, for it leads to the heart of the matter and illuminates anew the contemporary bearing of the educational thought of St. Augustine.

In view of the background sketched so far, it is clear that historical atheism, in practice, will be an attack on the biblical understanding of human history, and, as a consequence, upon the very essence of St. Augustine's educational theory and practice. The attack will be implemented by a persistent attempt to discredit the documents, namely the writings and records contained in the Bible, which apprize mankind of the *mirabilia Dei* and the economy of salvation. This negative phase in the propagation of historical atheism was the work of many men. Among them, however, one was central, the leader and the type of all the rest. He was Pierre Bayle (1647-1706), son of a Huguenot minister and refugee to Holland at the Revocation of the Edict of Nantes. Here he conducted a campaign against the foundations of Christianity as such, climaxed with the publication in 1697 of his *Historical and Critical Dictionary*.[23]

"If one wishes to understand the goal toward which Bayle's conception of history strives," states Cassirer, "one must compare his work with the last great attempt at a purely theological presentation of history, namely, with Bossuet's *Discourse on Universal History*." [24] Bossuet, as we have seen, had one end in view: to understand the plan of redemption and salvation in universal history, to see the historic life of mankind with eyes open to the Bible. With St. Augustine he perceived the great advent of world history in which even the mighty empires of antiquity played a Providential role in preparing the fullness of time. Here the incarnation is central, the life of Christ is the most important life, and the Church organized by Christ goes out into human affairs as a divine institution.

All this is precisely what Bayle denies. The central tendency of his "criticism" is a consistent, persistent, calculated attack on the miracles recorded in the Bible, on the idea of the miraculous, on the historicity of the Bible, on the value of religion for moral uplift and social welfare, on the notion that atheism is something harmful to men and society, or even particularly bad. "Bayle accomplished scarcely less for history," writes Cassirer, "than Galileo did for natural science. . . . It is he who carries out the 'Copernican revolution' in the realm of historical science. For he no longer bases history on some dogmatically given objective content which he finds in the Bible or in the doctrine of the Church. . . . The criticism of historical sources, which was at first his sole purpose, expands as he proceeds until it becomes a sort of 'Critique of Historical Reason.' " [25]

Bayle had his predecessors, Spinoza for example, and Richard Simon's *Critical History of the Old Testament,* published in 1678, which so delighted the sceptics and libertines who were preparing the Enlightenment. "It was not to be expected that the Bible would escape the critical onslaught," writes Hazard. "The symbol, as it was, of Authority, it was only natural to submit it to the searching eye of criticism." [26] "And then the sceptics," he continues, "what an ally he [Simon] was for them! They were not capable of examining the sacred texts for themselves, but they were only too ready to believe anything that tended to diminish the authority, and derogate from the power, of the Scriptures." [27]

But it was Bayle who summed up this caustic and negative spirit, and spread it far and wide by means of his *Dictionary.* Voltaire called his works "the library of the nations." Frederick the Great compiled an abridgment for publication in Germany. "The Bible of the eighteenth century," Faguet called it. It was read beyond Bayle's fondest expectations: the first edition was sold out almost immediately. Edition followed edition. Then came the translations.

Bayle, it is clear, is the one who stands at the origins of historical atheism. "We shall find," writes his American biographer, "that Bayle returns, again and again, to the defense of atheism. . . . Such a sweeping condemnation of Christianity as a moral force has seldom been made." [28]

Bayle's technique is the choice of persons for treatment who furnish him an apt occasion for his philosophy. St. Augustine, for example, for whom he has a particular animosity, receives an article of only seventy-five lines, mostly devoted to the immorality of his early life. Bayle excuses himself. "If those Gentlemen had not too lightly passed over St. Augustine's irregular life," he writes, "I might wholly have dispensed with this article." [29] But the "remarks" occasioned by the seventy-five lines overflow into column after column of footnotes, and extend the space devoted to St. Augustine to seven folio pages. The impact is a calculated derogation from the position of the leading Christian writer on the biblical understanding of human history.

Bayle derogates in another way. Only one-sixth of the persons to whom he devotes his articles lived in antiquity. "Old Testament worthies were treated when they afforded Bayle an opportunity to belittle the seeming importance of such persons as David and Abraham." [30] The Middle Ages were not important: "The thousand years that separated Augustine from Laurentius Valla were very much slighted." Over two-thirds of the persons were of the sixteenth and seventeenth centuries. "The *Dictionary* was thoroughly modern and appealed because of its numerous articles on contemporaries, and its references to events of the time." [31]

This constitutes the first sign of a basic shift in historical understanding. The contemporary period becomes preponderant. Nothing particularly significant happened in ancient history; medieval history is best passed by; only modern history has important meaning. This approach will become explicit, it will ripen; eventually it will control the pattern of historiography and modern textbook composition.

This, however, is practically the only positive note in Bayle's work, and it must be sought under the surface. "At the risk of committing a flagrant generalization," write Beller and Lee, "it may be said that Bayle's chief importance as a thinker was destructive. . . . [His] positive views were of very little relevance beside the enormous impact of the shattering criticism he leveled against the orthodoxies of his time." [32]

Let so much, then, sketch the negative phase of the origin and nature of historical atheism. "Bayle's . . . 'profanation of sacred history' . . . was essential, in order to clear the ground for the men of the next age—Voltaire was the most important —who were to write cultural history." [33] "Voltaire was, when all is said and done, Bayle's greatest pupil." [34]

Voltaire and Positivism: The Secular Doctrine on Human History

Voltaire is the symbolic personality whose life and work clarifies and constitutes the second phase of the origin and nature of historical atheism. It entails a new positive understanding of human history to replace the one which has suffered demolition, so the Enlightenment believes, at the hands of Bayle and his school.[35] Here the mind selects from the immense material of history *en philosophe* and passes judgment upon it *en philosophe*. These two activities constitute the function of historical understanding. To express the new type of historical understanding which he has in mind, Voltaire coined the phrase "Philosophy of History," with a connotation and a significance altogether new and in sharpest contrast with the biblical view of St. Augustine and his use of it as a *doctrina christiana* in the schools.[36]

Voltaire launches the two modern centuries of philosophical thought on the past of mankind with his *General History*. In the course of his years of work on this vast multivolumed narrative of universal history, he had published a treatise on the principles of his historical thinking entitled "The Philosophy of History," which has become the introduction to the definitive edition.[37] It is difficult to exaggerate the suddenness with which Voltaire's contrasting presentation of the meaning and direction of universal history impacted upon the mind of the West. While he had his antecedents, as we have noted, the fact remains that only a few decades separated Voltaire from Bossuet.[38] He wrote, furthermore, with Bossuet's work before him, with its refutation constantly in view.

Voltaire's intention in narrating the movement of human history is clear from his plan and procedure of composition. He begins his philosophical survey with China. This is an abrupt departure from previous historiography which provides Voltaire with a device for omitting the Bible, as well as for teaching how excellently a civilization can originate and progress without revealed religion. From his first page Voltaire embarks resolutely upon his project, which is to eliminate, root and branch, the biblical understanding of universal history. This is historical atheism: the exclusion of God through the refusal to consider the wonderful work of his interventions in the course of human events. Voltaire's chapters proceed from China to India, to Persia and thence to the Mohammedan world, in which he finds much to praise. He comes rather quickly upon the Christian West without a providential world-historical preparation for Christianity. The Church emerges suddenly, without reason, portrayed as a mere retarding factor in social progress. The major portion of Voltaire's work concentrates on the Christian centuries, teaching the basic principle that human progress and social welfare are a function of departure from the Church and the direct result of the elimination of Christianity from social influence. Voltaire's presentation of universal history is a revolutionary departure from the Augustinian tradition and a subversion of the biblical understanding of human history.

Not only does Voltaire teach a new principle of historical understanding; he also reflects the characteristic tendency of human thinkers to embody their teaching in a social group, in order to give it social being and solidity. This opens the prospect of an approach in education by which the social group embodying the idea will be perpetuated among men. Voltaire's historical understanding is a light, an illumination, a spirit of insight and understanding. It will be enshrined not only in books, but it will be embodied in a social group which will possess and carry forward this enlightenment, this wisdom and knowledge on the substance and mode of human development. For there is no body of wisdom and knowledge more fundamental for man than this light on the meaning and direction of human history, touching as it does the life of each individual person. Persons tend to perceive values and to choose ends for their individual lives in the light of their view of human life in general and of mankind as a whole.[39]

In the case of Voltaire's historical understanding, the realization in a social group took place in his own lifetime, in the sect of Freemasonry, and in what Voltaire called the Republic of Letters. This embodiment of the Voltairean historical knowledge and wisdom can be seen even better in the work of Voltaire's disciple, Auguste Comte. This founder of Positivism in philosophy, with its three stages of history and its law of secular progress as a simplified application of the basic position of Voltaire, likewise embodied his teaching in a social group by means of his concept of "The Priesthood of the Scientists." Thus Comte establishes an ultimate doctrinal authority, placing wisdom and knowledge on human origins, human progress and human destiny in the hands of specialists in research and in the body of human scholars as such. Positivism rises in this way to dominance as a characteristic intellectual position and embodiment of knowledge and wisdom on human affairs, in contrast with the mind of the Church and the tradition of Christian culture. In Comtean Positivism this "Priesthood of Science" is not found primarily in the area of natural science, but rather in a newly conceived social science which he places at the apex of human intellectual life. This social science was to establish itself by the discovery of the "laws" of human social living. It was Comte's ardent faith and hope thus to bring social life under control, to render the future predictable, and to make man his own providence unto himself.[40] The Voltairean historical understanding took deep root in the Comtean developments and became the common intellectual outlook in secularized institutions of learning in the Western world.

The embodiment of this teaching in a social group would not be complete nor would it possess its necessary equipment for continued life in society without its characteristic view of education and indeed a jealous attitude toward the education of youth. For the "body" of the "enlightened" depends on this application in the field of education for its social growth and progress. A typical approach to educational theory and practice becomes in this way an integral part of the embodiment of this knowledge and wisdom concerning the meaning and direction of human history. Here we are at the roots of the educational theory and policy of the sect of Freemasonry and of secularism in general as an exclusive philosophical position on the agency and the content of education. It would be difficult to exaggerate the impact of this educational movement on contemporary times, for it is nothing else than the dynamic process of the embodiment of this new wisdom and knowledge on human origins, progress and destiny. The pressure of *la science athée* even mounts within the Church of God, manifesting itself in the temptation to place the embodiment of knowledge and wisdom on religious matters in the group of scholars and specialists in the Sacred Sciences rather than in the Successors of the Apostles, in whom as a body the *charisma veritatis* dwells.[41]

Hegel and Marx: Wisdom Embodied in Secular Society

St. Augustine, in a typical contemporary misunderstanding of his thought, has been interpreted as a "theologian of history" erecting an arbitrary construct in the pattern termed by Professor Aiken "the characteristic nineteenth-century propensity to promulgate grandiose philosophies of history and irrefutable laws of historical development. . . ."[42]

His philosophy of history is, of course, entirely different from these modern substitutes for his biblical understanding, for it is based upon the teaching of witnesses who share the divine knowledge of the contingent panorama. Since the modern secular doctrines advance an alternate teaching on the human family, however, they take root in the education of youth and fashion a place and a procedure for themselves on the order or curriculum of studies. This encroaches, on the one hand, upon the position of St. Augustine in the schools of Christendom; but it also illuminates, on the other hand, the general background for perceiving the continuing relevance of Augustine to the Christian education of youth. To highlight this eminence of Augustinian thought by its contrast with the modern substitutes, we shall sketch the development of Voltaire's secular philosophy of history by his two chief followers, Hegel and Marx.

Hegel's natural tendency in philosophical thought was to speculate regarding the meaning and direction of history. All of his philosophical treatises have this goal in mind, for they relate to the comprehension of the dialectic, which is Hegel's understanding of the historical process. Hegelianism, in other words, moves the treatise on the philosophy of history to that central position hitherto occupied by metaphysics. With Hegel the philosophy of history actually becomes first philosophy, and it maintains that position as a dominant characteristic of contemporary thought.

Hegel's *Philosophy of History* manifests a striking parallel with Voltaire's work. It is difficult to avoid the thought that he planned his work with Voltaire's model explicitly in view, so close is his basic outline.[43]

Hegel begins his narration of the panorama of universal history with China, fully in the pattern of Voltaire. After a lengthy description of the oriental world, not so admiring as that of Voltaire, for Hegel finds the Spirit less incarnate in those earlier times, Hegel moves, exactly as Voltaire, from the Far East to the Near East and thence to the West.[44] More striking even than this external parallel with Voltaire is his

qualitative imitation of the earlier author in his omission of
the Bible and the choice of Israel. Thus Hegel, too, adopts
the basic position of secularism in its presentation of human
development, and presents the panorama of human history
without the embodiment of the divine plan in the historic
Chosen People, issuing forth under the New Testament in
the body of Christ, which is the Church, the new Israel of
God.[45]

The reason for Hegel's omission of the institutions of
the divine economy of salvation described in the Bible, the
Chosen People of the Old Law, and the new, reborn Chosen
People of the New Testament, the new Israel of God, the
Catholic Church, namely, which is the body of Christ, is not
far to seek. Hegel has a "re-constructed" or "modern" understanding of Christianity which does not permit him to see it
as embodied in the concrete institution established by the
New Testament. He has a new concept of the body in which
wisdom and knowledge on human development are to be
found. With this interesting parallel to Voltaire and Comte,
we come to the very center of the Hegelian philosophy of history.

"The State," Hegel writes, " . . . must be comprehended
as an organism." [46] Immediately we are in a world of thought
which has a body of some kind in view, an organism in society. History is a series of " . . . progressive embodiments." [47]
Thus history is nothing else than "the successive phases
of Spirit that animate the nations in a necessitated grada-
tion. . . . " [48] These embodiments, Hegel teaches explicitly,
are nothing else than the units of civil society, the states and
nations of history. Writing in his *Philosophy of Mind* on
the nature of "civil society, and with it the State," Hegel
says: "The universal substance, as vital, exists only so far as
it organically *particularizes* itself." [49]

This is a doctrine atheistic by implication, for Hegel
makes it clear that nothing really exists apart from the concrete being of this State. It particularizes the Spirit, and thus
becomes itself deified and sacred.[50] "The State is the world

which the Spirit has made for itself," he writes. "We must therefore worship the State as the manifestation of the divine on earth." [51] This is a most explicit affirmation of a new concept of the embodiment of spirit, knowledge and wisdom, this time in the secular state itself. One cannot but think of the concluding phrases of the Catholic creed, the expression of faith in the Holy Spirit and in the Holy Catholic Church. Hegel has transferred the embodiment of spirit from the Church and the City of God, moving among the generations of men toward the *parousia,* to civil society, embodied in the various national states of history. In the succession of these states, successive phases of the Spirit, Hegel finds the meaning and the process of universal history. The various nations, he writes, are inhabited by particular spirits, and "out of this dialectic (between them) arises the World-Spirit, the unlimited World-Spirit, pronouncing its judgment . . . upon the finite nations of the world's history. For the history of the world is the world's court of justice." [52] *Die Weltge-schichte ist das Weltgericht:* "World history is the last judgment." With this famous sweeping statement we have Hegel's central teaching on the meaning and direction of history. His philosophy of the dialectic and his elaborate metaphysical treatises on the phenomenology and process of mind are related always to this concrete embodiment of thought in the units of civil society. The state has become, in a sense, something deified and sacred, embodying the World-Spirit, and moving from the Orient toward the West, to its culmination in "The German World" and indeed in the Prussia of Hegel's own century.

It is no surprise to find that Hegel, like Voltaire, not only teaches a doctrine on the meaning and the direction of history, but sees his teaching embodied in this manner in a characteristic social group. This social entity possesses it as its wisdom and knowledge on human origins, the human process of dialectical development, and the human destiny which Hegel describes. This is nothing else than another secularized form of the Christian understanding of history, and its embodiment in an authorized teaching body which simulates the Sacred Magisterium. In Hegel's teaching, it follows directly, there is a characteristic educational system fostered and operated by the state,[53] to teach this Hegelian understanding of the dialectical process, the movement of the World-Spirit across the past toward culmination in the German world and in the modern German State.

Turning to Marxism, it is Lenin himself who tells us that it is impossible to understand Marx without understanding Hegel. It is well known that Marxism is in part an application of the Hegelian dialectic and view of historical development which restates the Hegelian position exclusively in terms of economic factors. This eliminates the concept of *Geist* and reduces the Hegelian philosophy to a materialism: matter-in-process because imbued (somehow) with Hegel's dialectic.

The Marxist view of life, accordingly, is a philosophy of history. It presents the panorama of human development on precisely the same secularized pattern, completely omitting the divine economy of salvation, but retaining from the biblical understanding the linear and purposive movement of human development, culminating now in the Marxist vision of contemporary affairs and the Marxist hope of an imminent glorious transformation of human society and hence of human nature.[54]

"Up to the present the dialectic has evolved four distinct productive regimes, and Marx divides past history into four epochs. 'In broad outlines,' Marx writes in his *Critique of Political Economy,* 'we can designate the Asiatic, the ancient, the feudal, and the modern bourgeois modes of production' as progressive epochs in the economic formation of society." [55]

Once again the secularized or Voltairean view of human development recurs, with its complete omission of the divine economy of salvation, recorded in the Bible and institutionalized in the Chosen People of the Old Law and in the new Israel of God issuing from the Incarnation. On the

other hand there is the simplified view of development from
the Orient through classical antiquity on a linear movement
from East toward the West and contemporary times. The
basic pattern is the same in Voltaire, in Positivism, in Hegel,
and now again in Marxism. There is the same phenomenon,
furthermore, of the embodiment of this knowledge and wisdom on human origins, development and destiny in a social
grouping which will be the carrier both of history and of
historical understanding. This embodiment in the case of
Marxism takes place, broadly speaking, in the proletariat,
but more strictly in the Communist Party which is the mind
of the proletariat, its leader, its guide—and its ruler.

In the same way, a characteristic education is imposed,
rigorously integrating the entire curriculum, all the syllabi
and textbooks in every branch, wherever the Communist
party assumes power. Thus the embodiment of this philosophical construct on human development and destiny becomes a dynamic process which moves with time in society
through the formation of the oncoming generation.

The Contemporary Relevance of St. Augustine

"The present age is a critical one," wrote Santayana on
the eve of the great wars of the present century, "and interesting to live in. The civilization characteristic of Christendom has not disappeared, yet another civilization has begun
to take its place. . . . Our whole life and mind is saturated
with the slow upward filtration of a new spirit—that of an
emancipated, atheistic, international democracy." [56] Not
least among the factors which have produced this phenomenon is the historical atheism of Voltaire, Comte, Hegel, Marx
and their followers, and its gradual introduction into the
schools of Christendom. Seen against the background of
Christian historical understanding, these philosophies of history all represent a secularized theological position in historical thought and a movement away from the Augustinian
and biblical understanding. They are cut to a common pat-

tern which derives from Voltaire. Each retains the linear concept of history from the Christian background and foundation of Western culture. Each one begets, furthermore, a secular *Ersatzreligion* by embodying the philosophical construct concerning universal history in a social group, and by believing and hoping that this social group will lead history to its climax precisely by possessing this historical knowledge and wisdom.

"One of Voltaire's greatest achievements," writes Brumfit, "is his success in replacing Bossuet's picture of the history of the world with one which, in its general outlines, is that of historians of the present day." [57] If this is true, and there is good reason to grant it when one considers on the one hand the academic position of theology and religion, and on the other hand the approach of contemporary historiography and textbook writing in the social studies for the schools, then we have arrived not only at a perspective on the origin and nature of historical atheism; we have also touched upon a most significant educational influence upon young people today, and have established the prerequisite for a consideration of the contemporary significance of the principles of St. Augustine in Western education and in contemporary Christian formation of youth.

Notes from Chapter Eight

[1] Cf. Colossians, 1, 15 ff.

[2] Cf. M. Roger, *L'enseignement des lettres classiques d'Ausone à Alcuin: Introduction a l'histoire des écoles Carolingiennes* (Paris: A. Picard, 1905), p. 438: "L'école monastique n'est pas l'école romaine modifiee; c'est un organisme nouveau." The monastery and cathedral schools were not the direct continuation of the schools of rhetoric, but a new creation which traces directly to St. Augustine's *De doctrina christiana.* His work saved the heritage of civilization from the inner decay which had fastened upon it long before the pagan schools were snuffed out in the chaos of the barbarian invasions. It is this which analyzes concretely the justification for the general admission of the world-historical greatness of the Bishop of Hippo and his unique importance at the historic juncture which Toynbee defines as the point of affiliation between the classical civilization and Western Christendom and which Karl Jaspers calls the "axial period" of universal history.

[3] Conf. I, 15 (24); P.L. 32, 672.

4 That St. Augustine's thought on educational theory and practice became institutionalized in the schools of the West is commonly admitted. See, for example, F. X. Eggersdorfer, *Der heilige Augustinus als Pädagoge und seine Bedeutung für die Geschichte der Bildung* (Freiburg: Herdersche Verlagshandlung, 1907), pp. 201-238; Augustine is the "Gesetzgeber" (p. 209) for all the great and seminal organizers of schools and curricula from Cassiodorus to Hraban Maur. It is difficult, however, to obtain information on the precise way in which "religion" and "history" were taught in the new order of studies. "Despite the vast amount written on Augustine's philosophy of history," writes Professor William M. Green, "little notice has been given to a well-defined plan for instruction in history devised by him and widely adopted in the schools of later days." Cf. his article, "Augustine on the Teaching of History," *University of California Publications in Classical Philology*, 12 (1944), 315. For the study of this fundamental point there are the general bibliographies and introductions to the medieval mind. An excellent and readily available bibliography opening upon this area of Christian scholarship is to be found in Helen Waddell, *The Wandering Scholars* (New York: Doubleday Anchor, 1955), pp. 306-337. H. O. Taylor, *The Medieval Mind* (Cambridge: Harvard University Press, 1949), contains many leads. For the fact that the Augustinian understanding of human history actually became the mind of the West, see Gonzague de Reynold, *Le toit chrétien* (Paris: Plon, 1957), Vol. VII of his monumental *La Formation de l'Europe,* esp. Part II, "La conception chrétienne du monde et de l'histoire," pp. 222-233, and ch. 10, "La caractère historique: la nouvelle histoire," pp. 234-252. See also Thomas Michels, *Das Heilswerk der Kirche: Ein Beitrag zu einer Theologie der Geschichte* (Salzburg: Verlag Anton Pustet, 1935), and Etienne Gilson, *The Spirit of Medieval Philosophy* (New York: Scribner's, 1940), Ch. 19, "The Middle Ages and History," pp. 383-402. This chapter was the inspiration of the unpublished dissertation of Benoît Lacroix, *Les débuts de l'historiographie médiévale: ses origines, son esprit, ses méthodes* (Toronto: Pont. Inst. of Med. Studies, 1947), the nearest approach to a comprehensive study of this basic aspect of our civilization available so far. A *Kurzbericht* appeared in *Mediaeval Studies,* 10 (1948), 219-224. Then there is Hans Wolter's "Geschichtliche Bildung im Rahmen der Artes Liberales," in Josef Koch (Ed.), *Artes Liberales: Von der antiken Bildung zur Wissenschaft des Mittelalters* (Leiden: E. A. Brill, 1959), pp. 50-83, with copious references. Finally, Pierre Riché, *Education et culture dans l'Occident barbare* (Paris: Editions de Seuil, 1962).

5 Perhaps the best general treatment of this entry of St. Augustine into the pedagogical theory and practice which characterized the formation of Christendom is still the concluding chapter of Eggersdorfer, *op. cit.,* pp. 201-238, "Der Einfluss des hl. Augustin auf die Pädagogik der Folgezeit," together with M. Roger, *op. cit.* Cf. also W. Wühr, *Das abendländische Bildungswesen im Mittelalter* (München: Franz Ehrenwirth Verlag, 1950). "An der Wende der Zeiten," he writes, "das Werk Augustins und die Gründung Benedikts massgebend wurden für die neuen Bildungseinrichtungen der kommenden Jahrhunderte," (p. 15). Cf. pp. 20-24, "Augustin von Hippo." "Jede Geschichte mittelalterlichen Pädagogik muss bei der Gestalt des afrikanischen Kirchenvaters von Hippo beginnen . . . weil Augustin in einem doppelten Sinn der Gesetzgeber des gesamten frühmittelalterlichen Bildungslebens wurde: Gesetzgeber der Bildungsidee und eines Teiles der wesentlichsten Bildungseinrichtungen," (p. 20). It should be noted that Wühr

(p. 24) seems to miss the point of *De catechizandis rudibus*, referring it as such and without the necessary qualifications to the future *Bildungssystem* for Christian youth rather than to the older institution for receiving adult converts. It is the *De doctrina christiana* which constitutes the key work for the formation of Christendom. A short general introduction is to be found at the end of Marrou's *History of Education in Antiquity* (New York: Sheed and Ward, 1956), "Appearance of Christian Schools of the Mediaeval Type," pp. 330-339, and "Epilogue: The End of the School of Antiquity," pp. 340-350. The comprehensive study, still valuable, is E. Troeltsch, *Augustin, die christliche Antike und das Mittelalter im Anschluss an die Schrift De civitate Dei* (Munich: 1915), with good appreciation of the importance of Augustine's ethics and philosophy of culture for the coming centuries. Troeltsch points out that Augustine's works entered Christendom as a sort of *Universalbibliothek* in theology and philosophy and were used in the schools like the Bible itself and later Aristotle. Cf. p. 158. It is the merit of Troeltsch to warn against the "dialectical" Hegelian view of the transition from antiquity to the Middle Ages, with "beinahe ein Dogma . . . dass Augustin das Mittelglied dieses dialektischen Übergangs gewesen sei" (p. 161). This is the basic defect of the otherwise scholarly work of Heinrich Scholz, *Glaube und Unglaube in der Weltgeschichte: Ein Kommentar zu Augustins De civitate Dei* (Leipzig: J. C. Hinrich'sche Buchhandlung, 1911). Troeltsch himself, however, due to his unwillingness to accept the Christian era as a whole, as manifesting one unified apostolate of the Church of God, falls into a similar failure to grasp the place and role of St. Augustine in universal history. Cf. pp. 160-171, his contrasting of St. Thomas Aquinas with St. Augustine, and his consequent inability to see the correlation of the two fundamental minds in the unfolding development of the mission and work of the Church in the regeneration and renewal of human culture. The facts themselves seem rather to demand a perception of the Christian era simply as a unitary process proceeding victoriously, even in the face of this world, until the recent rise of secularism and atheism, with St. Augustine, St. Thomas Aquinas and the Papal encyclicals since 1740 as the pivotal points on the linear movement of the Christian age of universal history. "When the fullness of time came God sent his Son": the Christian era as a whole is this fullness of time, a seamless robe which should not be torn by unwarranted contrasts, figments of imaginations which feed upon inadequate and impoverished "modern" philosophies of history.

6 Cf. the C.S.E.L. edition by C. Zangemeister, *Pauli Orosii historiarum adversum paganos libri VII* (Vindobonae: Apud C. Geroldi filium, 1882). For the English translation, cf. I. W. Raymond, *Seven Books of History of Orosius* (New York: Columbia University Press, 1936). For Orosius' relationship to St. Augustine, cf. Theodore E. Mommsen, *Medieval and Renaissance Studies* (Ithaca: Cornell University Press, 1959), "Orosius and Augustine," pp. 325-348, and the chapter "Orosius," in Karl Löwith, *Meaning in History* (Chicago: University of Chicago Press, 1949, pp. 174-181. In general, there is a lack of research on Orosius, perhaps significant in the light of contemporary problems of the curriculum, as Erik Peterson remarks: "Merkwürdigerweise ist über Orosius so gut wie gar nicht gearbeitet worden" (*Der Monotheismus als Politisches Problem* (Leipzig: Jakob Hegner, 1935), p. 150). James T. Shotwell, for example, in his *History of History* (New York: Columbia University Press, 1939), gives Orosius only three pages. Perhaps

the best study is in the unpublished work of Benoît Lacroix, *op. cit.,* "Orose et l'histoire," pp. 89-113.

7 Lacroix, *op. cit.,* p. 112.

8 For this, the work of Denis the Little, with a discussion of his well-known error in calculating the birth of Christ, cf. the article "Ère" in D.A.C.L., tome V, 350 ff.

9 Cf. Löwith, *op. cit.,* p. 249: "Orosius' work was officially approved by a papal bull in 494 and was henceforth used as a textbook of history and quoted throughout the Middle Ages by men like Otto of Freising. . . . Alfred the Great made an Anglo-Saxon version of Orosius. Only from Dante on was the Augustinian pattern of history weakened by the followers of Joachim." For King Alfred's work, a standing witness to his concern for the deepening of Christian and biblical thought among his English people, cf. Henry Sweet (ed.), *King Alfred's Orosius* (London: N. Trübner, 1883).

10 Lacroix, *op. cit.,* p. 110.

11 In addition to the general approaches to this new Western historiography noted above, cf. Johannes Spörl, *Grundformen hochmittelterlichen Geschichtsanschauung* (Müchen, Max Hueber, 1935), and L. Arbusow, *Liturgie und Geschichtsschreibung im Mittelalter* (Bonn: Ludwig Röhrscheid, 1951). See also W. Levison, "Bede as a Historian," in A. H. Thompson (Ed.), *Bede: His Life, Times and Writings* (London: Oxford Univ. Press, 1935), pp. 111-151, excellent for the insight which it provides into the teaching of history in these times; and A. D. v. den Brincken, *Studien zur lateinischen Weltchronistik bis in das Zeitalter Ottos von Freising* (Dusseldorf: Michael Triltsch Verlag, 1957).

12 Charles C. Mierow (transl.), *The Two Cities: A Chronicle of Universal History by Otto, Bishop of Freising* (New York: Columbia University Press, 1928), pp. 61-62.

13 Cf. Joseph De Ghellinck, " 'Pagina' et 'Sacra Pagina': Histoire d'un mot et transformation de l'objet primitivement désigné," *Melanges Auguste Pelzer* (1947), pp. 23-59. For the general fact and the development of teaching directly from the Bible, see H. Rost, *Die Bibel im Mittelalter: Beiträge Zur Geschichte und Bibliographie der Bibel* (Augsburg: M. Seitz, 1939); C. Spicq, *Esquisse d'une histoire de l'exégèse latine au moyen âge* (Paris: Bibliotheque thomiste, 1944); B. Smalley, *The Study of the Bible in the Middle Ages* (Oxford, The University Press, 1941, 1952). Also Robert E. McNally, *The Bible in the Early Middle Ages* (Westminster: The Newman Press, 1959). For a synthetic survey of this biblical learning and teaching, cf. Jean Leclercq, *The Love of Learning and the Desire for God* (New York: Fordham University Press, 1960), esp. Chap. V, "Sacred Learning," pp. 87-109.

14 Fernand Van Steenberghen, "L'organisation des études au moyen âge et ses répercussions sur le mouvement philosophique," *Revue philosophique de Louvain,* 52 (1954), p. 577. Cf. also F. Cavallera, "Saint Augustin et le livre des Sentences de Pierre Lombard," *Archives de Philosophie,* 7 (1930), pp. 186-199; J. De Ghellinck, *L'Essor de la littérature latine au XIIe siècle,* Vol. I-II (Paris: Desclée, 1946), esp. II, Ch. 5, "L'histoire," pp. 89-163.

15 For this point, see M. D. Chenu, *Introduction à l'étude de Saint Thomas d'Aquin* (Paris: J. Vrin, 1954), Ch. XI, pp. 255-276: "*Summa; Histoire* sainte et *ordo disciplinae;* La construction de la Somme."

16 Gerald F. Van Ackeren, *Sacra Doctrina: The Subject of the First Question of the Summa Theologica of St. Thomas Aquinas* (Romae: Officium

libri Catholici, 1952), pp. 115-116. Cf. Victor White, *Holy Teaching: The Idea of Theology According to St. Thomas Aquinas* (London: Blackfriars Publications, 1958).

17 Cf. Thomas Aquinas Collins, "Theology and Sacred Scripture," in R. J. Deferrari (ed.), *Theology, Philosophy and History as Integrating Disciplines* (Washington: Catholic University of America Press, 1953), p. 163: ". . . in his day a theologian began as a *lector biblicus* with the Bible as a text and ended his career with the same text as a Master of the Sacred Page. During his seventeen years as a Master, the text of St. Thomas was the Bible, as far as his daily classes were concerned." Out of this teaching we have his commentaries on the books of the Bible; cf. M. D. Chenu, *op. cit.,* Ch. VII, "Les Commentaires . . .," pp. 199-226: "L'évangelisme de base;" "Magister in sacra pagina," etc. For further study of the fact that Christian doctrine presented the theology of history, see the valuable suggestions and references in Chenu, pp. 60, 201 ff., 223-225.

18 For the direct and massive dependence of Bossuet upon St. Augustine, cf. Georges Hardy, *Le De civitate Dei source principale du Discours sur l'histoire universelle* (Paris: E. Leroux, 1913).

19 Hilaire Belloc, *A Companion to Wells' Outline of History* (London: Sheed and Ward, 1926), p. 67.

20 Oscar Halecki, "The Place of Christendom in the History of Mankind," *Journal of World History,* I (1954), pp. 934-936.

21 For a recognition of this fact from a professional although hostile source see James T. Shotwell, *The History of History* (New York: Columbia University Press, 1939), pp. 325-377; "Eusebius of Caesarea," he writes, "the Father of Church History, worked out . . . the chronology of the world which was to be substantially that of all the subsequent history of Europe down to our own time . . ." (p. 350).

22 Conf., I, 16; John K. Ryan, *op. cit.,* p. 58.

23 Peter Bayle, *The Historical and Critical Dictionary* (London: Knapton, 1734), in four folio volumes, translated by Desmaizeaux. Cf. E. A. Beller and M. du P. Lee (ed.), *Selections from Bayle's Dictionary* (Princeton: Princeton University Press, 1952), for the articles which reveal best his philosophy of attack upon the Bible, esp. "David," pp. 96-125.

24 Ernst Cassirer, *The Philosophy of the Enlightenment* (Princeton: Princeton University Press, 1951), p. 207. Cf. Eduard Fueter, *Geschichte der neueren Historiographie* (München und Berlin: R. Oldenbourg, 1936), p. 288: "A treatise on the philosophy of history, outside the biblical and theological framework, really did not exist prior to the Enlightenment."

25 Cassirer, *loc. cit.*

26 Paul Hazard, *The European Mind* (London: Hollis and Carter, 1953), p. 180.

27 *Ibid.,* pp. 196-197.

28 Howard Robinson, *Bayle the Sceptic* (New York: Columbia University Press, 1931), p. 32.

29 Pierre Bayle, *Dictionary* (Edition of 1734), Vol. I, p. 564.

30 Robinson, *op. cit.,* p. 140.

31 *Ibid.,* p. 141.

32 Beller and Lee, *op. cit.,* "Preface," p. xxxi.

33 *Ibid.,* p. xxv.

34 *Ibid.,* p. xxxii.

35 Cf. J. H. Brumfit, *Voltaire, Historian* (London: Oxford University Press, 1958), p. 141: "But if his criticism is often superficial, it has two qualities which go a long way to atone for this weakness. In the first place it is never silent. . . . The second characteristic of Voltaire's criticism is its total lack of respect for established authority. This, of course, is most clearly seen in his attitude to the Bible." Cf. also *ibid.*, p. 3: " 'Le Pyrrhonisme de l'histoire' became the watchword of men like Bayle . . .," and p. 32: "If Voltaire looks on Bossuet as an opponent, he regards the sceptics, and particularly Bayle, as allies." Brumfit remarks on Voltaire's "thorough knowledge of Bayle, with whose work he is acquainted in the 1720's and whose *Dictionnaire historique et critique* is later to become the Bible of the *philosophes* of Potsdam" (*ibid.*, p. 33).

36 Cf. Voltaire's clear statement of his intention in his *Essai sur les moeurs:* "Vous voudriez que des philosophes eussent écrit l'histoire ancienne parce que vous voulez la lire en philosophe. Vous ne cherchez que des vérités utiles, et vous n'avez guère trouvé, dites-vous, que d'inutiles erreurs. Tâchons de nous éclairer ensemble: essayons de déterrer quelques monuments précieux sous les ruines des siècles" (*Essai* (1785), tome I, p. 5).

37 M. de Voltaire, *General History*, trans. W. F. Fleming (New York: The St. Hubert Guild, 1901). For the "Philosophy of History," lacking in this English translation of the *Essai sur les moeurs*, see Condorcet's edition of the *Essai sur les moeurs et l'esprit des nations*, t. 16-19 of the *Oeuvres completes de Voltaire* (Paris: La société litteraire, 1786), "Introduction," t. 16, pp. 5-242. "The term 'philosophy of history,' " states Karl Löwith, "was invented by Voltaire, who used it for the first time in its modern sense, as distinct from the theological interpretation of history"; see his *Meaning in History* (Chicago: University of Chicago Press, 1949), p. 1, and in general his Chapter V, "Voltaire," pp. 104-114. Actually it formed a part of the campaign of the "enlightened" to steal the venerable name of philosopher for the particular cast of thinking which characterizes the Voltairean school. The use of the phrase "philosophy of history" belongs by a special right to the Christian philosophy founded by St. Augustine, distinguished as the thinker who above all others turned philosophy toward the consideration of the meaning and direction of history. For Voltaire's position in historiography, see J. H. Brumfit, *Voltaire: Historian* (London: Oxford University Press, 1958), with copious bibliography; also R. V. Sampson, *Progress in the Age of Reason: The Seventeenth Century to the Present Day* (Cambridge: Harvard University Press, 1956), esp. Ch. V, "Universal History," pp. 95-123, and Ch. VIII, "The Philosophy of History," pp. 158-182; Sister Thomas Aquinas O'Connor, "Voltaire's Use of Sources in Writing Hisory," *The Historical Bulletin*, 29 (1951), pp. 183-197. For the insertion of Voltaire in the larger picture of the Christian era, cf. Gustav Schnürer, *Katholische Kirche und Kultur im 18. Jahrhundert* (Paderborn: Ferdinand Schöningh, 1941). For the Voltairean approach as a continuing and developing position in these two centuries, see Gonzague de Reynold, *L'Europe Tragique* (Paris: Editions Spes, 1935), e.g., Ch. II, "Nous sommes en revolution," pp. 41-72; and Reinhart Koselleck, *Kritik und Krise: Ein Beitrag zur Pathogenese der bürgerlichen Welt* (München: Verlag Karl Alber, 1959), esp. 3. Kap., "Krise und Geschichtsphilosophie," pp. 105-157.

38 Cf. Eduard Fueter, *Geschichte der Neueren Historiographie* (München und Berlin: R. Oldenburg, 1936), p. 288: "Eine 'geschichts-philosophische'

Spekulation existierte ausserhalb des biblischen-theologischen Schemas bis zur Aufklärung so gut wie gar nicht." Cf. pp. 349-362, "Voltaire und seine schule: Die Begründung der Aüfklarungs-historiographie," and the extension of the Voltairean School to English-speaking lands by David Hume and Edward Gibbon, *ibid.*, pp. 364-366. Fueter summarizes Voltaire's impact as "Die Verschiebung des historischen Standpunkts," p. 336. See also Friedrich Meinecke, *Die Entstehung des Historismus*. Erster Band: *Vorstufen und Aufklarungshistorie* (München und Berlin: R. Oldenburg, 1936, esp. 2 Kapitel, "Voltaire," pp. 78-124; and above all the lucid monograph of Werner Kaegi, "Voltaire und der Zerfall des christlichen Geschichtsbildes," *Corona,* 8 (1938), pp. 76-101. Bayle and Fontenelle, Spinoza, Hobbes and Locke were all real antecedents of Voltaire, but more hidden from the public view and the social scene: miners and sappers of the historic edifice of the biblical understanding of human history.

39 The social embodiment of the secular doctrine on the historic life of mankind is itself a secularized form of the century-long tradition of Christian culture. St. Augustine's *City of God* concerns the Catholic Church as the body of Christ, the embodiment of the incarnation and revealed wisdom extended in space and time, socially, among the natural generations of the fullness of time. For a study of the Enlightenment as the first sketch of a City of Man, reflecting the City of God even while departing from it to build anew, cf. Carl L. Becker, *The Heavenly City of the Eighteenth Century Philosophers* (New Haven: Yale University Press, 1932), and the more recent collection of commentary on his work by Raymond O. Rockwood (ed.), *Carl Becker's Heavenly City Revisited* (Ithaca: Cornell University Press, 1958).

40 Cf. Henri de Lubac, *The Drama of Atheist Humanism* (New York: Sheed and Ward, 1950), Part II, "Auguste Comte and Christianity," pp. 75-159, in particular, "The Priesthood of the Scientists," pp. 136-141, and "Sociocracy," pp. 147-159, with its direct relevance to the project of social reconstruction by means of education launched in the United States by Dewey and his school of thought. For a detailed exposition of this pattern of thought, see René Hubert, *Les sciences sociales dans l'Encyclopédie* (Paris: Alcan, 1923). For a succinct definition of the concept of historical atheism, see Pope St. Pius X in *Pascendi* (*Denz.* 2073).

41 Cf. Pope St. Pius X, "Sacrorum antistitum" (*Denz.* 2147): "Retineo . . . de charismate veritatis certo, quod est, fuit eritque semper in episcopatus ab Apostolis successione."

42 Henry D. Aiken (ed.) *The Age of Ideology* (New York: The New American Library, 1956), p. 263. "The period in modern philosophy between Immanuel Kant and Ernst Mach," he writes, "was a period in which metaphysics, having lately been done in by David Hume and solemnly pronounced dead by Kant, underwent a semi-miraculous reincarnation in the absolute idealism of Fichte and Hegel, lived a vigorous new life in the evolutionary naturalism of Herbert Spencer, and, as some think, found its eternal home in the dialectical materialism of Karl Marx. The Age of Ideology was also a period in which the philosophy of history, that gaudiest of metaphysical disciplines, came into full flower, bringing with it a whole crop of grand theories concerning the nature of historical development and the destiny of man" (p. 13). It is clear that St. Augustine's historical and pedagogical doctrine is both imitated and engaged all along the line.

43 Cf. G. W. F. Hegel, *The Philosophy of History*, trans. J. Sibree (New York: The Colonial Press, 1899); the "Introduction" is reprinted with omis-

sions in J. Loewenberg (ed.), *Hegel Selections* (New York: Scribner's, 1957), pp. 338-442.

44 The West for Hegel is, of course, "The German World," the fourth and concluding part of the work (*op. cit.*, pp. 341-457). "The German World took up the Roman culture and religion in their completed form" (p. 342), and proceeded to develop in three periods; ". . . the first half of the sixteenth century forms . . . the beginning of the third period. Secularity appears now as gaining a consciousness of its intrinsic worth—becomes aware of its having a value of its own in the morality, rectitude, probity and activity of man. . . . This third period of the German World extends from the Reformation to our own times. . . . Not till this era is the Freedom of Spirit realized" (pp. 344-345). Hegel, therefore, like Voltaire, is also a philosopher of secularism—not in opposition to the Christian name, however, but by a consistent redefinition of the basic concepts denoted by this name. Thus Hegel becomes a founding father of Modernism in religion, the philosophical continuation of the Hegelian Right into our own times even as Leninism extends the Hegelian Left. There is indeed a centrality of Hegel in contemporary thought.

45 Cf. Hegel, *op. cit.*, p. 222, for the only reference, in passing, to the Jewish religion, and its complete omission from his discussion of "The Oriental World," pp. 111-222, and of "The Greek World," pp. 223-277. In his discussion of "Christianity," pp. 318-336, as a part of "The Roman World," it is clear that he omits an embodiment of it in the two religious institutions of the Bible, the Synagogue and the Church, as completely as does Voltaire himself.

46 J. Loewenberg, *op. cit.*, p. 446.

47 *Ibid.*, p. 442.

48 *Ibid.*

49 *Ibid.*, p. 238 (Hegel's emphasis).

50 Cf. *ibid.*, p. 450: "The State must be regarded as a great architectonic edifice, a hieroglyph of reason, manifesting itself in reality . . . the self-determining and the completely sovereign will. . . ."

51 *Ibid.*, p. 447.

52 *Ibid.*, p. 468.

53 The Hegelian components of the educational philosophy of John Dewey, whose doctoral dissertation was a study of the German philosopher, frequently pass unrecognized; Dewey himself, however, draws attention to the fact, which merits greater attention. Cf. P. A. Schilpp, *The Philosophy of John Dewey* (New York: Tudor, 1951), pp. 17-18.

54 For a penetrating analysis of the illogical nature of this expected cessation of the dialectical process, illogical because retained from the biblical teaching of the Western mind in opposition to the logic of the secularization, see Christopher Dawson, *Religion and the Modern State* (London: Sheed and Ward, 1935), Ch. V, "Communism and the Christian Interpretation of History," pp. 73-101; "When we come to the next cycle, to that of the proletarian revolution," writes Dawson, "Marx's historical sense deserts him and he does exactly what he blames the liberals for doing—he eliminates history. . . . Clearly (this is) . . . the victory of the Marxian apocalyptic over the Marxian philosophy" (pp. 92-3).

55 M. M. Bober, *Karl Marx's Interpretation of History* (Cambridge: Harvard University Press, 1950), p. 46. See also Karl Federn, *The Materialist Conception of History: A Critical Analysis* (London: Macmillan, 1939), esp.

Ch. V, "The Historical Epochs according to Marx," pp. 157-199; Isaiah Berlin, *Karl Marx: His Life and Environment* (London: Oxford University Press, 1939, 1948), especially Ch. III, "The Philosophy of the Spirit," pp. 35-60, for Marx's dependence upon Hegel, and Ch. VI, "Historical Materialism," pp. 121-144, for the alteration of Hegel. For Marx's own thought on history, cf. the bibliographies in the works cited. "No formal exposition of Historical Materialism was ever published by Marx himself. . . . The most extended statement of the theory occurs . . . in the *German Ideology*. . . . The framework of the new theory is undeviatingly Hegelian" (Berlin, *op. cit.*, pp. 121-122). But Marx and Engels' famed *Manifesto of the Communist Party* (New York: International Publishers, 1932), is actually a popular presentation of this philosophy of history. For a systematic treatment by an immediate disciple, see G. V. Plekhanov, *In Defence of Materialism: The Development of the Monist View of History* (London: Lawrence and Wishart, 1947), Ch. V, "Modern Materialism," pp. 138-255; for the comprehensive contemporary study, Gustav A. Wetter, *Der dialektische Materialismus: Seine Geschichte und sein System in der Sowjetunion* (Wien: Verlag Herder, 1956), with extensive bibliography, pp. 617-629.

[56] George Santayana, *Winds of Doctrine* (New York: Scribner's, 1937), p. 5. Santayana first published this striking essay on "The Intellectual Temper of the Age" in 1913.

[57] Brumfit, *op. cit.*, p. 76. Voltaire worked consciously toward a new manner of understanding and writing world history, one which was to replace the biblical view just as Newtonian physics had replaced the previous scientific theories: "Peut-être," he writes, "arrivera-t-il bientôt dans la manière d'écrire l'histoire ce qui est déjà arrivé dans la physique. Les nouvelles découvertes ont fait proscrire les anciens systèmes . . ." (quoted in Brumfit, *ibid.*, p. 98). Cf. the trenchant insight of Fritz Kern in *Historia Mundi* (Bern: Francke Verlag, 1952), Vol. I, p. 11: "Dieses religiöse Geschichtsverständnis, wie es vom Propheten Amos, von Augustin und anderen geprägt würde, ist in unseren Tagen nicht völlig ausgestorben. Es wurde zum Beispiel durch den Geschichtsphilosophen Christopher Dawson vornehm erneuert. Jedoch andere Gedankenströme sind mächtiger—und la faute en est à Voltaire, wie man in Frankreich sagt. Seit dem Jahrhundert der Aufklärung ist die alte Einstimmigkeit gebrochen." These insights bring into good focus the nature of the apostolate of the classroom in our time and illuminate the role of the Catholic school in the contemporary world.

9

The Relevance
of St. Augustine
for Modern Education

"Y OUR future is rich in promise," Pope Pius XII once
wrote to a group of American students, "because you
cherish the priceless heritage of the past." One of the most
important components of this Catholic educational heritage
is the legacy that descends from St. Augustine, contained in
the wealth of doctrine and of practice enshrined in his writings and in the educational activity of his life. Reduced to its
most fundamental principles, the educational teaching of
St. Augustine presents a Christian and human curriculum
in two phases. The first concerns the arts and disciplines of
human culture, which St. Augustine restores to its integrity
and crowns with philosophy. Indeed, as we have seen, he
includes philosophy, "the science of wisdom and of virtue,"
within the number of these arts. The second phase of the
curriculum is Christian doctrine, *doctrina christiana,* which
culminates in the sacred sciences of the priestly curriculum,
the theological study of revealed truth. Perhaps the best commentary on the Augustinian educational heritage is the fact
that this plan or order of studies still exists and functions
in the seminaries. In preparing young men for the priesthood, the Catholic Church still cherishes the circle of the

arts, then advances the student to philosophy, and completes his preparation for the priesthood with the theological sciences. Basically, also, the method and procedure in this curriculum of sacred learning is still the *enarratio*, the study of the Sacred Scriptures, joined with *quaestiones*, systematic, exact, and scientific investigations and elaborations of particular points or theses of doctrine. The purpose, furthermore, remains the same: the professors of the sacred sciences still continue the historic effort to achieve a *summa* in the mind of the student, the integrated view of knowledge and of life in the light of revealed wisdom. The lines of development lead directly from St. Augustine's *De doctrina christiana* to the *Sentences* of Peter Lombard and the *Summa theologica* of St. Thomas Aquinas, and onward to the contemporary faculties of sacred learning.[1] The course of studies in the seminaries, therefore, is a heritage, fully appreciated only when it is seen as an educational tradition which descends from the Fathers of the Church. It is not too much to say, when viewed in this way, that it offers a venerable model, *mutatis mutandis*, for the curriculum of studies in all other Catholic institutions of learning. For all of them, each in its own way, represent institutionalized arrangements of the educational means for the quest of wisdom on God and the soul by Catholic youth.

The General Features of St. Augustine's Educational Philosophy

St. Augustine's educational doctrine is Christian philosophy at work in the human formation of youth. It is applied philosophy. Since pedagogical science is concerned with the practical human activity of choosing and organizing instruments and means and putting them into operation in view of purposes in human development, it is a subdivision of practical philosophy directly related to the science of ethics.[2]

St. Augustine's teaching rejects the very idea of an educational system resting upon and functioning in terms of an autonomous theoretical basis, as it is called, separate from philosophy as such.[3] For the Bishop of Hippo at the fountain-head of Catholic pedagogy, as for Maritain, De Hovre, and Jordan in our own times, it is true to say that "the structure of education is merely a copy of a philosophical prototype, that educational systems are but reflected images of philosophical creeds." [4] For this reason, the fact that it is Christian philosophy, not Neoplatonism, which imbues the basic pedagogical works of St. Augustine, becomes a matter of first importance. It is in terms of his position in the heritage of this abiding, perennially true, and soundly human philosophy that St. Augustine's educational teaching retains its significance and practical value for the Catholic educator today.

When contrasted with contemporary positions in educational theory and practice which have been tried and found wanting, St. Augustine's pedagogical doctrine stands out with special strength and relevance. His philosophy of God and the soul, his concept of order in the universe and in the studies which develop and sharpen the inner eye for perceiving that order, especially his sweeping recognition of the objective nature of truth and its refraction in varying modes and degrees in the various arts and sciences of the teaching profession, all provide the contemporary Catholic educator with solid reasons for retaining his basic approach to Christian teaching and learning as a precious key to the secrets of qualitative excellence in educational practice.

Underlying these educational positions is the bedrock of St. Augustine's metaphysical realism, which gives his teaching its objectivity in pedagogical matters. His concept of truth is objective, not subjective, coming down upon the teaching profession as a light which reveals an objective order of being, truth, and value. Both the human teacher and the human learner exist and function within this objective order and see their role in subordination to it. The experiences of the learner occupy a properly defined subordinate position and importance; concern with the experiences of the learner is replaced by concern for sound and true attitudes on the part of the learner, attitudes of respect and appreciation for the subject matter, the branches of knowledge, the various arts and disciplines of human culture.[5] Regardless of the name given to this objective and ordered educational structure, whether it is called the *encyclios paideia* or the circle of the sciences or simply the curriculum, as in recent usage, in St. Augustine's educational theory and practice the structure remains erect and intact, safe from the dissolving effect of subjective metaphysical positions which have weakened the grasp of the teaching profession on the very idea of an objective educational structure and reality. "When philosophy stood stainless in honor and wise in judgment," Pope Leo XIII writes, "then, as facts and constant experience showed, the liberal arts flourished as never before or since; but, neglected and almost blotted out, they lay prone since philosophy began to lean to error and join hands with folly." [6] It is this foundation of the culture of the human arts and disciplines upon the solid rock of an objective metaphysics of truth and value which characterizes the educational wisdom of St. Augustine and which provides his most important contribution to contemporary educational theory and practice.

Augustinian Pedagogy in the Schools

St. Augustine's educational wisdom, in its most general terms, applies to all Catholic schools, for it reduces to two aspects of educational order. The first is the order of the school itself as a way of life for the students. This embraces everything denoted under the concept of the atmosphere of the institution, which reflects the quest for wisdom, the search for God, and the concern for the things of the soul characteristic of the students. Without this orientation of the total atmosphere of the student body under the direction of the faculty as a whole, the school will be unable to function in its proper manner. The second aspect is the order of studies which provides the framework for the specific activity of the institution, the formal element which distinguishes a school from all other social institutions.

Catholic education on all levels finds to this day in the teaching of St. Augustine an example of both principle and practice. On the elementary level, for example, the deep respect for all the branches of learning in St. Augustine's educational teaching brings with it a philosophical appreciation for the skills and tools by which alone learning can be acquired. On the level of higher education, perhaps the most fundamental principle of Augustinian educational wisdom is the insight into the place and role of philosophy both as a content taught and as a method of teaching. This is the essential factor in realizing that authentic and genuine humanism which is philosophical and not merely philological in mode and content. It is on the secondary level of education, however, that St. Augustine's educational doctrine perhaps finds its most significant and detailed application in our time. For his emphasis on the full circle of the liberal arts and disciplines, including the sciences of mathematics and of nature, is relevant to the high school curriculum in a special way. In addition to this, his philosophical principles of method in teaching the mathematical and scientific disciplines, the unified Christian wisdom which he brings to the trivium, to English, namely, and the social studies, and his catechetical manner of organizing the academic discipline of religion, form a body of educational teaching particularly important for the high school level.

From the viewpoint of the teacher, St. Augustine's philosophy of wisdom, unifying all of the arts and sciences and disciplines of learning toward the quest for God and the things of the soul, unlocks the door to a genuine apostolate of the classroom. From the viewpoint of the curriculum-planner, the supervisor, and school administrator, St. Augustine's position in the field of education and the principles which he teaches offer a means to preserve our educational heritage and to recover it where to some degree it has been lost. For the Catholic high school of today functions in a special situation created by a departure of the modern world from *doctrina sacra,* especially in the area of universal history and the social studies in general. In the practical academic problems created by the necessity of operating high schools in an intellectual and educational climate affected by the rise and spread of modern secularism and atheism, the educational philosophy of St. Augustine offers a guiding light.

The chief problem facing the Catholic school administrator today is the preservation of his doctrinal and educational heritage in the very structure and functioning of his institution, in order that he may succeed in shaping and forming Catholic minds in his students. So successful has been the rise and spread of modern secularism that its characteristic positions in educational theory and practice, especially in matters pertaining to the place of religious doctrine on the curriculum and to the relevance of theistic teaching in the arts and disciplines of human culture, have come to pose definite problems in the philosophy of the curriculum and of teaching. The secularized pedagogical views on these points have come to seem themselves "traditional," and the Catholic educational heritage somehow anomalous. It even is possible for the Catholic educator to have difficulty in perceiving educational truth, as well as to experience difficulty in explaining the Catholic philosophy of the curriculum lucidly and convincingly to non-Catholic educational authorities. In both of these tasks, the study of St. Augustine's educational principles and practices is profoundly helpful to the modern Catholic educator in the more effective realization of his own mission and apostolate.

In view of these considerations, we shall touch upon two of the more immediate ways in which St. Augustine's educational teaching and practice seem to relate to the problems and responsibilities of the Catholic high school educator in our time. One concerns the problems created by the rise and spread of modern secularism; the other offers the basic approach in school administration which solves the problem created by the pressures of a secularized general social environment.[7]

Meeting the Challenge of Doctrinal Secularism

The Catholic Church, in the words of the First Vatican Council, has always promoted the culture of the human arts and disciplines, teaching that they lead to Almighty God if they are taught and learned in the right way.[8] There is a direct implication in these words that the culture of the human arts and disciplines can be carried on in a wrong way. All these arts and disciplines should make a positive contribution to wisdom in the minds of the young people. Each one has its own natural, not artificial, contribution to make toward a deeper knowledge of God and the soul. It is this positive educative action on the part of all the arts and disciplines of the school curriculum which enables the Catholic institution of learning to function properly in the face of the rise and spread of modern secularism.

In the documents of the Holy See, this characteristic of the arts and disciplines of the school curriculum has been stressed more than once.

"A teaching, even if irreproachable, in all the branches of knowledge," states Pope Pius XII in an allocution to a group of Catholic teachers, "even when completed by the addition to it of religious instruction superior in quality, does not suffice. Each of the sciences has, directly or indirectly, some relationship with religion. This is true not only of theology, philosophy, history and literature, but also of the other sciences: juridical, medical, physical, natural, cosmological, paleontological, philological. . . . It is necessary, therefore, even in cases where the teaching does not directly touch religious truth and religious conscience, that it should be imbued with religion, with the Catholic religion." [9]

It is this same characteristic of the arts and disciplines of human culture which Pope Pius XI has in mind when he writes: "To be a fit place for Catholic students . . . it is necessary that all the teaching and the whole organization of the school, and its teachers, syllabus, and textbooks in every branch, be regulated by the Christian spirit . . . and this in every grade of school, not only the elementary, but the intermediate and the higher institutions of learning as well." [10]

St. Augustine's educational wisdom provides background and insight into the reason for these papal statements. The study of his educational teaching makes it possible for teachers and curriculum-planners today in Catholic schools to perceive better the mind of the Church expressed in these and similar documents of the Holy See, and to appreciate the contribution of each of the arts and disciplines of human culture to the knowledge of God and the soul. This is, as we have seen, the very core of St. Augustine's philosophy, and the point at which his philosophical teaching imbues his educational practice. It is the constantly recurring theme of St. Augustine's educational wisdom that all of the arts and disciplines form an order of studies oriented toward wisdom itself, namely, a knowledge of God and the soul.

Vast perspectives open in this manner upon the rise and spread of modern secularism, a disturbing fact in modern times, and one which denotes a deep-seated flaw in the educational process of modern civilization. This challenge can be met only by a careful study of the culture of the human arts and disciplines, in order that the teaching and the learning of them may take place, as the Vatican Council stated, in the right way. Each and every one of these arts and disciplines ought to be a quest for wisdom: its relationship to God ought to be clarified explicitly for the youthful minds. When this is done, the culture of the human arts and disciplines orients the students toward the theistic concept of human life and destiny which is the very essence of wisdom. Where this is not done, the culture of the human arts and disciplines becomes flat and neutral. The various subject matters are taught in a manner or mode or light that prevents the mind from perceiving the intrinsic and objective relationship of that subject matter to the Supreme Being.

St. Augustine's insistence upon a philosophical method of teaching is related directly to the cultivation of this knowledge of God and the soul in the minds of youthful students. This knowledge is not something that can be imparted and acquired in religion classes alone; it is rather the function of the school as a whole and of every component of its curriculum. The philosophical wisdom of St. Augustine provides the modern educator in this way with the perspectives upon the answer to the challenge of modern doctrinal atheism, a fundamental educational answer and not a mere superficial gesture.

Finally, it should be noted that St. Augustine's teaching provides the principles for answering an educational problem that he did not have to face, but that is closely related to the rise and spread of modern secularism. This is the strong current in recent times which denies or disparages this objective order of arts and disciplines which constitutes the educational process of human culture. Subjective philosophical currents have introduced a trend into educational thought toward a new definition of the curriculum in terms of inner experiences of the learner, detracting from this objective order of studies. This tendency and trend in modern educational theory and practice has the effect of disrupting the contribution of education toward theistic wisdom in the minds of modern youth. For the ultimate term of this development is to dislocate the objective order of arts and disciplines which are substanial in character and therefore suitable instruments for the cultivation of the light of intelligence, and a consequent tendency to replace them by trivialities of all sorts. In St. Augustine's time, the philosophical presuppositions for such a redefinition and misconception of the nature of education were lacking, hence he did not attend explicitly to the problem; in his thinking, however, there is a constant reference to the order of learning, the order of studies, as an objective educational entity and structure. Here again, therefore, the educational wisdom of St. Augustine provides the modern educator, concerned with the essential values of Western civilization, a solid foundation for retaining this objective approach and understanding in education, in the face of the educational currents which derive from subjectivistic metaphysical positions.

In two senses, accordingly, St. Augustine's educational teaching retains intact the objective character of the educational reality. He insists, on the one hand, upon its ordered structure as a series of arts and disciplines which young people must cultivate in order to become educated. On the other hand, St. Augustine's teaching provides the modern educator, by his philosophy of God and the soul, with the secret of qualitative excellence in this cultivation. Augustinian pedagogical wisdom, therefore, will inspect each of the arts, sciences, and disciplines in order to ascertain its particular objective relationship to the Supreme Being. This done, it will organize the teaching and the cultivation of each subject matter in such a way as to include, and not to omit, the ascent from this particular subject matter to God and the consequent return to a sharper insight into the nature and the greatness of the human soul. *Noverim me, noverim Te.*

It follows directly that the entire school, the syllabus and textbooks in every branch, as Pope Pius XI expresses it, and all the teachers and all the teaching, contributes in a unified manner toward the quest and the possession of wisdom on the part of the youthful mind. This is the true solution to the question of the integration of subject matter; it is a spiritual and doctrinal synthesis which exists first in the content and in the teaching, in order to come to be in the mind of the learner. This educational embodiment of wisdom for young people, that their schools be for them "the safe way in which [they] should walk," was a spiritual privilege which St. Augustine lacked in his own youth and which he dedicated his life to provide in the educational undertaking which so many of his works reflect.[11] Were St. Augustine to inspect the modern school, there is little doubt but that he would prescribe the same regeneration and renovation of all the arts and disciplines in terms of wisdom upon God and the soul which he provided for his own time. For this is the direct solution to the problems inherent in a barren and sub-human educational approach which permits or prepares the rise and spread of modern atheism.

The Seven Steps in Adolescent Development

St. Augustine's educational wisdom meets the problems and conditions which result from secularism with a fundamental *sanatio in radice*. Secularism implies a tendency to view education as if it were an essentially profane and secular area, even when a religious course is added, a secular area implemented by what have come to be called secular subjects. St. Augustine's teaching reaches to the root of the secularized attitude and approach, and accomplishes a healing regeneration and renewal by his concept of education as an integral part of the spiritual life and development of the Christian soul.[12] This provides the proper occasion to summarize his elevated understanding of human development in general.

Of fundamental importance in St. Augustine's educational teaching is his rejection of vitalism and what we may call biologism in education. It was not his view of human development that education is in any sense a merely natural process. The body grows in this fashion, he teaches, but the growth of the soul proceeds in an entirely different manner. This growth of the soul results from the cultivation of the human arts and disciplines, under the causality of teaching. There is a philosophical abyss between the teaching of St. Augustine on education and the process-philosophies of contemporary times in which education becomes equated with mere vitalistic growth-processes, and the teaching profession finds itself reduced to the status of a mere guide, standing by to remove impediments or perhaps to exhort.

St. Augustine stresses the growth of the soul in terms of

seven degrees of development which correspond closely to the doctrine of spiritual writers on the advance of the soul in the spiritual life. Indeed, the most fundamental understanding of St. Augustine's educational doctrine is precisely this insight into the relationship between the Christian education of youth and the development of the interior spiritual life of their souls.

The seven levels of the mental growth of man, the seven degrees or stages of the growth and development of the soul, are so many steps by which the mind rises in quest of wisdom to its possession. It is a process, St. Augustine says, by which "we become gentle through piety." [13] This is the fundamental principle of Christian humanism in education, in which St. Augustine states the ideal of Cardinal Newman's gentleman at the very beginning of the tradition of Christian schools and scholars.

This Augustinian educational wisdom which sees adolescent development in terms of a spiritual ascent to wisdom is the charter of Christian teaching. It provides the philosophical foundation for an authentic apostolate in every classroom of the Catholic school, in all the branches of learning, all the arts and disciplines of human culture.

The first of these levels, St. Augustine tells us, is the fear of God. This the young person must have in order to avoid pride. Pride is the great obstacle in the classroom, for it creates the disposition in which knowledge puffs up and hence is hindered from bearing its fruit. The second step is piety, "through which the student must need believe in and yield to the authority of the holy books." [14] A general attitude toward the Bible, therefore, is fundamental in Catholic education, on the part of all the teachers and all students. It is this which introduces the spirit of faith into the Catholic educational institution and which provides the necessary prerequisite for installing the Sacred Scriptures in their rightful position on the curriculum. This centrality of position, of course, applies primarily to the discipline of sacred doctrine, but all of the other arts and disciplines of the curriculum retain a conscious and explicit relationship to the Sacred Scriptures.

The fourth step, knowledge, is the study of the Sacred Scriptures themselves. The chief fruit which St. Augustine expects here is a growth in the love of God and neighbor, and of an interior humility, as the young person perceives with increasing clarity the discrepancy between the ideal held up for man by the Word of God, and the fallen reality which one perceives within himself. "He thus begins upon the fourth step," continues St. Augustine, "that of fortitude, where he hungers and thirsts for justice. In this state he withdraws himself from every deadly pleasure of passing things. In turning aside from these, he turns toward the love of eternal things, namely, the unchangeable Trinity in Unity." [15]

In and through his academic education, therefore, the student is gradually sharpening his intelligence to perceive the way of wisdom as the way of Christian living. Academic teaching, for St. Augustine, is always an apostolate of the classroom.

These four steps prepare the way for the fifth, sixth, and seventh, which lift the young person up to wisdom itself. "Such a child of God mounts to wisdom, which is the last and seventh step, and this he fully enjoys with perfect calm and serenity. . . . From that fear until we arrive even at wisdom, it is through these steps that we make our way." [16]

It is a philosophically sound concept of education, therefore, which the philosophical wisdom of St. Augustine holds out to the contemporary Catholic schoolman. It offers the philosophical insights and principles necessary for conducting the culture of the human arts and disciplines in that right way mentioned by the First Vatican Council. This right way of human teaching unifies all of the branches of learning and points them onward and upward toward God himself. They become instruments by which the soul of the young person is given a theistic orientation; a real and efficacious developmental path opens before the youthful mind, toward a growing educated appreciation of what it is to be a human soul, a spiritual reality animating a mortal body. *Noverim me, noverim Te.* St. Augustine's educational wisdom provides the foundation, therefore, for a teaching in the Catholic school of today which meets the double challenge of both an ambient secularism and a doctrinal atheism. It is a guide in educational theory and practice which shapes the minds of students by a systematic and substantial academic teaching, accomplished by means of the full circle of the human arts and disciplines. This develops the youthful mind, when it is carried on in the right way, toward that better understanding and appreciation of revealed wisdom which always has been the purpose and the crowning achievement of the Christian school.

Notes from Chapter Nine

[1] Cf. Fernand Van Steenberghen, "L'organisation des études au moyen age et ses répercussions sur le mouvement philosophique," *Revue philosophique de Louvain,* LII (1954), 577: "Le plan du célèbre ouvrage de Pierre Lombard, *Summa Sententiarum,* est inspiré directement du *De doctrina christiana;* or, on sait la place unique qu'occupent les *Sentences* dans l'histoire de la théologie au moyen âge." For the synthesizing of the *quaestiones* by St. Thomas Aquinas in a manner which remains closely rooted in the Augustinian *enarratio,* cf. M. D. Chenu, *Introduction à l'étude de saint Thomas d'Aquin* (Paris: J. Vrin, 1954), esp. pp. 258-265, "Histoire sainte et 'ordo disciplinae.' "

[2] Cf., for example, Johannes Di Napoli, *Manuale Philosophiae* (Roma: Marietti, 1956), III, 405-460, where human education is treated as a branch of philosophy developed in this manner, as the systematic knowledge of a special type of human acts and human activity directly and immediately concerned with the end of man.

[3] There is a growing tendency to view the philosophy of education as pure problem-solving devoid of roots in the principles and doctrine of philosophy as such. Cf. the symposium, "The Aims and Content of Philosophy of Education," *Harvard Educational Review,* XXVI (1956), 93-205; for a summary of recent efforts to promote this view, cf. George F. Kneller, "Philosophy, Education and Separatism," *Educational Theory,* XII (1962), 34-44.

[4] De Hovre-Jordan, *Philosophy and Education* (New York: Benziger, 1931), "Introduction," p. xxix. Speaking of the "restoration of educational philosophy," Jacques Maritain writes in the preface of the same work: "As a matter of fact, the great battles of education are being waged today beyond the frontiers of education properly so called; in other words, in the domain of philosophy. Rightly speaking, the term 'educational philosophy' should

be substituted for 'educational psychology' or 'education.' And because, in the practical order, ends play the role of principles, it is only by thus attaching and subordinating itself to philosophy that education will be able to acquire that real scientific character, a mocking counterfeit of which Positivism pretends to offer" (*ibid.*, p. viii).

5 For a comprehensive summary of St. Augustine's doctrine on the liberal arts, cf. John E. Wise, *The Nature of the Liberal Arts* (Milwaukee: Bruce, 1947), chap. vi, "St. Augustine," pp. 63-89. For the educational relevance of the recent continental schools of psychotherapy, which relate mental health to an objective order of truth and value, cf. for example Karl Dienelt, *Erziehung zur Verantwortlichkeit: Die Existenzanalyze V. E. Frankls und ihre Bedeutung für die Erziehung* (Wien: Österreichischer Bundesverlag, 1955).

6 Pope Leo XIII, *Aeterni Patris* (Aug. 4, 1879); *The Great Encyclical Letters of Pope Leo XIII*, p. 55.

7 Cf. Charles Boyer, "Presentazione sulle 'cinque vie' di s. Tommaso," *Doctor Communis*, VII (1954), 1: "The scandal of our time is the spread of atheism. . . . No human error can be more serious. . . . If there is anything urgent for the honor of God and the welfare of men, it is certainly the battle with modern atheism. . . ." With regard to secularism, there is the fundamental Statement of the Hierarchy of the United States, "On Secularism" (Nov. 14, 1947); cf. R. M. Huber (ed.), *Our Bishops Speak* (Milwaukee: Bruce, 1952), pp. 137-145.

8 Cf. Conc. Vat. (Oec. XX), Sess. III (24 Apr., 1870); *Denz.* 1799.

9 Pope Pius XII, "Allocution" (21 Sept. 1950); cf. for a similar statement, Pope Leo XIII, *Militantis Ecclesiae* (Aug. 1, 1897).

10 Pope Pius XI, *Divini illius magistri*, Encyclical on Christian Education of Youth (Dec. 31, 1929); *Selected Papal Encyclicals* (London: Catholic Truth Society, 1933), p. 38.

11 *Conf.*, I, 15 (24); Ryan, *op. cit.*, p. 58.

12 The importance of this point in St. Augustine's thinking is indicated by his frequent return to the discussion of it. Cf. *De vera religione*, 26 (48-49); *De doctrina christiana*, II, 7 (9-11); *De quantitate animae*, 33 (70)-35 (79). St. Augustine states explicitly that his analysis of "the seven levels of the soul's greatness" is intended for the field of education, "to serve the purpose of instruction," *De quan. animae*, 35 (79). For an extended discussion, in relation to the influence of this concept upon Dante, cf. Rand, *op. cit.*, pp. 258-266.

13 St. Augustine, *De doctrina christiana*, II, 7 (9); *Christian Instruction*, trans. John J. Gavigan (New York: Cima Publishing Co., 1947), p. 67.

14 *Ibid.*, II, 7 (10); *op. cit.*, p. 68.

15 *Ibid.*, II, 7 (11), *op. cit.*, p. 69.

16 *Ibid.; op. cit.*, p. 70.

10

St. Augustine
and Contemporary
Religious Education

TEACHING belongs to the very essence of the apostolate of the Church.[1] This teaching includes all the disciplines of the curriculum, but its principal concern is the teaching of religion, the revealed truth of Christ. In the pedagogical theory and practice of St. Augustine, religion itself is an academic discipline, a coherent and luminous body of intellectual knowledge which assumes a rightful place on the order or curriculum of studies together with the arts and disciplines of human culture. The academic teaching of this Christian doctrine, in the particular manner proper to its nature, is in a special sense the apostolate of the classroom. These positions summarize the principles of St. Augustine in religious education and provide the point of departure for a discussion of their relevance and application in the classrooms of religion in modern schools and colleges.

The Holy See has called attention to these things and has laid down the practical consequences for priest-educators in the Church of God. "From the pages of the Gospel," states the supreme organ of papal government charged with these matters, "from the Epistles of the Apostles, and from the entire history of the Church, it is clearly seen that the priest of Christ is not only a minister of divine worship and a sacred officer of the liturgy, but he is also an educator and instructor in the formation of the mind and the will of others. Furthermore, according to the command of Christ to the Apostles the office of *teaching* has precedence over the sacramental and liturgical ministry: 'Go, therefore, and make disciples of all nations, baptizing them in the name of the Father, and of the Son, and of the Holy Spirit' (Mt. 28:19).

"The Apostles, obeying this divine command, placed the work of teaching ahead of any other activity; for St. Paul himself could affirm, 'Christ did not send me to baptize, but to preach the Gospel' (1 Cor. 1:17). The reason for the precedence of the teaching office is evident: one cannot enrich the soul with grace if it has not been first enlightened with the truth." [2]

St. Augustine is the abiding image and model of such a priest of Christ, such an educator and instructor in the formation of the mind and the will of others, both in the example of his apostolate and in the pedagogical writings which he bequeathed to posterity. It is fitting to conclude this study of the great Bishop with a consideration of the practical application of his principles in the contemporary apostolate of the classroom in religion and theology.

For the primary purpose of the Christian institution of learning is contained in the religion program. St. Augustine's principles illuminate the fact that this program is broader than the course in Christian doctrine, and, at the same time, that it centers upon the genuine and substantial academic teaching of a definite body of intellectual knowledge. It is, furthermore, an academic teaching which functions in a unique way, for this discipline is unique in its very nature, different from the other arts and disciplines which constitute the curriculum. The religion program consequently is a many-faceted one. Only by giving it due consideration in the light of all the fundamental principles involved and by determining accurately the practical steps necessary for its implementation and improvement, can the modern educational administrator and supervisor of studies counter and eliminate the two deeply erroneous views which are met sometimes in discussion of the Christian education of youth.[3] The first is the view that the Catholic schools and colleges are not accomplishing an effective and fruitful work in religious formation; the second is the opinion that these institutions can be perhaps dispensed with in view of a so-called "new knowledge" in religious education which, under the influence of anti-intellectualist philosophy, thinks to separate effective and "vital" catechesis, on principle, from academic teaching in the classroom. Views such as these lend practical significance and contemporary relevance to the pedagogical doctrine of St. Augustine, for his principles and practices contain their full and luminous refutation.

Religion and the Curriculum as a Whole

The principles of St. Augustine introduce a fundamental distinction at the very outset.[4] The implementation of the religion program can be approached from the viewpoint of the religion course considered separately and in itself; we can also approach the larger question of the religion program as it embraces the teaching of all the other subjects, the guidance and counseling program, and indeed the entire life and atmosphere of the institution as a whole. It is of deeply basic importance to establish the fact that the question of teaching religion and theology in Catholic schools and colleges cannot be settled adequately from the viewpoint of the course in Christian doctrine alone.

In order to clarify this point, let us sketch a quick picture of the consequences which follow upon the attempt to improve the religion program by concentrating exclusively on the religion course, considered solely in itself.

In this approach, first of all, religion tends to become a thing apart: it exists in a hermetically sealed capsule, a cinderella among the offerings of the curriculum, without credit, without intellectual standing, often without administrative consideration, and lacking a real and living contact with the academic structure and intellectual content of the school.[5]

It follows, furthermore, in the logical development of this approach, that the other components of the curriculum will tend to become imbued with tendencies of thought introduced from the secularized environment, from alien currents of thought, and from the naturalistic pedagogy of the day. These tendencies, when they move, as they inexorably do, toward their full logical self-expression, gradually bring our young people to view the mathematical and the natural sciences in a mechanistic way, in a false neutrality, closed to the intelligible reality of the spiritual order, mutely silent, devoid of any real witness to God. The voices of these arts and disciplines of human culture become still: they fail to bear witness to the youthful mind concerning the Creator and Designer of the universe. We have here a point of deepest significance and concern for the religious educator, one which relates closely to the rise and spread of modern secularism and atheism.

Literature, the component of the curriculum called English, comes to be an area of proud existentialist self-expression, the voicing of opinion and the adoption of posture and attitude on a basis of mere personal view, solicited and encouraged prior to and apart from the sound principles acquired by solid education. The step to situation ethics is but a short one.

In the area of the social sciences, the youthful mind comes gradually to perceive their object of study in a secularized way, looking upon the human panorama in past and present as an exclusively profane area of earthly activity, unrelated, either personally or socially, to the economy of salvation. One learns to see *en philosophe*. Thus social welfare, in the characteristic illusion of secularism, comes gradually to be perceived in separation from religion, and personal living is projected in a profane and secular view of time, rather than in terms of the redemption. The young people in this way gradually lose the effective and practical power to think of earthly living in terms of the sacred.

Turning from the academic disciplines to the practical area of counseling, the guidance program comes sometimes to be viewed as a structure taken from naturalistic pedagogy, lifted bodily from other systems of education, where its invention has been due precisely to the lack of a religious foundation and orientation in the education of youth. It is not impossible, when an educational structure is introduced from the outside in this fashion, that alien currents of thought concerning human life and conduct, Neo-Freudianism for instance, are introduced together with the structure itself. Thus the area of moral guidance and spiritual direction, which is the authentic heritage of the Catholic school in the Christian formation of youth, comes to be seen out of relationship to this practical area of the life and atmosphere of the school.[6]

It is for these reasons that Pope Pius XI in the encyclical on the Christian Education of Youth stresses the fact that "to be a fit place for Catholic students . . . it is necessary that all the teaching and the whole organization of the school and its teachers, syllabus and textbooks in every branch, be regulated by the Christian spirit, under the direction and maternal supervision of the Church; so that religion may be in very truth the foundation and the crown of the youth's entire training; and this in every grade of school, not only the elementary, but the intermediate and the higher institutions of learning as well." [7] The striking statement of Pope Pius XII, "Each of the sciences has, directly or indirectly, some relationship with religion," is simply a commentary on the teaching of his predecessor. "It is necessary, therefore," he concludes, "even in cases where the teaching does not directly touch religious truth and religious conscience, that it should be imbued with religion, with the Catholic religion." [8]

As the present century opened, Pope Leo XIII, in his prophetic way, emphasized the same fundamental concept of the work of the Catholic schools in his encyclical on the great catechist, St. Peter Canisius. "Instruction is full of danger," he writes, "when the religious element is nullified or even weakened. Let no one think that piety can be with impunity severed from teaching and instruction. . . . It is *essential* not merely that youth be taught religion at fixed hours, but that all the other subjects of their educational course should breathe in the fullest measure the spirit of Catholic truth. . . . Let religion thoroughly dominate and inform every subject of instruction whatever." [9]

There is a remarkable consistency and an urgency of emphasis in these repeated statements of the Sacred Magisterium. Pope Pius XII in his last years, already in this second half of the twentieth century, uses measured and incisive words: "A mistake commonly made in religious instruction and education," he writes, "even when given according to a full and well arranged syllabus, is to confine it to a fixed period in the timetable. For a genuine Christian education more is needed. . . . It needs to fertilize all the teaching, even the secular teaching. . . . It consists in seeing *all* things and getting others to see *all* (objects of study) in the full light of divine Truth." [10]

As a matter of fact, this constant teaching of the Holy See throughout every decade of our century simply applies the fundamental pedagogical insight of the First Vatican Council in its Constitution on the Catholic Faith, already cited for its relationship to St. Augustine's educational doctrine. The Catholic Church, the Council states, has been throughout the Christian era the chief patron of education, and has fostered the culture of all the human arts and disciplines, not only because of the cultural progress and social benefit which accrue thereby to earthly living, but also because "the culture of the human arts and disciplines leads the soul to God, if they are studied in the right way.[11]

There is here a clear implication, deeply significant in view of the rise and spread of modern secularism and atheism, that the human arts, sciences and disciplines can be studied and cultivated in a wrong way. In such a case they would not lead the souls of young people to God.[12] This is a matter of basic importance for the contemporary religious educator, and one in which the pedagogy of St. Augustine, with its constant concern for the ordering of the studies toward God and the soul, is supremely relevant.

In this way, then, a solid first position, rooted in the pedagogy of St. Augustine, emerges in the consideration of the implementation and the improvement of the program in Christian doctrine. For this is a problem which cannot be solved by concentrating exclusively on the religion course. The curriculum as a whole must be given attention in a skillful and pedagogically sound manner, according to the principles laid down by the Holy See, which are indeed the very fundamentals of sound educational philosophy. They constitute, furthermore, a basic contact of St. Augustine's doctrine with contemporary religious education, for he is above all the thinker who plans the entire order or curriculum of studies gradually to illuminate, ever more brightly, the reality of God and the soul. Otherwise, the way is open to an unfortunate dichotomy between the course in Christian doctrine and the other disciplines of the curriculum, and indeed even the practical activities and the very life of the institution. Where this dichotomy exists, the religion course in itself, even when staffed by teachers of superior ability, and equipped with textbooks and teaching aids of outstanding quality, will be unable to function as effectively as it should. It will be unable to implement properly the apostolate of the classroom. The institution as a whole will suffer in Catholic efficiency and purposiveness as an instrument of intellectual and spiritual formation, for it will continually take away from its own young people with one hand what it offers to them with the other.

Christian Doctrine in Itself: Simultaneously Academic and Catechetical

Having arrived at this point, it is important to state that the element of fundamental significance nevertheless remains the course in religion or theology in itself. Unless the course in Sacred Doctrine is organized properly, taught effectively by the teacher in person, and implemented adequately by the syllabus and textbooks used by the teacher, the purpose of the school will not be achieved for the young people, even though the other arts and disciplines are taught in the right way, as the First Vatican Council stated, and even if the guidance and counseling program is in the fullest sense a moral and spiritual direction of youth.

In this matter of the proper organization of the religion course in itself, the curriculum planner and the teacher face a basic and central challenge: it is to avoid a second type of dichotomy, introduced by fundamentally wrong and philosophically unsound approaches, between academic teaching on the one hand, and the catechetical apostolate on the other, as if the two were in some kind of contrast or conflict.[13]

Nothing could be farther from the truth. Again it is St. Augustine whose educational theory and practice illuminate the pedagogical truth of the matter. The religion teacher of today succeeds into a heritage of Sacred Doctrine which descends from the Fathers of the Church and from apostolic times. Christian doctrine in the schools of Christendom always has been a program organized by the Fathers of the Church to contain and to continue the basic positions and approaches of the catechumenate of the early Church. In this catechumenate adult converts were prepared for intelligent membership in the Church; the Fathers of the Church carried its basic biblical and catechetical mode of teaching into the classrooms of the schools which they planned for young people in the coming centuries when most of the adults in Western civilization were born into the Catholic faith.[14]

This same kind of teaching is needed in the course of Christian doctrine in modern Catholic secondary schools and colleges for they correspond to the initiation schools common to mankind as a whole, which prepare young adults for responsible membership in society, and they continue the heritage of *doctrina christiana* handed down from the schools of Christendom. As Pope Pius XII points out, however, this teaching must be developed on the various levels of education, so that it is intellectually commensurate with the level of teaching in all of the other arts and sciences and disciplines of the curriculum. "Today it is not this or that article of the Creed," he writes, "but the very foundations of religion, the Church, Christ as the God-man, indeed God himself, which are under attack." Hence the necessity of an instruction in religion designed to be ever more complete and profound on the various levels of education. The Holy Father proceeds to point out the challenge to young people in the natural sciences, in technological pursuits, and in the social sciences. "Catholic youth," he concludes, "you desire to be truly and fully what you are. To the irreligion and unbelief with which you are surrounded, oppose your faith, firm, living, full of works. But your faith can only be firm and luminous if you know it, not superficially, but clearly and deeply." [15]

Pope John XXIII emphasizes the same principle of sound approach in Christian formation in his universally-acclaimed Encyclical *Pacem in terris*. "It is our opinion, too," he writes, "that the above-mentioned inconsistency between the religious faith, in those who believe, and their activities in the temporal sphere, results—in great part if not entirely—from the lack of a solid Christian education."

"Indeed, it happens in many quarters and too often that there is no proportion between scientific training and religious instruction. The former continues and is extended until it reaches higher degrees, while the latter remains at the elementary level."

"It is indispensable, therefore, that in the training of youth, education should be complete and without interruption, namely, that in the minds of the young, religious values should be cultivated and the moral conscience refined in a manner to keep pace with the continuous and ever more abundant assimilation of scientific and technical knowledge." [16]

Thus it is fundamentally unsound to approach the course in high school religion as a light and intellectually unchallenging continuation of a basically elementary level of teaching, while the young people are carrying an intellectual content in the other arts, sciences and disciplines which stands on a higher level of education. The young people will feel, and say, that they have had all of that before. The high school religion teacher in such a case faces an almost impossible task in gaining their interest and their personal sacrifice of study-time for Christian doctrine. In the present years of decided emphasis upon the academic disciplines, and of the recovery of the true nature of the secondary level of teaching which is such a bright spot in the educational picture today, there is a specific need for a substantial teaching, definitely on the secondary level of education, in the classroom of religion. The Catholic faith is not an emotional response nor a mere sentiment, but rather an intellectual assent. Since this is the case, this intelligent assent must itself be educated on the various levels of education: it must be broadened and deepened by the arduous, gradual, daily work of academic teaching and learning. This is the genuine apostolate of the classroom, a solid and substantial *doctrina christiana* in St. Augustine's sense, a teaching which deepens the perception of religious truth in the youthful intelligence, similar to the deepening perception of truth in the areas of humanistic studies and in the mathematical and natural sciences.

At the same time, Catholic educational philosophy always

has recognized that the content of Sacred Doctrine differs from the other intellectual offerings of the curriculum, in that it is an illumination of the whole soul of the young person, intelligence and will simultaneously, and not of the intelligence alone. It is a teaching which moves the will at the same time that it illumines the intellect, and relates therefore always to the concrete value judgments, the personal choices and decisions, of daily practical living. Thus the very nature of Sacred Doctrine, as St. Thomas Aquinas points out, tends to make of this teaching a *catechesis*, a catechetical apostolate of the classroom, in and through the very act of teaching.[17] This is because Sacred Doctrine concerns persons as well as intelligible truths, the Divine Persons, especially Christ our Lord Incarnate, and the persons of the friends of God whom the economy of salvation holds up as models for imitation and as examples to be followed. There is, furthermore, as the same patron of the Catholic schools tells us, the fact that much of Sacred Doctrine is implemented directly by God's own book, the Sacred Scripture, which makes the teaching concrete and immediately real, affecting the will and the emotions at the same time as it imparts its light of understanding for the intelligence.

There is, finally, the further fact that the proper approach to the religion class sees it as a part of the pastoral work and mission of the Church. Whoever holds a mandate to enter a classroom of Christian doctrine, is sent by ecclesiastical authority to carry out one of the aspects of the teaching mission of the Church, which is the very constituent element of the apostolate given to the Church by Christ himself.[18] Hence the teaching ought to be designed deliberately for pastoral and catechetical effectiveness. This is done in two chief ways, by the constant practical relevance, made explicit by the teaching, of the doctrine to daily personal living, and by conducting the class in a manner which brings the teacher to know each of the students separately and personally. This makes of the academic teaching a living catechesis of the

Sacred Doctrine which is taught. The teacher in the class-room of religion is something more than just a teacher, in this world's sense; he is a teacher as Christ our Lord was a teacher: a good shepherd who tends his flock by giving the truth of God.

In these two basic ways, then, the teaching of Christian doctrine in the classroom can be established upon solid foundations. First, by giving due pedagogical attention to the curriculum as a whole, seeing to it that all the arts, sciences and disciplines are taught in the right way, in the light of divine truth. This, furthermore, in such a way as not to overlook the atmosphere of the school as a whole and the practical aspects of its life which are embodied in the guidance and counseling program. Secondly, by giving a proper attention to the syllabus of Christian doctrine and to the religion class in itself, so that the teaching be on the one hand genuinely and truly academic, as solid and as intellectually substantial as any of the other disciplines of the curriculum, and on the other hand fully, completely, and simultaneously catechetical: both in accordance with the authentic heritage of the Church. Upon such presuppositions one can consider certain practical measures which might be suggested as applications of Augustinian theory and practice in contemporary religious education.

Christian Doctrine and Curriculum Planning

The order or curriculum of studies leads the souls of young people to God, St. Augustine teaches, because it includes among its disciplines the Christian doctrine of revealed truth and Christian philosophy, the science of wisdom and virtue, and because it teaches all the other arts and disciplines in such a way that each bears its proper and characteristic witness to God. Thus "the very law of God," he writes, ". . . is transcribed, so to speak, on the souls of the wise, so that they know they live a better and more sublime life in proportion as they contemplate it more perfectly with their understanding and observe it more diligently in their manner of living. Accordingly this science [of divine things] imposes a twofold order of procedure on those who desire to know it, of which order one part pertains to the regulating of life, and the other pertains to the directing of studies." [19]

The Catholic institution of learning, in other words, is an instrument of Christian formation, a genuine and effective "school of perfection," the safe way which St. Augustine had in mind for young people to walk.[20] This is the very essence of the heritage from the Fathers of the Church, the fact that the Catholic faith is learned in two ways: first, by participation in the sacred mysteries, a participation which regulates in a Christian manner the daily life of the young people; secondly, by instruction, in the same way as any other body of intellectual knowledge is learned, ascending in academic method and mode with the ascent of the young person upon the levels of education. We shall give brief consideration to some contemporary considerations regarding each of these two areas of school life distinguished by the principles of St. Augustine.

The first embraces the area of spiritual direction, guidance, counseling, and the entire life of the institution. The school is not life; yet the fact remains that the young people who attend it are living their lives, and their young lives already are Catholic lives. The liturgy, in other words, is something which they understand and participate in already, and indeed in most cases quite well from their grade school training, and which they ought to be living to the fullest extent in their respective parishes. In their high school and college studies, they will be deepening their perception of the Christian idea which underlies the liturgy, but usually they will not need to be learning about the liturgy in its externals, which for them would often be tedious and repetitious. In other words, it is not so much the liturgy as an object of study as the living of it which concerns the teacher and administrator on the secondary level and beyond. The young people should be living the liturgy as conscious members of the Church, whose life is the liturgy.[21]

By the same token, educational guidance aside, the entire area of moral guidance and counseling ought to be one thing with the heritage of spiritual direction which always has characterized and distinguished Catholic institutions of learning. This approach to guidance and counseling will govern both individual work with souls and the total atmosphere of the school. Here the religion program will achieve its lasting results for souls. As St. John Bosco writes, "Frequent confession and frequent Communion, and daily Mass, are the solid columns which must support the educational edifice, if teachers are to hope that it will last in the souls of youth. . . . When educational institutions overlook the frequenting of the sacraments, they cannot prosper." [22] St. John Baptist de La Salle, another great educational founder in the recent times in the Church, takes exactly the same position. "You must take measures," he writes, "that your students go to confession frequently and keep themselves disposed to receive Holy Communion as frequently as possible." [23] This is, of course, not to say that the school is the same thing as the parish church, or that the school should supplant the parish in its proper function. The school administrators cooperate with the local pastors in developing a suitable local program for this side of the Catholic life of the young people, a life which they are learning to understand in a more educated manner through the excercise of the proper function of the institution of learning.

Turning to the second area mentioned by St. Augustine, the order of studies, we come to the syllabus of academic instruction in Christian doctrine. There are, of course, various ways of organizing the content of revealed truth for instruction on the various levels of education. The way, or syllabus, which will be sketched here is derived from St. Augustine's treatises *De catechizandis rudibus and De doctrina christiana* and is simply a contemporary adaptation of his catechetical and academic teaching of the Bible. The teaching of religion to the maturing adolescent must come to grips with the great questions of human life and destiny. This is done effectively in St. Augustine's approach, that of sacred history, for it teaches how to project personal living in sacred time, to think and to make the concrete value judgments of life in terms of God and the Sacred. Academic teaching in this way is an initiation of the young people in accordance with the universal tradition of mankind, and constitutes a catechetical apostolate rightly proportioned to the exigencies of modern civilized and literate life. Such a syllabus, furthermore, continues the heritage of Christian education which is ours from the times of the early Church, and incorporates in the apostolate of the classroom today the solid fruits of the biblical, catechetical and liturgical movements which characterize the life of the contemporary Church.[24] We shall divide the syllabus into four sections corresponding to the standard major divisions of the secondary and college levels of education.

The first section, devoted to a catechesis of God and his moral law, is the study of an objective and divine set of human values. For the secondary level, this has the advantage of locating a solid and detailed study of the moral law early in the student's adolescence. It has, furthermore, the advantage of beginning with God, establishing the entire maturing intellectual life of the student upon the recognition of the primacy of God in all human affairs. This special attention to an explicit catechesis of God in himself is needed in our time in a new way, due to the rise and spread of modern secularism and atheism. Presupposing the catechetical instruction of the elementary level, this teaching of God and the moral law is scriptural and Christocentric, and not a philosophical or ethical approach which prescinds from revelation.

The second section is devoted to the study of salvation history and the life of Christ, a catechesis, namely, of the Bible. The syllabus should be designed to promote actual use of the Bible, aiming at a familiar love for the Sacred Scriptures as its outcome, in the hope that it will abide as a distinguishing characteristic of Catholics in the future. At the same time, the fundamental doctrines of the creation, elevation and the fall, the promise and plan of redemption, the Incarnation and the redemption, should be taught in a systematic manner commensurate with the secondary or college level. Since the framework of teaching is basically biblical, there will be a study of the Old Testament preparation, followed by a detailed consideration of the life of Christ in the Gospels. The important apologetical questions of our time concerning human origins should be treated fully, and the progress of mankind toward the coming of Christ should be portrayed as an advent under the providence of God. Thus the world-historical greatness and stature of the figure of Christ will be made clear to the students, who will study his life in the Gospels realizing that he is the center and the Lord of history.[25]

The third section is devoted to the study of the living Catholic Church, the body of Christ. Here the teacher embarks upon the difficult yet challenging and fruitful task of a catechesis of the Christian era, which will give to the young people a sound and true interpretation of these times of the Church which are our own. The teaching will manifest the relationship between religion and social welfare, between the Catholic Church and the foundations of Western civilization, and between the unity of faith and the unification of the peoples of the earth which is taking place before our eyes. Thus it is a catechetical teaching which brings the youthful mind to see that the history of the Church, as Pope Leo XIII points out, constitutes in itself a splendid and conclusive demonstration of the truth and divinity of Christianity.[26]

Finally, in the fourth section, the syllabus studies the life of faith in the modern world, personal holiness and the social apostolate. This is actually a "modern problems" course, understood in the Catholic sense, centered upon the treatises on grace and the virtues and on the social documents of the Holy See. As Pope John XXIII states in *Mater et Magistra,* "We reaffirm that Christian social doctrine is an integral part of the Christian conception of life." It is in the senior year of high school or college, when personal living is projected in the social conditions, challenges, spiritual dangers and apostolic opportunities of our time, that this principle of Christian social doctrine is realized in Catholic classrooms. The outline of the fourth section, naturally, gives an important place to marriage and the home. The syllabus described here ends with a concluding unit on vocations, callings, and the four last things which stand at the end of human life on earth.

It may be well to mention certain characteristics and advantages of this syllabus or manner of organizing the content of Christian doctrine, and to point out its roots in the principles of St. Augustine.

It is, first, a return to the sources in Catholic education, parallel to that return to the sources in the Scriptures and the Liturgy which characterizes the life of the Church today. For this syllabus simply applies in the present St. Augustine's plan for teaching Christian doctrine, as he says, "from the text: *In the beginning God created heaven and earth,* down to the present period of Church history.[27] This actually continues the biblical mode of teaching which characterized the catechumenate of the early Church, and which was organized into academic teaching by St. Augustine himself in his educational treatises. For, while there are many ways of organizing syllabi and plans for presenting the content of Christian doctrine in the high school, it seems better to return to the sources, and to follow the instructions of the great teachers of the early Church.

Secondly, the syllabus offers a comprehensive coverage of Christian doctrine, for all the branches of sacred theology are covered at one place or the other, in a manner proper to the secondary or college level of education.

Thirdly, the presentation of doctrine is strongly biblical

in both content and mode, without neglecting the necessary systematic exposition of doctrine proper to the secondary, or, *mutatis mutandis*, to the higher level of education.

Fourthly, since the syllabus is biblical in its basic framework, and Augustinian and patristic in its fundamental inspiration, it conveys to Catholic youth the panorama of universal history, and the concept of the human family as a whole in its temporal development and destiny, which is that of the Bible and of the Catholic faith. The view of universal history which derives from the Word of God is presented to the young people, by the very fact that the content of Christian doctrine is organized upon this biblical and Augustinian plan.[28] Since a concept of universal history is the focal point of apologetical interest in our time, due to the fact that most of the anti-Christian currents of thought today are contrasting and opposed philosophies of history, an apologetical efficiency is built in this way into the very structure of the syllabus. This is especially true of Marxist Communism, which, from the doctrinal and educational standpoint, is a materialistic view of human history and destiny in direct antithesis to the syllabus of doctrine just outlined. This method of organizing Christian doctrine on the biblical framework of universal history provides Catholic young people with the fundamental equipment for a personal intellectual victory over the contemporary challenge of secularism and atheistic communism. An apologetical efficiency, close to the needs and issues of our time, is built in this fashion into the very structure of the religion program.

Fifthly, this syllabus has a special academic significance. It tends to break the wall of separation between religion and the rest of the curriculum, especially in the area of the social studies, and to open an avenue of approach for the religion course to the academic heart of the school, to a central position on the curriculum, and to the highest place in intellectual substance and importance among all the other arts, sciences and disciplines of the curriculum.[29]

Sixthly, and finally, due chiefly to the sum total of the

foregoing factors, this syllabus tends to heal that fatal dichotomy between "academic teaching" on the one hand and "the catechetical apostolate" on the other, which confuses minds regarding the value and indeed the critical necessity of the Catholic schools for Catholic youth.[30] For it sees the teaching as catechetical and academic at one and the same time, and perceives the mandate to teach as a delegated participation in the very apostolate of the Hierarchy of the Church.

Teachers of the Sacred Page

These reflections on the contemporary relevance of St. Augustine have dwelt upon objective structuring in religious education rather than upon the person of the religion teacher. This has been, first, because the Church has at hand a corps of teachers of Christian doctrine unique in both quality and quantity. It is safe to say that none of the other arts, sciences and disciplines possesses a body of teachers to surpass, either in preparation or in dedication, the teachers of religion and theology in the schools and the colleges.[31] The problems of development and improvement, it seems safe to say, have not to do with the teachers, but rather with the objective structuring and the basic pedagogical principles which have been considered. Secondly, the underlying approach of the teacher and curriculum planner, perhaps the most important factor of all in the program of Christian doctrine, opens too large an area of thought and analysis for comprehensive consideration in this study of St. Augustine. This is the question of a "vital" teaching of religion: how its nature is to be defined and its mode is to be described. Suffice it to say that the higher levels of Sacred Doctrine have been wrestling for over fifty years with the matter and the problem of what is termed a "vital" teaching of religion.[32] It is to be expected that these questions and problems eventually would have an impact on the secondary and college level of teaching as well. From the viewpoint of the improvement of the religion program, it seems clear that our primary concern as teachers should be to guard against currents of thought and modes of expression which use the phrase "vital teaching" in too naturalistic a sense and indeed even sometimes in an anti-intellectual way.[33] For this tends to undermine the true nature of Sacred Doctrine and even to imply a non-intellectual concept of faith. This is the position which fosters the unfortunate dichotomy between academic teaching and the catechetical apostolate, and which tends to undermine the idea of Catholic education by obscuring its relationship to religious formation.[34]

The fact is that the life that concerns teachers of Christian doctrine in the academic classrooms is a higher life than the natural, the organismic, the biological; it is the supernatural and divine life of grace. Its vital experiences, its vital pulsation and its vital acts are the acts of faith, hope and charity. These are the acts of the supernatural life, and it is the increase of educated perceptiveness and motivation in regard to them which the labor of classroom teaching brings as a priceless benefit to young Catholic students. This is the genuine orientation of a vital teaching of the Catholic religion, one which keeps the academic approach really and soundly catechetical.

A sound and prudent use of the holy Bible in this teaching, in accordance with the heritage in religious education which descends from the early Church and which sees the teachers as actual *magistri in sacra pagina*, is one of the keys to this much-sought vital teaching of Christian doctrine.[35] It results not from a "new knowledge" or a recently discovered "novel approach"; it is rather a heritage in religious education which has borne rich spiritual fruit for souls in the schools of Christendom. It is the very essence of St. Augustine's *De doctrina christiana*. "In all those books," he writes, speaking of the Canon of the Scriptures, "those who fear God and are meek in their devotion seek the will of God. The first care of this task and endeavor, as I have said, is to know these books. . . . The more anyone learns about these, the more capable of discernment he is. For, among those things which have been clearly expressed in the Scriptures, we discover those which involve faith and the rules of living, namely hope and charity, of which I treated in the previous book." [36]

The second key to a vital teaching of Christian doctrine St. Augustine points out when he makes an effective catechesis depend upon enjoying the work, and this in turn upon one's life of prayer. "Our chief concern," he writes, "is what means we should adopt to ensure that the catechizer enjoys his work; for the more he is able to do so, the more agreeable will he prove. And a directive indeed for this is ready at hand. For if in the case of material wealth *God loves a cheerful giver*, how much more in that of spiritual? But that the catechist may have this cheerfulness in the hour of need depends on the mercy of Him who has given these commandments." [37]

These two fundamental principles, these two keys to an effective and vital teaching of revealed truth, the use of the Bible in the order and plan of the curriculum, namely, and a supernatural catechetical approach on the part of the teacher born of the interior life, contain the very heart of St. Augustine's pedagogical doctrine and constitute his abiding relevance to religious education. His principles produce an objective structuring of the curriculum and a subjective methodology in the teacher which makes of the teaching a powerful orientation of the students upward toward God and the things of the soul. This makes of teaching an apostolate of the classroom, a contribution to the salvation of the immortal souls who form the class roster in religion. The teacher contributes to this apostolic work by the very act of teaching: for what he teaches is a saving doctrine, a divine truth, full of light and power. It saves souls. It must be properly implemented, however, and put in the first place by the educator: then all the rest, the good citizenship and the apostolic living of the young people, when they leave their Catholic halls of learning, will be added to him.

Notes from Chapter Ten

1 Cf. Pope Pius XI, *Deus Scientarum Dominus* (May 24, 1931): From the time when our Saviour gave his Church her divine mandate to teach all nations, she has been "the infallible teacher of divine Truth, and hence the chief patron of the entire body of human teaching as well." This human teaching is the culture of the human arts and disciplines of which the First Vatican Council speaks, as we have noted more than once in the course of this study, in its statement that the Catholic Church always has promoted this culture, teaching that it leads the souls of young people to God, if the arts and disciplines are studied in the right way. Cf. Vat. Council, Sess. III (Apr. 24, 1870; *Denz.* 1799).

2 *Instruction of the Sacred Congregation of Seminaries and Universities,* issued by Joseph Cardinal Pizzardo, Prefect, Dec. 21, 1944; cf. *Acta Apostolicae Sedis*, 37 (1945), pp. 173-176.

3 A discussion of the improvement of the apostolate in the contemporary classroom of religion or theology in no way implies a criticism of the Catholic schools and institutions of learning in the past. Self-criticism can be good; it can also be overdone and become unhealthy. Above all, self-criticism in the Church can be founded upon false principles. For example, one can discuss the improvement of the Catholic school religion program as if the Church of the past, lacking what is called the "new knowledge" and "recently-discovered approaches," did not know how to teach religion and to carry on an effective apostolate. The principles which underlie such opinions must be rejected root and branch: they lead all too readily to a denigration of the past, unwarranted by the facts, and to an equally unwarranted enthusiasm for the new in the sense of the novel. On the other hand, one can carry on this discussion in the legitimate sense of *vetera novis augere,* seeking ways and means of lessening the enervating influence and the distorting pressure which this world, with its views and its customs and sometimes its educational procedures, brings to bear upon the historic and indeed timeless educational mission of the Church. One can subscribe wholeheartedly to this latter type of needed thought concerning the problems of the educational apostolate today. As a matter of fact, those who have worked with American Catholic young men in the Armed Forces, or who have observed the body of Catholic professional men serving each community in the United States, know well how fine a work the Catholic educational system has been doing, and how right the American Hierarchy has been in its historic apostolate of the Catholic school. It is clear that the Catholic schools and colleges are vital for the life and growth of the Church, not only for vocations, but also for the sound mothers and fathers of future families and for a genuinely Catholic lay leadership in contemporary society. At the same time, there is a constant need to study the improvement of the program of Christian doctrine, in order to build the edifice of Catholic education further

upon the foundations which have been laid so well. St. Augustine offers indispensable and abidingly valid pedagogical principles for such study.

4 These principles, relevant to the bearing of the curriculum as a whole upon the teaching of religion are discussed in Chapter VI above, "The Culture of the Human Arts and Disciplines," pp. 149-179, and in Chapter IX, "The Relevance of St. Augustine for Modern Educaton," pp. 289-302. Here we shall discuss this particular application in a more explicit manner.

5 Cf. George Delcuve, S.J., "Church History and Catechesis," *Lumen Vitae*, 14 (1959), p. 241: Father Delcuve calls for a study of the Church which does not fail to present "her radiation throughout humanity, her value for civilization"; this type of study, he states, "is especially valid in these days of outrageous secularization which in action and in thought seeks to isolate religion."

6 The consequences of approaching the area of religion from the viewpoint of the religion course alone, without considering the indispensable function of all of the other arts, sciences, disciplines and activities of the institution, can lead to a distorted public image of the Catholic school, especially the high school, charged as it is with formation and initiation of youth in the vital period of passage to Christian adulthood. Indeed, it can at last seem to pastors and parents as a school which differs little from the secular school of the day, and it can seem not to fulfill adequately the motives which parents have at heart in desiring a Catholic education for their sons and daughters. The tendencies consequent upon this approach, furthermore, are not designed to motivate the continued sacrificial giving on the part of pastors and people upon which the Catholic school system depends.

7 Pope Pius XI, "Divini illius Magistri," *A.A.S.*, 22 (Feb. 22, 1930), p. 77, already cited in Chapter VIII above. It should be noted that there is a natural reference of each art, science and discipline of human culture to the intelligible order and the divine reality, which should be made explicit in the teaching. This is the central point of St. Augustine's doctrine on the manner of teaching the arts and disciplines. When this is done each of the studies contributes toward the ever more educated ascent of the youthful mind to God. It is this *rite pertractentur (Denz.* 1799) which the Supreme Magisterium has in mind, and not a false, sugary and artificial addition of "religious matter" *ab extra*, as it were, as something extraneous to the matter at hand. Sound principles and fundamentals of teaching know how to find the objective truth of this matter, lest the arts and disciplines be taught in the wrong way, either as an opiate which dulls the eye of the youthful mind to non-material reality, or as an artificial procedure which repels the will and the taste from religion.

8 Pope Pius XII, "En vous souhaitant" (Sept. 21, 1950), *Discorsi e Radiomessagi* (Rome: Tipografia Poliglotta Vaticana), XII, pp. 219-220; cf. Chapter VIII above, p. 295, for the entire passage. The Holy See has emphasized this point repeatedly and ever more explicitly, as if there is difficulty in clarifying it to the contemporary mind in a way fully commensurate with the apostolate of the classroom.

9 Pope Leo XIII, *Militantis Ecclesiae* (August 1, 1897).

10 Pope Pius XII, "Con lieta gratitudine" (May 6, 1951), *Discorsi e Radiomessagi* (Rome: Tipografia Poliglotta Vaticana), XIII, pp. 76-77. Pope John XXIII continued this teaching of the Supreme Magisterium in, if possible, even more vigorous terms. Cf., for example, his Allocution, *Osservatore*

Romano (July 12, 1961): "Christian civilization is founded upon the practical doing of the truth, a truth which penetrates minds and hearts and is accompanied by divine grace. For this reason, we have a particular blessing for those who are concerned with the right formation of children. The heads of families in every country of the earth ought to demand that their children be educated according to the solid tradition of the past." (". . . devono esigere che i loro figliuoli siano educati secondo la solida tradizione antica.") Cf. also his Allocution to the Central Commission of Conc. Vat. II, *A.A.S.,* 53 (June 20, 1961), 503: ". . . that the new generations arising as a hope of better times be educated properly."

11 *Constitutio dogmatica de fide catholica,* c. 4; Vat. Counc. Sess. III (Apr. 24, 1870); *Denz.* 1799.

12 The implications for religious education contained in the wrong way of studying the disciplines usually called world history, Western civilization, modern problems, and the social sciences in general, are sufficiently clear in Chapter VIII above, in the rise of the recent effort to view past, present and future humanity, as Voltaire says, *en philosophe.* It would lead beyond the scope of the present study to analyze the pedagogical connection between the Voltairean philosophy of history and a wrong way of teaching the mathematical and the natural sciences. From the viewpoint of contemporary religious education, to summarize the matter, there are two important principles in the manner of teaching these disciplines. The first, as Pope Pius XII states, is to teach in a way that allows the youthful mind to understand the voice of creation, (Wis. 13:1-2), perceiving that "this same idea of God finds fresh confirmation in every new discovery and every fresh advance of science" (Address to the Pont. Academy of Science (Nov. 22, 1951); cf. P. J. McLaughlin, *Modern Science and God* (Dublin: Clonmore and Reynolds, 1952), p. 55. The second is to make available to young people, in an adequate and objectively true manner, the cultural history of the Western scientific tradition. Above all, they should be allowed to know the historical fact that contemporary atheism derives in no sense from the genuine men of science in this long and honorable tradition, but rather from the recent "philosophers of history," litterateurs and publicists who have been attempting to "capture" the tradition of natural science which is indigenous in Christendom, indeed since Augustine's seminal action in his restoration of the real disciplines to the *enkyklios paideia.* This they do by turning the mind away from the intelligent understanding of the data of empirical science which St. Thomas Aquinas summarized succinctly in his *Fifth Way,* and toward a new fictitious "understanding" that scientific knowledge implies the philosophical views of mechanism, materialism and atheism. In this fashion they construct a new philosophical doctrine, *la Science athée;* it is the intellectual illusion which they have been able to propagate far and wide in the contemporary world, that atheism *is* science and that the meaning of modern science is atheism. Cf. Herbert Butterfield, *The Origins of Modern Science* (New York: Macmillan, 1951), pp. 127-128: "It is important to note that the literary man intervenes at this crucial stage of the story and performs a second function—the translation of the scientific achievement [from Copernicus to Newton] into a new view of life and the universe. . . . It was not the new discoveries of science in that epoch but, rather, the French *philosophe* movement that decided the next turn in the story and determined the course Western civilization was to take. The discoveries of seventeenth-century science were translated into a new outlook and a new

world-view, not by scientists themselves, but by the heirs and successors of Fontenelle." From France this movement of atheistic philosophical interpretation and pedagogy, ever more successful in arrogating to itself the tradition and heritage of the mathematical and natural sciences, penetrated throughout the nineteenth century into the other countries of Western civilization and into their educational systems. In the present century it continues its spread to the other peoples and cultures of the entire world and enters into their educational processes and traditions with shattering effect. Cf. Christopher Dawson, *The Movement of World Revolution* (New York: Sheed and Ward, 1959). This is an important aspect of the new situation which contemporary religious education faces, and it serves to emphasize the relevance of the pedagogy of St. Augustine, St. Thomas and the great educators in Western culture generally: the teaching of these sciences and disciplines in the right way which leads the minds of young people to God.

13 Cf. the *Instruction of the Sacred Congregation of Seminaries and Universities, loc. cit.,* for an indication that the mind of the Church knows nothing of such a dichotomy: "Consequently of greatest importance for priests are *Pedagogy* which treats of education in general, *Educational Methods* which refers to teaching in general and to its methodology, *Catechetics* which is Educational Methods applied to the teaching of Religion."

14 The elucidation of this point is the burden of Chapter VII, above, "Christian Doctrine: The Renewal of Sacred History," especially the manner in which the catechetical teaching of the Bible in the catechumenate was transposed, *mutatis mutandis,* into the academic teaching of the Bible in the schools. Cf. esp. pp. 210-230.

15 Pope Pius XII, "Nel Vedere" (Sept. 12, 1948, to the Youth of Italian Catholic Action), *Discorsi e Radiomessaggi* (Rome: Tipografia Poliglotta Vaticana), X, pp. 208-209. This Allocution of the Head of the Church illuminates the fallacy which misconceives the teaching of religion to young people in Catholic schools and colleges an application to them in a direct and mechanical way of the catechetical approaches suitable to young children or to the catechizing of converts in less-developed mission lands. We are concerned with students on the secondary level of formal education in one of the most advanced cultures on earth, and one deeply imbued with secularism and irreligion. The words of the Holy Father throw a further light upon the consequence among us of a half-century of Deweyism and of the approach of the 1918 Cardinal Principles Report. By an undetected osmosis views can take root that the high school ought to be conceived as an upward extension of the grade school. This unfortunate and egregious educational error is at variance with the authentic human heritage in education, which sees the high school as a qualitatively excellent downward extension from the college among the people. This is true democracy in educational thinking and planning, and it has had its great representatives in the United States from Jefferson to William Torrey Harris and on to the present. It would be indeed unfortunate if the "Dewey dispensation" of adolescents from serious academic work should find its last stronghold, of all places, in the area of religion in the Catholic high school. On the other hand, brilliant perspectives for leadership open for Catholic education in the decades ahead, provided the philosophy preferred by the Church is applied rigorously and consistently to the practical arrangement and the processes of the various levels of education.

16 Pope John XXIII, Encyclical Letter "Pacem in Terris" (April 11,

1963), in the "Pastoral Exhortation" at the end of his discussion of the principles of peace on earth and human social welfare. These ardently desired values depend upon a solid Christian education, formally as such, which will provide "new generations arising as a hope of better times."

17 Cf. St. Thomas Aquinas, *In Epist. ad Hebraeos*, V, lect. 2; Parma Edition, Vol. XIII, pp. 712-713: "Sacra ergo doctrina est cibus et potus, quia animam potat et satiat. Aliae enim scientiae tantum illuminant intellectum, haec autem illuminat animam . . . et etiam nutrit et roborat animam. . . . In ipsa non tantum traduntur speculanda sicut in geometria, sed etiam approbanda per affectum. . . . In aliis ergo scientiis sufficit quod homo sit perfectus secundum intellectum; (here however) . . . quod sit perfectus secundum intellectum et affectum." This world of religious education differs *toto coelo* from that of the anti-intellectual vitalists and existentialists. Cf. Thomas C. Donlan, O.P., *Theology and Education* (Dubuque: William C. Brown, 1952), p. 97. Sometimes compromises are sought between an "intellectual" approach with an academic manner of teaching and other approaches which represent the underlying positions of vitalism and existentialism, as if an appreciation for and love of revealed truth on the part of the young people can be purchased by dispensing from the arduous task and diligent work demanded for any worthwhile human learning. In the long run, however, such attempts at a "happy medium" will not wear well in the schools, nor defend their continuing necessity in the apostolate. The manner of teaching Christian doctrine should be fully and completely commensurate with the level of education concerned, whether secondary or college, and the syllabus and textbooks ought to compare intellectually with those used in the other arts and disciplines of the curriculum. It is not a denatured and watered-down form of the teaching, but the very teaching itself, in its presentation of Sacred Doctrine in the manner fully proper to the level of education concerned, which is the catechetical apostolate of the classroom. This is the authentic and legitimate sense of a "vital" teaching of religion in the classrooms of Catholic institutions of learning. It moves the will at the same time that it illumines the intellect: but the illumination of the intellect proceeds in the same way, as far as the intellectual level and challenge of the teaching are concerned, as in physics, mathematics, history, and so for the rest. Nothing else will provide an adequate foundation, either in theory or in practice, for the respect due among educated Catholics to Christian doctrine as a body of truth.

18 Cf. the Letter of the Holy See to the Third National Congress of France for Religious Education (*Osservatore Romano*, April 23, 1960): "No other mandate in the Church is more closely connected with the announcement of the Gospel, hence none is exercised in more direct dependence upon the Magisterium of the Pope and the Bishops. . . . Catechetical teachers do not teach in their own name, but in the name of the Church. . . . It is indispensable that all who carry out this apostolate, on whatever level, be fully conscious of the fact." For a lucid example of the way sound contemporary thought evaluates teaching and scholarship in terms of the apostolate, cf. Joseph M. Escriva, *The Way* (Chicago: Scepter, 1954), "Study," pp. 90-95.

19 De ordine, II, 8 (25); Robert P. Russell, *op. cit.*, p. 301. In this chapter St. Augustine describes the Catholic school in terms of what we today call the whole atmosphere of the institution, its extra-curricular activities and the concrete functioning of its guidance and counseling program on be-

half of individual students and of the student body as a group. Youths, he states, are to live in a strictly Christian manner, "to be so obedient that it would be embarrassing to give them commands. . . . By no means are they to become proud. Let them live in a fitting and decent manner. Supported by faith, hope and love, let them have God the object of their worship, their thinking, and their striving. Let them desire tranquillity and a definite course for their own studies and for those of all their associates; and for themselves and for whomsoever else such things are possible, a good mind and a quiet life." Such an institution, obviously, does far more than instruct the intellect; the entire chapter must be read, for it contains the seminal description of the moral and spiritual atmosphere which has characterized the Catholic school throughout the Christian era: *schola nostra* in fullest contrast with *schola illa,* the secularized educational institution of the Classical civilization.

20 Cf. *Confessions,* I, 16 (25); John K. Ryan, *op. cit.,* p. 58.

21 One should guard against misunderstanding at this point. While the high school and college programs are careful to avoid needless repetition, they are definitely a teaching of the biblical and doctrinal foundations of the Sacred Liturgy, and a development *by means of the teaching,* of a more intelligent, perceptive and convinced active participation in the Mass and sacramental life of the Church.

22 Quoted *apud* S. Ferranti, "Attualità e perennità della pedagogia lasalliana," *Osservatore Romano* (July 13, 1960), 6.

23 *Ibid.*

24 Cf. Joseph B. Collins, S.S., "Kerygmatic Catechesis and Religious Education Today," *The American Ecclesiastical Review,* 147 (December, 1962), 361-373, esp. 369-371 for "the over-all plan, a detailed outline of the history of salvation." The three basic steps in this teaching which gives "a loving consciousness of the essential factors in the Way of Salvation" are I: God the Father; II: God Sends His Son, and III: The Catholic Church, the Mystical Body of Christ (369). Father Collins speaks with keen insight of the "pedagogical apportionment" which must be accomplished in syllabus, texts and teaching on the different educational levels and situations of Christian doctrine. (Cf. 370.)

25 By viewing the matter superficially or within the categories of the positivist and secularist concept of "history," one might repeat for emphasis, it is possible to misconceive such a course in Sacred Doctrine as a mere "social science project" or even as a program which puts religion in second place. For those, however, who see the life of mankind on earth in terms of St. Augustine's doctrine on "science" and "wisdom," esp. in *De Trin.,* Books XII, XIII and XIV, no such misapprehension of the economy of salvation and the teaching of it in the schools is possible. Cf. Chapter VII above, pp. 238-243, and Pierre Ranwez, S.J., "Religious and Profane Education," *Lumen Vitae,* 6 (1951), 453: "Perhaps a mistake has been in the separating of secular history from Bible history or Church history; the sacred and the profane have not run parallel lines. All history is sacred, and it is for the teacher to show its significance to his pupils."

26 Cf. Pope Leo XIII, *Saepenumero considerantes* (August 18, 1883): "Incorrupta rerum gestarum monumenta si quis tranquillum et praejudicatae opinionis expertem intendat animum, per se ipsa Ecclesiam et Pontificatum sponte magnificeque defendunt."

27 St. Augustine, *De catechizandis rudibus,* 3 (5); transl. by J. P. Christo-

pher, *St. Augustine: The First Catechetical Instruction* (Westminster: The Newman Press, 1952), p. 18.

28 Sometimes an objection is raised to the study of Church History, the life of the Church across the centuries, as if Catholic young people were mere organisms of the present without historical roots and perspective. Such an approach to the syllabus of Christian doctrine unfortunately fits too well the program of those who wish, as they say, to wipe the slate of history clean. It tends, like their program, to deracinate the young generation and to cut it off from the natural and supernatural heritage of mankind.

29 Cf. the facts and conclusions of Edwin J. Weber, S.M., "Pity the Poor Religion Course," *Journal of Religious Instruction* (Oct., 1944-Jan., 1945), a careful and scholarly study even more relevant and significant today than when it was first published.

30 Cf. *Codex Iuris Canonici*, can. 1372-1383; Peter Guilday (ed.), *The National Pastorals of the American Hierarchy, 1792-1919* (Westminster: The Newman Press, 1954); Raphael M. Huber (ed.), *Our Bishops Speak* (Milwaukee: Bruce, 1952), *passim*.

31 This is not to overlook the need for a program of methodological preparation, grounded in a sound philosophical as well as catechetical approach, for the academic teaching of religion on the secondary and college level. Trained teachers are as necessary here as in the program of the Confraternity of Christian Doctrine. But the potential is at hand, and can only be diverted by the intrusion of anti-intellectual and non-academic views into the area of Sacred Doctrine.

32 Cf. Raimondo Spiazzi, O.P., "L'enciclica 'Pascendi Dominici Gregis' di San Pio X e il problema di una 'teologia vitale,'" *Divinitas*, 2 (1958), 25-50; also Andreas H. Maltha, *Die Neue Theologie* (München: Manz Verlag, 1960), "Allgemeine Characteristik," pp. 11-38. Father Maltha analyzes as "Erstes Charakteristikum" a "Neigung zu Intuitionismus," pp. 21 ff. "Typisch für die Intuition ist auch: Was man intuitiv erkennt, weiss man sogleich. Darum fort mit all den vielen Syllogismen, bei denen man von dem einen oder anderen Ausgangspunkt ausgehend über Zwischenglieder zu der ewigen Wahrheit zu kommen versucht. Lasst uns lieber Liturgie erleben . . . , mit der Kirche empfinden, als mühsame Exegese betreiben, lieber Parabeln lesen, als sich mit Dialektik beschäftigen" (p. 24). When such one-sided views take root, genuine teaching and learning will suffer. A quick and easy intuition will be desired, instead of the arduous daily task which education in the human situation demands, a climb along a path through the disciplines of human culture. The "order of studies," planned by St. Augustine to include Christian doctrine, will come at last to seem an area exclusively devoted to the "secular" subjects. The pedagogical truth of the matter lies in a quite different direction. In the words of a Bishop who is an experienced classroom teacher, "The only way to teach Latin is to teach it; and I would say the only way to teach religion is to teach it."

33 Those who use in pedagogical analysis the terminology and the concepts of vitalism and existentialism, speak much of commitment and a vital response, stressing that Christ our Lord came to impart a life, not a mere abstract doctrine, and maintaining that the teaching of religion must be "experiential," proceeding in terms of an inner experience rather than in those of an intellectual discipline. Rightly understood, these comprise the desired outcomes of Holy Teaching which all religious educators have in mind; understood, however, in terms of the philosophies of "life," rather

than of objective being and truth, with their intuition and experience rather than intellectual development and the attendant habits and acts of the will, these positions soon subvert not only Catholic education but indeed the very idea of human education as such. In a philosophically sound concept of man, which recognizes the spiritual powers of the person as well as the human situation of gradual organic maturation, all these outcomes will be seen in their inescapable connection with a laborious ascent upon a path or order of academic studies and disciplines among which Christian doctrine is included and given a central position. This is the very essence of St. Augustine's educational philosophy, the same Augustine who valued the human intellect as the divine image in man: "Intellectum valde ama" expresses a position in religious education as valid today as when it was spoken by the Bishop of Hippo. It is this which illumines human free will and develops in young persons the power of making Christian value judgments in the actions and decisions of daily personal living. By this teaching of religion on the order of studies the culture of the human arts and disciplines becomes a Christian culture and produces, in the words of Pius XI, the man of true and finished Christian character.

[34] Cf. the trenchant words of the late Aloisius Cardinal Muench, in J. J. Graham, *Faith for Life* (Milwaukee: Bruce, 1939), "Foreword," pp. v-vii: "In discussing texts and books useful for religious instruction one hears these days again and again the phrase, 'Religion is something that must be lived.' The meaning of it, upon further explanation, is that religion has remained too doctrinal and that dogma has sterilized human conduct. Religion has been too much a thing of the head and too little a thing of the heart. It must become a religion of personal experience. The student of Modernism detects an undercurrent of Modernistic theology in this conception of religion. Modernism . . . clothed its subjective conception of religion in theological language; today it speaks a popular language and seeks to make religion purely a matter of personal experience. Indeed, religion must be lived. The Church has always taught this. One of the qualities of faith is, that faith must be a living faith. So said the catechism that taught those of a generation ago. The Saints are proof that the Church's teachings make of religion a thing to be lived. In brief, their lives give evidence that right religious conduct comes out of right religious ideas. Ideas are basic to action. Ideas, said the schoolmen, are not only a source of cognition but also of operation. Sound action without sound ideas is impossible. In this connection Cardinal Newman's sermon delivered to the students of the Catholic University of Ireland in 1856 on the 'Intellect, the Instrument of Religious Training,' bears rereading. As a virtue, religion is exclusively personal and subjective. Its motive power, however, disposing and prompting men to religious activity, is derived from objective religion—the great facts of religion. These must be known before religion can be lived as it should be lived. The better they are known, the better it can be lived." The eminent author goes on to point out that religion in this sense is a body of truth, an objective discipline of intellectual knowledge, on a par with the other sciences. "Religion," he concludes, "is as objective and scientific in its approach to its facts as chemistry or history." For a philosophical analysis of these matters, cf. P. A. Naber, S.J., *Philosophia vitae sive existentiae: De metaphysica hodierna anti-intellectualistica* (Roma: Pontificia Universitas Gregoriana, 1937). For an excellent study of the manner in which an academic and substantial teaching of Christian doctrine relates to the practical

and personal living of the Christian life, cf. G. Gieraths, "Die Bedeutung des D. Thomas für die Frömmigkeit," *Freiburger Zeitschrift für Philosophie und Theologie,* 8 (1961), 121-143.

[35] St. Augustine has much to offer the contemporary religious educator on the nature of this sound and objectively correct use of the Holy Bible in Christian teaching; indeed, it is in his attitude toward the Bible as well as in his planning of the curriculum to provide a fitting place for it in education, that the Bishop of Hippo is most relevant to the contemporary classroom. The present writer has elaborated on these matters elsewhere from the viewpoint of recent Papal documents, which bring the Patristic approach to the Scriptures into our times, and the discussion need not be repeated here. Cf. "Sacred Scripture in the Catholic High School," *The Catholic Biblical Quarterly,* 17 (April, 1955), 136-153; "St. Augustine's Method of Teaching Religion on the Framework of Universal History," *Catholic High School Quarterly Bulletin,* 16 (October, 1958), 1-30; "Teaching Sacred Scripture in High School," *National Catholic Education Association Bulletin* (August, 1961), 259-268. In general it is an emphasis on the divine authorship of the Bible and its doctrinal content, a teaching of the Bible rather than about the Bible, without, however, overlooking the findings of scholarship concerning the human authorship. For a comprehensive discussion, cf. Maurice Pontet, S.J., *L'éxègese de S. Augustin Prédicateur* (Paris: Aubier, 1945), *passim;* esp. p. 152, for a penetrating comparison between the Patristic approach to the Bible, one more suitable to the religion classroom of school and college, and the scientific study of recent times, which is more properly at home in advanced studies. "It is apparent," he writes, "that an exegesis such as St. Augustine's is quite far removed from that of the modern criticism, whether non-Catholic or indeed even within the Church. . . . The divine aspect of the Bible, its living spirit, so to speak, are less observed and less perceived. While the Fathers approach the Scriptures from within and move within them in a very free and simple manner, the Moderns approach them from the outside. . . . St. Augustine knew neither the advantages or the perils of this method. He comes to the Bible less as a scholar than as a child of God. This is a fundamental difference. To interpret the Bible, he thinks, like his predecessors among the Fathers, that it is not necessary to go outside the inspired Book, for it contains within itself its own explanation." Cf. F. Spadafora, "I Vangeli e la critica moderna," *Divinitas,* 7 (1963), 236-242; speaking of the seminary programs, he writes, p. 242, of "the lament which is heard rather universally: so much time is lost in the subsidiary material, in questions, that is, of literary criticism, while the essential suffers underemphasis: the explanation and direct study of the Word of God. One circles around without arriving at the substance of the matter. Proportionately, the time devoted to biblical exegesis is already much restricted and even insufficient. . . . Then, as if this were not enough, the time is used on outmoded questions and systems, instead of proceeding in a positive manner. This is an evil of the day which seems to be growing, due to an unsound and dangerous approach, arising and tenaciously fostered precisely where one would least imagine. Exegesis, the explanation of the Sacred Text, has become a Cinderella, while special introductions, vivisectional literary analyses and fantasy in research upon literary forms are the order of the day." From the viewpoint of sound pedagogy, not only in the seminaries but *a fortiori* in the schools and colleges, St. Augustine would be in fullest sympathy with the approach desired by Msgr. Spadafora.

36 *De doctrina christiana*, II, 9 (14); John J. Gavigan, *op. cit.*, pp. 71-72. For an excellent exposition of St. Augustine's doctrine on this essential content of religion, "clearly expressed in the Scriptures," cf. Stanislaus J. Grabowski, *The Church: An Introduction to the Theology of St. Augustine* (St. Louis: Herder, 1957), the chapter on "Faith, Hope, and Charity," pp. 295-394.

37 *De catechizandis rudibus*, 2 (4); J. P. Christopher, *op. cit.*, p. 17.

Epilogue

The Idea of a Human School

THE idea of a human school, the very idea of human education, phrases suggested by Cardinal Newman's *Idea of a University*, state the nature and the significance of the contact of St. Augustine with this basic fundamental of civilized social living. For schools, formally as such, have not always been visible on the human scene. A school is a social entity connected with civilization as such, with the life of mankind during these most recent and relatively brief six thousand years: four thousand prior to the Incarnation and these two thousand of the on-going contemporary Christian Era. In the historic process of civilized life across this span of time there must be a dynamic agent of cultural movement, one of specific and indeed unique design. Education is this dynamic factor, and the school is its concrete institutionalized form. It is specifically and uniquely human, found neither among the animals nor the angels: it is the very location and substance of humanism. For it is the agent of a movement in time which is able to preserve an abiding cultural sameness amid the biological flux and succession of the generations, the abiding values of the natural and supernatural heritage of mankind—and at the same time to allow for a many-sided social and cultural progress.

Such is the school in the civilized mode of living. It is the outgrowth of the earlier institution for the initiation of youth in prehistoric times, yet quite different in the complexity of the social heritage into which it introduces the oncoming generation of young people, and especially in the dynamic factor of progressive elaboration of the social heritage which it makes possible. It is of the essence of the primitive initiation that it was relatively simple and relatively static. It is of the essence of the school that it holds in hand a complex content which grows by accumulation and deeper insight, indeed according to an increasingly visible law of acceleration.

The initiation of youth in the long times of prehistory, however, and the education of youth during these brief six thousand years have in common that their very idea includes the moralization of youth, in the original meaning of the word, as well as instruction in technology, the temporal and utilitarian aspects of the heritage of culture. Education is an institution which furnishes youth not only with knowledge but also with moral lessons and spiritual formation. It teaches the principles of human behavior as such, but more importantly it illustrates the human ideal by means of attractive archetypes, admirable patterns, heroic examples and models for emulation. Indeed, these paradigms of human perfection are invested with the sacred and they point the mind and will of youth toward an order and a destiny higher than the merely earthly. It is the very idea of human initiation and education that it should teach sacred history and that its literature should hold up for young people heroic and even divine models and examples provided for mankind *in illo tempore* as part of the goodness and mercy of God. As Pope John XXIII points out in the striking Allocution "Abbiamo negli occhi" (Feb. 3, 1963), the great non-Christian peoples and cultures participate visibly to this day in this educational process and live socially upon its benefit, even though suffering sadly from human loss and decline during the long expectation of the Gospel with its transforming and renewing power. "The great peoples of Central Asia and of the Far East," he says, "whose light of civilization preserves definite traces of God's Primitive Revelation, . . . will be called one day by Providence to permit the light of the Gospel to penetrate their cultural values. . . ."

It is in this world-historical perspective that the role and significance of St. Augustine for human education come fully into view. For the Homeric *paideia*, like the cultural traditions of the Orient, could not sustain a true and integral humanism, but rather suffered a process of demoralization and secularization which left it in the fulness of time an empty shell, a cultivation of the spoken word apart from the inner word of truth on God, man and human destiny. The Church of Christ is a teaching Church which was sent into this stream of civilized life with divine truth and power to regenerate and renew man individually from within, and to reach his social life and institutions by means of reborn and rejuvenated persons. St. Augustine is an educator within this efficacious teaching and regenerating apostolate of the Church to all peoples and nations during the Christian Era. The cultivation of the Word, the *Logos*, receives a new and higher meaning in the universe and thoughtworld of the Incarnation, and it is this meaning which the Bishop of Hippo grasps and incorporates in the concrete structure of the curriculum and practice of the school. This regenerates the school and renews the historic educational institution as such. Pedagogy and teaching for St. Augustine are a *doctrina christiana;* and its fruit in society is that renewed and regenerated state of the civilized life of mankind which we call Christian culture. This Christian culture is a historic reality. It stands written into the substance of the Christian Era and indeed is the very qualitative meaning of the term. For the Christian Era is the ongoing process of the regeneration and renewal of civilized life as such, the climax of these recent six thousand years which have succeeded the far longer, far simpler and far more static times of prehistory.

The sacred history of the pedagogy proper to this Christian culture is the Bible itself, replacing Homer and occupying the academic center of the order of studies; and the models and paradigms which illustrate attractively the principles of true humanism and truly human ideals, are now Christ the Lord, his virginal Mother, and his Saints. "He is the image of the invisible God," writes St. Paul, "the firstborn of every creature . . . All things have been created through and unto him, and he is before all creatures, and in him all things hold together." (Col. 1:15-17). This is the very idea of human education, and the concept which explains the practical measures which St. Augustine took when planning the Christian school and its order of studies so as to embrace and to transmit, with all the essentials intact and in proper balance, the natural and supernatural heritage of mankind.

Our problem today on all levels of education, seen so clearly and experienced so acutely by Cardinal Newman on the level of higher education, is the slow attrition and the revolutionary subversion of this pedagogical heritage which relates so directly to man's civilized state. This is the problem posed by the recent secularization of history and of literature and the removal of the Bible from that place in the education of youth which the educational theory and practice of St. Augustine provided for it. Education begins to lose its very idea, to degenerate toward a mere instruction in technical matters and to leave the moralization of youth, or demoralization, to the vagaries of the mass media. Without the historic sacred teaching of abiding principles of behavior and of permanent models and examples of human perfection to emulate and to imitate, with the consequent respect for law and the rights of one's neighbor, it is difficult to see how effective social life can be maintained except on an increasingly sub-human basis of force, secret police and the use of the reign of terror.

St. Augustine's theory and practice of education, seen in this light, possess an abiding relevance to contemporary life, and, far from being outmoded, are directly related to this fullness of time, to this regeneration and renewal of man's life on earth during the Christian Era, in a manner which becomes more visible with each passing decade of contemporary history. Much work needs to be done, of course, to bring his chronology, that of Eusebius and St. Jerome, up to date with the brighter light upon the historic and prehistoric past of mankind which has become available in the last century or so. But this better and more complete knowledge of his own past which man now has at hand does not outmode the intellectual achievement of Augustine. Rather it vindicates him anew and invests both his philosophy of history and his pedagogy with a new contemporaneousness. For the most fundamental successions in human social life, the succession of the Testaments and the succession of the largest social and cultural entities of mankind in relationship to the Testaments, are visible again, as he saw them, but now more wonderfully patterned than even St. Augustine could have known. The Christian Era is indeed the regeneration and renewal of the social life of mankind, as he knew, but the long night of prehistory, which had preceded these six thousand years of civilized life, largely escaped his view. Our present knowledge only serves to emphasize what he saw, to bring the work of the Church for human and civilized values on earth into even better relief, and to underline forcefully and strikingly the importance of *doctrina christiana*, the Christian education of youth, for civilization and its characteristic values.

There is a temptation abroad today to see human civilization in the light of a false philosophy, as if it could embody itself in a form which is supra-individual and quasi-autonomous. This intellectual temptation would have us believe that natural evolution and cultural evolution are the same phenomenon of man. This is a fallacy and an extrapolation which Augustine the Educator would reject root and branch as an offense against the very idea of human education. Indeed, he would brand it as a concept which flies against the very essence of the human situation. The culture of persons by means of the cultivation of the Word, the *Logos*, is the human, the humanistic, avenue of approach to the life of society and to its renewal. There is no apostolate but that which the Church of God has been carrying on throughout the Christian Era. Religious education is not suddenly different from the historic work of Christian schools and scholars which we of the present are charged to carry on. A new sweeping practical success for the Church by abandoning the historic apostolate of *doctrina christiana*, holy teaching, as if there were a process in culture sweeping modern man upward to new progress without the labor of teaching and learning in the school, is quite simply a chimera. It misses the very point of Augustine's philosophical analysis of the idea of human education as the providential plan for mankind. There is no process but the process of education; it is carried out not automatically but by the diligent labor of teaching, and by the arduous task of learning, according to the order of studies which is the pedagogical embodiment of what the Holy See calls the natural and supernatural heritage of mankind. It is an order of studies, a culture of the human arts and disciplines, which has been elaborated gradually by the labor of the generations across these recent six millennia of man's civilized life, and which is marvellously illuminated with principles, values and models by the light from on high. It is a *doctrina sacra ac christiana*. There is no other process or key to progress. *Aut illo ordine*, in the words of the Bishop of Hippo, *aut nullo modo*.

Appendix I

Selected References
The Basic Structure
of St. Augustine's Pedagogy

"Quoniam multi mei anni mecum effluxerant, forte duodecim anni ex quo ab undevigesimo anno aetatis meae, lecto Ciceronis Hortensio, excitatus eram studio sapientiae . . ."—*Conf.*, VIII, 7 (17); P.L. 32, 757.

"Proponebatur enim mihi negotium animae meae . . . ut dicerem verba Junonis . . . O vera vita mea, Deus meus, . . . Nonne ecce illa omnia fumus et ventus? Itane aliud (negotium) non erat ubi exerceretur ingenium et lingua mea? Laudes tuae, Domine, laudes tuae per Scripturas tuas suspenderent palmitem cordis mei, et non raperetur per inania nugarum turpis praeda volatilibus. Non enim uno modo sacrificatur transgressoribus angelis."—*Conf.* I, 17 (27), P.L. 32, 673.

"Didici enim in eis multa verba utilia; sed et quae in rebus non vanis disci possunt: et ea via tuta est in qua pueri ambularent." —*Conf.* I, 15 (24); P.L. 32, 672.

"Deus pater veritatis, pater sapientiae, pater verae summaeque vitae, pater beatitudinis, pater boni et pulchri, pater intelligibilis lucis, pater evigilationis atque illuminationis nostrae, pater pignoris quo admonemur redire ad te. Te invoco, Deus veritatis, in quo et a quo et per quem vera sunt, quae vera sunt omnia . . .

Deus intelligibilis lux, in quo et a quo et per quem intelligibiliter lucent, quae intelligibiliter lucent omnia. Deus cuius regnum
est totus mundus, quem sensus ignorat . . . Deus a quo exire,
emori; in quem redire, reviviscere; in quo habitare, vivere est.
Deus quem nemo amittit, nisi deceptus; quem nemo quaerit,
nisi admonitus; quem nemo invenit, nisi purgatus."—*Solil.*, I,
1 (2-3): P.L. 32, 870.

"A: Ecce oravi Deum. R: Quid ergo scire vis? A: Haec ipsa omnia
quae oravi. R: Breviter ea collige. A: Deum et animam scire
cupio. R: Nihilne plus? A: Nihil omnino. R: Ergo incipe quaerere."—*Solil.* I, 2 (7); P.L. 32, 872.

"Deus semper idem, noverim me, noverim te."—*Solil.* II, 1 (1);
P.L. 32, 885.

"Num aliam putas esse sapientiam nisi veritatem in qua cerni-
tur et tenetur summum bonum?"—*De lib. arbit.*, II, 9 (26); P.L.
32, 1254-1255.

"O Veritas, lumen cordis mei, non tenebrae meae loquantur mihi.
Defluxi ad ista et obscuratus sum; sed hinc etiam, hinc adamavi
te. Erravi et recordatus sum tui . . . Et nunc ecce redeo aestuans
et anhelans ad fontem tuum . . . Tu me alloquere . . . Credidi
Libris tuis. . ."—*Conf.* XII, 10 (10); P.L. 32, 830.

"Verbum tuum per quod fecisti omnia, in quibus et me, Unicum
tuum . . . in quo sunt omnes thesauri sapientiae et scientiae
absconditi (Col. 2:3), Ipsum quaero in Libris tuis. Moyses de
illo scripsit. (Joan. 5:46): hoc ipse ait, hoc Veritas ait."—*Conf.*
XI, 2 (4); P.L. 32, 811.

"Sint castae deliciae meae Scripturae tuae; nec fallar in eis, nec
fallam ex eis. Domine, attende . . . et audi, clamantem de pro-
fundo . . . Largire . . . spatium meditationibus nostris in abdita
legis tuae, neque enim frustra scribi voluisti tot paginarum
opaca secreta . . . confitear tibi quidquid invenero in Libris
tuis . . ."—*Conf.* XI, 2 (3); P.L. 32, 810.

"Narratione autem historica cum praeterita etiam nominum instituta narrantur, non inter humana instituta ipsa historia numeranda est; quia jam quae transierunt, nec infecta fieri possunt, in ordine temporum habenda sunt, quorum est conditor et administrator Deus."—*De doctrina christiana,* II, 28 (44); P.L. 34, 56.

"Tenenda est nobis christiana religio, et eius Ecclesiae communicatio quae catholica est, et catholica nominatur . . . Huius religionis sectandae caput est historia et prophetia dispensationis temporalis divinae providentiae, pro salute generis humani in aeternam vitam reformandi atque reparandi."—*De vera religione,* 7 (12-13); P.L. 34, 128.

"Haec est religio, quae universalem continet viam animae liberandae; quoniam nulla nisi hac liberari potest. Haec est enim quodam modo regalis via, quae una ducit ad regnum, non temporali fastigio nutabundum, sed aeternitatis firmitate securum . . . Haec est igitur animae liberandae universalis via, id est universis gentibus divina misericordia concessa; cuius profecto notitia ad quoscumque iam venit, et ad quoscumque ventura est . . . (sed) mittentis consilium non est humano ingenio penetrabile."—*De civitate Dei,* X, 32 (1-2); P.L. 41, 312-313.

"Sicut enim Aegyptii non solum idola habebant et onera gravia, . . . set etiam vasa atque ornamenta de auro et argento; . . . sic doctrinae omnes Gentilium non solum . . . superstitiosa figmenta . . . sed etiam liberales disciplinas usui veritatis aptiores, et quaedam morum praecepta utilissima continent, deque ipso uno Deo colendo nonnulla vera inveniuntur apud eos. . . ." —*De doctrina christiana,* II, 40 (60); P.L. 34, 63.

"Disciplina disputandi verane, an falsa est? Quis dubitet veram? Sed vera est etiam grammatica . . . Omnis ergo vera est disciplina."—*Solil.* II, 11 (19); P.L. 32, 893-894.

"Nec Lastidianum et Rusticum consobrinos meos, quamvis nullium vel grammaticum passi sint, deesse volui, ipsumque eorum

sensum communem, ad rem quam moliebar, necessarium putavi."
—*De beata vita.* 1 (6); P.L. 32, 962.

"Per idem tempus quo Mediolani fui, Baptismum percepturus,
etiam Disciplinarum libros conatus sum scribere . . . per corporalia cupiens ad incorporalia quibusdam quasi passibus certis
vel pervenire vel ducere . . . de Grammatica, . . . de Musica,
. . . De aliis vero quinque disciplinis similiter inchoatis; de
Dialectica, de Rhetorica, de Geometria, de Arithmetica, de Philosophia, sola principia remanserunt, quae tamen etiam ipsa perdidimus: sed haberi ab aliquibus existimo."—*Retr.* I, 6; P.L. 32,
591.

"Philosophia est enim, a cuius uberibus se nulla aetas queretur
excludi . . . Posteaquam in agro vivere coepimus, cum eos ad
studia hortans atque animans, ultra quam optaveram paratos et
prorsus inhiantes viderem, volui tentare pro aetate quid possent:
praesertim cum Hortensius liber Ciceronis iam eos ex magna
parte conciliasse philosophiae videretur. Adhibito itaque notario
. . . , nihil perire permisi."—*Contra Acad.* I, 1 (4); P.L. 32, 908.

"Quid ergo anima, inquam? nulla ne habet alimenta propria? an
eius esca scientia vobis videtur? Plane, inquit mater; nulla re alia
credo ali animam quam intellectu rerum atque scientia . . .
Manifestum esse dixerunt. Recte igitur dicimus eorum animos,
qui nullis disciplinis eruditi sunt, nihilque bonarum artium
hauserunt, jejunos et quasi famelicos esse . . . , ita et illorum
animi pleni sunt morbis quibus sua jejunia confitentur . . . Ut
corporum, ita animorum duo alimentorum genera inveniuntur;
unum salubre atque utile, alterum morbidum atque pestiferum."
—*De beata vita,* 2 (8); P.L. 32, 963-964.

"Tale aliquid sapientiae studiosissimis . . . magistri optimi faci-
unt. Nam ordine quodam ad eam pervenire bonae disciplinae
officium est . . . A: Et alio die: Da, quaeso, inquam, iam si
potes, illum ordinem . . . R: Unum est quod tibi possum prae-
cipere, nihil plus novi. Penitus esse ista sensibilia fugienda,
cavendumque magnopere, dum hoc corpus agimus, ne quo eorum
visco pennae nostrae impediantur, quibus integris perfectisque
opus est, ut ad illam lucem ab his tenebris evolemus . . . Itaque,

quando fueris talis ut nihil te prorsus terrenorum delectet, mihi crede, eodem momento, eodem puncto temporis videbis quod cupis."—*Solil.*, I, 13 (23-24); P.L. 32, 882.

"Facilius autem cognoscet ista . . . de summo Deo . . . et de anima ipsa sua . . . qui numeros simplices atque intelligibiles comprehenderit. Porro istos comprehendet, qui et ingenio valens . . . et studio vehementer incensus, memoratum disciplinarum ordinem, quantum satis est, fuerit persecutus. Cum enim artes illae omnes liberales, partim ad usum vitae, partim ad cognitionem rerum contemplationemque discantur; usum earum assequi difficillimum est, nisi ei qui ab ipsa pueritia ingeniosissimos, instantissime atque constantissime operam dederit . . . De rebus obscurissimis, et tamen divinis, . . . de his atque huiusmodi rebus, aut ordine illo eruditionis, aut nullo modo quidquam requirendum est."—*De ordine*, II, 16-17 (44-46); P.L. 32, 1015-1016.

"Ad istarum rerum cognitionem neminem aspirare debere sine illa quasi duplici scientia bonae disputationis, potentiaeque numerorum . . . Excipit enim hanc eruditionem jam ipsa philosophiae disciplina, et in ea nihil plus invenit quam quid sit unum, sed longe altius longeque divinius. Cuius duplex quaestio est: una de anima, altera de Deo. Prima efficit ut nosmetipsos noverimus; altera, ut originem nostram . . . Hic est ordo studiorum sapientiae, per quem fit quisque idoneus ad intelligendum ordinem rerum, id est, ad dignoscendos duos mundos, et ipsum parentem universitatis; cuius nulla scientia est in anima, nisi scire quomodo eum nesciat."—*De ordine*, II, 18 (47); P.L. 32, 1017.

"Sine temporali transitu stant etiam ipsae utique intelligibiles, non sensibiles. Ad quas mentis acie pervenire paucorum est; et cum pervenitur, quantum fieri potest, non in eis manet ipse perventor, sed veluti acie ipsa reverberata repellitur, et fit rei non transitoriae transitoria cogitatio. Quae tamen cogitatio transiens per disciplinas quibus eruditur animus, memoriae commendatur . . . (et) poterit recordando quodam modo ruminare, et in disciplinam quod sic didicerit trajicere. Quod si fuerit omnimoda oblivione deletum, rursus doctrina duce ad id venietur quod penitus exciderat, et sic invenietur ut erat."—*De Trinitate* XII, 14 (23); P.L. 42, 1010-1011.

"Tales sunt qui bene disciplinis liberalibus eruditi, . . . nec se tenent donec totam faciem veritatis, cuius quidam in illis artibus splendor iam subrutilat, latissime atque plenissime intueantur." —*Solil.* II, 19 (35); P.L. 32, 902-903.

"Reformamini, inquit, in novitate mentis vestrae . . . (Rom. 12:2) . . . Mente quippe renovatus, et conspiciens intellectum veritatem tuam, . . . ; doces eum iam capacem videre Trinitatem unitatis, et unitatem Trinitatis . . . Ita homo renovatur in agnitionem Dei; secundum imaginem eius qui creavit eum."— *Conf.* XIII, 22 (32); P.L. 32, 858-859.

"Haec autem omnia quae pro nobis Verbum caro factum temporaliter et localiter fecit et pertulit, secundum distinctionem quam demonstrare suscepimus, ad scientiam pertinet, non ad sapientiam. Quod autem Verbum est sine tempore et sine loco, est Patri coaeternum et ubique totum; de quo si quisquam potest, quantum potest, veracem proferre sermonem, sermo ille erit sapientiae: ac per hoc Verbum caro factum, quod est Christus Jesus, et sapientiae thesauros habet et scientiae . . . Scientia ergo nostra Christus est, sapientia quoque nostra idem Christus est. Ipse nobis fidem de rebus temporalibus inserit, ipse de sempiternis exhibet veritatem. Per ipsum pergimus ad ipsum, tendimus per scientiam ad sapientiam . . . ."—*De Trinitate,* XIII, 19 (24); P.L. 42, 1033-1034.

"Nec ideo laudanda es, quia eos [filios] habes, sed quia pie nutrire atque educare studes."—*De bono viduitatis,* 14, 18; P.L. 40, 441.

Appendix II

The Controversy on St. Augustine's Conversion

The Catholic Church always has considered the conversion of St. Augustine one of the most significant events of her life across the centuries, and has accorded it a liturgical honor second only to the conversion of St. Paul.[1] An integral part of that vast movement of persons to Christ which constituted the conversion of classical antiquity as a whole, no other personal history in that movement is so well documented. In addition to Possidius' life of St. Augustine, written by a man who lived with the Bishop of Hippo for many years, there are the many references scattered through Augustine's own works and his invaluable personal review of his writings in the *Retractationes* composed toward the end of his life. In addition to these more ordinary although copious sources, however, St. Augustine has left to posterity a conscientious history of his conversion in the *Confessions*. The universal respect for his intellectual and spiritual qualities, especially for the role of truth and truthfulness in his thought and character, have caused men through the intervening centuries simply to accept the unique self-revelation as the straight-forward historical truth on his conversion, uttered for men and before men, but to God himself. A traditional view of his conversion has resulted, based on the *Confessions*, "which can be summarized in two affirmations: in 386, St. Augustine was converted to Christianity; his life at Cassiciacum immediately afterwards was that of a fervent neophyte preparing for baptism by prayer and penance." [2]

347

In the face of this long acceptance, however, a controversy has arisen in recent times which obscures the nature of St. Augustine's life and work. "It may come as a surprise to many admirers of Augustine," writes Professor O'Meara, "to learn that for nearly three-quarters of a century a large number of important scholars have maintained that Augustine in 386 was converted not to Christianity but rather to Neo-Platonist philosophy." [3] Nor does the dispute show any sign of abating. Writing in 1960 in his introduction to the English translation of Portalié's survey of St. Augustine's doctrine, first published at the opening of the present century, Professor Vernon J. Bourke emphasizes the continuing difficulties in which the traditional view has become involved. "Concerning the personal life of Augustine," he writes, "one of the most significant controversies had started before Father Portalié wrote and has continued to the present day. This is the dispute about the details of his conversion . . . Father Charles Boyer strongly supported the historicity of the *Confessions* and maintains the sincerity of Augustine's religious conversion. More recent works have stressed the complexity of the problem." [4]

In view of the continuing life of the matter and the importance of the problem in itself, it may be worth while to review the controversy from the beginning in order, if possible, to clarify its various causes; this done, a solution will be proposed from the distinct, although closely related, viewpoints of Christian philosophy and the idea of Catholic education.

The Modern Criticism of the *Confessions*

The controversy is ordinarily dated from 1888, when Gaston Boissier in France and Adolf Harnack in Germany published apparently independent monographs which laid down the thesis that St. Augustine's earliest works, the *Dialogues of Cassiciacum,* are incompatible with the traditional acceptance of the historicity of the *Confessions.*[5]

Boissier launched the idea with enduring force into modern Augustinian scholarship that the *Dialogues of Cassiciacum,* documents written in the weeks following Augustine's resignation from the chair of rhetoric at Milan, portray a state of mind and soul in direct conflict with the account he himself gave a dozen years later when he had become the Bishop of Hippo.[6] The historicity of the *Confessions*, therefore, can not be simply accepted in the traditional way. The *Confessions* portray the conversion in one way, he maintains, and the "philosophical dialogues" in another: "Not that the facts are different, but the general coloration has been changed." [7] It is not that St. Augustine voluntarily altered the true picture. "Everyone agrees, on the contrary, that his sincerity is his greatest merit . . . but one must not forget that the Confessions were written eleven years after his baptism." Augustine fell into the common human habit of "perceiving one's past life in the light of present opinions and impressions." [8] Bossier sees rightly that St. Augustine's occupation at Cassiciacum is the crucial point. What was the activity, he asks, at *La retraite de Cassiciacum?* [9] He supervised the villa, he wrote letters—"and the rest of his time was given to study. But here we meet a surprising fact," continues Boissier. "This study is not devoted exclusively to the Sacred Scriptures, the only pursuit, it seems, which would befit a penitent. In the picture Augustine traces of his activities at Cassiciacum, there is hardly question of anything but the profane sciences, especially grammar and rhetoric. We note that the classical authors are analyzed at Cassiciacum with the greatest care. On one occasion an entire book of Vergil is explained in the period before dinner, and Augustine continues thus on the following days. (cf. *C. Acad.* I, 15; *De ord.* I, 26). It truly appears that Augustine is simply continuing his professional capacity as *rhetor* for a few selected students." [10] Boissier gives his interpretation of these facts with the remark that it is difficult to understand why Augustine devotes his first liberty to the school exercises for which he professes such disgust, and goes on to discuss the *Dialogues of Cassiciacum* as purely philosophical exercises, in the Platonic and Ciceronian literary genre.

Boissier arrives in this way at two Augustines, one of the *Confessions*, the other of the *Dialogues*. "Since these two personalities differ from each other," he asks, "can we know which is the true one, the philosopher or the penitent?" [11] The continuing discussion of these apparent alternatives, conceived as a dilemma, constitutes the controversy on St. Augustine's conversion.

Adolf Harnack states his intention to "get rid of a widespread prejudice" by viewing St. Augustine's conversion as "a course of development" quite natural for those times and indeed a commonplace process "such as not a few of Augustine's contemporaries passed through." [12] This prejudice, "for the existence of which, it is true, he is himself to some degree responsible," consists in understanding the *Confessions* as the report of "a wild wastrel or a heathen, who, after a life of vice, is suddenly overcome by the truth of the Christian religion. No view can be more mistaken." [13] Augustine as a matter of fact is simply a Christian boy who undergoes the normal effect of his immersion in the secularized state of society; he wins victory over himself at last, with the aid of the authority of the Catholic Church, "because in the message of this Church he has experienced the power of breaking with the world and devoting himself to God." [14]

"In his external life," continues Harnack, "this change presents itself as a breach with his past; and it is in this view that he has himself depicted it. To him there is here nothing but a contrast between the past and the present. But in his inner life, in spite of his own representations, everything appears to us a quite intelligible development. It is true—and we understand the reason—that he was unable to judge himself in any other way." [15] Harnack explains that no one, recounting his passage from sin and error over to God, can possibly call the earlier portion of his path the way of truth.

"But others, both contemporary and later, may judge differently; and in this case such a judgment is made specially easy. For the man who here speaks to us is, against his will, compelled to give evidence that, even before his conversion, he strove unceasingly after truth and moral force; and, on the other hand, the numerous writings he produced immediately after his 'break with the past,' prove that the break was by no means so complete as the *Confessions*—written twelve years afterwards—would have us believe. Much of what only came to maturity in him during those twelve years, he has unconsciously transferred to the moment of his conversion. At that time he was no ecclesiastical theologian. In spite of his resolve to submit himself to the Church, he was still living wholly in philosophical problems. The great break was limited entirely to worldly occupations and to his renunciation of the flesh; the interests that had hitherto occupied his mind it did not affect. Thus it is not hard to refute Augustine out of Augustine, and to show that he has in his *Confessions* antedated many a change of thought. Yet, at bottom, he was right. His life, essentially, had but two periods. . . ." [16]

Harnack arrives in this way, although somewhat hesitantly, at the same two distinct and contrasting Augustines, one of the *Dialogues of Cassiciacum*, the other of the *Confessions*.

It remained for others to undertake detailed study of this basic thesis of the two scholars; the thirty years following the publication of these monographs were to see several works, mostly doctoral dissertations tracing to the inspiration of Boissier and Harnack, which represent careful scientific efforts to gather the evidence for the new view of St. Augustine's conversion. Friedrich Loofs emphasized the role of Neoplatonism, a point which will receive increasing attention in the development of the new interpretation.[17] In 1908 the studies of Hans Becker and W. Thimme appeared, defending the new position with much critical apparatus, and deepening the contrast with the traditional view.[18]

Becker, dedicating his work to Harnack as his Major Professor to whom he owes his *Anregung*, gathers evidence to show that the *Confessions* represent the suddenness of Augustine's conversion, while the *Dialogues of Cassiciacum* enable the modern analyst to see the truth of the matter, namely, that "Augustine is a man who matured gradually," whose conversion was "a process." [19] Becker's procedure is to develop "a sharp opposition" between the *Confessions*, a construct designed to contrast "nature" and "grace," and the quite different psychology of the *Dialogues of Cassiciacum*.[20] These represent a positive attitude toward the culture of this world, in contrast with the penitential spirit of the *Confessions* and their tone of flight from the world. Noteworthy is the fact that Augustine in the *Dialogues* holds philosophy up as the guide amid the errors and temptations of life." [21] From the *Confessions* one would expect Cassiciacum to reflect struggles like those of Luther in the cloister cell at Erfurt, but Augustine actually reports "a country idyll," where "his chief concern is to arouse enthusiasm for philosophy in the minds of two young students." [22] Becker identifies this philosophy: "In his first five writings, the *Weltanschauung* of Augustine is still completely conditioned by the Neoplatonic philosophy. . . . Only three years later, in the *De moribus ecclesiae*, does the fixed faith of the Catholic Church appear for the first time." [23] "When Augustine went to Cassiciacum, therefore, his development toward Christianity was by no means accomplished . . . only in 387 or thereabouts can one say that he has found in Christianity that for which he had sought through his many years of search for truth." [24] "Augustine's development," Becker concludes, "followed a completely different path than he himself presents in his Confessions, and which has since become traditional. This is the result of the more recent research . . . ." [25]

In France, L. Gourdon had published a doctoral study eight years before the appearance of the works of Becker and Thimme, along similar lines, but with even more drastic conclusions. In the Confessions and the Dialogues, he writes, "we are in the presence of two conversions and two different men." [26] These works are in "flagrant contradiction" with each other.[27] "The conversion of St. Augustine, intimately linked with the general development of his thought and with his entire spiritual history, found its effective termination in the years just before A.D. 400. Although he himself tells us in the Confessions that his conversion was fully accomplished at one stroke in 386, we say that it took place slowly and gradually, that it took place little by little, and was only completed in the year 400." [28] "In 386, Augustine went through a crisis which converted him, first, to a good moral life, and secondly, to the Neoplatonist philosophy. Nothing else." [29]

These works received restatement and detailed elaboration in Prosper Alfaric's massive treatise which appeared in 1918 under the title, The Intellectual Evolution of St. Augustine, Vol. I, From Manicheism to Neoplatonism, the first of a projected three-volume study intended to be fully comprehensive and finally definitive.[30] In it he seeks to demonstrate with all the weight of critical scholarship the fact that the Confessions are historically unreliable, that Augustine was a Neoplatonist at Cassiciacum, and that the Dialogues of Cassiciacum are nothing else than the purely philosophical exercises of a disciple of Plotinus and Porphyry. The dissertation was conducted under the supervision of Salomon Reinach, L. Lévy-Bruhl, and C. Guignebert, names of a stature in critical scholarship on classical antiquity at the turn of the century, sufficient in themselves to highlight the fundamental nature of this dispute. The sharpness of the controversy is evident from Alfaric's summary of his position: "When Augustine received baptism, he accorded so little importance to this rite, that in the writings of this period, in which he frequently speaks of himself and of everything which interests him, he never made even the most distant allusion to his baptism. Hence he was at the time hardly Catholic. Without doubt he had accepted Christian tradition, but he considered it simply a popular adaptation of Platonic wisdom." [31]

"Augustine adopted Platonism before adhering to Christianity," Alfaric writes, "and only came to the latter because he judged it, after examination, to be in conformity with the former . . . And even subsequently to this, he held for some time much more strongly to the doctrine of Plotinus than to Catholic dogma." [32] "Morally as well as intellectually," Alfaric concludes, "it was Neoplatonism to which Augustine was converted, rather than the Gospel." [33] His final conclusion, already cited, follows directly from these positions. "In Augustine," Alfaric writes, "the Christian disappears behind the disciple of Plotinus. Had he died after publishing the *Soliloquies* or the treatise *On the Greatness of the Soul*, he would be considered simply a convinced Neoplatonist, more or less tinctured with Christianity." [34] Augustine's teaching does indeed modify Plotinus in adapting Neoplatonism to Christianity, according to Alfaric; "but he transforms Catholicism still more in adjusting it to the Neoplatonist philosophy, and he looks upon Catholicism as a lower form of wisdom, good only for weaker intelligences or those still novices in the quest." [35]

Such, then, is this fundamental change from the traditional understanding of St. Augustine's life and works in the period during and immediately after his conversion. The scholars whose work reaches a climax in Alfaric's volume share a common approach to the *Confessions* and a common denial of the historicity of Augustine's self-revelation; at the same time, it should be noted, the basic proof adduced rests upon the *Dialogues of Cassiciacum*. The entire problem turns about the manner in which these earliest writings are to be understood.[36]

From the beginning, other representatives of Augustinian scholarship took up the defense of the historicity of the *Confessions*, a defense which culminates in the writings of Father Charles Boyer, S.J., of the Gregorian University in Rome, works which have been crowned by the French Academy. So strongly consistent and so well documented was Boyer's defense, published in 1920, that Alfaric, apparently in view of it, did not proceed with his study: his second and third volumes have never appeared. It seems, therefore, that the proper juncture has been reached for a short survey of the chief works which prepared for Boyer's research, and for a summary of his contribution to the study of the problem.

The Defense of the *Confessions*

Friedrich Wörter, writing in 1892, seems to have been the first to take exception to the position of Boissier and Harnack, devoting a few pages of his traditional exposition of St. Augustine's development to the new theory.[37] He rejects what he considers an exaggerated contrasting of the *Confessions* and the *Dialogues of Cassiciacum*, in view of the explicit evidence in the latter that they are the work of a Catholic man. "Augustine was happy over his liberation from school and from the disciplines he had been teaching, rhetoric and the rest, but not because of a liberation from philosophy, with which he continued to concern himself after his conversion." [38] Wörter concedes that there are certain stages by which Augustine came to the Catholic faith, but it does not follow that his conversion was a purely natural process. "Harnack's position regarding St. Augustine depends upon viewing Christian life in general as a merely natural development." [39]

Portalié's article, "Augustin (Saint)," in the *Dictionnaire de théologie catholique* (Paris: Letouzey, 1902), touches the essentials of the defense, supporting Wörter, but again only briefly.[40] "The ten years from 386-396," he writes, "comprise a period when Augustine became acquainted with Christian dogma. During this time he developed in his mind a blend of Platonic philosophy and revealed doctrine. The principle which governed the evolution of his thought has been misunderstood recently and deserves a clear explanation. . . . Until modern times no one had doubted that Augustine was a Christian. . . . Today, however, some critics uncover a radical opposition between the philosophical dialogues . . . and the state of soul described in the *Confessions*." [41] After summarizing the statements of Harnack, Loofs and especially Gourdon, Portalié makes the points which form the nucleus of the defense of the *Confessions*, and which were to be fully elaborated in the future work of Boyer. "Wörter," he writes, "has anticipated and treated these assertions as they deserve. The discussion is quickly resolved by means of these solidly-established facts: (1) Augustine was baptized, as all admit, at Easter, 387. Who will believe that this was a meaningless and empty ceremony? (2) The material facts of the *Confessions* (and not only the state of his soul) would have to have been falsified with unashamed brazenness: the scene in the garden, the example of the solitaries, the reading of St. Paul, the conversion of Victorinus, the ecstasy of Augustine when reading the Psalms with Monica—all that fabricated after the deed was done! (3) Finally, Augustine composed such apologetic works as *On the Morals of the Catholic Church* in 388, when he would not even have been a Christian! The reader is free, moreover, to consult the dialogues themselves. Undoubtedly there is all the difference between the *Confessions* and the philosophical dialogues that such diverse literary types and purposes demand. The dialogues are a purely philosophical work. . . . How could works of this nature tell of the victories of grace? Only incidentally do they reveal the state of soul of the solitary, but they tell enough of it to prove that their author is the converted Augustine of the *Confessions*. The first thing to consider is the ruling purpose which directs these philosophical inquiries." [42]

The Abbé Jules Martin, in his contribution to the series *Les Grandes Philosophes*, follows a different approach: he ignores the controversy completely and simply allows a comprehensive and objective exposition of St. Augustine's philosophical thought, existing as a consistent entity throughout all his writings, to clarify the fact that it is the work of a Christian mind.[43] That this is his conscious intention is indicated by his statement in an earlier article: "The inspiration of the four dialogues is as Christian as that of the *Confessions*. This is so obvious that it would seem to be superfluous to point it out." [44] Due to Boissier's views, however, Martin proceeds to cite in great detail the passages of the *Dialogues of Cassiciacum* which demonstrate their Christian authorship and hence their basic harmony with the *Confessions*.[45]

In Germany Mausbach, writing on another topic after Becker and Thimme had published, adverted to the controversy in ten pages packed with facts in defense of the *Confessions*.[46] All in all, however, the defense thirty years after the launching of the controversy was still without a comprehensive and detailed *ex professo* statement of its case comparable to the weighty works of scholarship which the criticism of the *Confessions* had produced, and which apparently was culminating with the announcement of Alfaric's three-volume study.[47] It was the place and function of Charles Boyer, who dedicated his work to Portalié, to provide this type of scholarly investigation of the evidence concerning the historicity of the *Confessions*.[48] His work is characterized by keen theological and philosophical perception, but he intends his method of approach to be that of the positive historian concerned to respect, without distortion or suppression, the evidence of the documents. "We have arrived," he writes, "at the center of our study. Under what influence did that change of life called the conversion of St. Augustine take place? Christianity? Or Neoplatonism? This question is decisive . . . The results accumulated up to this point will give us powerful assistance in the research of the truth concerning this fact of history." [49]

To summarize Boyer's exposition and to place its chief points in a logical progression, he first disposes of Harnack's point of departure, the popular impression that St. Augustine's conversion resulted from some bolt out of the supernatural world which separated his life with miraculous suddenness into black and white. "The literary and oratorical preoccupations of St. Augustine's panegyrists," he writes, "frequently have led them to represent his conversion as a sudden, total transformation of his personality. . . . His life would be divided into two periods without rational connection. A miracle, without previous preparation, would have created a new Augustine at one stroke. It was felt that Augustine is to be understood in this way, by virtue of the mere fact that he attributed his conversion to the action of God and his Church. But the narrative of the *Confessions* presents an entirely different picture . . . It is this which Harnack has not sufficiently noted . . . [and] it is this which seems to have been the origin of the idea of narrating St. Augustine's personal history differently than he himself does, and of opposing the *Dialogues of Cassiciacum* to the *Confessions*." [50] It becomes basic in Boyer's work, therefore, to show that St. Augustine himself describes his conversion as a process which entailed several stages, especially the distinction between the "conversion of his mind" and the "conversion of his heart." [51] There was indeed a "process" and a "development," but not the purely natural or even vitalistic "evolution" which has been so often the presupposition of the new theory.

Boyer, in the second place, demonstrates by a careful analysis of the documents that St. Augustine returned to the Catholic faith prior to his reading of the Platonists.[52] This crucial point is frequently missed; indeed, Boyer can say that "ordinarily it has been presumed that Augustine was prepared for the act of faith by his reading of the Neoplatonists." [53] This is the lasting accomplishment of Boyer, for it removes the theory that Augustine was converted to Neoplatonism from any foundation in the facts. Boyer concedes a role to Neoplatonism in the formation of St. Augustine's mind from this point forward, but not that he was converted initially to Neoplatonism as such.[54]

As an outgrowth of this demonstration Boyer in the third place gathers much valuable material on St. Augustine's own thought, how it is different from that of Plotinus, and in what way it depends on the Neoplatonist teacher. He does not, however, come to a decisive position regarding the nature of St. Augustine's philosophy—whether it is "Christian Neoplatonism," or "Christian Philosophy."

Finally, Boyer discusses the kind of life which Augustine led at Cassiciacum in the weeks following his conversion, and the nature of the *Dialogues of Cassiciacum* which he composed during this time.[55] Solid evidence is presented from these philosophical works themselves that they exhibit the thought of a Catholic mind and reflect the life of a Catholic man. In this, Boyer amplifies the work of his predecessors. The opposed theory has been disposed to minimize or even to overlook this evidence; but when it is considered objectively, the supposed contrast between the *Dialogues of Cassiciacum* and the *Confessions* proves to be an artificial modern construct.[56] "The opposition," Boyer concludes, "which has been pretended between Augustine's Neoplatonism and his Christianity never was apparent to himself. In his mind, the elements of his philosophy existed with the articles of faith in an indivisible and ordered unity which took its form from the principle of authority." [57]

The defense of the historicity of the *Confessions*, conducted along these four lines, seemed to win an overwhelming victory; not only did Alfaric fail to publish his remaining volumes, but non-Catholic scholars, such as Nörregaard [58] and Holl [59], subscribed in their works to the basic positions established by Boyer. Pierre de Labriolle, five years after Boyer's work appeared, states that "a reaction is beginning to set in, favorable to the historicity of the *Confessions*." [60] Father Boyer himself was conscious of his success. "The historical validity of the *Confessions* of St. Augustine," he writes in 1932, "while disputed in these recent times with more ardor and assurance than even that of the poems of Homer, has emerged from the controversy more strongly confirmed and more clearly manifest than ever." [61] It seemed this time that the discussion was indeed resolved, as Portalié had put it thirty years before, by means of the solidly established facts.

Such, however, was once more not to be the case. "More recent works," to cite Professor Bourke again, "have stressed the complexity of the problem," and he refers to the studies of P. Courcelle and J. J. O'Meara. [62] Father Boyer himself has noted the new turn in the matter. "M. Pierre Courcelle," he writes in his review, "has taken up once more the examination of the historical value of the *Confessions* of St. Augustine. This discussion, which was quite lively thirty years ago, seemed to have concluded in favor of the incomparable autobiography. Very recently, however, the doubts have begun to be affirmed anew. . . ." [63] As a matter of fact, the controversy has returned vigorously to life, and indeed one must say that increasing concession is being made by Catholic scholars to the view which Boyer thought to have refuted, the view that St. Augustine was converted initially to Neoplatonism, and that the *Dialogues of Cassiciacum* do indeed reflect a largely philosophical state of soul, and therefore tend to refute the other Augustine of the *Confessions*. [64]

In his detailed study of St. Augustine's self-revelation Courcelle, in fact, has attempted to find an entirely new approach. [65] "The purpose of this study," he states, "is not to advance a solution to the controversy now half a century old, but to take the problem out of the beaten path." [66] This is to distinguish the theological from the biographical components, as he terms them, then to set literary history to work upon the resulting text. What the success has been in Boyer's view, is evident from his comments already cited. One thing, however, is clear: the defense of the historicity of the *Confessions* seems to labor anew under some hidden factor which has prevented it from winning a decisive and conclusive victory in this dispute.

What might this factor be? "The first thing to consider," Portalié wrote, long ago, "is the ruling purpose which directs these philosophical inquiries," the *Dialogues of Cassiciacum*.[67] The powerful resurrection of the opposed theory, but now in works far removed from the Harnack-Becker-Alfaric group of earlier years, can be appreciated best, perhaps, by studying its apparent effect upon the most recent and fundamental study of St. Augustine's conversion in the English language, that by Professor O'Meara.[68] His basic approach, in quite obvious contrast to the work of Boyer, appears in the topics of his Chapter IX, "Neo-Platonism for the Few: The Ascent of the Soul"; and Chapter X, "Neo-Platonism for the Many: The Universal Way." It was a "Conversion to philosophy," in A. D. Nock's sense, to be followed later by the submission of intellect and will to the Catholic faith.[69] What, then, will be Professor O'Meara's view of Augustine's ruling purpose at Cassiciacum and in the *Dialogues*?

"During those leisurely days of the autumn and early winter of 386," he writes, "Augustine with his mother, brother, son, some cousins, Alypius, Evodius, and two young men who were entrusted to him for instruction, spent their days attending to the chores in the house and in the fields, sitting under a tree by the meadow or, when it was wet, in the baths discussing philosophy and reading Cicero and Virgil. Augustine prayed and wrote when he was not otherwise engaged." [70] Out of this activity the *Dialogues* came forth. "Other writings were projected," continues O'Meara, "for he proposed to write a series of works treating of the disciplines introductory to philosophy and some (such as *On the True Religion*) may have been begun. It would seem that for the moment, at any rate, he proposed to devote himself to philosophy, philosophical or semi-philosophical writing, and the sweet companionship of his friends—while at the same time integrating all of this to his new life as a Christian. There is no hint of any further plan." [71]

It is indeed possible that Augustine had no plan at Cassiciacum beyond this "country idyll" and some general intention to "devote himself to philosophy." The question is whether such is the actual Augustine, the real Augustine of history as known by means of the documents which are available. The answer is contained in the present study as a whole, and especially in Chapter IV, "Paideia Theou: The Birth of Christian Philosophy, with its detailed analysis of the paideutic character of the so-called philosophical dialogues of St. Augustine.

Analyzed in this way from the point of view of the field of education, which to be sure is St. Augustine's own field since his decision upon a calling in life when he read the *Hortensius* as a student, it becomes apparent that his very works contain the correct answer to the question at hand. He does indeed have a further plan, beyond his need of a physical rest, beyond his interest in philosophy, indeed beyond his baptism itself, which he saw as a beginning. This further plan is a "difficult undertaking" in the field of Catholic education, a plan for qualitative excellence in education which has been maturing in his professional life and experience since he read Cicero's *Hortensius*. It is this paideutic tendency and character of his philosophical ideal which makes him in a fully legitimate sense the Christian Plato; it is this, furthermore, which makes his baptism his personal fulfillment and his conversion in the garden at Milan truly the conversion of *Augustinus rhetor*—as such.[72]

Christian Philosophy and a *Paideia* of God

This insight into the purpose of the philosophical dialogues makes it possible to examine the controversy on St. Augustine's conversion with the orientation needed for solving the protracted dispute and for identifying the factor which seems to have hindered the defense of the *Confessions* from winning a finally conclusive victory. This approach is simply to follow the admonition of Father Portalié himself.[73] These considerations are offered as a complement to the work of Father Boyer; they are intended on the one hand to round out certain aspects of his research, and on the other hand to call renewed attention to the abiding validity of the fundamental demonstrations which he accomplished.[74]

The controversy on St. Augustine's conversion has turned about two points, both having to do with Cassiciacum. The first is the question of the type of activity which Augustine was carrying on at the villa. The second concerns the kind of philosophy which occupied his mind. When the activity is seen as a purely philosophical exercise and the philosophy is thought to be Neoplatonism as the result of a standard conversion to philosophy, then indeed it will become possible to wonder why the *Dialogues of Cassiciacum* are animated as they are with a spirit so apparently unlike the *Confessions*. Then the modern reader will indeed begin to graft onto Augustine his modern misconception of the purpose which Augustine actually had in mind in the two types of works. In this way the modern reader can come to the interpretation of the new criticism, which wants to hold that the philosophical works written at Cassiciacum represent not Christian philosophy but Neoplatonism.[75] It is possible, however, and apparently it is also a fact supported by the relevant documents, that the *Dialogues of Cassiciacum* are philosophical in nature not because St. Augustine has not yet been fully converted to the Catholic faith, or because his state of soul is quite unlike his report in the *Confessions*, but because he has a practical reason, a ruling purpose, which involves philosophy in a very definite and specific way. When this practical purpose is seen to be educational in nature, always within his conversion to the Catholic Church and indeed within his decision to embrace a religious life, a helpful vantage point is gained for analyzing accurately the kind of philosophy which is occupying his mind. It is the educational perspective which reveals the dialogues clearly as works of Christian philosophy and not of Neoplatonism; not, however, as pure philosophy, but rather as applied philosophy, the seminal works of St. Augustine's Christian philosophy of education. It follows immediately that the concern for Vergil and the liberal studies in general, the love for philosophy, the continuing academic interests, and all the other points adduced in alleged conflict with the *Confessions* have their natural and rightful place in the life at the villa and in the *Dialogues of Cassiciacum*. There is no conflict with the *Confessions*. There are not two Augustines, nor does the later Augustine report inaccurately the man whom St. Ambrose was preparing for baptism. He was *Augustinus rhetor*, the man who always has been admired for his truthfulness, his love of truth, and his greatness of mind and soul: a greatness fully capable of having in mind so large a ruling purpose as the regeneration and renewal of the educational profession which was a part of his person and which all his life had constituted his concrete way in the quest for wisdom.

The perspective from the field of education serves also to illuminate certain points in the defense of the historicity of the *Confessions* which seem to be the factor which has hindered thus far its full and lasting victory over the recent theory of the two conversions and the two Augustines. A discussion of these points may serve to clarify the paideutic character of St. Augustine's early works, which has been advanced as a positive solution to the persistent attempt to portray a conflict between the *Confessions* and the philosophical dialogues.

The first point is the fact that the *Dialogues of Cassiciacum* have seldom been seen as emerging directly from the act of teaching and in relationship to the field of education. In the reflections which opened the controversy on St. Augustine's conversion, Boissier adverts explicitly to the academic character of the months at Cassiciacum. "It truly appears," he writes, "that Augustine is simply continuing his professional capacity as *rhetor* for a few selected students." [76] Boissier thus verges upon the solution to the controversy in the very act of launching it. But he veers away with the remark that it is difficult to understand why Augustine devotes his first liberty from the school exercises, for which he professes such disgust, to a program which seems to include those same school exercises: and he proceeds to discuss the *Dialogues of Cassiciacum* as purely philosophical exercises. Later writers, on both sides of the controversy, tend to follow Boissier in viewing the philosophical dialogues largely out of relationship with this continuing professional work in the field of education; in fact, sometimes the field of education simply drops out of sight.

Like Boissier, Boyer approaches more closely to the educational relationship than his successors in the defense, but again like Boissier he ends by missing the mark. Boyer notes the fact that Augustine was continuing his teaching profession at Cassiciacum, directing the academic work of students and even continuing the use of profane authors. "But these young people are Christians," he writes, "and their teacher is concerned with their total formation. . . . Everything which takes place now has a new value, and the studies on the lower level prepare for the highest ones. If Christianity always has counted so many teaching religious, we should not be surprised to see a convert continue as an apostolate what he had abandoned as an empty and a dangerous profession. Forming these young sons of his own friends must have appeared as a noble task to Augustine . . . , and at the same time an opportunity to oblige the benefactors who doubtless were continuing to assure his material needs." [77] This actually contains, *materialiter*, the key to the nature of the *Dialogues of Cassiciacum* and to the full refutation of the opposed theory. Augustine was continuing his professional work in the field of education, but now as an apostolate; Cassiciacum was a genuine school, indeed a Catholic school, the actual fountainhead of the educational institution of the coming Christian culture of the Western world. But in Boyer's account education is viewed as something incidental to Augustine's life at the villa, a mere private favor to his benefactors, or perhaps an unwanted task which he was obliged still to fulfill. Speaking *formaliter*, the entire larger reality of the situation is missed, the plan, the project, the "difficult matter he was undertaking" which engrossed Augustine's mind and formed the concrete setting and purpose of his philosophizing.[78] "More even than to rhetoric," notes Boyer, "a place of honor was given in the Dialogues to philosophy." [79] This is true, of course, but not sufficiently strong: it merely juxtaposes rhetoric and philosophy, and seems to miss the full importance of the use of Cicero's *Hortensius* at the villa: this was no school of rhetoric, in the sense of the classical past; it was *nostra schola*, a new departure in education in which philosophy is restored to its rightful place and full function. "The solitaries of Cassiciacum," continues Boyer, "devoted long hours to philosophical conversations," [80] on topics which renew the "profane dialogues" of Cicero.[81] This seems not to convey the real point of the Dialogues as exemplifying pedagogical method on the one hand, and as illustrating on the other hand the manner in which the most fundamental themes of Christian philosophy relate to purposes in the Christian education of youth. Noting how certain characteristic words, such as philosophy, science, wisdom and discipline, recur throughout the Dialogues, Boyer asks, "Is it not evident that Cassiciacum, in that year's-end of 386, was nothing

else than an oasis of independent philosophy?" [82] Boyer states
that Boissier, Loofs, Gourdon and Alfaric concluded in this manner, but were deceived in so doing: "There is nothing in this
view but an appearance." [83] He proceeds to prove, with points
fully valid as far as they go, that the reality was not the Neoplatonist philosophical group which these authors suppose, but
actually the practice of Christian perfection, one of the meanings
commonly given to the term philosophy in the early Church.[84]
The fact is, however, that these four words are school words, the
stock-in-trade of the teaching profession, especially when imbued
with the ideals of the *Hortensius*. When the defense omits the
ruling purpose of the philosophical dialogues in this way, it can
never really defeat the theory of the two Augustines.[85] The position of the opponents continues to seem plausible, and indeed
to rest upon plain evidence needing no arduous effort to clarify.
When, on the other hand, the *Dialogues* are viewed as the exemplified application of Christian philosophy to the renewal and
reform of education, the defense meets the new theory upon its
own ground, the historicity of the *Dialogues*, in a decisive rebut-
tal.

The second point is a certain lack of definiteness on this crucial question of the historicity of the *Dialogues of Cassiciacum*.
From the beginning of the controversy, the theory of the two
Augustines has planted its case squarely upon the historicity of
the philosophical dialogues.[86] This has opened the way to a
tendency on the part of the defense to support the historicity of
the *Confessions* by derogating from that of the *Dialogues of
Cassiciacum*.

On the one hand, Boyer feels a strong compulsion to admit
their historicity. "To begin with," he writes, "these writings are
'dialogues.' They belong to a literary genre which has its customs,
its liberties, its manner of speaking. A fictitious component is
admissible in it. Without doubt, these works of Augustine are
more real than the dialogues of Plato or Cicero. They were actually held." [87] Boyer cites several references to Augustine's use of
the stenographer, then makes his strongest statement in a footnote: "For our part, especially because of the manner in which
the *Retractationes* report the composition of the *De beata vita*
(*Retr.* I, II, P.L. 32, 588), we think that the *Dialogues of Cassic-*

iacum were in fact written according to the way they were held";
and he refers to Ohlmann and van Haeringen, the classic defenders of the historicity.[88]

On the other hand, however, Boyer immediately opens the
door to the conclusion, seemingly illogical in the face of his
reference to Ohlmann, that the *Dialogues* are not historical
because Augustine edited the stenographer's copy—which of
course he did.[89] "It would seem to us," he concludes rather
hesitantly, "not quite prudent to oblige oneself always to take
the *Dialogues* according to the rigor of the letter. The *Confessions*, on the contrary, pertain to a genre which is more incompatible with fiction." [90] In addition, Boyer continues, Augustine's
purpose in the *Dialogues* is not to narrate his personal history;
the passage of some time, furthermore, has its advantages, giving
perspective when one recounts a personal history. "One must expect," he concludes somewhat tortuously, "that the *Dialogues*,
despite their authority as an intimate journal, describe St. Augustine to us with more confusion, with a lesser sense of proportion,
and by that very fact, with less truth than the *Confessions*." [91] In
other words, Boyer, even while citing Ohlmann, is making a large
concession to the position that one must choose between the two
works of Augustine on this point of historical veracity, as if one
Augustine does indeed, as Harnack puts it, refute the other.

The third point is a further development of the second, the
fact that some defenders of the *Confessions*, since Boyer's works,
have tended to weaken still more, giving up altogether the concept of the historicity of the *Dialogues of Cassiciacum*. The
pressure which the new criticism has placed upon Augustinian
scholarship is readily visible, for example, in Professor O'Meara's
efforts to deny this historicity. "But in the main," he writes,
"although there may be much solid fact enshrined in them, the
dialogues of Cassiciacum are works of fiction and must be treated
with appropriate reserve." [92] "It was often customary in such
dialogues," Professor O'Meara continues, "to pretend that the
discussions actually took place and consequently a number of
conventions were employed to lend veri-similitude to the claim.
Among these conventions was the supposed even verbal accuracy
of the report of an actual discussion. Augustine conforms very
closely to the conventional practice in all these matters, and the

historicity of the discussions between him and his circle must inevitably be suspect." [93]

Professor O'Meara, in other words, adopts the position that the *Dialogues of Cassiciacum* are simply a literary genre in the philosophical tradition of Plato and Cicero. He grants, however, that it is "not unlikely . . . that Augustine attempted to hold the discussions, and either recorded them for editing afterwards, or wrote up discussions that had just taken place." [94] "Moreover," he concedes, "the prefaces to the works give without any doubt many historical facts, and there are other detailed points favoring the historicity of certain episodes." [95]

Here again there is the failure to meet the new theory on its own ground, a failure which gives the controversy its continuing life and has made it seem at last insoluble.[96] Professor O'Meara's defense seems to writhe under the torturing impact of the opposed theory, which rests, as we saw, precisely upon the historicity of the *Dialogues*, and the apparent foundation which this historicity would give to the charge that they reflect the work of a convert to Neoplatonism, not Christianity, and that they therefore render the *Confessions* historically unreliable.

Our purpose here has been to advance the view that the *Dialogues* emerge into a different position when they are seen from the field of education. When the years from the garden in Milan through his baptism up to his ordination are seen as one consistent intellectual period, in which Augustine turns to authorship because he now has a mission in the field of education, then the literary works of this period fall into a certain definite and natural perspective and into a natural, not an artificial, grouping. It is somewhat of a misnomer, it has been noted, to call the first four published works of St. Augustine the *Dialogues of Cassiciacum*, for this introduces the danger of setting them off artificially from the other works of this period when he is a layman working toward a suitable philosophy and program of education for Christian youth, one which he intends to organize and to pursue within the framework of the new institution of monasticism.

Reflecting upon St. Augustine's own numerous statements, we cannot avoid the conclusion that he is describing a factual situation in the *Dialogues of Cassiciacum*: he is not indulging a rhetorical device or a literary genre, not writing works of fiction.

The *Dialogues* have an authentic ring of historical validity to them which has provided the new theory with its enduring position in this controversy. This historicity of the *Dialogues* has seemed self-evident to Tillemont, to Ohlmann, to E. K. Rand, as well as to Marrou in our own day. [97]

It is of course possible that St. Augustine invented all of this and that the *Dialogues of Cassiciacum* are works of fiction. It seems to be a possibility, however, which is not supported by the evidence. Nor it is necessary, furthermore, to interpret the *Dialogues* in this fashion in order to defend the historicity of the Confessions and the integrity of St. Augustine as a bishop.

On the basis of the evidence adduced so far, it seems safe to say that the descriptions of Augustine's mind and activity at Cassiciacum which omit the field of education are not in accord with the facts. Augustine himself, as we have seen, tells us that he has a definite plan in mind, which he calls his "difficult undertaking." We stand here at the crux of the entire controversy, which seems ultimately to turn upon this view of Cassiciacum which omits its contact with the field of education. This point could be studied further in Augustine's letters to Nebridius, as well as in the content and significance of his treatises on the liberal arts and disciplines of human culture. All of these are in his mind at this time, an integral part of his "difficult undertaking." The central point about the activity at Cassiciacum is the fact that Augustine is conducting a school. O'Meara, we have seen, omits this more completely than either Boissier or Boyer. In connection with his activity along these lines St. Augustine is actively engaged in planning a new theory and practice of education, the reflection of the new Christian philosophy which he has found, introducing into education his philosophical insight into the spiritual reality of God, into creation from nothingness, and into the intellectual discernment of the providential order in the universe.

The view that Augustine "for the moment, at any rate," as Professor O'Meara says, intends to devote himself simply to "philosophy and philosophical writing and the sweet companionship of his friends," is not realistic.[98] Augustine was a teacher. The formation of youth is his very life: it has been so for years. He has never been a writer, nor has he ever manifested interest in philosophy purely and simply for its own sake. He has made con-

tact with monasticism under St. Ambrose at Milan: the idea of
the "service of God" has definitely entered his thought. The
central question is the manner in which Augustine conceives this
service of God. The evidence in the *Dialogues of Cassiciacum*
appears to place this definitely in the field of education. He looks
upon his service of God as a continuing contact with the field of
education. He intends to develop a Christian *paideia*, realizing
under the mighty power of Christ that aspiration of classical
antiquity which was embodied in Plato and Cicero.

Seen from the field of education, there is a striking consistency
and unity in Augustine's thought, as well as in his outward activity, from his reading of the *Hortensius* as a youth of nineteen
and the forsaking of the field of law for a career in education,
through his conversion at Milan and his writing of the *Dialogues
of Cassiciacum*, to the "school of perfection" at Thagaste and the
entire body of his published works up to his ordination as a
Catholic priest. When the *Dialogues of Cassiciacum* are understood as treatises in Christian philosophy at work in the field of
education, intended to exemplify the kind of teaching, content
and method which Augustine wished "our school" to possess in
contrast with "those other schools," the schools of rhetoric of
imperial Rome from which he had just resigned, then the controversy on his conversion no longer has an object. Everything
falls into its place exactly as Augustine states the case; nothing
is wrong with any of his works, nor with his sincerity in composing them. His *Confessions* describe the actual mind which he had
during his conversion and baptism. They form one piece with
the educational thought and practice at Cassiciacum. The *Dialogues of Cassiciacum* are fully historical, edited, of course, for
publication. They contain clear evidence that they are the work
of a Christian thinker or philosopher, a Catholic man who makes
unequivocal references to his faith, as Boyer successfully pointed
out. Neoplatonism is not concerned in any intrinsic or substantial way. Seen in the light of Augustine's "difficult undertaking,"
an educational program organized and implemented to constitute
a safe way for Christian youth, the *Dialogues of Cassiciacum* are
not in contrast or opposition with the *Confessions*, but in full
harmony and accord with them.[99] It seems possible that the entire controversy on the conversion of Augustine has arisen because

insufficient attention has been paid to the massive contact of the life and work of St. Augustine with the field of education.

St. Augustine and the Conversion of the Classical Civilization

A great fact stands written across the face of universal history. It is the fact that the Christian Era has followed upon the pagan times of antiquity. The classical civilization declined and fell. After it there developed in the Western world a new kind of social order called Christendom, or Western civilization. In such a gigantic succession in human social life, education could not but be involved, for it is the life-process, the dynamic factor, in both cultural continuity and cultural change. The decline and fall of the Roman Empire, the political and social embodiment of the classical culture, was one thing with the snuffing out of the schools of antiquity. When the light of history brightens again, in the times of Charlemagne, Alcuin and the rest, schools are returning to life and activity everywhere, and a new Athens, as Alcuin puts it, is coming into existence in the Western world. But, wonder of wonders, these new academic institutions are not the old classical schools simply restored; they are all monastery and cathedral schools, multiplying everywhere in the West even beyond the boundaries of that other, earlier, Rome. Their guiding light, furthermore, is the new paideia of God elaborated by St. Augustine. His works are everywhere the guide to the educational practices of *doctrina christiana*, and his philosophical thinking forms the educational theory of this new academic institution which transmits the essential values of this new Western world. It is a distinct civilization, therefore, indeed a new creation, as Toynbee says, but at the same time one which is affiliated to the Classical civilization of the past.[100]

There always has been among Western men some perception of St. Augustine's world-historical position and greatness, and of the importance of his conversion for universal history as an unfolding social process. It has been viewed also outside the Catholic Church as something more than another personal event taking place in the stream of world history.[101]

This is fully appreciated when his conversion is viewed from the standpoint of the field of education, for then it is seen to entail the conversion and the reform, the regeneration and the renewal, of the educational institution of the Western world and, potentially, of all mankind. The conversion of St. Augustine, the *rhetor* who embodied so fully and so magnificently the cultural and educational heritage of mankind, was perhaps the most important single factor and personal event in that process of affiliation, in Toynbee's sense, which links the heritage of the classical past with the Western and Christian civilization which has come to dominate the history of the Christian Era. Seen in this fashion, the conversion of St. Augustine involves both the fundamentals of Christian philosophy and the "philosophy of history" or meaning of the Christian Era.[102] The controversy on St. Augustine's conversion turns ultimately on the question whether it was good that mankind of classical antiquity turned to God in the Catholic Church, and whether it can be good for Western civilization, now becoming the World civilization, to turn away.

Notes from Appendix II

1 Cf. *Martyrologium Romanum* (Taurini: Marietti, 1932), p. 129: "24 Aprilis: Mediolani conversio sancti Augustini Episcopi, Confessoris et Ecclesiae Doctoris; quem beatus Ambrosius Episcopus veritatem fidei catholicae docuit, et hac die baptizavit." Permission to reprint this study of the conversion of St. Augustine, which appeared originally in substantially the same form in *Studies in Philosophy and the History of Philosophy*, Vol. II (Washington: The Catholic University Press, 1963) was given by the editor and copyright holder, Rt. Rev. John K. Ryan, and is gratefully acknowledged. This occasion is taken also to thank Rev. John P. Ashton for assistance in the preparation of the index.

2 Charles Boyer, *Christianisme et néo-platonisme dans la formation de Saint Augustin* (Rome: Officium Libri Catholici, 1953), p. 17.

3 John J. O'Meara, *The Young Augustine: The Growth of St. Augustine's Mind Up to His Conversion* (London: Longmans, 1954), p. 131. For a brief summary of the controversy, see *ibid.*, pp. 131-133. A comprehensive survey of the matter is contained in O'Meara's "Introduction" to his *St. Augustine: Against the Academics*, (Westminster, Maryland: The Newman Press, 1950), pp. 18-32; the controversy, he states, "has received little notice in English" (*ibid.*, p. 18). An earlier historical sketch is contained in Sister Mary Patricia Garvey, *Saint Augustine: Christian or Neo-Platonist? From his Retreat at Cassiciacum until his Ordination at Hippo* (Milwaukee: Marquette University Press, 1939), pp. 3-38; likewise antedating recent work, especially that of Courcelle and O'Meara, is Romano Guardini, *The Conversion of Augustine* (Westminster, Maryland: The Newman Press, 1960), a translation of a German original which appeared in 1935.

4 Vernon J. Bourke, in Portalié-Bastian, *A Guide to the Thought of Saint Augustine* (Chicago: Regnery, 1960), "Introduction," p. xxiv.

5 For a review of the few scattered tendencies to distrust the *Confessions* prior to 1888, cf. U. Mannucci, "La conversione di S. Agostino e la critica recente," in *Miscellanea Agostiniana* (Rome: Tipografia Poliglotta Vaticana, 1931), Vol. II, p. 26.

6 Cf. Gaston Boissier, *La fin du paganisme: Étude sur les luttes dernières religieuses en occident au quatrieme siècle* (Paris: Hachette, 1891), tome I, "La conversion de saint Augustin," pp. 339-379; previously published in *Revue des deux mondes*, 85 (Jan. 1, 1888), 43-69.

7 *Ibid.*, p. 340.

8 *Ibid.*, pp. 340-341.

9 Cf. *ibid.*, pp. 366-379, devoted to the discussion of this topic.

10 *Ibid.*, p. 368.

11 *Ibid.*, p. 376.

12 Adolph Harnack, *Augustin's Confessionen* (Giessen: J. Ricker'sche Buchhandlung, 1888); English translation, *Monasticism, Its Ideals and History; and The Confessions of St. Augustine* (London: Williams and Norgate, 1913), p. 138.

13 *Ibid.*, p. 139.

14 *Ibid.*, p. 140.

15 *Ibid.*

16 *Ibid.*, p. 141. Harnack's hesitancy and even self-contradiction are noteworthy. "As a whole," he writes on p. 127 of the same work, "in the presence of death itself, he makes it *(The Confessions)* as a witness of the truth. It was not to be a mingling of *Dichtung* and *Wahrheit;* but he meant, plainly and without reserve, to show in the book what he had been."

17 Cf. Friedrich Loofs, "Augustinus," in *Realencyclopädie für protestantische Theologie und Kirche* (Leipzig: J. C. Hinrichs'sche Buchhandlung, 1897, 3rd edition), Vol. II, pp. 257-285.

18 Cf. Hans Becker, *Augustin: Studien zu seiner geistigen Entwicklung* (Leipzig: J. C. Hinrich'sche Buchhandlung, 1908), and W. Thimme, *Augustins geistige Entwickelung in den ersten Jahren nach seiner "Bekehrung"* (Berlin: 1908).

19 Hans Becker, *op. cit.*, p. 16: "allmählich herangereift," "einen Prozess." The account of the episode in the garden at Milan in the *Confessions* has given rise to the traditional view of the suddenness of the conversion; "Dem wirklichen Verlauf seiner inneren Entwicklung, wie er selbst in den Tagen seines jungen Christentums gezeichnet hat, entspricht eine derartige Auffassung allerdings nicht," p. 17.

20 *Ibid.*, p. 12: "ein scharfer Abstand." The *Confessions* are written out of "a preconceived standpoint," according to a theological thesis which Augustine has in mind as a bishop: "Das Schema von Sünde und Gnade, nach dem er die Theologie und Kirche des Abendlandes bis in unsere Tage hinein orientiert hat, legt er mit aller Schärfe auch an sein eigenes Leben," p. 8.

21 *Ibid.*, p. 10; cf. his entire I Teil, "Psychologische Momente in der Entwicklung Augustins," pp. 9-62.

22 *Ibid.*, p. 13 and p. 15; "Immer und immer wieder weisst er auf die Philosophie hin als auf das Mittel, sich im Leben zurechtzufinden," p. 15. It is a peaceful, orderly and even a happy life, where Augustine takes the leading role in philosophical conversations; there is no sign of a penitential struggle, nor of a contrast with his earlier life. Cf. p. 14.

23 *Ibid.*, p. 56.

24 *Ibid.*, p. 59.

25 *Ibid.*, "Vorwort," P. III

26 Louis Gourdon, *Essai sur la conversion de St. Augustin: Thèse présentée à la faculté de Théologie Protestante de Paris* (Cahors: A. Coueslant, 1900), p. 46.

27 *Ibid.*, p. 51.

28 *Ibid.*, p. 87.

29 *Ibid.*, p. 45.

30 Cf. Prosper Alfaric, *L'Evolution intellectuelle de saint Augustin.* Vol. I, *Du manichéisme au néoplatonisme* (Paris: Emile Nourry, 1918).

31 *Ibid.*, "Préface," p. viii; translation of John J. O'Meara, *St. Augustine: Against the Academics, op. cit.*, p. 20.

32 *Ibid.*, pp. 380-381.

33 *Ibid.*, p. 399. The sweeping character of Alfaric's study is conveyed strikingly by his lengthy discussion, pp. 415-513, of St. Augustine's works published prior to his ordination in A.D. 391. Alfaric states his general conclusion in positive terms: "The doctrine which has been summarized here is seen to be essentially Neoplatonic and is inspired primarily by Plotinus," p. 515.

34 *Ibid.*, p. 527.

35 *Ibid.*, p. 515.

36 Cf. U. Mannucci, *op. cit.*, p. 25: The proof adduced by "la nuova critica" is the fact that St. Augustine, "dopo la presunta conversione . . . scrisse dei dialoghi, i famosi opuscoli di Cassiciaco . . . in cui—a tacere che serba un silenzio completo sull'evento di Milano—non trasparisce affatto l'uomo convertito, quindi già cristiano, ma solo il filosofo, il *Neoplatonico* in fieri . . ." [his emphasis].

37 Cf. Friedrich Wörter, *Die Geistesentwickelung des hl. Aurelius Augustinus bis zu seiner Taufe* (Paderborn: Ferdinand Schöningh, 1892), p. 210; for the discussion of the new view, cf. Chapter X, "Kurze Charakteristik des Lebenslaufes Augustins. Die Faktoren seiner Bekehrung," pp. 62-66. Wörter's summary of the Boissier-Harnack thesis shows his awareness of the role of philosophical presuppositions in the matter: "Augustin sei nicht . . . plözlich (durch göttliche Gnade) von der Wahrheit der Christlichen Religion ergriffen worden. Vielmehr allmählich, auf dem Wege wissenschaftlichen Strebens und Forschens habe sich seine Bekehrung nach ihrer intellektuellen Seite vollzogen . . . ," p. 63.

38 *Ibid.*, p. 65.

39 *Ibid.*, p. 64. Others have perceived the same factor at work in what Mannucci calls "the recent criticism," which views St. Augustine's conversion as "un procedimento del tutto naturale": cf. his "La conversione di S. Agostino e la critica recente" in *Miscellanea Agostiniana* (Roma: Tipografia Poliglotta Vaticana, 1931), Vol. II, p. 25. Cf. L. de Mondadon, "Les premières impressions catholiques de saint Augustin," *Etudes,* 119 (1909), p. 444: "Tendance extreme à minimiser le surnaturel." More recently, in his review of Courcelle's *Recherches sur les Confessions,* in *Doctor Communis IV* (1951), p. 110, Boyer calls attention to the same factor in connection with Courcelle's "pénible" twenty-page effort to minimize the episode in the garden at Milan: "On doit pourtant regretter qu'il ait trop cédé à cet esprit prétendu critique qui minimise ou meme supprime ce qui pourrait suggérer une intervention surnaturelle ou seulement providentielle." How can this be done, he asks, "sans accuser Augustin d'imposture?" The controversy, in addition to the

theological and philosophical presuppositions, involves the personal honor and integrity of Augustine as a man and a Catholic bishop, and by implication the honor of the Catholic clergy, as well as the inference, drawn, "più audacemente" by Alfaric, to use Mannucci's words, that Augustine found a higher and stronger motive of intellectual and moral progress in Neoplatonism than in the Christianity of Ambrose and Monica. It is for these reasons that the controversy has divided Augustinian scholars in the way pointed out by Karl Holl in his lecture before the Prussian Academy in 1922: "Diese Auffassung [Harnack's] hat sich bei den protestantischen Forschern, man darf sagen, durchgesetzt. Loofs, Scheel, Thimme Becker, Alfaric, geben sie mit wenigen Abwandlungen wieder. Ich begnüge mich mit dem Satz von Thimme: 'Dass Augustin in Cassiciacum durchaus nicht als ein gewöhnlicher christlicher Pönitent, eigentlich nicht einmal als werdender Christ, sondern als werdender Platoniker zu beurteilen ist' . . . Dagegen verhalten sich die katholischen Forscher Bardenhewer, v. Hertling, Mausbach ebenso entschieden ablehnend, ohne dass freilich von dieser Seite her ein ernsthafter Versuch unternommen worden wäre, die eigene Auffassung tiefer zu begrunden." K. Holl, *Augustins innere Entwicklung* (Berlin: Walter de Gruyter, 1923), pp. 8-9. We shall allow Holl's omission of Boissier and Boyer to pass without comment. In the present study, the primary interest is with the work of scholars who have defended the Confessions by the investigation of the historical evidence which illuminates the conversion of St. Augustine as a fact of history.

40 Cf. Portalié-Bastian, *A Guide to the Thought of Saint Augustine* (Chicago: Regnery, 1960), pp. 10-19.

41 *Ibid.*, pp. 14-15.

42 *Ibid.*, pp. 15-16. This "quick resolution of the discussion," however, did not take place: Thimme and Becker proceeded with their comprehensive studies from the opposed standpoint and published them, it has been noted above, in 1908. Obvious as the "solidly established facts" appeared to the defense, it seemed nevertheless to labor, from the beginning, under some factor which has prevented it from winning a decisive and conclusive victory in the dispute.

43 Cf. Jules Martin, *Saint Augustin* (Paris: Félix Alcan, 1901).

44 Jules Martin, "Saint Augustin à Cassiciacum: veille et lendemain de sa conversion," *Annales de philosophie chrétienne,* 39 (1898-1899), 307-308.

45 *Ibid.*, 308-316 and 410-428.

46 Cf. Joseph Mausbach, *Die Ethik des heiligen Augustinus* (Freiburg: Herder, 1909), Vol. I, pp. 5-16; reprinted without change in the new edition, 1929. "Trotz feiner Einzelbemerkungen Thimme's halte ich gegenüber seiner Auffassung das obengezeichnete [namely, from the *Confessions*] Entwicklungsbild aufrecht," p. 8, fn. 1. Mannucci (*op. cit.*, p. 28) considers that Mausbach's dense paragraphs "contengono in realtà tutti gli elementi atti à costruire una solida dimostrazione della giusta tesi."

47 Cf. Mannucci (*op. cit.*, p. 28): " . . . e non so se ciò provenga pel giusto disprezzo delle stravaganze di questa critica, o per la difficoltà del problema, che presuppone un lungo studio."

48 Cf. Charles Boyer, *Christianisme et Néo-platonisme dans la formation de saint Augustin* (Paris: Gabriel Beauchesne, 1920). For the purposes of the present study, the new edition, revised by the author (Rome: Officium Libri Catholici, 1953), was compared with the first edition; unless otherwise noted, citations will be made from the revised edition. There is, however, no substantial change of any kind in the new edition; it simply brings the references

up to date. Cf. also his summary, "La dialectique de la conversion de saint Augustin" in *Essais sur la doctrine de saint Augustin* (Paris: Gabriel Beauchesne, 1932), pp. 1-40, and his study of St. Augustine's philosophy, *L'idée de vérité dans la philosophie de saint Augustin* (Paris: Gabriel Beauchesne, 1920).

49 Charles Boyer, *La formation* . . . (1953), p. 115.

50 *Ibid.*, pp. 123-124. Cf. p. 127: "L'auteur [des *Confessions*] présente son histoire, non pas d'un point de vue rationaliste, certes, mais comme un développement rationnel. S'il entend bien que la suite de ses événements n'avait rien de nécessaire, et qu'elle a été créée par sa propre liberté et par l'action divine, il la croit néanmoins ordonnée et intelligible, et c'est pourquoi il estime, en la racontant, glorifier Dieu."

51 *Ibid.*, chap. III, "La conversion de s. Augustin," pp. 115-134, *passim;* for an *ex professo* discussion of these stages, cf. "La dialectique de la conversion de saint Augustin," in *Essais* . . . (*op. cit.*), pp. 1-40. "Le retour d'Augustin à la foi ne constitue que l'une des étapes de ce que l'on appelle sa conversion. . . . Bien avant de se donner pleinement à Dieu, à cette heure de grace qu'il vécut dans son jardin de Milan, le brillant rhéteur était revenu à la foi de son enfance. Avant la conversion du coeur avait eu lieu la conversion de l'esprit," pp. 3-4. It should be noted that Wörter, *op. cit.*, p. 65, had pointed out that there were stages in Augustine's return to the faith, and that Jules Martin distinguishes the formation of his "sens chrétienne et intelligence chrétienne," his "conviction chrétienne totalement formée," and the later "décision de vivre en parfait religieux" which took place in the garden. Cf. his *Saint Augustin* (Paris: Felix Alcan, 1901), p. 16.

52 Cf. Boyer, *La formation* . . . (1953), pp. 47-74, for the *ex professo* demonstration of this point.

53 Charles Boyer, *Essais* . . . (1932), p. 4.

54 Cf. Boyer, *La formation* (1953), pp. 172-173, "Role considerable du néo-platonisme dans la formation de saint Augustin," but "Sa subordination au christianisme."

55 *Ibid.*, Chap. IV, "Cassiciacum," pp. 135-167.

56 Becker (*op. cit.*, pp. 10-11) admits eight texts of the *Dialogues* which bear witness to their harmony with the *Confessions*, but judges that they are too few. "Mais saint Augustin n'eut-il révélé qu'une seule fois," asks Boyer, "dans les *Dialogues*, la réalité de son christianisme, ne devrait-on pas l'en croire?" *La formation* . . . (1953), p. 150.

57 Boyer, *La formation* . . . (1953), pp. 193-194.

58 Cf. D. Jens Nörregaard, *Augustins Bekehrung* (Tübingen: Verlag von J. C. B. Mohr, 1923). This work, which was first conceived in Harnack's seminar at Berlin in 1911, ended as a refutation of Alfaric independent of Boyer and arriving at substantially the same conclusion: "Der Neuplatonismus war in Wirklichkeit nur eine ganz kurze Zeit das Primäre für Augustin, in dem er vor der Bekanntschaft mit ihm in einer solch ständigem Berührung mit christlichen Gedanken gewesen war . . . und schon so stark zum Christentum hineingezogen worden war, dass die neue Philosophie für ihn ein Mittel wurde, sich das Christentum aneignen zu können," p. 242.

59 Cf. Karl Holl, *op. cit.*

60 Pierre de Labriolle (transl.) *Saint Augustin: Confessions* (Paris: Société d'Edition "Les Belles Lettres," 1925), "Introduction," p. xxii. "It is imprudent," he adds, "to substitute for St. Augustine's testimony des conjectures infiniment plus incertaines."

[61] Charles Boyer, *Essais* . . . (1932), p. 1.

[62] Vernon J. Bourke, in Portalié-Bastian, *op. cit.*, "Introduction," p. xxiv.

[63] Charles Boyer, Review of Courcelle's *Recherches*, in *Doctor Communis*, 4 (1951), 109. The new delicacy of the question is reflected in Father Boyer's carefully-worded "Préface de la nouvelle édition" of *La formation* . . . (1953): ". . . il nous semblait . . . très opportun de maintenir à l'usage des hommes d'études une interprétation des *Confessions* qui a pour elle l'autorité des textes et l'appui d'une longue tradition. . . . Là où les innovations nous semblaient contraires à la vérité, nous l'avons dit sans détour, comme sans passion. Notre désir de ne mécontenter personne ne pouvait nous enlever le souci de conserver entière à nos contemporains la lumière qui rayonne de la formation d'Augustin, telle qu'il l'a lui-meme déerite sous le regard de Dieu." As noted already, the fact is that Father Boyer's new edition is actually not new; it is a verbatim reprint of his original work, with the addition of some footnote references to the more recent literature. The only significant addition to the text is his "Examen d'un position récente," pp. 107-113, a sharply critical analysis of Courcelle's failure to remain faithful to the documents. "Chose étrange, plus d'une fois, M. Courcelle, si attentif à des détails minimes, ne voit pas les faits principaux; absorbé par l'étude d'un grain de sable, la montagne lui échappe," p. 112. In his review in *Doctor Communis*, *loc. cit.*, p. 111, Boyer is quite specific: it is his careful demonstration that St. Augustine returned to the Catholic faith *before* he read the Neoplatonist books which is being overlooked. "M. Courcelle n'admet pas qu'Augustin soit revenue à la foi chrétienne avant de lire Plotin. Mais pourquoi ne discute-t-il pas les textes où s. Augustin l'affirme?" Boyer mentions Conf. VI, 5 (7); VII, 5 (1); VII (11); one should add *La formation* . . . (1953), pp. 47-74, the *ex professo* demonstration.

[64] Cf., for example, Karl Adam, *Saint Augustine: The Odyssey of His Soul* (New York: Macmillan, 1932), for an early instance of the spirit of concession on this point, apparently motivated by the desire to have Augustine appear in marked contrast to St. Thomas. Cf. pp. 7-8. Boyer's demonstration that Augustine returned to the faith prior to his reading of the Platonist books is missed entirely. Cf. pp. 16-18. ". . . He was redeemed by a second great experience, the reading of Neoplatonist writings. . . . That was the knowledge which freed him and banished all doubt," p. 18. "But he saw Catholicism at that time in a Neoplatonic light. Or rather, he then identified Christianity in essentials with Neoplatonism . . . ," p. 21. Conf. VII, 17 represents a "Neoplatonist ecstatic contemplation," p. 22. It is all as if Boyer's works, and those of his forerunners in this defense, had never been written.

[65] Cf. Pierre Courcelle, *Recherches sur les Confessions de saint Augustin* (Paris: E. de Boccard, 1950).

[66] *Ibid.*, p. 12.

[67] Portalié-Bastian, *op. cit.*, p. 16.

[68] Cf. John J. O'Meara, *The Young Augustine: The Growth of St. Augustine's Mind up to His Conversion* (New York: Longmans, 1954). On the other hand, witness the recent strong affirmation of Boyer's position by M. F. Sciacca, *St. Augustin et le Néoplatonisme: la possibilité d'une philosophie chrétienne* (Louvain: Publ. Univ. de Louvain, 1956), p. 2: "A l'église il est venu (*Conf.* VII, 9) . . . *avant et indépendamment* de la lecture des livres des platoniciens" (his emphasis).

[69] *Ibid.*, p. 142; cf. pp. 131-155, *passim*.

[70] *Ibid.*, p. 192.

71 *Ibid.*

72 Seen in this perspective, the *Dialogues of Cassiciacum* are something of a misnomer, for St. Augustine wrote several other works up to his ordination which, as it frequently has been noted, bear an obviously similar stamp. Indeed, many of his works up to his ordination and even beyond to the *De doctrina christiana,* which climaxes his "difficult undertaking," form part of this plan for the renovation of the heritage of *paideia,* to make of it a *tuta via* for Catholic youth. The key to the understanding of his philosophical works is this paideutic character, and the fact that he was working simultaneously on school textbooks designed to animate and illuminate the liberal arts with this new clear-eyed Christian philosophy of God and the soul. Does this not define in the concrete framework of his life-long professional interest, his intense quest for wisdom in the very structure and process of education? Cf. St. Augustine's own statement at the end of his life as a bishop, *Retr.* I, 5 (6).

73 Cf. Portalié-Bastian, *A Guide to the Thought of St. Augustine* (Chicago: Regnery, 1960), p. 16: "The first thing to consider is the ruling purpose which directs these philosophical inquiries." In pointing out that Boyer's study of St. Augustine's life and work in the months at Cassiciacum does not penetrate to a full perspective on this plan and purpose, it should be noted that the same has been true in general of both the exponents of the "new criticism" and the defenders of the historicity of the *Confessions,* including also Portalié: "There (at Cassiciacum) he devoted himself to true philosophy . . ." (*Ibid.,* p. 13); "The dialogues are a purely philosophical work . . ." (P. 16). It is the paideutic character of the philosophizing and the ruling purpose of elaborating a Christian paideia which is omitted from the picture. (pp. 11-19).

74 Cf. for example, the complete omission of Boyer's works from the "Select Bibliography" given by O'Meara, *op. cit.,* pp. 210-211, which includes in a total of 31 titles, 13 in French.

75 Or perhaps some philosophical entity, which probably has its real existence more in modern writings than in ancient minds, called Christian Neoplatonism. It is clear that the controversy on St. Augustine's conversion touches at several points the recent entirely distinct controversy on the existence and the nature of Christian philosophy. Those who hold that Christian philosophy is simply the philosophical thought held by the world in general at a given time, adopted and adapted because it seems timely to do so in the interests of communication, will not want to see Christian philosophy in St. Augustine, but rather "Christian Neoplatonism." It is beyond the scope of the present study to pursue this particular question further. Cf. Luigi Bogliolo, *Il problema della filosofia cristiana* (Brescia: Morcelliana, 1959), and Etienne Gilson in his "revue critique" of Alfaric's volume (*Revue philosophique,* 88 (1919), 508: "Le seul fait qu'Augustin ait admis dès le début la création et l'égalité des personnes divines suffirait à établir qu'il fut immédiatement catholique et non plotinien."

76 Boissier, *op. cit.,* p. 368; cf. the passages already cited.

77 Charles Boyer, *La formation,* etc. (1953), p. 141.

78 *De beata vita,* 1 (6), already cited.

79 Charles Boyer, *ibid.,* pp. 141-142.

80 *Ibid.,* p. 142.   81 *Ibid.*

82 *Ibid.*

83 *Ibid.* "Mais il n'y a là qu'une apparence." This amounts to a con-

cession of the basic position asserted by his adversaries; his attempt to circumvent it is somewhat off the mark: hence the continuation of the controversy.

[84] Cf. Boyer, *ibid.*, pp. 142-147. Boyer's third argument notes that "the subjects discussed in the Dialogues constitute the foundations of the religious life" (*ibid.*, p. 146). This is indeed true, for they are the basic themes of Christian philosophy. They are also, *ipso facto*, the themes in terms of which the Catholic philosophy of education conceives the ends of education. Speaking of the *De ordine*, Boyer terms its subject "Providence and evil," problems which engaged Augustine all his life (ibid., p. 147). The fact is that *De ordine* is a treatise on the order of studies necessary for preparing youthful minds to perceive the order of Providence in general. The same complete omission of the educational character, revelance and content of the *Dialogues* characterizes the second appendix of Boyer's work, "Analyse des *Dialogues* à Cassiciacum," pp. 181-202.

[85] The proponents of the new theory, it goes without saying, do not describe the paideutic character of the philosophical dialogues, for their entire position rests upon interpreting them as exercises in pure philosophy, in fact, as a Neoplatonism of some kind. The defenders of the historicity of the *Confessions* seem usually to portray the life at Cassiciacum in almost the same terms as their opponents, as noted already in the instance of Portalié. Wörter, *op. cit.*, p. 65, explicitly excludes the field of education from Cassiciacum: "Augustin freute sich, nicht die Philosophie, mit der er sich nach seiner Konversion gleichwohl beschäftigte sondern die Schule und die von ihm gelehrten Disziplinen, wie Rhetorik und dergleichen, aufgeben zu können." Thus the interpretation of "pure philosophy" is fostered; it is then but a short step to viewing Augustine's inner self as "purely philosophical," and at variance with the state of soul described in the *Confessions*. Mausbach, *op. cit.*, p. 12: "Die Gesellschaft, in der er auf dem Landsitze sich befand, bestand zum teil aus studierenden Jünglingen. . . ." No other reference is made, and the educational purpose thus is omitted entirely. Mannucci, *op. cit.*, p. 40, likewise misses the educational character of Cassiciacum, calling it simply a time for "lo studio delle questioni filosofiche"; this "aveva nulla di innaturale nelle condizioni d'animo in cui egli si trovava; al contrario, quelle studio gli era *allora* assolutamente necessario" (his emphasis). This is an excellent example of excessive concession to the opposed theory; it should be noted, furthermore, that it does not take into consideration Boyer's careful demonstration that St. Augustine was not philosophizing at Cassiciacum because of personal need. He had already won his way to the basic positions of Christian philosophy. Cf. finally H. Gros, "La valeur documentaire des Confessions," *La vie spirituelle* (1927), p. 173: "Les Dialogues représentent-ils le christianisme intégral? Ils ne visent pas à ce but. . . . Augustin s'y exprime en catéchumène lettré. C'est un néophyte du christianisme, mais un néophyte remarquablement averti." In this way, the *Dialogues* are misconceived exactly as the new criticism misconceives them; it is difficult as a result to prevent them from being used, plausibly, against the historicity of the *Confessions*. The insights of Eggersdorfer and Marrou have been noted, but those scholars seem not to have applied their perception of the nature of the dialogues to this controversy or to the larger question of the relationship of Augustine's entire life and work to the field of education. The same is true of F. E. Tourscher in his articles in *The Ecclesiastical Review*, 83 (1938), 113-124, and 89 (1933), 113-125.

⁸⁶ Cf. Gourdon, *op. cit.*, pp. 50-52, in his rebuttal of Wörter, whom he accuses of taking the *Confessions* as a historical source against the *Dialogues of Cassiciacum.* ". . . C'est employer, selon nous, une fausse méthode, car c'est méconnaître le *point de vue historique.*" P. 51, his emphasis. Gourdon lists the advantages of the dialogues as documents relating to Augustine's mind in the weeks of his conversion, and asks: "Pour toutes ces raisons, les *Dialogues* n'ont-ils pas une valeur historique supérieure à celle des *Confessions?*" P. 52. Thus the new theory seems to possess the calm security of an objectively sound position, and to enjoy the feeling of superiority given by its monopoly of the sound critical method. It seems to itself to represent the scientific approach.

⁸⁷ Charles Boyer, *La formation . . .* etc., (1953), p. 24.

⁸⁸ *Ibid.*, p. 25, n. 1: ". . . nous pensons que les *Dialogues de Cassiciacum* ont été de fait écrits à mesure qu'ils etaient tenus; cf. D. Ohlmann . . . et van Haeringen . . ." Cf. Desiderius Ohlmann, *De S. Augustini Dialogis in Cassiciaco scriptis* (Argentorati: Ex officina typografica "Der Elsässer," 1897), the solid demonstration that Augustine was reporting real discussions, not inventing a literary production, not producing a fiction. Ohlmann's work has abiding value.

⁸⁹ "Toutefois, il les retouchait . . . ," Boyer, *ibid.*, citing *Contra Academicos* I 1 (4).

⁹⁰ Boyer, *ibid.*: ". . . Les *Confessions* appartiennent au genre qui repugne davantage à la fiction.

⁹¹ *Ibid.*, p. 26; "On doit s'attendre à ce que les *Dialogues,* malgré leur autorité de journal intime, nous racontent saint Augustine avec plus de confusion, avec un moindre sentiment des proportions, et par là même avec moins de vérité que les *Confessions.*" This sentence seems to carry a contradiction within itself; furthermore, it seeks the solution to the challenge of the opposed theory once more by assuming some defect in St. Augustine's works. If ever there has been a writer whose works cannot be categorized according to degrees of truth, it is St. Augustine. In general, it seems a vain hope to solve this question, as some try to do, by assuming an inability in St. Augustine to think, to remember or even to write well, apart from his personal integrity. The difficulty actually may not be in St. Augustine at all, but in that of grasping the true nature of his works on our part so many centuries later.

⁹² J. J. O'Meara, *The Young Augustine, op. cit.*, p. 193.

⁹³ *Ibid.*

⁹⁴ *Ibid.*

⁹⁵ *Ibid.*, p. 193, cf. the same author's *St. Augustine: Against the Academics, op. cit.*, pp. 24-32. The indications of historicity, "being fictional, are worthless" (p. 25); ". . . their untrustworthiness as guaranteeing facts" (p. 29). Cf. also his "The Historicity of the Early Dialogues of Saint Augustine," *Vigiliae Christianae*, 5 (1951), 150-178.

⁹⁶ Cf., for example, H. I. Marrou, who relegates the controversy to a footnote with the remark, ". . . quand la critique s'exerce trop longtemps sur la même question elle arrive bientôt à un point mort; les arguments s'échangent et s'accumulent, sans grand profit . . .": *Saint Augustin et la fin de la culture antique* (Paris: E. de Boccard 1958). "Introduction," p. xiii, n. 1.

⁹⁷ Cf. Le Nain de Tillement, *Mémoire pour servir à l'histoire ecclesiastique,* (Paris: 1702), Vol. XIII, p. 87: "Jusqu'au moindre mot"; cf. Ohlmann,

op. cit. cf. Edward Kennard Rand, *Founders of the Middle Ages* (New York: Dover Publications, 1957); first edition, Harvard University Press, 1928), p. 256: ". . . he wrote certain dialogues, the record of actual conversations, taken down by a stenographer, doubtless somewhat embellished in their published form, that recall the day of Tusculum and prophesy the academies of the Renaissance, and the schools of Guarino and Vittorino." We could only add to this that they prophesy even better the *Questiones* of the twelfth century and the *Questiones Disputatae* of St. Thomas Aquinas, for they contain the vast edifice of education in Christendom, one cannot avoid the thought, almost as a *ratio seminalis.* Cf. finally H. I. Marrou, *op. cit.,* p. 309, n. 1: "L'historicité de ces dialogues paraît incontestable, bien qu'il se soit trouvé des érudits pour la contester. . . . Mais cf. *contra* Ohlmann. . . . Augustin fait plusieurs fois allusion au sténographe qui recueillait les echangées. . . ." In general, even Marrou's great work seems somewhat to reflect the distorting pressure of the opposed theory: "Le pas est fait," he writes, "Augustin n'est plus un rhéteur, mais un penseur, un philosophe . . ." (pp. 166-7).

98 Cf. J. J. O'Meara, *op. cit.,* p. 192. Note the striking similarity of Gourdon's picture of the country idyll, *op. cit.,* pp. 43-45: "Dominé par des souvenirs classiques, il profite de ses loisirs, et de la sociéte de quelques disciples et amis, pour imiter, en leur genre de vie, quelques illustres maîtres de l'antiquité. . . . Il ne rompt pas avec sa vie passé; il se nourrit encore de littérature, de poésie et de philosophie; il conserve les mêmes gouts et les mêmes besoins profanes." For Professor O'Meara, of course, Augustine is a Christian at Cassiciacum, while for Gourdon, he is not.

99 Cf. *Confessions,* I, 15 (24); P.L. 32, 672: "in rebus non vanis discere . . . : et ea via tuta est in qua pueri ambularent"; John K. Ryan, *op. cit.,* p. 58: "I learned many useful words in such studies, but they could have been learned from things that were not vain. This last is the safe way in which children should walk." Elaborating this way was the educational concern of the Fathers of the Church generally, and the continuation of it has been the mission and the apostolate of the Catholic educator down to the present times of the Church. St. Augustine, by virtue of his place among the Fathers, occupies a unique position in this historic Christian education of youth.

100 Cf. Arnold J. Toynbee, *A Study of History* (London: Oxford University Press, 1935), Vol. I, pp. 51-63; cf. Vol. VII, "Universale States," pp. 1-379, *passim,* for a wide variety of instances illustrating the fact that "the Catholic Church became . . . a beneficiary of the Roman Empire . . ." (p. 376).

101 Wilhelm Dilthey, *Einleitung in den Geisteswissenschaften* (Leipzig: 1883), Vol. I, p. 334, terms "die Nachwirkung seiner Schriften als eine weltgeschichtliche." Cf. J. Mausbach, *op. cit.,* Vol. I, p. 3: ". . . nur weltgeschichtliche Mässstabe zu seiner Würdigung ausreichen." For a good study and appreciation of this stature of Augustine in relation to the civilization which preceded his conversion and to that which was to come after it, cf. E. R. von Kienitz, *Augustinus: Genius des Abendlandes* (Wuppertal: Abendland Verlag, 1947); e.g., p. 8: ". . . eine der universalem Gestalten der Menschheit"; p. 12: "Augustin, der so machtvoll Hand anlegte bei der Grundlegung unseren abendländischen Kultur, scheint uns vor anderen berufen, Fährmann über die Würbel der Zeitenwende zum neuen Ufer eines neuen Weltentags zu sein."

102 Gaston Boissier sees St. Augustine's importance to the Christian Era in the simple fact that his philosophical dialogues contributed somewhat to

the survival of profane letters and secular culture. "Violà ce qui donne de l'intérèt aux *Dialogues philosophiques* . . . c'est par là que cette retraite de Cassiciacum, qui semble d'abord n'être qu'une crise passagère dans l'existence d'un homme, prend une certaine importance dans l'histoire même de l'humanité et mérite l'étude que nous venons de lui consacrer." "La conversion de s. Augustin," *Revue des deux mondes*, 85 (1888), 69. For Harnack, Augustine's personal conversion is an interesting study, one which can be solved by the theory of the two Augustines, but the social significance of his conversion, its meaning in the Christian Era, is a problem in quite another dimension. "Even if we keep in mind the state of the time," he writes, "how strange is it nevertheless that this rich and untiring spirit, striving after personal Christian piety, should only attain it by submitting to the authority of the Church! . . . The solution of this problem I shall not here attempt . . ." *op. cit.*, pp. 168-169. A wholly different concept of the conversion of St. Augustine, in which it is seen to launch a vast philosophical and theological development in the schools of Christendom, growing homogeneously across the Christian Era under the guiding light of the Magisterium of the Church, and placing the work of St. Thomas Aquinas in organic relationship to St. Augustine's program of *doctrina christiana*, is implied by the foundation at Rome in 1960 of the *Institutum Patristico-Mediaevale "Johannes XXIII."* Here the meaning of the conversion of St. Augustine for the Christian Era as a whole receives its full academic appreciation and elucidation in the present day. Seen in this light, the work of the Church in the Christian Era is the fundamental regeneration and renewal of man and his works; St. Augustine's conversion occupies a place of unique importance in this historic mission and accomplishment.

Bibliography

A Note on
the Study of
St. Augustine

The works of St. Augustine and the literature which grows in connection with them form a vast object of study, one which can offer a discouraging prospect and an engulfing experience. It is well to begin with a good life of the Bishop of Hippo, *Augustine's Quest of Wisdom* by Professor Vernon J. Bourke, for example, or Father Hugh Pope's *Saint Augustine of Hippo,* works which provide a framework for perceiving the origin and the nature of his successive writings. It is helpful to approach the *opera omnia sancti Augustini* in the three-fold pattern into which they naturally fall when seen in close relationship to the real Augustine of flesh and blood: The *Confessions* for the period before he wrote, prior to his baptism; his writings as a layman, those composed at Cassiciacum, Rome and Thagaste until his ordination; and the works associated with the several aspects of his priestly and episcopal apostolate. Brief introductory surveys of his thought and influence are to be found in Marrou's *St. Augustine and his Influence through the Ages,* in Guitton's *The Modernity of St. Augustine,* and in *A Monument to Saint Augustine* edited by M. C. D'Arcy, where the powerful synthesis by Christopher Dawson, "St. Augustine and his Age," is especially noteworthy.

Writing in 1918 at the term of his extensive study of the Augustinian literature in connection with his treatise on the conversion and intellectual evolution of St. Augustine, Alfaric ("Préface," p. I) laments the lack of an *Index Augustinianus*, the thick volume which a mere listing of the works devoted to St. Augustine would fill. He notes three items, however, which offer a "very ample introduction" to the vast material of Augustinian scholarship: Potthast, *Bibliotheca historica Medii Aevi* (Berlin: 1896), t. II 1186-1188; Chevalier, *Répertoire des Sources historiques du Moyen Age, Biobibliographie* (Paris: 1905), t. I, 371-382; and Portalié's article, "Augustin, (Saint)," in D.T.C. (Paris: 1902), I, col. 2268-2472. Translated by Ralph J. Bastian, S.J., and published as a separate book under the title *A Guide to the Thought of Saint Augustine* (Chicago: 1960), this work is probably still the best general introduction to the writings of St. Augustine, especially in view of Professor Vernon J. Bourke's preface, on the Augustinian literature which has appeared since Father Portalié wrote. Not to be overlooked is the *Companion to the Study of St. Augustine* (New York: 1955) edited by Roy W. Battenhouse.

Turning to consider the world of St. Augustine's *opera omnia* in itself and the universe of his personal thought, we are already in an immense body of writings, challenging in complexity and depth. "Augustine," says Etienne Gilson in his *Christian Philosophy of Saint Augustine* (Foreword, p. X), "always writes as though all of his readers will be able to see precisely how the point he is making at the moment fits into the whole scheme of his doctrine. In point of fact, this is beyond any beginner. On the contrary, we know from bitter experience that those who enter the vast land of Augustinism for the first time are liable to lose their way. It has been my hope that a simple map like this book might help them to find their bearings." Professor Gilson's introduction to the study of St. Augustine is indeed such a map for the philosophical doctrine which underlies all his writing; and a similar indispensable guide is available for the theological doctrine in *The Church: An Introduction to the Theology of St. Augustine* (St. Louis: 1957) by Stanislaus J. Grabowski. In the other languages similar treatises are available, for example the excellent brief "Introduction Générale" to the works and thought, by F. Cayré and F. Van Steenberghen, which prefaces Vol. I of the series, *Oeuvres de saint Augustin*. Finally, there is the unique fact that St. Augustine in his *Retractationes* toward

the end of his life reviewed his own books in nearly chronological order; the French bilingual edition (*Oeuvres de saint Augustin, XII*) has the advantage of the book-length introduction
and copious notes by the Patristic specialist Gustave Bardy.

Coming to the literature on St. Augustine and his writings,
we find ourselves in what Marrou rightly calls a jungle. It is an
immense thicket which never ceases to proliferate. How to orient
oneself? It is possible indeed to enter anywhere, for one thing
will lead to another in this wonderfully consistent realm of
thought and closely inter-related world of Augustinian scholarship. Usually, however, the leisure needed for this approach will
be lacking: some more direct and purposive plan to dominate the
literature in terms of a point or aspect of doctrine will be im-
perative. For this there is at hand for the literature prior to 1928
the serviceable *Bibliographia Augustiniana* by Nebreda (Rome:
1928), nearly that *Index* which Alfaric desired. This can be
checked and supplemented by S. Lambrino, *Bibliographie classique des années 1896 à 1914* (which continues from Klussmann,
Bibliotheca Scriptorum Classicorum), and by J. Marouzeau, *Dix
années de bibliographie classique, 1914-1924*. For the literature
since Nebreda to the present, the basic tool is J. Marouzeau's
L'année philologique, années 1924 et suivantes (Paris: 1927–).
These annual listings can be supplemented by the collective
works which appeared on the occasion of the two centenaries of
St. Augustine, 1930 and 1954, by the various encyclopedias and
dictionnaires, and by consulting the volumes of the periodicals
devoted to St. Augustine: *Augustiniana* (Louvain: 1951–). *Augustinus* (Madrid: 1956–), *Augustinianum* (Roma: 1961–), and
others. In 1954 the *Année Théologique (Augustinienne)* became
the *Revue des Études Augustiniennes* (Paris: 1954–), which,
together with its supplement, *Recherches Augustiniennes*, is now
a basic instrument for orientation in the flood of Augustinian
studies. The decade of the nineteen fifties is covered conveniently
by T. van Bavel, *Répertoire bibliographique de Saint Augustin,
1950-1960* (Steenbrugis: In Abbatia Sancti Petri, 1963).

For the more general picture, there are the histories of philosophy and of theology, the recent invaluable guide, *Biblio-
graphica Patristica: Internationale patristische Bibliographie*
(Berlin: 1959–), edited by W. Schneemelcher, and the patrologies.
"There is no bibliography of Augustinian studies in English,"

writes Marrou in his *St. Augustine and His Influence Through the Ages*, p. 190; "the best available is B. Altaner, *Patrologie*, 2nd ed. (expanded), 1950, pp. 364-398." The forthcoming Volume IV of *Patrology* (Westminster, Maryland: The Newman Press, 1950–) by Johannes Quasten will rectify this at last, for his work, which is appearing originally in English, will offer the most comprehensive and up-to-date study of the great Latin Fathers. Since St. Augustine comes toward the end of the movement of Patristic thought, since he stands under the tutelage of St. Ambrose, and since he embodies in his own work a true synthesis of his predecessors, Quasten's first three volumes, especially "The Cappadocian Fathers," III, pp. 203-301, become particularly relevant. For an informative discussion of the available bibliographical aids, cf. Quasten, I, pp. 19-20, "Bibliographies," and in general his "Introduction: The Concept and History of Patrology," *ibid.*, pp. 1-22.

The works and studies listed below are of course only partial and reflect a selection of areas of special interest made long ago: St. Augustine's experience of time, his philosophy and theology of history, his pedagogical principles and fundamentals, his catechetical practices. Even with selection, however, one ends with a feeling of inadequate mastery. Perhaps it is always so, a part of one's experience of the greatness of the Bishop of Hippo. In any case, these are simply works which have been helpful, in one way or the other, in the study of St. Augustine as an educator, and which may serve others as an entrance to Augustinian scholarship. They are offered in token of recognition to my own students, among whom I have always noted that spontaneous keen interest in St. Augustine which seems connatural to our time.

Primary Sources: Texts and Translations

Saint Augustine. *Opera omnia*, in Migne, *Patrologiae cursus completus, series latina*. Parisiis: Apud J.-P. Migne, Editorem, 1845, Vols. XXXII-XLVII, incl. This Maurist text is reprinted in the recent Spanish and French bilingual editions: *Obras de san Agustin en edicion bilingüo*. Madrid: Biblioteca de autores cristianos, 1950–; *Oeuvres de saint Augustin*. Paris: Desclée, 1936–.

A complete critical edition of the works of St. Augustine is still wanting; for purposes of this general study, therefore, the reprints of the Maurist text have been used. The *Corpus scriptorum ecclesiasticorum latinorum,* edited by the Academy of Vienna, 1866–, contains several works of St. Augustine in critical edition; the same is true of the *Corpus Christianorum.* Turnhout, 1952–. For the works available so far in critical edition, cf. Eligius Dekkers, *Clavis Patrum Latinorum,* Steenbrugis: In Abbatia Sancti Petri, 1961, altera editio, "Augustinus Episcopus Hipponensis," pp. 65-86.

———. *De beata vita liber unus.* Migne, P.L. 32, 959-976. Ludwig Schopp (trans.), "The Happy Life," in *Writings of Saint Augustine,* Vol. I. New York: Cima Publishing Co., 1948.

———. *Soliloquiorum libri II.* Migne, P.L. 32, 869-904. Thomas F. Gilligan (trans.), "Soliloquies," in *Writings of Saint Augustine,* Vol. I. New York: Cima Publishing Co., 1948.

———. *De ordine libri II.* Migne, P.L. 32, 977-1020. Robert P. Russell (trans.), "Divine Providence and the Problem of Evil," in *Writings of Saint Augustine,* Vol. I. New York: Cima Publishing Co., 1948.

———. *Contra academicos libri III.* Migne, P.L. 32, 905-958. John J. O'Meara (trans.) *St. Augustine Against the Academics.* ("Ancient Christian Writers," No. 12.) Westminster, Md.: The Newman Press, 1950. Also: Denis J. Kavanagh (trans.) "Answer to Skeptics," in *Writings of St. Augustine,* Vol. I. New York: Cima Publishing Co., 1948.

———. *De immortalitate animae liber unus.* Migne, P.L. 32, 1035-1080. Ludwig Schopp (trans.), "The Immortality of the Soul," in *Writings of St. Augustine,* Vol. II. New York: Cima Publishing Co., 1947.

———. *De quantitate animae liber unus.* Migne, P.L. 32, 1035-1080. Joseph M. Colleran (trans.), *St. Augustine: The Greatness of the Soul.* ("Ancient Christian Writers," No. 9.) Westminster, Md.: The Newman Press, 1950. Also John J. McMahon (trans.), "The Magnitude of the Soul," in *Writings of Saint Augustine,* Vol. II. New York: Cima Publishing Co., 1947.

———. *De magistro liber unus.* Migne, P.L. 32, 1193-1220. Joseph M. Colleran (trans.) *St. Augustine: The Teacher.*

("Ancient Christian Writers," No. 9.) Westminster, Md.: The Newman Press, 1950.

————. *De musica libri VI*. Migne, P.L. 32, 1081-1192. Robert C. Taliaferro (trans.), "On Music," in *Writings of St. Augustine*, Vol. II. New York: Cima Publishing Co., 1947.

————. *De libero arbitrio libri III*. Migne, P.L. 32, 1221-1299.

————. *De vera religione liber unus*. Migne, P.L. 34, 121-172. *St. Augustine: Of True Religion*. Translated by J. H. S. Burleigh, with an introduction by Louis O. Mink. Chicago: Henry Regnery Co., 1959.

————. *De moribus Ecclesiae et de moribus Manichaeorum libri II*. Migne, P.L. 32, 1300-1376.

————. *Disciplinarum libri*. For these works, left unfinished by St. Augustine and in doubtful preservation, see *Retr.* I, 6 and Migne, P.L. 32, Appendix, 1383-1474: *De gram., Principia dialectica, Categoriae decem, Principia rhetor*.

————. *De diversis questionibus octoginta tribus liber unus*. Migne, P.L. 40, 11-102.

————. *Enchiridion de fide, spe et caritate liber unus*. Migne, P.L. 40, 231-290. Translated with an introduction and notes by Louis A. Arand ("Ancient Christian Writers," No. 3.) Westminster, Md.: The Newman Bookshop, 1947.

————. *De catechizandis rudibus liber unus*. Migne, P.L. 40, 309-348. Bilingual edition on facing pages with introduction and copious notes by Joseph Patrick Christopher. Washington: The Catholic University, 1926. This work was adapted and revised as the translation in the Ancient Christian Writers series, No. 2, by Joseph P. Christopher: *St. Augustine: The First Catechetical Instruction*. Westminster, Md.: The Newman Press, 1946.

————. *De doctrina christiana libri IV*. Migne, P.L. 34, 15-122. Reprinted in convenient form, with some emendation by H. J. Vogels in the *Florilegium Patristicum*, fasc. 24. Bonn: Peter Hanstein, 1930. John J. Gavigan (trans.), "Christian Instruction," in *Writings of St. Augustine*, Vol. IV. New York: Cima Publishing Co., 1947.

————. *Confessionum libri XIII*. Migne, P.L. 32, 659-868. *The Confessions of St. Augustine*. Translated with an introduction and notes by John K. Ryan. New York: Doubleday Image Books, 1960. Several translations could be listed.

————. *De Trinitate libri XV.* Migne, 42, 819-1098. *On the Trinity.* Translated by Arthur West Haddan. Edinburgh: T. and T. Clark, 1873.

————. *De civitate Dei libri XXII.* Migne, P.L. 41, 13-804. *St. Augustine: The City of God.* Translated by D. B. Zema, Gerald G. Walsh, Mother Grace Monahan, and Daniel J. Honan, with a foreword by Etienne Gilson. Vol. I-III. New York: Fathers of the Church, 1950, 1952, 1954.

————. *Retractationum libri II.* Migne, P.L. 32, 583-658. For the text and French translation with a comprehensive critical commentary, cf. G. Bardy, *Les revisions.* Paris: Desclée, 1950.

Secondary Works

Adam, Karl. *Saint Augustine: The Odyssey of his Soul.* New York: Macmillan, 1932.

Adriani, Maurilio. "Il concetto di storia nel cristianesimo e nel marxismo," *Humanitas,* V (1950), 479-489.

Alfaric, Prosper. *L' évolution intellectuelle de saint Augustin.* Vol. I: *Du manichéisme au néoplatonisme.* Paris: Émile Nourry, Éditeur, 1918.

Alföldi, Andrew. *The Conversion of Constantine and Pagan Rome.* Oxford: At the Clarendon Press, 1948.

Allievi, L. "I fondamenti della pedagogia nel *De magistro* di s. Agostino e s. Tommaso," *Scuola Cattolica* (1937), 545-561.

————. "Catechesi primitiva," *Scuola Cattolica* (1942), 21-36.

Altaner, B. "Die Bibliothek des hl. Augustinus," *Theologische Revue,* II (1948), 73–78.

————. "Augustinus, Gregor von Nazianz und Gregor von Nyssa," *Revue Bénédictine,* 61 (1951), 54-62.

Amand, David. *Fatalisme et liberté dans l'antiquité grecque.* Louvain: Bibliothèque de l'Université, 1945.

Amari, G. *Il concetto di storia in Sant 'Agostino.* Roma: Edizioni Paoline, 1950.

Arbesmann, R. "The Idea of Rome in the Sermons of St. Augustine," *Augustiniana,* IV (1954), 305-324.

Arbusow, Leonid. *Liturgie und Geschichtsschreibung im Mittelalter.* Bonn: Ludwig Röhrscheid Verlag, 1951.

Arendt, Hannah. "The Modern Concept of History," *Review of Politics,* 20 (1958), 570-590.

Arnold, Poelman, Dondeyne, Tilmann, Garrone, and others. *Catéchèse pour notre temps.* Brussels: Lumen Vitae, 1960.

Arnou, R. *De platonismo Patrum.* Rome: Apud aedes Universitatis Gregorianae, 1935.

Aron, Raymond. *Introduction à la philosophie de l'histoire.* Paris: Librairie Gallimard, 1948.

———. *The Dawn of Universal History.* New York: Praeger, 1961.

Auvray, P. "S. Jerome et s. Augustin," *Recherches de science religieuse,* XXIX (1939), 594-610.

Balthasar, H. U. von (ed.). *Die grossen Ordensregeln.* Einsiedeln: Benziger, 1948.

———. *Theologie der Geschichte.* Einsiedeln: Johannes Verlag, 1950.

Bandas, Rudolph George. *Catechetics in the New Testament.* Milwaukee: Bruce, 1935.

Barbagallo, C. *Lo stato e l'istruzione publica nell'Impero romano.* Catania: F. Battiato, 1911.

Bardenhewer, Otto. *Patrologie.* Freiburg: Herdersche Verlagshandlung, 1901.

Bardy, Gustave A. *The Christian Latin Literature of the First Six Centuries.* St. Louis: B. Herder, 1930.

———. "L'église et l'enseignement pendant les trois premiers siècles," *Revue des sciences religieuses,* 12 (1932), 1-28.

———. *Saint Augustin: l'homme et l'oeuvre.* Paris: Desclée de Brouwer, 1940.

———. *A l'école de saint Augustin.* Ecully: Oeuvre Populaire d'Education, 1947.

———. *La conversion au christianisme durant les premiers siècles.* Paris: Aubier, 1949.

———. "Définition de la cité de Dieu," *L'Année théologique Augustinienne,* XII (1952), 113-129.

———. "La formation du concept de 'Cité de Dieu' dans l'oeuvre de saint Augustin," *L'Année theologique Augustinienne,* XII (1952), 5-19.

———. "Les origines des écoles monastiques en Occident," *Sacris Erudiri,* 5 (1953), 86-104.

———. "Manichéisme," *Dict. Théol. Cath.,* t. IX, col. 1841-1895.

Bareille, G. "Catéchèse," *D.T.C.,* 2, 1877-1895.

————. 'Catéchuménat," *D.T.C.*, 2, 1968-1987.

Barion, Jakob. *Plotin und Augustinus: Untersuchungen zum Gottesproblem.* Berlin: Junker und Dünnhaupt, 1935.

Barnes, Harry Elmer. *A History of Historical Writing.* New York: Dover, 1962.

Barrachina, Ignatio. *Hombre-Mundo-Redencion: Concepto Agustiniano del Hombre bajo el signo de Adán o de Cristo.* Valencia: Editorial Federico Domenech, 1954.

Batiffol, Pierre. *Le catholicisme de saint Augustin.* Paris: J. Gabalda, 1920.

Battenhouse, Roy W. (ed.) *A Companion to the Study of St. Augustine.* New York: Oxford University Press, 1955.

Bauer, Adolf. *Die Chronik des Hippolytos im Matritensis Graecus 121.* Leipzig: J. C. Hinrichs'sche Buchhandlung, 1905.

————. *Ursprung und Fortwirken der Christlichen Weltchronik.* Graz: Leuschner und Lubensky, 1910.

Bauer, Wilhelm. *Einführung in das Studium der Geschichte.* Tübingen: Verlag von J. C. B. Mohr, 1928.

Bavel, Tarsicius J. van, O.E.S.A. *Recherches sur la Christologie de saint Augustin: L'humain et le divin dans le Christ d'après saint Augustin.* Fribourg (Suisse): Éditions Universitaires, 1954.

Beck, Kurt. *Die Überwindung heidnisch-damonischer Gottheiten durch die Christliche-missionarische Botschaft.* Oberhausen: VVA Druck, 1952.

Becker, Hans. *Augustin: Studien zu seiner geistigen Entwicklung.* Leipzig: J. C. Hinrichs'sche Buchhandlung, 1908.

Benoit, P. "Un adversaire du christianisme au III siècle: Porphyre," *Revue Biblique*, 54 (1947), 543-572.

Berdyaev, Nicholas. *The Meaning of History.* London: Geoffrey Bles, 1945.

Berlinger, Rudolph. "Le temps et l'homme chez saint Augustin," *L'Année theologique Augustinienne*, XIII (1952), 260-279.

Bernheim, Ernst. *Lehrbuch der historischen Methode.* Leipzig: Düncker und Humblot, 1908.

Bertrand, L. *Saint Augustin.* Paris: A. Fayard, 1913.

Biard, Pierre. "Histoire du salut au coeur de la catéchèse," *Catéchèse*, I (Oct. 1960), 11-20.

Bihlmeyer-Tüchle. *Kirchengeschichte.* Vol. I: *Das christliche Altertum.* Paderborn: Schöningh, 1951.

Bindemann, Carl. *Der heilige Augustinus.* Berlin: Verlag von Hermann Schultze, 1844, 1855.

Blass, F. W. *Die attische Beredsamkeit.* Leipzig: B. G. Teubner, 1892.

Blondel, Maurice. "L'unité originale et la pensée permanente de la doctrine philosophique de saint Augustin," *Revue de métaphysique et de morale,* XXXVII (1930), 424 ff.

Boissier, Gaston. *La fin du paganisme.* Tome I-II. Paris: Hachette, 1891.

————. "La conversion de saint Augustin," *Revue des Deux Mondes,* LXXXV (1er Janvier, 1888), 43-69.

Bolgar, R. R. *The Classical Heritage and Its Beneficiaries.* Cambridge: At the University Press, 1958.

Boman, Thorlief. *Das hebräische Denken im Vergleich mit dem Griechischen.* Göttingen: Vandenhoeck und Ruprecht, 1952.

Boublik, Vladimiro. *La predestinazione: S. Paolo e S. Agostino.* Roma: Libreria Editrice della Pontificia Università Lateranense, 1961.

Bourke, Vernon J. *Augustine's Quest of Wisdom: Life and Philosophy of the Bishop of Hippo.* Milwaukee: Bruce, 1945.

Boyancé, Pierre. *Le culte des Muses chez les philosophes Grecs: Études d'histoire et de psychologie religieuses.* Paris: E. de Boccard, Éditeur, 1937.

Boyer, Charles. *L'idée de vérité dans la philosophie de saint Augustin.* Paris: Gabriel Beauchesne, 1920.

————. *Christianisme et Néo-platonisme dans la formation de saint Augustin.* Paris: Gabriel Beauchesne, 1920.

————. *Saint Augustin.* Paris: Librairie Lecoffre, 1932.

————. *Christianisme et Néo-platonisme dans la formation de saint Augustin.* 2d ed. Rome: Officum libri Catholici, 1953.

Brandon, S. G. F. *Time and Mankind: An historical and philosophical study of mankind's attitude to the phenomena of change.* London: Hutchinson, 1951.

Bréhier, Émile. *The Philosophy of Plotinus.* Chicago: The University of Chicago Press, 1958.

Brezzi, Paolo. *Cristianesimo e Impero Romano.* Roma: A.V.E., 1944.

————. *La concezione agostiniana della Città di Dio.* Galatina (Lecce): Liceo P. Colonna, 1947.

————. "Il carattere e il significato della storia nel pensiero di
S. Agostino," *Revue des Etudes Augustiniennes,* I (1955),
149-160.

Brucculeri, A. "Il pensiero sociale di S. Agostino," *Civiltà Cattolica,* 81 (1930), 437-451.

Burger, Jean-Daniel. *Saint Augustin: Un père de l'église.* Neu-
chatel: A la Baconnière, 1948.

Busch, Benedictus. "De initiatione christiana secundum sanctum
Augustinum," *Ephemerides liturgicae,* LII (Jan.-Mar. 1938),
158-178.

————. *De initiatione christiana secundum doctrinam Sancti
Augustini.* Romae: Typis Polyglottis Vaticanis, 1939.

Butterfield, Herbert. *History and Human Relations.* London:
Collins, 1951.

————. *Man on His Past: The Study of the History of Historical
Scholarship.* Cambridge: At the University Press, 1955.

Callahan, J. F. *Four Views of Time in Ancient Philosophy.* Cambridge: Harvard University Press, 1948.

————, "Basil of Caesarea: A New Source for St. Augustine's
Theory of Time," *Harvard Studies in Classical Philology,*
LXIII (1958), 437-454.

Camelot, P. "Clément d'Alexandrie et l'utilisation de la philosophie grecque," *Recherche de sciences réligieuses,* XXI
(1939), 540-569.

Capelle, B. "L'introduction du Catéchumenat à Rome," *Recherches de théologie ancienne et médiévale,* V (1933), 129-154.

Carcopino, J. *Daily Life in Ancient Rome: The People and the
City at the Height of the Empire.* London: Routledge, 1941.

Carr, Edward Hallett. *What is History?* New York: Knopf, 1962.

Casamassa, A. "Le fonti della filosofia di S. Agostino," *Acta
heldomadae augustinianae thomisticae,* 1931, pp. 88-96.

Caturelli, Alberto. *La doctrina agustiniana sobre el maestro y
su desarrollo en santo Tomas de Aquino.* Cordoba, Argen-
tina: Universidad de Cordoba, 1954.

Cayré, Fulbert. "La Contrition et la Vision Médiate de Dieu
d'après Saint Augustin: Présupposés Philosophiques,"
E.Th.L. 4 (1929), 23-39, 205-29.

————. "La notion de sagesse d'apres s. Augustin," *L'Annee theologique,* 4 (1943), 453-456.

————. Dieu présent dans la vie de l'esprit. Paris: Desclée, 1951.

————. *L'Existentialisme.* Paris: Tequi, 1947.

Ceillier, R. *Histoire générale des auteurs sacrés et ecclesiastiques.* Paris: Chez Louis Vivès, 1861.

Chaix-Ruy, J. "La cité de Dieu et la structure du temps chez Saint Augustin," *Augustinus Magister,* II, 923-931.

————. *Saint Augustin: temps et histoire.* Paris: Études Augustiniennes, 1956.

————. *Donoso Cortés: Théologien de l'histoire et prophète.* Paris: Beauchesne, 1956.

Champomier, J. "Naissance de l'humanisme Chrétien," *Bulletin de l'association Guillaume Budé,* 3 (Nouvelle Serie) (1947), 58-96.

Cioffari, V. *Fortune and Fate from Democritus to St. Thomas Aquinas.* New York: Columbia University Press, 1935.

Clark, D. L. *Rhetoric in Greco-Roman Education.* New York: Columbia University Press, 1957.

Clark, Mary T. *Augustine, Philosopher of Freedom.* New York: Desclée, 1958.

Cochrane, Charles Norris. *Thucydides and the Science of History.* London: Oxford University Press, 1929.

————. *Christianity and Classical Culture: A Study of Thought and Action from Augustus to Augustine.* New York: Oxford University Press, 1944.

Cole, P. R. *Later Roman Education in Ausonius, Capella, and the Theodosian Code.* New York: Columbia University Press, 1902.

Collingwood, R. G. *The Idea of History.* New York: Oxford University Press, 1946.

Colomer, Eusebio. "Cristianismo e Historia: Esbozo de una Teología de la Historia," *Razón y Fe,* 160 (Diciembre 1959), 405-418.

Combès, G. S. *Augustin et la culture classique.* Paris: Plon, 1927.

Comeau, Marie. *La rhétorique de saint Augustin d'après les Tractatus in Joannem.* Paris: Boivin, 1930.

Congar, Y. M. J. "Civitas Dei et Ecclesia chez S. Augustin," *Revue des Études Augustiniennes,* III (1957), 1-14.

Connolly, K. H. "The So-called Egyptian Church Order and Derived Documents," *Texts and Studies,* VIII, 4. Cambridge: At the University Press, 1916.

Costello, Charles Joseph. *St. Augustine's Doctrine on the Inspiration and Canonicity of Scripture.* Washington: Catholic University Press, 1930.

Courcelle, Pierre. *Les lettres grecques en occident de Macrobe à Cassiodore.* Paris: E. de Boccard, 1948.

——. *Recherches sur les Confessions de saint Augustin.* Paris: E. de Boccard, 1950.

Courtade, Gaston. "Le sens de l'histoire dans l'Écriture et la classification usuelle des sens scripturaires," *Recherches de Science Religieuse,* 36 (1949), 136-141.

Crombrugghe, C. van. "La doctrine christologique et sotériologique de saint Augustin et ses rapports avec le néoplatonisme," *Revue d'histoire ecclésiastique,* 5 (1904), 237-257 and 477-504.

Cullmann, Oscar. *Christus und die Zeit: Die urchristliche Zeit- und Geschichtsauffassung.* Zürich: Evangelischer Verlag A. G. Zollikon, 1946.

Cumont, F. "Le culte egyptien et le mysticisme de Plotin," in *Monuments Piot,* t. XXV (1921-22), 77-92.

Cunningham, William. *S. Austin and His Place in the History of Christian Thought.* London: C. J. Clay, 1886.

Curti, Merle (ed.). *Theory and Practice in Historical Study: A Report of the Committee on Historiography.* New York: Social Science Research Council, 1946.

Curtius, Ernst Robert. *Europäische Literatur und lateinisches Mittelalter.* Bern: Francke, 1948. (English translation, New York: 1953.)

Cushman, R. E. "Greek and Christian Views of Time," *Journal of Religion,* XXXIII (1953), 254-265.

Dahl, A. *Augustin und Plotin.* Lund: Univ.-Bokhandel, 1945.

Daniélou, Jean. "S. Irénée et les origines de la théologie de l'histoire," *Recherches de Science Religieuse,* 34 (1947), 227-231.

——. *Théologie du Judéo-Christianisme.* Paris: Desclée, 1958.

——. "La catéchèse dans la tradition patristique," *Catéchèse,* I (Oct. 1960), 21-34.

————. *The Lord of History.* London: Longmans, 1958.

D'Arcy, M. J. (ed.) *A Monument to St. Augustine.* London: Sheed and Ward, 1930.

————. *The Meaning and Matter of History.* New York: Farrar, Straus and Cudahy, 1959.

Davidson, Thomas. *The Education of the Greek People and Its Influence on Civilization.* New York: D. Appleton, 1894.

Deferrari, R. J., and Keeler, M. J. "St. Augustine's City of God. Its Plan and Development," *American Journal of Philology* (1929), 109-137.

DeGraff, Thelma. "Plato in Cicero," *Classical Philology*, 35 (1940), 143-153.

Dekkers, Eligius. *Clavis Patrum Latinorum.* Steenbrugis: In Abbatia Sancti Petri, 1961. (2 ed.)

Deman, Th. "Saint Augustin, maître de culture chrétienne," *La vie spirituelle*, LXII (1940), 158-187.

Dempf, Alois. *Die Hauptform mittelalterlicher Weltauschauungen: eine geisteswissenschaftliche Studie über die Summa.* München: R. Oldenbourg, 1925.

————. *Sacrum Imperium.* Milano: casa Editrice Giuseppe principato, 1933.

Dentan, Robert C. (ed.). *The Idea of History in the Ancient Near East.* New Haven and London: Yale University Press, 1955.

De Sinéty, R. "Saint Augustin et le transformisme," *Archives de Philosophie*, VII (1930), 244-272.

Diano, Carlo. "Il concetto della storia nella filosofia dei Greci," *Grande Antologia Filosofica*, Vol. II, 247-404.

Díaz de Cerio, Franco. "La Historia en la formación del hombre moderno," *Revista de la Universidad de Madrid*, IX (1960), 513-536.

Dinkler, Erich. *Die Anthropologie Augustins.* Stuttgart: Kohlhammer, 1934.

Dobson, J. F. *Ancient Education and Its Meaning to Us: Our Debt to Greece and Rome.* London: Longmans, 1932.

Döllinger, J. J. *The Gentile and the Jew in the Courts of the Temple of Christ.* London: Gibbing, 1906.

Dominguez-del Val, N. "Cultura y formacion intelectual en los monasteros agustinianos de Tagaste, Cartago e Hipona," *La Ciudad de Dios*, CLXIX (1956), 426-455.

Dorsch, C. "SS. Augustinus und Hieronymus über die Wahrheit der biblischen Geschichte," *Zeitschrift für Katholische Theologie* (1911), 421-448, 601-661.

Douais, C. "St. Augustin et la Bible," *Revue Biblique* II (1893), 62-81, and III (1894), 110-135; 410-432.

Drever, James. *Greek Education: Its Practice and Principles.* Cambridge: At the University Press, 1912.

Duchrow, Ulrich. "Zum Prolog von Augustins De doctrina christiana," *Vigiliae Christianae,* 17 (1963), 165-172.

Dujovne, Léon. *La Filosofia de la Historia en la Antigüedad y en la Edad Media.* Buenos Aires: Ediciones Galatea-Nueva Visión, 1958.

Eggersdorfer, F. X. *Der heilige Augustinus als Pädagoge und seine Bedeutung für die Geschichte der Bildung.* Freiburg: Herdersche Verlagshandlung, 1907.

Ehnmark, E. *The Idea of God in Homer.* Uppsala: Almquist and Wiksells, 1935.

Eibl, Hans. *Augustin und die Patristik.* München: E. Reinhardt, 1923.

————. *Augustinus: vom Götterreich zum Gottesstaat.* Olten (Schweiz): O. Walter, 1951.

Eliade, Mircea. *Birth and Rebirth: The Religious Meanings of Initiation in Human Culture.* New York: Harper, 1958.

————. *Cosmos and History: The Myth of the Eternal Return.* New York: Harper, 1959.

Ellsperman, Gerard Leo. *The Attitude of Early Christian Latin Writers Toward Pagan Literature and Learning.* Washington: The Catholic University of America Press, 1949.

"Etudes sur Saint Augustin (430-1930)," *Archives du philosophie,* Vol. VII, Cahier 2. Paris: Beauchesne, 1930.

Fabo de Maria, Pedro. *La Juventud de San Agustin ante la critica moderna.* Madrid: Bruno del Amo, Editor, 1929.

Fabre, Lucien. *Saint Augustin.* Paris: Hachette, 1951.

Fabro, Cornelio. "La storiografia nel pensiero cristiano," *Grande antologia filosofica,* V, 311-503. Milano: Marzorati, 1954.

Falconi, Carlo. "Cristo come senso della storia nel pensiero del filosofo martire di Sichem," *Humanitas,* V (1950), 330-343.

Fellermeier, J. "Die Illuminationstheorie bei Augustinus und Bonaventura und die aprioristische Begründung der Erkennthis durch Kant," *Ph.J.B.*, LX (1950), 296-304.

Festugière, A. J. *Le monde gréco-romain au temps de Notre-Seigneur.* Paris: Blond and Gay, 1935.

———. *Personal Religion Among the Greeks.* Berkeley: University of California Press, 1954.

Figgis, John Neville. *Christianity and History.* London: James Finch, 1905.

———. *The Political Aspects of St. Augustine's City of God.* London: Longmans, 1921.

Finaert, Joseph. *Saint Augustin rhéteur.* Paris: Société d'Edition "Les Belles Lettres," 1939.

Fink-Errera, Guy. "San Agustin y Orosio," *La Ciudad de Dios,* CLXVII (1954), 455-549.

Flood, J. M. *St. Augustine: A Biographical Sketch.* Dublin: Clonmore and Reynolds, 1960.

Foran, E. A. *The Augustinians from St. Augustine to the Union, 1256.* London: Burns, Oates and Washbourne, 1938.

Fotheringham, J. K. (ed.). *Eusebii Pamphili Chronici canones latine vertit, adauxit, ad sua tempora produxit S. Eusebius Hieronymus.* Londini: Apud H. Milford, 1923.

Frick, Carl. *Die Quellen Augustins im XVIII Buche seiner Schrift De civitate Dei.* Höxter: Druck von C. D. Flotho, 1886.

Friedländer, L. *Darstellungen aus der Sittengeschichte Roms in der Zeit von August bis zum Ausgang der Antonine.* Leipzig: S. Hirzel, 1910.

Fuerst, A. N. *The Systematic Teaching of Religion.* Vols. I-II. New York: Benziger Brothers, Inc., 1939.

Fueter, Eduard. *Geschichte der neueren Historiographie.* Berlin: R. Oldenbourg, 1936.

Fuller, Edmund (ed.). *The Christian Idea of Education.* New Haven: Yale University Press, 1957.

Garraghan, Gilbert J. *A Guide to Historical Method.* New York: Fordham University Press, 1946.

Garvey, Sister Mary Patricia. *Saint Augustine: Christian or Neo-Platonist? From His Retreat at Cassiciacum until His Ordination at Hippo.* Milwaukee: Marquette University Press, 1939.

Geffcken, Johannes. *Der Ausgang des griechisch-römischen Heidentums*. Heidelberg: Carl Winter, 1929.

Gemelli, A. (ed.). *S. Agostino: pubblicazione commemorativa del XV centenario della sua morte*. Milano: Vita e Pensiero, 1921.

Gennep, A. van. *Les rites de passage*. Paris: E. Nourry, 1909.

Gilmore, A. A. "Augustine and the Critical Method," *Harvard Theological Review*, XXXIX (1946), 141-163.

Gilson, Étienne. "Pourquoi S. Thomas a critiqué S. Augustin," *Archives d'histoire doctrinale et littéraire du Moyen Age*, I, 5-127.

————. *The Spirit of Medieval Philosophy*. New York: Scribner's, 1940.

————. *God and Philosophy*. New Haven: Yale University Press, 1941.

————. *Philosophie et incarnation selon Saint Augustin*. Montréal: Institut d'Études Mediévales, 1947.

————. *The Christian Philosophy of Saint Augustine*. New York: Random House, 1960. (Translation of *Introduction à l'étude de s. Augustin*.)

————. *Les métamorphoses de la Cité de Dieu*. Paris: J. Vrin, 1952.

Ginsberg, H. L. *Studies in Daniel*. New York: Jewish Theological Seminary, 1948.

Girard, Paul Frédéric. *L'éducation athénienne*. Paris: Hachette, 1891.

Glover, T. R. *The Influence of Christ in the Ancient World*. New Haven: Yale University Press, 1929.

Godin, André. "The Historical Function: For a Religious Education of the Christian in Time," *Lumen Vitae*, XIV, No. 2 (June 1959), 245-265.

Gomperz, H. "Isokrates and Sokratik," *Wiener Studien*, XXVII (1905), 163-207; and XXVIII (1906), 1-42.

Gooch, G. P. *History and Historians in the Nineteenth Century*. London: Longman's, 1952.

Gottschalk, Louis. *Understanding History*. New York: Knopf, 1950.

————. *Generalization in the Writing of History: A Report of the Committee on Historical Analysis of the Social Science*

Research Council. Chicago: University of Chicago Press, 1963.

Gourdon, Louis. *Essai sur la conversion de St. Augustin. Thèse présentée à la faculté de Théologie Protestante de Paris.* Cahors: A. Coueslant, 1900.

Grabmann, M., and Mausbach, J. *Aurelius Augustinus: Die Festschrift der Görres-Gesellschraft zum 1500 Todestage des hl. Augustinus.* Köln: J. P. Bachem, 1930.

Grabmann, Martin. *Die Geschichte der scholastischen Methode.* Freiburg: Herder, 1909.

————. *Der göttliche Grund menschlicher Wahrheitserkenntnis nach Augustinus und Thomas von Aquin.* Münster: Aschendorff, 1924.

————. *Die Grundgedanken des heiligen Augustinus über Seele und Gott.* Köln: J. P. Bachem, 1929.

————. Der Einfluss des heiligen Augustinus auf die Verwertung und Bewertung der Antike im Mittelalter," *Mittelalterliches Geistesleben,* II (Munich, 1936), 1-24.

————. *Die theologische Erkenntnis—und Einleitungslehre des hl. Thomas von Aquin auf Grund seiner Schrift "In Boethium de Trinitate."* Freeburg in der Schweiz: Paulus Verlag, 1948.

Grabowski, Stanislaus J. *The Church: An Introduction to the Theology of St. Augustine.* St. Louis: B. Herder, 1957.

Grasberger, Lorenz. *Erziehung und Unterricht im klassischen Alterthum.* Vols. I-III. Würzburg: Die Stabel'sche Buchhandlung, 1864, 1875, 1880.

Green, William M. *Augustine on the Teaching of History.* Los Angeles: University of California Press, 1944.

————. *Initium omnis peccati superbia: Augustine on Pride as the First Sin.* Berkeley: University of California Press, 1949.

Greenwood, David C. *Saint Augustine.* New York: Vantage Press, 1957.

Guardini, Romano. *The Faith and Modern Man.* New York: Pantheon Books, 1952.

————. *The Conversion of Augustine.* Westminster: Newman, 1960.

Gudeman, A. "Sind die Dialoge Augustins Historisch?" *Silvae Monacenses* (1926), 16-27.

Guidi, I. "L'Historiographie chez les Sémites," *Revue Biblique,* 3 (1906), 509-519.

Guignebert, C. "La culture antique et saint Augustin," *Revue de l'histoire des Religions,* CXXII (1940), 25-41.

————. "Saint Augustin et la fin du monde antique," *Revue Historique,* CLXXXIX (1940), 403-413.

Guilday, Peter (ed.). *The Catholic Philosophy of History.* New York: Kenedy, 1936.

Guitton, Jean. *Le temps et l'eternité chez Plotin et St. Augustin.* Paris: Boivin et cie., 1933.

————. *The Modernity of Saint Augustine.* Baltimore: Helicon Press, 1959.

Guthrie, W. K. C. "The Pre-Socratic World-Picture," *Harvard Theological Review,* XLV (1952), 87-104.

Guzzo, Augusto. *Agostino dal "Contra academicos" al "De vera religione."* Torino: Edizioni di Filosofia, 1957.

Gwynn, A. *Roman Education from Cicero to Quintilian.* Oxford: At the Clarendon Press, 1926.

Haecker, Theodor. *Der Christ und die Geschichte.* Leipzig: Jakob Hegner, 1935.

Halecki, Oscar. *The Limits and Divisions of European History.* New York: Sheed and Ward, 1950.

Hamman, Adalbert. *La Rédemption et l'histoire du monde.* Paris: Editions Alsatia, 1949.

Hanssler, Bernhard. "Christus Herr der Geschichte," *Katechetische Blätter,* 84 (März, 1959), 115-124.

Harnack, Adolf von. *Augustin's Confessionen.* Giessen: J. Ricker-'sche Buchhandlung, 1888.

————. *Monasticism: Its Ideals and History; and The Confessions of St. Augustine.* London: Williams and Norgate, 1913.

Harrington, Wilfrid. "A Biblical View of History," *Irish Theological Quarterly* (1962), 207-222.

Hausheer, H. "St. Augustine's Conception of Time," *Philosophical Review* (1937), 503-512.

Heinrici, D. *Das Urchristentum in der Kirchengeschichte des Eusebius.* Leipzig: Verlag der Dürr'schen Buchhandlung, 1894.

Hendrikx, E. "Die Bedeutung von Augustinus 'De Civitate Dei' für Kirche und Staat," *Augustinianum,* I (Aprilis, 1961), 79-93.

Henry, Paul. *Plotin et l'Occident.* Louvain: Spicilegium Sacrum Lovaniense, 1934.

――――. "The Christian Philosophy of History," *Theological Studies,* XIII (1952), 419-432.

――――. *Saint Augustine on Personality.* New York: Macmillan, 1960.

Herring, Pendleton (ed.). *The Social Sciences in Historical Study: A Report of the Committee on Historiography.* New York: Social Science Research Council, 1954.

Hessen, Johannes. *Augustins Metaphysik der Erkenntnis.* Leiden: E. J. Brill, 1960.

Hewitt, J. F. K. *Primitive Traditional History: The Primitive History and Chronology of India, south-eastern and south western Asia, Egypt and Europe.* London: J. Parker, 1907.

Highet, G. *The Classical Tradition.* New York: Oxford University Press, 1959.

Hislop, Ian. "Aquinas, Augustine and the Intellectus Agens," *Dominican Studies,* VI (1953), 180-183.

Hoare, F. R. (ed.). *The Western Fathers.* New York: Sheed and Ward, 1954.

Hoffman, Ross. *Tradition and Progress.* Milwaukee: Bruce, 1938.

Hoffmann, E. *Pädagogischer Humanismus.* Zürich: Artemis Verlag, 1955.

Hofinger, Johannes. *Teaching All Nations: A Symposium in Modern Catechetics.* London: Burns, Oates, 1961.

Holl, Karl. *Augustins innere Entwicklung.* Berlin: Walter de Gruyter, 1923.

Horst, Ulrich. "Über die Frage einer heilsökonomischen Theologie bei Thomas von Aquin," *Münchener Theologische Zeitschrift,* 12 (1961), 97-111.

Hubaux, Jean. *Les Grands Mythes de Rome.* Paris: Presses Universitares de France, 1945.

――――. "Saint Augustin et la crise cyclique," *Augustinus Magister,* II (1954), 943-950.

Hulsbosch, A. "Sagesse créatrice et éducatrice: 1. Job 28," *Augustinianum,* I (July, 1961), 217-235.

Huttman, Maude A. *The Establishment of Christianity and the*

Proscription of Paganism. New York: Columbia University Press, 1914.

Hyde, Walter W. *Paganism to Christianity in the Roman Empire.* London: Oxford University Press, 1946.

Jaeger, Werner. *Paideia: The Ideals of Greek Culture.* Translated by Gilbert Highet. Vols. I-III. Oxford: Blackwell, 1936.

————. *Humanistische Reden und Vorträge.* Berlin: Walter de Gruyter, 1960.

————. *Early Christianity and Greek Paideia.* Cambridge: Harvard University Press, 1961.

Jedin, Hubert. "Kirchengeschichte als Heilsgeschichte?" *Saeculum,* V (1954), 119-128.

Jentsch, Werner. *Urchristliches Erziehungsdenken: Die Paideia Kyriu im Rahrmen der hellenistisch—Judischen Umwelt.* Gütersloh: C. Bertelsmann Verlag, 1951.

Johnson, J. W. "Chronological Writing: Its Concepts and Development," *History and Theory,* 2 (1962), 124-145.

Jolivet, Régis. *Saint Augustin et le néo-platonisme chrétien.* Paris: Denoël et Steele, 1932.

————. *Dieu, soleil des esprits: ou, la doctrine augustinienne de l'illumination.* Paris: Desclée, 1934.

————. *Essai sur les rapports entre la pensée grecque et la pensée chrétienne.* Paris: J. Vrin, 1931.

Journet, Charles. *The Wisdom of Faith.* Westminster: The Newman Press, 1952.

Kafka, Gustav. *Geschichtsphilosophie der Philosophiegeschichte.* Berlin: Junker und Dünnhaupt, 1933.

Keeler, L. *Sancti Augustini doctrina de cognitione.* Rome: Pont. Univ. Gregoriana, 1933.

Kertész, A. N. *Doctrine S. Augustini de memoria mentis.* Romae: Pontificia Universitas Gregoriana, 1944.

Keseling, Paul. "Augustiniana," *Theologische Revue,* XLIX (1953), 81-98.

Kienitz, Erwin Roderich von. *Augustinus: Genius des Abendlandes.* Wuppertal: Abendland-Verlag, 1947.

Kirsch, J. P. *Die Geschichte der Kirche: Ein Zeugnis ihrer höheren Sendung.* München: Kösel und Pustet, 1918.

Klibansky, Raymond, and Patton, H. J. *Philosophy and History: Essays Presented to Ernst Cassirer.* Oxford: Clarendon Press, 1936.

Klibansky, Raymond (ed.). *Philosophy in the Mid-Century: A Survey.* Vol. III, *Values, History and Religion.* Firenze: La Nuova Italia Editrice, 1958.

Koch, Josef (ed.). *Artes Liberales: Von der antiken Bildung zur Wissenschaft des Mittelalters.* Leiden: E. J. Brill, 1959.

Körner, Franz. *Sein und der Mensch: Die existenzielle Seinsentdeckung des jungen Augustins.* Freiburg-München: Verlag Karl Alber, 1959.

Kreutzwald, Heinrich. *Zur Geschichte des biblischen Unterrichts.* Freiburg: Verlag Herder, 1957.

Labriolle, Pierre de (transl.). *Saint Augustin: Confessions.* Paris: Societe d'Edition "Les Belles Lettres," 1925.

Lacroix, Benoît. *L'Histoire dans l'antiquité.* Paris: J. Vrin, 1951.

Ladner, Gerhart B. *The Idea of Reform: Its Impact on Christian Thought and Action in the Age of the Fathers.* Cambridge: Harvard University Press, 1959.

Laistner, Max. "Some Reflections on Latin Historical Writing in the Fifth Century," *Classical Philology,* 35 (1940), 241-258.

———. *Christianity and Pagan Culture in the Later Roman Empire.* Ithaca: Cornell University Press, 1951.

Lambert, H. C. M. *The Nature of History.* London: Oxford University Press, 1933.

Lavasseur, J.-M. *Le lieu théologique: Contribution à une ontologie et introduction à une méthodologie.* Trois-Rivières, Canada: Editions du Bien Public, 1960. (Dissertation, Angelicum, Rome.)

Le Blond, Jean Marie. *Les conversions de saint Augustin.* Paris: Aubier, 1950.

Lebreton, J. "Sainte Monique et saint Augustin: La vision d'Ostie," *Recherches de sciences religieuses,* 28 (1938), 457-472.

Leclercq, H. "Catéchèse-catéchisme-catéchumène," *D.A.C.L.,* II, 2530-2579.

———. "École," *D.A.C.L.,* IV, 1730-1883.

———. "Historiens du Christianisme," *D.A.C.L.,* LXII, 2533-2735.

Leclercq, Jean. "Disciplina," *Dictionnaire de spiritualité*, III, 1291-1302.

———. "Prédication et rhétorique au temps de saint Augustin," *Revue bénédictine*, LVII (1947), 117-131.

———. *The Love of Learning and the Desire for God: A Study of Monastic Culture*. New York: Fordham University Press, 1961.

Lesaar, Heinrich Hubert. *Saint Augustine*. New York: Benziger, 1931.

Levi, A. "Il concetto del tempo nelle filosofie dell'età romana," *Rivista Critica di Storia della Filosofia*, VII (1952), 173-200.

Linhardt, Robert. *Die Sozialprinzipien des hl. Thomas von Aquin*. Freiburg: Herder, 1932.

Loewenich, Walther von. *Menschsein und Christsein bei Augustin*. München: C. Kaiser, 1947.

Lomask, Milton. *St. Augustine and His Search for Faith*. New York: Farrar, Straus and Cudahy, 1957.

Loofs, Friedrich. (1858-1928). "Augustinus," *Realencyclopädie für protestantische Theologie und Kirche*. (Leipzig: J. C. Hinrichs'sche Buchhandlung, 1897, 3rd ed.), Vol. II, 257-285.

Lot, Ferdinand. *The End of the Ancient World*. New York: Barnes and Noble, 1953.

Löwith, Karl. *Meaning in History*. Chicago: University of Chicago Press, 1949.

———. "Die Dynamik der Geschichte und der Historismus," *Eranos-Jahrbuch*, 21 (1952), 217-254.

MacKenna, Stephen (transl.). *Plotinus: The Enneads*. New York: Pantheon, 1957.

Mahdi, Muhsin. *Ibn Kaldun's Philosophy of History*. London: Allen and Unwin, 1957.

Maier, Franz Georg. *Augustin und das antike Rom*. Stuttgart: W. Kohlhammer, 1955.

Malevez, L. "La vision chrétienne de l'histoire," *Nouvelle Revue théologique*, 71 (1949), 113-134 and 244-264.

Mangenot, E. "Catéchisme," *D.T.C.*, II, 1895-1968.

Mannucci, U. "La conversione di S. Agostino et la critica recente," *Miscellanea Agostiniana*, Vol. II (Roma: 1931), 23-47.

Manrique, Miguel A. *The Epistemology of St. Augustine.* Washington: Catholic University, 1953.

Manser, G. M. "Augustins Philosophie in ihrem Verhältnis und ihrer Abhängigkeit von Plotin, dem Fürsten des Neuplatonismus," *Divus Thomas,* 10 (1932), 3-22.

Maritain, J. "De la sagesse augustiniènne," *Mélanges augustiniens,* (1931), 385-411.

Marrou, H.-I. "Autour de la Bibliothèque du Pape Agapit," *Mélanges d'archéologie et d'histoire,* XLVIII (1931), 157-165.

————. *L'ambivalence du temps de l'histoire chez saint Augustin.* Paris: J. Vrin, 1950.

————. *De la connaissance historique.* Paris: Éditions du Seuil, 1954.

————. *A History of Education in Antiquity.* New York: Sheed and Ward, 1956.

————. *Saint Augustine and His Influence Through the Ages.* London: Longmans, 1957.

————. *Saint Augustin et la fin de la culture antique.* Paris: Éditions E. de Boccard, 1958.

Martin, Jules. *Saint Augustin.* Paris: Felix Alcan, 1901.

Masnovo, Amato. *S. Agostino e S. Tomaso: concordanze e sviluppi.* Milano: Vita e pensiero, 1950.

Mausbach, J. *Die Ethik des heiligen Augustinus.* Bd. I-II. Freiburg: Herder, 1909.

Mayer, Johann. *Geschichte des Katechumenates und der Katechese.* Kampt: Jos. Kafl, 1868.

Mehl, Roger. "Philosophy of History or Theology of History?" *Cross Currents* (Winter 1953), 162-181.

Melchior, Sister M. "Saint Augustine, Student and Teacher," *The Catholic Educational Review,* 52 (1954), 306-317.

Meulenbroek, B.-L. "The Historical Character of Augustine's Cassiciacum Dialogues," *Mnemosyne,* ser. III, t. XIII (1947), 203-229.

Michels, Thomas. *Das Heilswerk der Kirche: Ein Beitrag zu einer Theologie der Geschichte.* Salzburg: Verlag Anton Pustet, 1935.

Milburn, R. L. P. *Early Christian Interpretations of History.* London: Black, 1954.

Miscellanea Agostiniana: *Testi e Studi Pubblicati a Cura dell-'Ordine Eremitano di S. Agostino nel XV Centenario.* Roma: Tipografia Vaticana, 1930. Vols. I-II.

Mommsen, Theodore E. *Medieval and Renaissance Studies.* Ithaca, N. Y.: Cornell University Press, 1959.

Mondadon, Louis de. "Les premières impressions catholiques de saint Augustin," *Études* 119 (May 20-June 5, 1909), 441-459.

———. "Saint Augustin professeur," *Études,* 1910, 5-34.

Monnot, P. "Essai de synthèse philosophique d'après le XIe livre de la Cité de Dieu," *Archives de Philosophie,* VII, 2 (1930), 142-185.

Monroe, Paul. *Source Book of the History of Education for the Greek and Roman Period.* London: Macmillan, 1901.

Moriones, Franciscus (ed.). *Enchiridion theologicum sancti Augustini.* Madrid: Biblioteca de Autores Cristianos, 1961.

Morris, Nathan. *The Jewish School: An Introduction to the History of Jewish Education.* London: Eyre and Spottiswoode, 1937.

Mueller, F. "De 'historiae' vocabulo atque notione," *Mnemosyne,* 54 (1926), 234-257.

Muller, Herbert J. *The Loom of History.* New York: Mentor Books, 1961.

Munoz Vega, Pablo. *Introduccion a la sintesis de San Augustin.* Romae: Apud aedes Universitatis Gregorianae, 1945.

Nardi, Bruno. *Il pensiero pedagogico del Medioevo.* Firenze: Coedizioni Giuntine-Sansoni, 1956.

Nebreda, Euloge. *Bibliographia Augustiniana.* Rome: Tipogr. Cuore di Maria, 1928.

Nef, John. "A New Christian View of History?" *Thought* (1962), 347-356.

Niebuhr, Richard. *Christ and Culture.* New York: Harper, 1951.

Niemann, Albert. *Augustin's Geschichtsphilosophie.* Griefswald: Druck von Julius Abel, 1895.

Nilsson, M. P. *Primitive Time-Reckoning: A study of the origins and first development of the art of counting time among the primitive and early culture peoples.* Lund: C. W. K. Gleerup, 1920.

———. *Die hellenistische Schule.* Munich: Verlag C. H. Beck, 1955.

Nock, A. D. *Conversion.* New York: Oxford University Press, 1933.

Nörregaard, J. *Augustins Bekehrung.* Tübingen: Verlag von J. C. B. Mohr, 1923.

North, R. "Prophetismus ut Philosophia Historiae," *Verbum Domini,* 29 (1951), 321-333.

Nourrisson. *La philosophie de saint Augustin.* Vols. I-II. Paris: Didier, 1865 et 1869.

O'Connor, William Patrick. *The Concept of the Human Soul According to St. Augustine.* Washington: The Catholic University, 1921.

Ogg, George. "Hippolytus and the Introduction of the Christian Era," *Vigiliae Christianae* (March, 1962), 2-18.

Oggioni, E. *S. Agostino filosofo e pedagogista.* Padora: CEDAM, 1949.

Ohlman, Desiderius. *De S. Augustini dialogis in Cassiciaco scriptis.* Argentorati: Ex officina typographica "Der Elsässer," 1897.

O'Meara, John J. "The Historicity of the Early Dialogues of Saint Augustine," *Vigiliae Christianae,* V (1951), 150-178.

———. *The Young Augustine: The Growth of St. Augustine's Mind up to His Conversion.* London: Longmans, Green, 1954.

———. *Charter of Christendom: The Significance of the City of God.* New York: Macmillan, 1961.

Ong, Walter. "Cyclicism and Evolution," *Thought,* 34 (1959), 547-569.

Oster, Henri. *Le grand dessein de Dieu dans la pastorale et la predication.* Paris: Les Editions du Cerf, 1957.

Otto, Stephan. "Das Problem der Zeit in der voraugustinischen Theologie," *Zeitschrift für Katholische Theologie* (1960), 74-87.

Padovani, Umberto A. *La Città di Dio di S. Agostino: teologia e non filosofia della storia.* Milano: Vita e Pensiero, 1931.

———. *Filosofia e teologia della storia.* Brescia: Morcelliana, 1953.

———. "Il problema della storia," *Atti dell'VIII Convegno di studi filosofici Cristiani,* Brescia: Morcelliana, 1953.

Palanque, J. R., et al. *The Church in the Christian Roman Empire.* New York: Macmillan, 1953.

Palazzini, Pietro. "Educazione della coscienza," in *La Coscienza.* Roma: Edizioni Ares, 1961.

Parodi, Bonaventura. *La Catechesi di Sant' Ambrogio: Studio di pedagogia pastorale.* Genova: Scuola Tipografica Opera SS. Vergine di Pompei, 1957.

Pellegrino, Michele. *Le "Confessioni" di Sant'Agostino: Studio introduttivo.* Roma: Editrice Studium, 1956.

Penati, Giancarlo. "Riflessioni su alcune recenti interpretazioni filosofiche della storia," *Rivista di filos. neoscol.,* 55 (1963), 219-231.

Peterson, Erik. *Die Kirche aus Juden und Heiden.* Salzburg: Verlag Anton Pustet, 1933.

————. "Kaiser Augustus im Urteil des antiken Christentums," *Hochland,* XXX (1933), 289-299.

————. *Der Monotheismus als politisches Problem: Ein Beitrag zur Geschichte der politischen Theologie im Imperium Romanum.* Leipzig: Jakob Hegner, 1935.

Pegis, Anton C. "The Mind of St. Augustine," *Medieval Studies,* VI (1944), 1-61.

Petruzzellis, Nicola. *Il valore della storia.* Napoli: Mezzogiorno, 1959.

Phelan, Thomas W. "St. Augustine and the Recent Excavations of the Christian Monuments of Hippo," *Theological Studies,* 20 (1959), 422-431.

Philippson, R. "Sind die Dialoge Augustins historisch?" *Rheinisches Museum für Philologie,* 1931, 144-150.

————. "Il concetto greco di tempo nelle parole aion, chronos, kairos, eniautos," *Revista Critica di Storia della Filosofia,* IV (1949), 81-97.

Plagnieux, Jean. "Influence de la bette antipélagienne sur le 'De Trinitate': ou Christocentrisme de Saint Augustin," *Augustinus Magister* II (1954), 817-826.

Pohlenz, M. "Kronos und die Titanen," *Neue Jahrbücher für das klassische Altertum,* XXXVII (1916), 549-594.

Polman, A. D. R. *The Word of God According to St. Augustine.* Grand Rapids, Michigan: Wm. B. Berchmans Publishing Co., 1961.

Pontet, M. *L'exégèse de saint Augustin prédicateur.* Paris: Aubier, 1945.

Pope, Hugh. "The Teaching of the Bible for the Ministry," *The Ecclesiastical Review,* LXXXVIII (Jan.-June, 1933), 16-27.

————. *Saint Augustine of Hippo: Essays Dealing with His Life and Times and Some Features of His Work.* Westminster, Maryland: The Newman Press, 1949.

Portalié, Eugène. *A Guide to the Thought of Saint Augustine.* Chicago: Regnery, 1960.

Pöschl, Viktor. "Augustinus und die römische Geschichtsauffassung," *Augustinus Magister,* II (1954), 957-963.

Possidius, St. *Sancti Augustini vita scripta a Possidio Episcopo.* Trans. by H. T. Weiskotten. Princeton: Princeton University Press, 1919.

Poujoulat, Jean. *Histoire de Saint Augustin, sa vie, ses oeuvres, son siècle, influence de son genie.* Paris: J. Lafitte, 1845.

Prümm, K. *Religionsgeschichtliches Handbuch für den Raum der altchristlichen Umwelt.* Rome: Päpstliches Bibel-Institut, 1954.

Puniet, P. de. "Catéchuménat," *D.A.C.L.,* II, 2579-2621.

Quasten, Johannes. *Patrology.* Vols. I-III. Utrecht: Spectrum Publishers, 1950, 1953, 1960.

Quispel, G. "Zeit und Geschichte im antiken Christentum," *Eranos-Jahrbuch* XX (1951), 115-140.

Rand, E. K. *Founders of the Middle Ages.* Cambridge: Harvard University Press, 1928.

————. *The Building of Eternal Rome.* Cambridge: Harvard University Press, 1943.

————. "The Humanism of Cicero," *Proceedings of the American Philosophical Society,* LXXI (1932), 207-216.

Ranke, Leopold von. *Universal History, The Oldest Historical Group of Nations and the Greeks.* New York: Harper, 1885.

Rentschka, Paul. *Die Dekalogkatechese des hl. Augustinus.* Breslau: R. Grosser, 1905.

Rey, A. *Le retour éternel et la philosophie de la physique.* Paris: Flammarion, 1927.

Reynold, Gonzague de. *Le toit chrétien. (Formation de l'Europe,* Vol. VII.) Paris: Librairie Plon, 1957.

Riché, Pierre. *Éducation et culture dans l'occident barbare, VIe-VIIIe siècles.* Paris: Editions du Seuil, 1962.

Rickaby, Joseph. *St. Augustine's City of God: A View of the Contents.* Burns, Oates, 1925.

Roger, M. *L'enseignement des lettres classiques d'Ausone à Alcuin: Introduction à l'histoire des écoles carolingiennes.* Paris: A. Picard, 1905.

Rondet, H. "L'Anthropologie religieuse de saint Augustin," *Recherches de science religieuse,* 29 (1939), 163-196.

Rongione, Louis A. "Saint Augustine, the Catechist," *Journal of Religious Instruction,* XV, No. 5 (Jan. 1945), 461-469.

Rosan, L. J. *The Philosophy of Proclus: The Final Phase of Ancient Thought.* New York: Cosmas, 1949.

Rost, H. *Die Bibel im Mittelalter: Beiträge zur Geschichte und Bibliographie der Bibel.* Augsburg: M. Seitz, 1939.

Rostovtseft, M. *The Social and Economic History of the Hellenistic World.* Vols. I-III. Oxford: Clarendon Press, 1942.

Rowley, H. H. *Darius the Mede and the Four World Empires: A Historical Study of Contemporary Theories.* Cardiff: University of Wales Press Board, 1935.

Ryan, John K. "Augustinianism," *The Encyclopedia Americana,* II (1957), 545-547.

————. "Saint Augustine," *The Encyclopedia Americana,* II (1957), 544-545.

Samaran, Charles (ed.). *L'histoire et ses méthodes.* Paris: Gallimard, 1961.

Schapiro, J. Salwyn. "The Esquisse of Condorcet," in James T. Shotwell (ed.), *Essays in Intellectual History,* New York: Harper, 1929, 165-185.

Schilling, Otto. *Die Staats- und Soziallehre des hl. Augustinus.* Freiburg: Herder, 1910.

Schlegel, Friedrich. *Vorlesungen über die Universalgeschichte.* Paderborn: Ferdinand Schöningh, 1960.

Schmid, Reinhold. *Marius Victorinus Rhetor und seine Beziehungen zu Augustin.* Kiel: E. Uebermuth, 1895.

Schmidt, R. "Aetates Mundi, die Weltalter als Gliederungsprinzip der Geschichte," *Zeitschrift für Kirchengeschichte,* 67 (1956), 288-317.

Schneider, Wilhelm. *Die Questiones disputatae de veritate des Thomas von Aquin in ihrer philosophiegeschichtlichen Beziehung zu Augustinus.* Münster: Aschendorff, 1930.

Schnürer, Gustav. *Die Anfänge der abendländischen Völkergemeinschaft.* Freiburg: Herder, 1932.

————. *Kirche und Kultur im Mittelalter.* Erster Band. Paderborn: Ferdinand Schöningh-Verlag, 1936.

Scholz, Heinrich. *Glaube und Unglaube in der Weltgeschichte.* Leipzig: J. C. Hinrichs'sche Buchhandlung, 1911.

Schöne, Alfred. *Die Weltchronik des Eusebius in ihrer Bearbeitung durch Hieronymus.* Berlin: Weidmannsche Buchhandlung, 1900.

Schorlemmer, P. "Augustinus als Erzieher der Kirche," *Hochkirche,* XII (1930), 263-267.

Schroeteler, J. (ed.). *Die Pädagogik der nichtchristlichen Kulturvölker.* München: Kösel und Pustet, 1934.

Schütz, Anton. *Gott in der Geschichte.* Salzburg: Verlag Anton Pustet, 1936.

Schuetzinger, Caroline Eva. *The German Controversy on St. Augustine's Illumination Theory.* New York: Pageant Press, 1960.

Schumacher, H. "The Historical Value of Genesis, Chapter II," *Homiletic and Pastoral Review,* 23 (1923), 579-587; 699-706; 803-810; 917-924; 1027-1033; 1138-1144.

Sciacca, M. F. *Sant'Agostino.* Vols. I-III. Brescia: Morcelliana, 1949.

————. *Saint Augustin et le néoplatonisme: la possibilité d'une philosophie chrétienne.* Louvain: Publ. Univ. de Louvain, 1956.

Seeberg, E. "Geschichte und Geschichtstsanschauung dargestellt an altchristlichen Geschichtsvorstellungen," *Zeitschrift für Kirchengeschichte* (1941), 309-331.

Semple, W. H. "Augustinus Rhetor: A Study, from the *Confessions,* of St. Augustine's Secular Career in Education," *The Journal of Ecclesiastical History,* I (1950), 135-150.

Sérant, Paul. "Le prétendu 'sens de l'histoire'," *Revue des Deux Mondes* (1962), 399-411.

Sethe, Paul. *Epochen der Weltgeschichte: von Hammurabi bis Kolumbus.* Frankfurt aur Main: H. Scheffler, 1954.

Seyrich, G. S. *Die Geschichtsphilosophie Augustins nach seiner Schrift de civitate Dei.* Chemnitz: Adam, 1891.

Shotwell, James T. (ed.). *Essays in Intellectual History.* New York: Harper, 1929.

————. *The History of History.* New York: Columbia University Press, 1939.

Sihler, E. G. *From Augustus to Augustine.* Cambridge: University Press, 1924.

Simard, Georges. *Les maîtres chrétiens de nos pensées et de nos vies.* Ottawa: Éditions de l'Univ. d'Ottawa, 1937.

———. "Philosophie et théologie de l'histoire d'après la Cité de Dieu," *Revue Univ. Ottawa,* VII (1937), 441-448.

Simon, Paul. *Aurelius Augustinus: Sein geistiges Profil.* Paderborn: Schöningh, 1954.

Sizoo, A. *Augustinus: Leven en Werken.* Kampen: J. H. Kok, 1957.

Sleidanus, Johannes. *The Key of historie.* London: W. Sheeres, 1627.

Smalley, B. *The study of the Bible in the Middle Ages.* Oxford: University Press, 1941.

Solignac, A. "L'existentialisme de Saint Augustin," *Nouvelle revue théologique,* LXX (1948), 3-19.

Soltau, G. C. W. *Die Aufänge der römischen Geschichtsschreibung.* Leipzig: Haessel, 1909.

Spalding, J. F. *The Teaching and Influence of St. Augustine.* New York: J. Pott, 1886.

Spiazzi, R. *La civiltà cerca Cristo.* Milano: Vita e Pensiero, 1949.

Spicq, C. *Esquisse d'une histoire de l'exégèse latine au Moyen Age.* Paris: Bibliotheque Thomiste, 1944.

Srawley, J. H. (ed.), *The Catechetical Oration of St. Gregory of Nyssa.* London: S.P.C.K., 1917.

Stakemeier, E. *Civitas Dei: Die Geschichtstheologie des heiligen Augustinus als Apologie der Kirche.* Paderborn: Schöningh, 1955.

Stark, Werner. *Social Theory and Christian Thought.* London: Routledge and Kegan Paul, 1959.

Stelzenberger, Johannes. *Conscientia bei Augustinus: Studie zur Geschichte der Moraltheologie.* Paderborn: Schöningh, 1961.

Stern, Fritz (ed.). *The Varieties of History from Voltaire to the Present.* New York: Meridian Books, 1956.

Straub, J. "Christliche Geschichtsapologetik in der Krisis des römschen Reiches," *Historia,* I (1950), 52-81.

———. "Augustins Sorge um die regeneratio imperii," *Historisches Jahrbuch,* LXXIII (1953), 36-60.

Strauss, Gerhard. *Schriftgebrauch, Schriftauslegung und Schriftbeweis bei Augustin.* Tübingen: J. C. B. Mohr, 1959.

Swain, J. W. "The Theory of the Four Monarchies: Opposition History under the Roman Empire," *Classical Philology* (1940), 1-21.

Sweet, Henry (ed.). *King Alfred's Orosius.* London: N. Trübner, 1883.

Teggart, Frederick J. *Theory and Processes of History.* Los Angeles: University of California Press, 1941.

Testard, Maurice. *Saint Augustin et Cicéron. Vol. I: Cicéron dans la formation et dans l'oeuvre de saint Augustin.* Vol. II: *Répertoire des textes.* Paris: Études Augustiniennes, 1958.

Theiler, W. "Review, Courcelle, Confessions de S. Augustin," *Gnomon,* 25 (1953), 113-122.

Thieme, Karl. *Gott und die Geschichte.* Freiburg: Verlag Herder, 1948.

Thils, Gustave. *Théologie et réalité sociale.* Paris: Casterman, 1952.

———. *Théologie des réalités terrestres.* Vol. I-II. Paris: Desclée, 1946.

Thimme, W. *Augustins geistige Entwicklung in den ersten Jahren nach seiner Bekehrung (386-391).* Berlin: Trowitzsch & Sohn, 1908.

———. *Augustins Selbstbildnis in den Konfessionen: Eine religionsgeschichtliche Studie.* Gütersloh: C. Bertelsmann, 1929.

Thompson, James Westfall. *A History of Historical Writing.* Vol. I-II. New York: Macmillan, 1940.

Thompson, T., and Srawley, J. H. *St. Ambrose on the Sacraments and on the Mysteries.* London: S.P.C.K., 1950.

Thonna-Barthet, O. S. A. *L'Évangile commenté par saint Augustin.* Paris: Lethielleux, 1930.

Thonnard, F. J. "Ontologie Augustinienne," *L'Année théologique Augustinienne,* XIV (1954), 41-53.

———. "Saint Augustin et les grands courants de la philosophie contemporairie," *Revue des Études Augustiniennes,* I (1955), 69-80.

Thyssen, Johannes. *Geschichte der Geschichtsphilosophie.* Berlin: Junker U. Dünnhaupt, 1936.

Tillemont, Le Nain de. *Mémoire pour servir l'histoire ecclésiastique des six prémiers siècles.* Paris: 1702.

Tillich, Paul. *The Interpretation of History.* New York: Scribner's, 1936.

Tornielli, Agostino. *Annales Sacri, et ex profanis praecipui, ab orbe condito ad eundem Christi passione redemptum.* Antverpiae: Novetum et Meursium, 1620.

Tourscher, F. E. "Augustine's First Studies in Philosophy: His Influence on Catholic Culture," *American Ecclesiastical Review,* 83 (1930), 113-124.

———. "Saint Augustine's Philosophy: Right Thinking and Right Living," *American Ecclesiastical Review,* 89 (1933), 113-125.

Toynbee, Arnold J. *Greek Historical Thought: From Homer to the Age of Heraclitus.* London: J. M. Dent, 1924.

Trapé, A. (ed.). *Sanctus Augustinus Vitae Spiritualis Magister.* Roma: Edit. Analecta Augustiniana, 1956.

———. "A proposito di predestinazione: S. Agostino ed i suoi critici moderni," *Divinitas,* VII (1963), 243-284.

———. *S. Agostino e le grandi correnti della filosofia contemporanea.* Tolentino: Macerata, 1954.

Tresmontant, C. *Essai sur la pensee hébraïque.* Paris: Ed. du Cerf, 1953.

Trieber, C. "Die Idee der vier Weltreiche," *Hermes,* XXVII (1892).

Troeltsch, Ernst. *Augustin, die christliche Antike und das Mittelalter: Im Anschluss an die Schrift de civitate Dei.* München: R. Oldenbourg, 1915.

———. *Christian Thought: Its History and Application.* New York: Meridian Books, 1957.

Ussher, James. *Annales Veteris Testamenti.* Londini: Crook and Baker, 1650.

Vaccari, A. "La theoria nella scuola esegetica di Antiochia," *Biblica,* I (1920), 3-36.

Van den Eynde, D. *Les normes de l'enseignement chrétien dans la littérature patristique des trois premiers siècles.* Paris: Gabalda, 1933.

Van Bavel, T. "Répertoire bibliographique de saint Augustin," *Augustiniana,* III (1953), 354-375.

Van der Meer, F. *Augustine the Bishop: The Life and Work of a Father of the Church*. London: Sheed and Ward, 1961.

Van Haeringen, J. H. *De Augustini ante baptismum rusticantis operibus*. Groningae, 1917.

Van Steenberghen, F. "La philosophie de s. Augustin d'après les travaux du centenaire," *Revue néoscholastique de philosophie*, XXIV (1932), 366-387; XXXV (1933), 106-126 and 230-281.

Vecchi, Alberto. "Il concetto di filosofia e il problema del corso storico nel 'De vera religione' di S. Agostino," *Actes du XIeme Congrès Internationale de philosophie*, XIV (1953), 282-291.

Vega, A. C. *St. Augustine*. Philadelphia: Peter Reilly Co., 1931.

———. *Introducción a la filosofía de San Agustin*. Madrid: Biblioteca de Autores Cristianos, 1946.

Versfeld, Marthinus. *A Guide to the City of God*. New York: Sheed and Ward, 1958.

Vismara, Silvio. "Il pensiero storiografico del Bossuet," *Rivista di Filosofia Neo-scholastica*, XX (1928), 24-41.

———. "La storiografia nella cultura graeco-romana, nel pensiero neo-cristiano e in Sant'Agostino," *Rivista di filosofia neo-scholastica*, 20 (1928), 261-278.

Vogels, Heinrich Joseph. *St. Augustins Schrift De consensu Evangelistarum*. Freiburg: Herdersche Verlagshandlung, 1908.

———. *Die heilige Schrift bei Augustinus*, im Grabmann-Mausbach (eds.), *Aurelius Augustinus*. Köln: Verlag J. P. Bachem, 1930.

Walsh, P. G. *Livy: His Historical Aims and Methods*. Cambridge: At the University Press, 1961.

Ward, Leo R. *God and World Order*. St. Louis: Herder, 1961.

Webster, Hutton. *Primitive Secret Societies: A Study in Early Politics and Religion*. New York: Macmillan, 1908.

Weiss, Adalbert G. *Die altkirchliche Pädagogik dargestellt in Katechumenat und Katechese der ersten sechs Jahrhunderte*. Freiburg: Herder, 1869.

Weiskotten, Herbert T. (ed.). *Sancti Augustini vita scripta a Possidio Episcopo*. Princeton: Princeton University Press, 1919.

Weller, Philip T. (ed.). *Selected Easter Sermons of St. Augustine.* St. Louis: Herder, 1959.

Wilberforce, Robert Esaac. *The Five Empires: An Outline of Ancient History.* London: J. Hughes, 1852 (8th ed.).

Willis, G. G. *Saint Augustine and the Donatist Controversy.* London: S.P.C.K., 1950.

Wilmart, A. "La tradition des grands ouvrages de saint Augustin," *Miscellanea Agostiniana,* II, 257-315.

————. "Operum S. Augustini elenchus a Possidio eiusdem discipulo Calamensi episcopo digestus," *Miscellanea Agostiniana,* II, 149-233.

Wise, John E. *The Nature of the Liberal Arts.* Milwaukee: Bruce, 1947.

Wolfsgruber, C. *Augustinus.* Paderborn: Schöningh, 1898.

Woody, Thomas. *Life and Education in Early Societies.* New York: Macmillan, 1949.

Wörter, Friedrich. *Die Geistesentwicklung des hl. Augustin bis zu seiner Taufe.* Paderborn: Ferdinand Schöningh, 1892.

Wühr, Wilhelm. *Das abendländische Bildungswesen im Mittelalter.* München: Franz Ehrenwirth Verlag, 1950.

Wytzes, Jelle. *Der Streit um den Altar der Viktoria.* Amsterdam: H. J. Paris, 1936.

Zangemeister, Carolus (ed.). *Pauli Orosii Historiarum adversum paganos libri VII.* Vindobonae: Apud C. Geroldi filium, 1882.

Zarb, S. M. *Chronologia operum S. Augustini secundum ordinem Retractationum digesta.* Romae: Apud Pont. Institutum "Angelicum," 1934.

————. "Chronologia tractatuum s. Augustini in evangelium primamque epistulam Ioannis apostoli," *Angelicum,* 10 (1933), 50-110.

————. "Chronologia Enarrationum s. Augustini in Psalmos," *Angelicum,* 12 (1935), 52-81, 245-261; 13 (1936), 93-108, 252-282; 14 (1937), 516-537; 15 (1938), 382-408; 16 (1939), 267-295.

Zeschwitz, Carol Adolph Gerhard von. *Der Katechumenat, oder die Kirchliche Erziehung nach Theorie und Geschichte: Ein Handbuch für Seelsorger und Pädagogen.* Leipzig: J. C. Hinrichs'sche Buchhandlung, 1863.

Ziebarth, E. *Aus dem griechischen Schulwesen: Eudemos von Milet und Verwandtes.* Leipzig: B. G. Teubner, 1914.

Zumkeller, Adolar. *Das Mönchtum des heiligen Augustinus.* Würzburg: Augustinus-Verlag, 1950.

Index

417

tellectual discipline to the order of studies, 221, 224-225, 228, 300-301, 304; is simply sacred or salvation history, 243; taught on framework of universal history, 239-240, 255, 258, 262-267, 284, 317-322; see: Bible; Salvation history; Method of teaching, St. Augustine's; Historical theism; academic teaching of, 217 ff., 228, 245, 289-290; see: Apostolate of the classroom; Academic teaching simultaneously catechetical; relation of, to the human arts and disciplines, 308-311; unique among curricular disciplines, 305, 314; and the curriculum as a whole, 306-311; the integrating factor in education, 220; see: Wisdom; *Si rite pertractentur;* God, ascent of mind to; Christian humanism; separation of, from rest of disciplines, 306-311; see: Modernism; Historical atheism; Secularism, pedagogical doctrine of; practice of, 214; see: Formation; Apostolate of the classroom; Catholic education, nature and purpose of; Catholic schools, need for; Practice of, dependent on solid education, 312-313; see: Pope John XXIII; Holy See; curriculum doctrine of; benefit of, to society, 170; see: Renewal of education and civilization; Christian era, interpretation of; barred from modern curriculum, 254; see: Secularism; Historical atheism; Philosophies of history, victory over

Religion program, broader than religion classes, 297, 305, 306, 310; see: Curriculum-planning, Catholic; Catholic education, nature and purpose of

Religious education, 5, 7, 9, 14, 21-22, 113, 187-188, 239, 241, 305 ff., 322-325; basic idea of, 229; foundation of, 204; traditional among men, 16-17; must be proportioned to levels of education, 312-313; method of, 212 ff., 217; use of Bible in, 333; right way of teaching history, 256; mistake in separating "sacred" and "profane" history, 253; common mistake in, 309; see: Religion; Formation; Apostolate of the classroom; Academic teaching simultaneously catechetical

Religious knowledge, 6; supernatural origin of, 187; see: Religion; Religious education

Reminiscence, Plato's doctrine of, 12

Renewal, of academic history, 20

Renewal, of the Catholic Church in North Africa, 120-121, 131; see: Bishop, educational apostolate of the; Saint Augustine, apostolate of

Renewal, of cognitive powers of man, 193; see: Christian philosophy, aided by revelation

Renewal, false contemporary concept of, 340

Renewal of education and civilization, 41, 81, 82, 86, 91, 95, 105-106, 107, 110, 114, 120, 127-130, 132, 137-138, 141, 146, 148, 173, 177-179, 185-186, 188-189, 190 ff., 196, 199 ff., 203, 223, 226, 242-243, 247, 267, 298-299, 337, 363-364, 368-370, 376; see: Christian era, interpretation of; Universal history, meaning and direction of

Renewal of human life, 4, 22; see: Regeneration; Culture, renewal of; Renewal of personal life

Renewal, of mankind's educational institution, 75, 217-230, 246; see: Renewal of education and civilization; Christian era, interpretation of

Renewal of *paideia,* 173; see: Renewal of education and civilization; Renewal of personal life

Renewal, of personal life, 211, 301; see: Baptism; Liturgy; *Catharsis;* Renewal of education and civilization

Renewal, religious, 192

Renewal, of the teaching profession, 361-362

Res gestae, 237; see: History, St. Augustine's definition of

Resignation, from professional chair, 57, 62

Retractationes: see *Libri retractationum*

A NOTE ON THE TYPE

IN WHICH THIS BOOK IS SET

This book is set in Baskerville, a Linotype face, created from the original types used by John Baskerville, the eighteenth-century typefounder and printer. This type has long been considered one of the finest book types ever developed. The letters are wide and open and have a businesslike approach. The finer hairlines give exquisite delicacy. The heavier strokes give color and strength. The relation of the two in combination gives a brilliant effect and makes for easy reading. The book was composed and printed by the Wickersham Printing Company of Lancaster, Pa., and bound by Moore and Company of Baltimore. The typography and design are by Howard N. King.